The Word Became Flesh

E. Stanley Jones

ABINGDON
NASHVILLE

THE WORD BECAME FLESH

A Festival Book

Copyright © 1963 by Abingdon Press

All rights reserved
Festival edition published by Abingdon, January, 1979

ISBN 0-687-46128-6

Scripture quotations unless otherwise noted are from the Revised Standard Version of the Bible, copyrighted 1946, 1952, © 1971, 1973 by the Division of Christian Education of the National Council of The Churches of Christ in the U.S.A. and are used by permission.

Quotations from The New English Bible. © the Delegates of the Oxford University Press and the Syndics of the Cambridge University Press 1961, 1970. Reprinted by permission.

Quotations noted Moffatt are from The Bible: A New Translation, by James Moffatt; copyright 1935 by Harper & Row.

"I See His Blood Upon the Rose" by Joseph Mary Plunkett, used by permission of Harper & Row, Publishers, Inc.

"Jesus of the Scars" by Edward Shillito is copyright 1928 Christian Century Foundation. Reprinted with permission from *The Christian Century*.

INTRODUCTION

Each time I have written a book I have said to myself, in some form or other, "Well, this is it. If I can say what I want to say on this subject, I would satisfy a life intention." And I have meant it. I did not mean, of course, that I had the presumption to think I was going to say the last word on that subject, or the best word. That would be folly. But I did mean that for me this subject is it—if I could say and live what I am writing, then it would meet my deepest need—and the need of others.

But as I look back I see that each book, while meeting a need of my own, and possibly the needs of others, did not move to the very Center, nor did it comprehend the Whole, gathering up the Christian faith into a total concept. This book, I believe, comes nearer the Center and more nearly comprehends the Whole than any I have written. At the close I shall probably send it forth with a sigh, "Well, I haven't said it! I have picked up some pebbles along the beach, but the great ocean depths are yet to be explored." While I shall be dissatisfied with my offering, I shall be convinced that whether I have said it or not, the thing itself is the Center—the Word Became Flesh is the Center. This is it! And the circumference is the working out of that Word Became Flesh in the sum total of life.

If I were to put my finger on the most important verse in Scripture, I would unhesitatingly put my finger on this one: "And the Word became flesh." The whole passage reads this way:

And the Word became flesh and dwelt among us, full of grace and truth; we have beheld his glory, glory as of the only Son from the Father. . . . And from his fullness have we all received, grace upon grace. For the law was given through Moses; grace and truth came through Jesus Christ. No one has ever seen God; the only Son, who is in the bosom of the Father, he has made him known (John 1:14-18).

This verse—"the Word became flesh"—is the Great Divide. In all other religions it is Word became word—a philosophy, a moralism, a system, a technique, but for all time and all men everywhere, "the Word became flesh"—the Idea became Fact.

As a missionary and an evangelist for over half a century, I have stood amid the thought currents of the world—"where cross the crowded ways of life." These "ways of life" meet in India as in no other place in the world. Here men take religion seriously, ready to live and die for it. And here in large measure the religious battle of the world is being fought. Among the great philosophical nations of the world—Greece, India, and China—India alone stands and fights for her ways of life. Greece has produced her philosophers, but go to Greece today—you will be shown monuments and archaeological ruins, but no one will debate with you on Mars' Hill the relative merits of the various philosophies of ancient Greece. A Mecca for photographers, but not for pilgrims. In China the temples are places of picnics or now, under the Communists, places of indoctrination for Marxism. Apparently the religious issues are wiped out.

But in India it is different. There the old faiths have vitality still. It is true that many of the gods are worm-eaten. In India the gods lose their vitality and vigor every fifty or sixty years and have to be revived by certain reviving ceremonies and rites. Said a Hindu to me: "Ishwara [God] is growing old and decrepit, is not of much use to us now." While there is a decay of temple Hinduism, nevertheless philosophical Hinduism is still strong and militant and even invades the West. Even in our Christian Ashrams in America I get the questions: "What do you think of Reincarnation and Karma?" "Are we one with God, as Vedanta says, or more truly stated, Are we God?"

The reaction of India to the Christian Gospel has gone through three stages: (1) It isn't true. (2) It isn't new. (3) It isn't you. The first stage was short-lived. The Gospel was so self-verifying to the human mind that it could not be waved out as untrue. The second stage, "It isn't new," has lingered and is still in vogue—"Everything you have in your faith is found in our sacred books." The third stage, "It isn't you"—"You don't live it"—is here and is the usual argument against the Christian Gospel. There we must humbly acknowledge the truth of what they say. They have a point—a real one. The stage India is in at present is a combination of "It isn't new" and "It isn't you."

I have lived with this combination for years. Everything I have presented in the Christian Gospel has been met by a bland reply: "Yes, what you say is good; we have the same in our sacred books." When I arrived in India fifty-four years ago and was traveling from Bombay to Lucknow, I found myself in a compartment with an educated Mohammedan, and I said to myself: "I am a missionary. I'd better go to work." So I read him the whole of Sermon on the Mount. When I finished, he quietly replied: "Yes, we have the same thing in the Koran." Whether it was true or not was beside the point for him—he must get rid of the uniqueness of the Christian faith.

When I put up the teaching concerning turning the other cheek and going the second mile and loving your enemies, the Hindus would reply: "Yes, our sacred books tell us that we are to be like the sandalwood tree, which, when smitten by the ax, pours its perfume upon the ax that smites it." I had to acknowledge its beauty while inwardly raising the question, "Then where is the uniqueness of the Christian faith?" When I came to the cross, which certainly must be unique, I thought, I would be met by the statement of the Rig Veda: "Prajapati, the Lord of creatures was himself their sacrifice—he gave himself for them," and the blue-throated Shiva (one of the Hindu trinity) "drank poison that we might ambrosia taste," and the patch of blue on his throat is the lodged poison. Everything I brought up had its parallel. Then where was the uniqueness? I was puzzled.

Then it dawned on me. In all these statements from the Hindu scriptures it was the Word become word—the sandalwood illustration was an exhortation, not an exhibition; Prajapati, the Lord of creatures, giving himself for men in sacrifice was a statement with no historical basis; and the blue-throated Shiva was a legend, a myth. In Jesus the Word had become flesh—"Father, forgive them; for they know not what they do." And Jesus, the Lord of creatures, did give Himself for them on a cross. And He did drink the poison of our sin that we might taste the ambrosia of forgiveness and a new life.

The center of the faith of the modern Hindu is the Bhagavad-Gita where Krishna, a Hindu divinity, on the eve of a battle says things which strangely parallel the Christian faith. But here, too, it is the Word become word—it is a philosophical discourse put into the mouth of a divine Krishna who never lived. The historical Krishna is hardly the kind of character who could be looked up to and emulated. The philosophical Krishna is the Word become word—a philosophy or moralism.

Then I got hold of this difference: in all other religions it is the Word become word, but only in Jesus Christ did the Word become flesh. Then everything fell into its place. I had the Key, and this Key fitted everything in East and West. In the West we have studies in comparative religion in our theological seminaries and universities. In these courses the teachings of the various religions are outlined, and parallels are pointed out. The Christian faith emerges a little more moral, a little more consistent in its view of God and man, and a little higher in general, but nothing very unique. So many students came out of these institutions with little or no convictions and with nothing to preach—nothing except a philosophy or moralism, but no Gospel, no Good News. That is the paralysis that lies upon the Christian ministry; for the most part they are preaching the Word become word—a moralism, an exhortation to be good. Hence the barrenness.

I was being interviewed on TV by a brilliant commentator, who came to the point by saying: "You go throughout the world preaching. What do you have to preach that others do not have? It was a good question—and valid. Just what did I have?" The answer was simple and simply given: "I have Jesus Christ—the Word become flesh."

This brought a difference not only in degree, but in kind. The Christian faith is not just a little better than other faiths—a little more moral, more free from contradictory elements, more lofty in its conceptions. It is that, but it is more—it is different in kind. Religions are man's search for God. The Gospel is God's search for man. Therefore, there are many religions, but only one Gospel. Religions are the Word become word; the Gospel is the Word become flesh.

This verse: "And the Word became flesh" sets the Gospel off in a class by itself. And yet while it is in a class by itself, a *sui generis,* nevertheless it relates it to everything—God, life, the material, everything. For it is planted in life—spiritual, material, social. But planted in life it is different, apart, unique. No wonder William Barclay, perhaps the greatest authority on John's Gospel, could say, "Here we come to the sentence for the sake of which John wrote the Fourth Gospel: 'The Word became flesh.' " And then goes on:

Augustine afterwards said that in his pre-Christian days he had read and studied the great pagan philosophers and their writings, . . . but he had never read that "the Word became flesh." The one thing that no Greek would ever have dreamed of was that God could take a body. To the Greek the body was an evil, a prison-house in which the soul was shackled, a tomb in which the spirit was confined. Plutarch, the wise old Greek, did not even believe that God could control the happenings of this world directly; He had to do it by deputies and intermediaries, for as Plutarch saw it, it was nothing less than blasphemy to involve God in the affairs of the world. Philo could never have said it. He said: "The life of God has not descended to us; nor has it come as far as the necessities of the body." The great Roman Stoic Emperor, Marcus Aurelius, [said] "Despise the flesh—blood and bones and a net-work, a twisted skein of nerves and veins and arteries." "The composition of the whole body is under corruption."

And yet, in the face of all that—the highest thought of the day—the Gospel quietly says: "And the Word became flesh." It reversed everything and revealed Everything. No wonder Barclay could add: "It might well be held that this is the greatest verse in the whole New Testament."[1]

Without this verse the Christian faith is the Word become word—an idea, a philosophy, a moralism; with it the Christian faith is the Word become flesh, a fact—a Redemptive Fact, the Supreme Fact.

[1] *The Gospel of John,* tr. William Barclay (Philadelphia: The Westminster Press, 1955) I, 44, 45, 46.

Compared with this the differences between the Christian way and other ways are marginal and indecisive, but this is central and decisive. And compared with this the questions of the manifestations of the Christian faith are marginal and indecisive: If the manifestation of the Christian faith is not the Word become flesh—a decision—then it is the Word become word—a discussion, hence sub-Christian.

This book will deal with these two phases: Is this idea the Word become word, or the Word become flesh? And is this manifestation of the idea of the Word become word, or the Word become flesh? The one deals with faith and the other with life, and the touchstone in both cases is—the Word became flesh.

Someone asked me which of my twenty-three books I liked the best. My reply was: "Please don't make me choose between my babies." But if I were asked as to the message I would like to leave, I would unhesitatingly choose the message of *The Way*. My readers apparently have not agreed with me for it hasn't sold as much, for instance, as *The Christ of the Indian Road* and *Abundant Living*, each of which has sold over a million copies. I must not have said it too well. But the message of *The Way* seems to me the most important thing I have been trying to say through the years. If the Christian faith is written not merely in the Scripture but also into the nature of things, then that is not only important—it is decisive. In this present book I have reiterated the message of *The Way* in the first part of the book, since it fitted the present theme, hoping that this re-emphasis would call attention again to what I consider the most important thing in the Christian faith, namely, that the Christian Way is *the* Way and that "Way" is written not merely in texts of Scripture but into the texture of our beings.

I have used repeatedly in this book the phrases, "The Word became word," and "The Word became flesh." I have done so deliberately, for these phrases side by side bring into focus the issues in this book and in the world of faith. If we can make the transition from one to the other, we can be saved—we and our world. If not? Well, "The Word become word" has run its course and is near bankruptcy. Nothing can save us except that transition to "The Word became flesh."

The question arose in my mind: Shall I make this a book reading straight through without a daily division for daily devotion, or shall I make it a devotional book—a page a day? The publishers advised the devotional form. And rightly, I believe. For in the devotional one reads not merely for information, but for transformation. He reads to become a better person; consciously or unconsciously he wants the literature to become life, the worship to become work. In other words he wants the Word to become flesh. So the devotional is more in line with the title. It can be read straight through for information, for one there runs through the whole, but it can also be read for transformation. And that is the real purpose of this book—transformation to individuals and society. To discuss "the Word became flesh" as a proposition is to make the Word become theology; but to discuss it, not as a proposition, but as a proposal for change and action—that would be nearer "the Word became flesh."

If it means to the reader what it is increasingly meaning to the writer, then the purpose of this book will be accomplished. What for me began as a question is now turning into a quest—a quest to embody in some way, however faint and imperfect, the Word become flesh.

E. STANLEY JONES

CONTENTS

Section I—The Word Became Flesh in Jesus

9

10

11

Section II—The Word Becomes Flesh in Us

14

Plague-stained Hands I Saw the Meaning of the Christian Faith" • "O God, Make Me like Christ" • "Lord, Do Not Hold this Sin Against Them" • "Now Them" • "Now I See the Meaning of Christianity" • A Bootblack: "I Love to Work for Jesus—I Do It for Him"

"What Is This? Viewing Cherry Blossoms Wearing a Long Sword!" • "Drunk with the Wine of His Own Wordiness" • Afraid of Fallout and Producing It All the Time • "In All These Things We Are More Than Conquerors" • Not Ghost but Embodied Beings • Spiritualization—First Refuge of the Skeptical Mind • The Body Is Holy If Wholly His

"We Do Not Work to the Victory But from the Victory" • The Gospel Is Different: It Is God Taking the Initiative • "It's Pouring Down—It's Pouring Down—Take It" • Living in a State of Yesness to God • "I Refuse to Accept My Limitations" • Holding to Crusts • "Has Anyone Told You Today?"

Can the Flesh Be Redeemed? • Sixty to Eighty Percent of Patients Have Psychosomatic Complaints • "It's the Surly Bird Who Gets the Germ" • All Mental Illnesses Are a Retreat Out of Life • A Prescription for Health: The Nine Beatitudes • "Always Right, Hence Always Wrong" • Inward Conflict Chief Cause of Illness

"It Is Inherent for the Christian to Propagate His Faith" • Not God's Lawyer but His Witness • "Suffering from a Hallucination?" • Lay Witnessing the Center of Our Faith • Separating What God Had Joined • A Tongue-tied Colonel Freed Through Witnessing • "Let Him Who Hears Say 'Come' "

The Motive and Incentive for Missions? • We Do What He Did • John 3:16 and I John 3:16 • "I Know That My Redeemer Liveth" • "But I Decided to Stay" • The World Is a Mission Field and God the First Missionary • "I Wouldn't Do That for a Million"

The Incarnation and the Kingdom • "We Wanted Something That Would Bring Life into Total Meaning" • "Everything

16

WHY "THE WORD"?

The phrase "the Word" was not really indigenous to Hebrew thought. It used "the word of the Lord," "Thy word," but not "the Word" as a separate entity. But it was indigenous to Greek thought, so the early Christian writers did not hesitate to reach out beyond the Hebrew heritage and take hold of any conception to express that which was beyond expression. For they saw that the Gospel was bursting with universal meanings and could not be confined to the Jewish language and culture to express that which was beyond language and culture. A universal faith would require a universal medium for its expression. That universal medium could only be life—the one thing universal to us all. But even that universal "life" would be insufficient—it would have to be "Life," the Life of God and man, the Life of the God-man. The Word would have to become flesh.

But on the way to reveal the Word become flesh, the writer would use "the Word," for it is expressive: "In the beginning was the Word, and the Word was with God, and the Word was God" (John 1:1). Why was Jesus here called "the Word"? Well, one's words are the expression of the hidden thought. If you should stand before an audience without a word, hoping that the audience would get your thought, intuitively and immediately, it would end in futility. Only as the hidden thought is put into a word is the thought communicated.

Here is the hidden God, like the hidden thought, and we cannot know what He is like unless He communicates Himself through a word. If one says, "I can know God in my heart intuitively and immediately, without the mediation of a word," then the answer is: "But your 'heart' then becomes the medium of communication and knowing the heart as one does with its sin and crosscurrents and cross-conceptions he knows it is a very unsafe medium for the revelation of God." God must reveal Himself.

O God, my Father, Thou art the hidden God. How can I, bounded by my senses, know Thee except as Thou shalt show Thyself to me? I cannot read Thee unless I get a Word from Thee. But I know that Word cannot be verbal, for Thou art not verbal, but vital. Amen.

AFFIRMATION FOR THE DAY: *If the word is the expression of the hidden thought, I shall be, in some real way, the expression of the hidden God.*

THE WORD IS THE SON OF THE THOUGHT

We saw yesterday that without a word the thought cannot be expressed. The word is the thought become available. When you get hold of my words, you say: "Now I have hold of his thought." The words are the thought mediated to us. The words are not a third something standing between you and the thought—they are the thought become available. He who takes hold of the words takes hold of the thought itself. The word and the thought are one.

Here is the hidden God, and He expresses Himself through the Word. When you take hold of that Word, you do not take hold of something standing between you and God—that Word, Jesus, is God available. Jesus is not a third person standing between you and God. When you take hold of Him, you take hold of God Himself. He is a mediator only in the sense that He mediates God to you. When you know Him you know God. Just as the thought and the word are one, so Jesus could say, "I and the Father are one."

But the word is the offspring, or son, of the thought. So Jesus is the offspring, or Son, of the Father. And just as the thought is greater than the word, for all expression means limitation—you have to look around to get the right word to express the thought—so the unexpressed God is greater than the expressed God. God had to limit Himself in coming to us in human form. So Jesus could say, "The Father is greater than I."

There seems to be a contradiction: "I and the Father are one," and "The Father is greater than I." But there is not. Just as the thought and the word are one, so God, the Thought, and Jesus, the Word, are one. But just as the unexpressed thought is greater than the expressed thought, the word, so God the Father, the unexpressed, is greater than God the Son, the expressed. They are one, and yet the Father is greater than the Son. For God was self-limited when He became human.

Did He have to become human to show Himself?

O God, our Father, we are at the very crux of our quest—didst Thou have to become human? Help us not to make a misstep here, for we go astray in life if we go astray in thought. May we think Thy thoughts after Thee, for we would be Thy life after Thee. Amen.

AFFIRMATION FOR THE DAY: *I offer my mind, my soul, my flesh to reveal God to someone today.*

DID GOD HAVE TO BECOME HUMAN?

We ended yesterday with the question: Did God have to become human to show Himself? Wasn't there some other way? A less expensive way? A less humiliating way?

Well, there are a number of ways He might reveal Himself. He can reveal Himself through nature. But not perfectly. I look up to God through nature and come to the conclusion that God is Law. But the revelation is a very impersonal kind of law. The discovery of atomic energy has driven many thoughtful scientists to God. From whence this awe-ful energy, so awe-ful and so law abiding? All this drives men to a dependable Creator. But that energy tells you little about the character of God except His might. Said a chaplain, "That plane holds more power than was expended in the last war." But the revelation of God's character in an atom is questionable. That atom can burn millions to ashes, or it can lift the life of millions to a higher level if it is harnessed to the collective good. The character of God revealed in the atom is morally neutral. The song we sing, "How great Thou art," tells of looking at the stars and hearing the rolling thunder and concluding that God is "great," but "great" in what? The stars look down on us indifferent as to our moral character, and the rolling thunder and the flashing lightning may hit a brothel or a baby with no moral discrimination. So nature's revelation of God is equivocal.

Then God reveals Himself through prophet and teacher and sage, but not perfectly, for the medium of revelation is imperfect and the message coming through that imperfect medium partakes of that imperfection. Besides, it is the Word become word—verbal.

Then there is the method of revelation through a book. We must be grateful for every inspired word which has come down to us through a book—grateful, but not satisfied. For two reasons: first, a book is impersonal and God is the infinitely Personal; second, a book is the Word become word, not the Word become flesh.

O Father, we search through various ways and various media to find Thee. For we are homesick for Thee. For Thou art our Home, and apart from Thee we wander from thing to thing and from place to place seeking, seeking. Our hearts are restless till they rest in Thee. Amen.

AFFIRMATION FOR THE DAY: *I shall be an imperfect medium, but nevertheless a medium, through which people can see God today.*

CAN GOD REVEAL HIMSELF PERFECTLY
THROUGH A BOOK?

We paused yesterday to ask whether God could reveal Himself perfectly through a book, however sacred it may be. The Sikhs of India treat the Granth Sahib, their sacred book, as though it were a person. They fan it in hot weather, offer it food, and put it to sleep under mosquito curtains. To them it is a person. But however they may attempt to make the book personal, it is still impersonal. The Vedas of the Hindus are supposedly eternal, but we know that ofttimes there are historical references in them. They are of time and are impersonal. The Koran is supposedly dictated by God, but if it were, it would still be impersonal; hence the Word become word. There are those in our day who put out books with such titles as *God Speaking,* which were supposedly dictated to the listening scribes. From the contents, it would seem that they are, at their best, the highest thoughts of the writers translated as the voice of God, for nothing beyond high human thinking has been revealed—and some of it is not even high—it is very, very ordinary. But if it were dictated by God, it would still be the Word become word.

Then there are those who in religious circles sit in séances waiting for some word from God through a medium, who in turn is supposed to get some word from a person in the next life. Apparently, what has "come through" has added little or nothing to our knowledge of God, and little or nothing to our knowledge of the hereafter—nothing except what the human mind would project into the future and call revelation. In any case, if it were real it would be inadequate, for it would be the Word become word and, a very second-hand or third-hand word at that. But there are those who go into contortions and trances and speak supposedly as God. "Who is he?" I inquired of a disciple when people at every railway station fell at the feet of a "holy man." "He is God. He can tell you anything." But I could see he was a spastic and his contortions of speech were supposed to be the result of divine possession.

O God, we project ourselves and our thoughts into the heavens and call it Thy voice and Thy revelation. We are sick, nigh unto death, at the echoes of our own voices. We want some authentic Word from thee—the Word for which we have been waiting. Amen.

AFFIRMATION FOR THE DAY: *Regarding God, I shall be not a second-hander but a first-hander.*

SEEING GOD THROUGH IMPERFECT MEDIA

We are considering how God could reveal Himself perfectly. We continue to look at the question of whether a book can be a perfect revelation. Words get meaning from the life that surrounds them. If I should use the word "home" before an audience, to some it would mean "heaven," to some "hell," according to the life which surrounded the word. Literature can never rise higher than life. For life puts content and meaning into the literature. Suppose God should give us a book from heaven with all His will written into it—would that be a perfect revelation of God? Hardly. For we would read into those words our highest experience of those words. I would see the word "love" in the book, and I would read into it my highest experience of love. But my highest experience of love is not love—it is my highest experience of love which is partial, incomplete. I would see the word "purity" in the book, and I would read into it my highest experience of purity; but my highest experience of purity is not purity. I would see the word "God," and I would read into it my highest experience of God; but my highest experience of God is not God.

I would pull these words to the level of my highest experience, and so would you, so the book would not be so much a revelation of God as a revelation of us. What then do we need for a perfect revelation of God ? A life must come among us—a Divine Life which will lift these words from the level to which we have dragged them and put a new content into them—a Divine Content through the Divine Illustration. We would then no longer see these words through what we are but through what He is. We think that has happened. A Life came among us and lived publicly for thirty-three years. We no longer see the word "love" in the light of our poor, partial love, but in the light of a Love that prayed for enemies upon a cross: "Father, forgive them for they know not what they do." The Word of love became flesh.

O, Father, we see Thee faintly and distortedly through the lattice of nature and through the lattice of Thy followers, but we begin to see Thee through the Life of Thy Son. And what we see sets our hearts on fire to see more and yet more. In His name. Amen.

AFFIRMATION FOR THE DAY: *My light may be poor, but it will be light, not darkness.*

THE QUEST FOR THE PERFECT REVELATION

We continue our quest for the Perfect Revelation. If God should give us a book from heaven as His revelation of Himself, we would read into those words our highest experience of those words. But now the new possibility has come. I can see those words through a Divine Illustration of the meaning of those words. I see the word "purity," and I no longer read into it my highest experience of purity, which is partial and incomplete, but I see it in the light of a Purity which shared my temptations, minus my falls. I see Purity—the Real Thing. I no longer see the word "God" in the light of my imagination of God, but in the light of this authentic uncovering of the nature of God in understandable terms—human terms. I look up through Jesus, the Son, and I now know what God is like. He is a Christ-like God, and if He is; then He is a good God and trustable. I could think of nothing higher, I could be content with nothing less.

If God isn't like Jesus, I am not interested in Him. For the highest I know in the realm of character is to be Christlike. I said that in India, and a Hindu wrote to me: "You took my breath away. This is Bhakti [devotion] par excellence. You said you wouldn't be interested in God if He were not like your Guru [Master]." But my Guru is no human Guru—He is God's authentic self-revelation. When the disciples said, "Show us the Father—it sufficeth us," Jesus quietly said: "He that hath seen me hath seen the Father," and it was one of the greatest moments in human history. In the Congo when those in charge were about to pull up the idol from the idol-pit, the people fell back terror-stricken. They cried: "If we look on the face of 'our father,' we will die." But here, as we look on the face of "Our Father" in the person of Jesus, then we do not die, but live! We see God not terrible but tender, not forbidding but forgiving. We see in Jesus God as He is—really is!

O Son of God, we thank Thee for showing us the Father. We would never have known what He was like had we not looked on Thy face. Seeing Him in Thy face, we rest not satisfied but stirred—stirred to be like what we see in Thee. Read our gratitude. Amen.

AFFIRMATION FOR THE DAY: *Perhaps I cannot be authoritative but I can be authentic.*

THE SILENCE OF ETERNITY HAS BEEN BROKEN

We come now to gather together what we have been saying this week. We must reject as inadequate or inaccurate the attempts to find God through nature—the nature worshipers; the attempt to find Him within ourselves—the "I" worshipers; the attempt to find Him through teachers, gurus, priests—the men worshipers; the attempt to find Him in legalism—the written law worshipers; the attempt to find Him in slogans and affirmation—the cult of the Positive, the Positive worshipers; the attempt to find Him in the quiet of submissiveness—the worshipers of Silence, of Quietism. In any of these you may find glimpses of God, but if you are to see God face to face you must see Him in the face of Jesus Christ. For Jesus is God approachable, God available, God simplified, God lovable. The Word has become flesh.

There was, and is, no other way for God to reveal Himself except in understandable terms, human terms. He had to show His character where your character and mine are wrought out, namely, in the stream of human history. The Word had to become flesh, or else not be the Word; it would be something else—words!

Lao-tse, the great Chinese philosopher said: "The Word that can be uttered is not the Divine word; that Word is Silence." He is right, in a way, for the Divine Word cannot be uttered. That would be the Word become word. But the alternative is not silence. Lao-tse had to say the alternative was silence for he knew of no Word become flesh, knew no Jesus Christ. So it had to be silence. But "the silence of eternity" has been broken, it has been interrupted by love, by the appearance of Incarnate Love—Jesus.

The statement of Lao-tse, himself a philosopher, that the Word that can be uttered is not the Divine Word, sweeps from the board of adequacy all attempts to utter the Divine Word through philosophy, laws, reason, and theology. They are all the Word become word. The only method of revelation is the Word become flesh.

O God, my Father, I thank Thee that when all other ways were inadequate Thou didst open the way to us. When we couldn't come to Thee, Thou didst come to us, come to us in lowly form, human form. And now we can come to Thee through the Way. Amen.

AFFIRMATION FOR THE DAY: *The Silence of Eternity shall become revealed in me today.*

GOD THROUGH PHILOSOPHY AND MORALISM

There have been two great attempts to find God apart from the Word became flesh. They are the attempts of philosophy and the attempts of moralism. The attempt of philosophy has been seen in the great philosophical nations—Greece, India, and China. The great philosophical systems were all three completed just before the time of the coming of Jesus. They took men as high as man could go by philosophical reasoning. Beyond these systems the human race will not progress in philosophical thought. The human brain strained itself to the utmost and having reached its apex went progressively bankrupt as an adequate method of finding God. At its highest, in the Vedanta philosophy of India, the philosopher could only say of Brahma: *"Neti, Neti"*—"Not that, Not that." That was the very highest it could say, and its word was negative. The Word of philosophy was word and that word was "No." It had no positive affirmation to make about the nature and character of God. It was the tacit acknowledgment of bankruptcy. Lao-tse said the final word about God is Silence and Shankarachariya, the great philosopher of India, said the final word about God is "Not that." They both came out to zero.

If the attempt to find God by philosophy was completed just before the coming of Jesus, so the attempt through moralism, or the Law, was also completed just before His coming. The attempt to find God through Law was a noble attempt of a great people, the Hebrews. Never was such a moral system built up as was embodied by the Law, and never was the end product so disappointing. It produced the Pharisee, who stood in his pride and said, "I thank God I am not as other men." And Jesus pronounced the doom of this attempt at finding God when He said: "Unless your righteousness exceeds that of the Scribes and Pharisees, you will never enter the Kingdom of heaven." Their highest could not reach the Kingdom. Both philosophy and moralism fall short.

O Father, when our best was not good enough, and when our highest could not reach the Kingdom, Thou didst come Thyself to lift us to Thyself. What mercy. What humility. What grace. We are speechless before the wonder of it. Read our thankful hearts. Amen.

AFFIRMATION FOR THE DAY: *May no one looking at me ever say in his quest for God, "Not that."*

"THE LAW CONTAINS BUT A SHADOW"

We ended yesterday on the attempt to reach God by moralism, by the Law. The inadequacy, even bankruptcy, of this method is expressed in the Epistle to the Hebrews:

"For the Law contains but a shadow, and no true image, of the good things which were to come; it provides for the same sacrifices year after year, and with these it can never bring the worshipers to perfection for all time. . . . That is why, at his coming into the world, he [Christ, RSV] says:

> Sacrifice and offering thou didst not desire,
> But thou has prepared a body for me.
> Whole-offerings and sin-offerings thou didst not delight in.
> Then I said, "Here am I: as it is written of me in the scroll,
> I have come, O God, to do Thy will" (10:1, 5-7 NEB).

"The Law contains but a shadow, and no true image." It was the Word become word, hence, a shadow and no true image. Then it follows that if the Law is but a shadow, all discussion and argument about the Law are but shadow-boxing. And all preaching of moralism to whip up the will to do good and to be good is but shadow-preaching. It ends in futility.

When sacrificers of animals and products of nature were at the end of their rope—God did not "desire" them—and when all man's endeavor to gain salvation by offering his moral acts and good deeds fell short—for God did not "desire" them—then the Unexpected happened: "But Thou hast prepared a body for me"—the Word became flesh. "Here am I . . . I have come, O God, to do Thy Will"—the will of God became a Person—embodied in that Person it was the Will become flesh.

This was the Substance—all else is but "shadow." So the Substance superseded all shadow manifestations. It now holds the field as the only real way of Revelation, that way—the Word became flesh.

Dear God and Father, we see clearly now that only as Thou didst come to us, could we find Thee and know Thee. Now we know Thee and find Thee in available form—find Thee in the God-Man. And what a find! Our hearts sing with gratitude. Amen.

AFFIRMATION FOR THE DAY: *My body is at Thy disposal to reveal Thy will.*

HASN'T RESOURCES WITHIN HIMSELF

Job asks, "Who by searching can find out God?" The answer is plain in history: No one! For what we find in our upward search for God is not God, but the projection of our thoughts into the heavens and calling it God. It is the Word become word—and earthbound. We create God in the image of our imagination. And this is "no true image." Apart from Jesus we know little or nothing about God, and what we know is wrong. The Word must become flesh or the Word is a vast question mark.

India is the greatest illustration of the truth of the above. If God the Father could have been discovered through philosophy, then the philosophers of India could have discovered Him. For centuries they have piled words on words, but through this multiplicity of words they have not discovered the Word. Someone has facetiously defined philosophy as "the search in a dark room for a black cat which isn't there." But there is more than usual truth in that jibe. For philosophic reason has searched in a dark universe for a philosophical God who isn't there. The highest philosophical thought of India, the Vedanta, came to the conclusion that Brahma, in its highest state, the *Niraguna* (without relationships) is *Sat*—Truth, *Chit*—intelligence, *Ananda*—bliss. Truth, intelligence, and bliss, but no Love. Reason made God in its own image—bliss through truth and intelligence. But without Love God is a cold, uninviting Abstraction. Therefore "Vedanta is the philosophy of a few, the religion of none." Through philosophy you have come out to a God who is other than God the Father. God the Father could only be revealed by Revelation. No one could imagine or think that the God of the Universe would take a body and become man to redeem man. A love like that just doesn't exist—not in the categories of philosophy. Here only seeing is believing. We would never have believed it unless we had seen it. The Word had to become flesh to become credible. Unless the eye had seen and the ear heard it would never have entered into the heart of man what God has prepared for us.

O God, our Father, our hearts are filled with an unutterable joy—a joy too deep for words. We are not knocking at the gates of heaven; Thou art knocking at the lowly doors of our hearts. What grace, what humility, what love! What we couldn't dream—we see! Thank Thee, thank Thee. Amen.

AFFIRMATION FOR THE DAY: *I haven't resources in myself to complete myself, but I know how to take what He offers.*

PRINCIPLES INSTEAD OF A PERSON?

In *Conversion* we mentioned Dr. Hocking, the philosopher, who said that as a philosopher he could not say, "The Word became flesh," though he said that he saw it. There is a sequel to that. I mentioned the above story to his son who is also a philosopher, at Emory University, and he replied, "That is interesting, for when someone asked my father what verse in the Scripture was the most precious to him, he replied, 'Behold, I stand at the door and knock; if anyone hears my voice and opens the door, I will come in to him and eat with him, and he with me.' " That is interesting, for one would have thought that the great philosopher would have chosen, "Ye shall know the truth and the truth shall make you free," for that would have been down his philosophical alley, but no, he chooses this personal approach from the Unseen, this fact of God coming to us and knocking at the door of our hearts, the Word of Love made flesh. Dr. Hocking, the philosopher, could see this personal approach but could not say it; but Dr. Hocking, the person, sees it, loves it, and says it, and cherishes it as the most precious thing in Scripture and in his life. There is the difference between philosophy and real religion—one is cold, calculating, and uncommitted; the other is warm, uncalculating, and committed with a life committal.

That is where Dr. Q. Hobart Mowrer, Research Professor of Psychology at the University of Illinois, is so right in his diagnosis of Freudianism—psychoanalysis, and so wrong when he switches to religion and says, "As long as different religious groups fasten upon personages, which are of necessity unique, they will remain apart; but when they begin *to look at the principles which they have in common,* reconciliation and union are by no means improbable." He would take the principles of the Christian faith and push to the edges the Person. He would take the stream, but not the source; the rays of the sun, but not the sun.

O my Father, they want the impersonal but not the Personal. But it is Thou that my soul most deeply craves. I can take no halfway house and call it a home. Thou art my home and nothing this side of Thee can ever satisfy the deepest cravings of my heart. Amen.

AFFIRMATION FOR THE DAY: *The personal is too big to be satisfied with the impersonal.*

CHRISTIANITY IS CHRIST

We paused yesterday to look at the suggestion of Dr. Mowrer that the emphasis should be on the principles in the Christian faith and not on the Person. But the Person is the Christian faith. Christianity has its doctrines but it is not a doctrine; has its creeds but it is not a creed; has its rites and ceremonies but it is not a rite or ceremony; has its institutions but it is not an institution. Christianity is Christ. Christians are people who believe in God and man and life through Christ. We do not begin with God, for if you do you, do not begin with God but with your ideas of God which are not God. We do not begin with man, for if you do, you begin with the problems of man. And if you begin with a problem you will probably end with a problem, and in the process you will probably become a problem. Of one modern minister it was said, "Without a problem spake he not unto them." This is a problem-obsessed age, and we have become problems dealing with problems. A man was offered a better job—he turned it down: "I'd be a two-ulcer man in a five-ulcer job." A retired bishop said, "Since I've been retired I am frustrated; and unhappy." We don't begin with God, and we don't begin with man, we begin with the God-Man and from Him we work out to God, and from Him we work down to man. In His light we see life—all life. For He is the revelation of God and man—the revelation of what God is and what man can become—he can become Christlike.

The words of William Temple, Archbishop of Canterbury, sum up the Christian position: "The supreme revelation is given in the life and person of Jesus. The revelation is not His teaching or His acts but Himself. . . . Christianity is not a dedication to a system of rules or of thought, but a dedication to a Person. This is unique among the religions of the world." Mowrer wants the Word become word; the Christian faith presents the Word become flesh. Hence power.

O blessed Savior, Thou art a Savior just because Thou art God available—available to our needs, for Thou dost meet us amid those needs. Thou hast lived among our needs and hast shown us how to live where we live. Now I not only hear, I see. Amen.

AFFIRMATION FOR THE DAY: *I, the personal, am made by the Personal, and for the Personal, and cannot rest this side of Him.*

"THE PRINCIPLE OF MOTHERHOOD"?

We are considering whether the principles of the Christian faith apart from the Person, Jesus, would be adequate or effective, and the answer is a decided "No." For it is the Person who puts content into the principles. Apart from the Person the principles would mean something else, something very different. Take the statement: "A new commandment I give to you, that you love one another; even as I have loved you" (John 13:34). Without the last portion, "even as I have loved you," there would have been nothing new in the commandment. The old content—the content gathered from contemporaneous life—would have remained. That content would have been eros—possessive love—and not agape—sacrificial love. Jesus put the agape content into love by His illustration of agape love. But even agape love is not the norm now—the norm is Christlike love which is a norm all its own, *sui generis*.

Principles may be low in content; they are also always low in power. They are moonlight, secondhand, not sunlight, firsthand. Suppose a child is crying for its mother, and you say, "Don't cry, little child, I'll give you the principle of motherhood." The child would reply: "I want my mother." In India where the highest God, Brahma, is impersonal, Tulsi Das, a great Indian poet says, "The Impersonal laid no hold on my heart." Too cold, too unresponsive. No wonder someone described the Vedantic philosophy, which expounds the philosophy of the impersonal Brahma, in this way: "It is the philosophy of a few, the religion of none." There are no temples to Brahama—no worship of it. Philosophy about Brahma, but no religion. Religion sets up when a person seeks communion with a Person. Then the principles embodied in the Person take on power and vitality, and we *want* to practice the principles because He practiced and embodied them. Then principles become power, but only as they are embodied in a Person—otherwise, no. They fall faintly upon the human heart.

O blessed and only wise God, Thy method is sound. Thou hast shown us in Thy Son that Thou art practicing what Thou dost require of us. In Thee the Word is always flesh. "For by all that God requires of me, I know that He himself must be." I thank thee. Amen.

AFFIRMATION FOR THE DAY: *Let all my principles become personal in me today.*

JESUS PUTS A FACE ON GOD

We are discussing the relation of principles and the Person. When people speak of God as "the Divine Principle," they may talk to themselves about God, but they cannot talk to God. You cannot talk to a Principle; you can only talk to a Person. So a religion founded on "the Divine Principle" must be, of necessity, a religion of dialogue with yourself, affirming to yourself certain principles. This is this side of, and other than, the religion of communing with your Heavenly Father, a person with a Person.

Christianity "puts a face on God." Jesus is God's face. And that "one dear Face, far from vanishes, rather grows . . . and becomes my universe that feels and knows." And Browning further adds: "O heart I made, a Heart beats here." The Psalmist asks: "He that made the eye shall He not see; He that made the ear shall He not hear?" And we may add: "He that made the human personality shall He not be Personal?" He can't be less than Personal, for personality is the highest category of being we know. And when I say, "God is Personal," I don't mean He is corporeal—an enlarged Man seated in the heavens. In personality there are at least four things: intelligence, feeling, will, self-consciousness. So when we say that God is personal, we believe He thinks, He feels, He wills, He has self-consciousness. He may be more than that; He cannot be less. And the Impersonal is less.

We cannot say our prayers to a principle, nor worship an axiom. The woman in Ceylon, who when self-government came and the first election was introduced, was seen with folded hands saying her prayers to a ballot box—the new god who decided things. But prayers to a ballot box decided nothing; the number of votes within the box did.

Prayer and worship is response on the part of the person to the response of the Person. It is communion, or it is self-hypnotism.

So principles let you down unless they are embodied.

O Father God, when I talk with Thee I know I am not listening to the echo of my own voice. I know my Father's voice. And the Voice is not mine projected into the heavens, for it often runs counter to my voice—and rightly so, for it is redemptive. I thank Thee. Amen.

AFFIRMATION FOR THE DAY: *My person responds to the Eternal Person fully and forever.*

"WHY DON'T YOU PREACH PRINCIPLES?"

We are discussing whether principles, apart from the Person, in religion would be sufficient. A Hindu said to me: "Why don't you preach principles to us and leave out the person of Christ?" The answer is simple and twofold: The principles without the person are powerless. An exact statement of truth, or an exact statement of ethical moralism, leaves us cold and unmoved. Only as principles are embodied in a person do they become power. And second, we would never have known what the principles meant had we not seen them illustrated in the Person.

We who are persons yearn for the Personal. Browning puts it in these vivid words:

" 'Tis the weakness in strength, that I cry for! my flesh, that I seek
In the Godhead! I seek and I find it! O Saul, it shall be
A Face like my face that receives Thee; a Man like to me,
Thou shalt love and be loved by, for ever: a Hand like this hand
Shall throw open the gates of new life to Thee! See the Christ stand!"
"Saul"

Suppose there is no flesh in the Godhead, no Face like my face there—is the Godhead attractive? Will the Godhead evoke loyalty and love? The answer is in the Brahma of Hinduism. We have noted that Brahma has three attributes—truth, intelligence, bliss, but no love. If Brahma, the It, had love, it would relate Itself to men and things. Brahma is the unrelated. Love is absent from the Highest. But love is the highest in man. Then man has something higher than that which is found in the Highest. Then God is a disappointment. If love is absent from the Highest, then the Highest will do nothing to help you up the ladder to Itself. You get there if you get there. And you get there by contemplation, by meditation, by self-affirmation: *"Aham Brahma": "*I am Brahma." But that is the Word become word, not the Word become flesh.

O Father, I thank Thee that I seek the highest in Thee—love—and find it there. But I would never have found it had I not been shown it—shown it in Thy Son. In Him we see, not merely hear. And the seeing is believing. So I believe. Amen.

AFFIRMATION FOR THE DAY: *I see in God my weakness in His Strength, my littleness in His Greatness—I nestle.*

"HE HATH VISITED AND REDEEMED"

We are driven to the conclusion that the only way for God to reveal Himself to us is for the Word to become flesh. So the Scripture reads: "And the Word became flesh and dwelt among us, full of grace and truth; we have beheld his glory, glory as of the only Son from the Father. . . . And from his fullness have we all received, grace upon grace. For the law was given through Moses; grace and truth came through Jesus Christ. No one has ever seen God; the only Son, who is in the bosom of the Father, he has made him known" (John 1:14-18).

"And dwelt among us." The revelation of God was not a momentary rift in the clouds that surround the mystery of the hidden Divine—a momentary insight as to what God is like, a fleeting vision. No, He "dwelt among us." He dwelt among us from the cradle of the manger to the grave of the tomb. It was long enough for Him to reveal God's character in operation amid the surroundings where your character and mine are wrought out. He met life as you and I meet it—as a man. He called on no power not at our disposal for His own moral battle. He performed no miracle to extricate Himself from any difficulty. If He had power, He had power to restrain power, holding it only for the meeting of human need in others. He never performed a miracle just to show power or to confound an enemy. He lived a normal life, so normal that it became the norm. He dwelt among us as one of us.

Another passage says: "He hath visited and redeemed his people." The only way to redeem His people was to visit them. He couldn't sit on a cloud and utter commands, or pick us up and take us to heaven with celestial tongs, not soiling His fingers with the messy business of human living. No, He dwelt among us—amid our poverty, amid our temptations, amid our problems and choices, amid our oppositions and disappointments. He lived among us and showed us how to live by living.

Gracious Savior, Thou didst come where we are to take us where Thou art. Thou didst show us Life in the midst of life. And now we know what Life is like; we have seen it—in Thee. And what we see is so infinitely beautiful that we are on fire to see more. Amen.

AFFIRMATION FOR THE DAY: *I walk today with One who has all the wisdom, all the power, all the grace I need.*

"I TAKE A BITE, YOU TAKE A BITE"

We are considering the verse: "And the Word became flesh and dwelt among us." He really dwelt among us. He resisted the temptation to live in any way except "among." The first temptation in the wilderness was to feed himself upon miracles *apart* from the people—make stones into bread. He rejected that—He would eat as we eat. The second temptation He also rejected—the temptation to live above the people, standing on a pinnacle of the temple, and throwing Himself down, only to be carried back again on angels' hands. He would not live *above*. The third temptation was the temptation to live *as*—to live as we live, taking the devil's suggestion to worship him—to adopt his methods, to gain the kingdoms of the world. No, He would not live apart, above, or as—He would be with us, but different. He would identify Himself with us in everything, except our sin.

During the war a G.I. saw a starved little girl and offered her a sandwich, but her mind had been so poisoned by propaganda that she wouldn't take it—it might be poisoned. So the G.I. took a bite and then said to her: "I take a bite, you take a bite"; "I take a bite, you take a bite." She melted and began to play the game of "I take a bite, you take a bite." In Jesus we find God seriously playing that game with us: "I take a bite, you take a bite." Jesus "tasted death for every man," but He also tasted life with every man. He asks us to do nothing but what He himself does. If we are born in poverty and rejection, remember He was born in a stable, for there was no room for them in the inn. "He was tempted in all points like as we are." He knows us—from within.

In Holland I saw a church bell ringing inside a cross. Befitting. The music came out of pain. There is music in the Gospel, but it's music which is not surface jazz—it is pain set to music—pains become paeans. The Victory is not apart, or above, but in. He "dwelt among us."

O Jesus, when Thou dost speak it is Deep speaking to deep. We know that You know. And knowing You love, how can we help loving in return? We do with all our ransomed beings. We love Thee; we love Thee. Give us a greater capacity to love Thee. Amen.

AFFIRMATION FOR THE DAY: *All my crosses shall have bells within them, and I shall ring them when pain wrings me.*

"FULL OF GRACE AND TRUTH"

We continue to look at this amazing passage: "And the Word became flesh and dwelt among us, full of grace and truth." "Full of grace and truth." The first thing in the Christian faith is "grace"—an act—an act of outgoing, forgiving, redeeming grace. Grace is first, for the first thing in God is love, and grace is love in action—it is the word of love become flesh. If grace is "unmerited favor," so, here, it is Love favoring us when we are not favorable, loving us when we are not lovable, accepting us when we are not acceptable, redeeming us when by all the rules of the book we are not redeemable. Grace is love applied, the word of love become flesh. That is the distinctive thing in the Christian faith.

Suppose it had read: "Full of truth and grace." Then the emphasis would have been upon "truth" in God. "God is truth," said Mahatma Gandhi, for he, inheritor of the emphasis on philosophy from the Hindu centuries, would approach it with emphasis on truth. But that would be the Word become word—"God is truth" is a word about the Word. But the first thing in God is not truth but love. The Christian Scriptures never say, "God is truth," for that would have classed the Christian faith as a philosophy. But the Christian faith is not primarily a thought; it is primarily an act—an act of Love invading history to redeem men. It is Grace in action.

Then where does "truth" come in? It comes in after "grace." For you have to see "truth" and not merely hear about it. If truth is not seen in action, it is not seen; for truth not in action is less than truth—it is truth verbal, not vital. I am not truth unless I am truth in my relationships, in my acts. For truth that is not acting is truth static, which is less than truth.

So we see "truth" through "grace"—grace is truth in gracious act. We see the nature of truth through the revelation of the act. Otherwise truth would be the Word become word; now we see it as the Word become flesh.

O Savior, Thou dost not only save us, Thou dost save truth—save it from being a proposition and made it into a Person. Thou didst say, "I am truth," and lo, Truth is lovable and livable and not a dry-as-dust proposition. I am at Thy feet, Gracious Truth. Amen.

AFFIRMATION FOR THE DAY: *All my justice shall have kindness in it, and all my kindness shall have justice in it.*

A PERSON TO BE FOLLOWED

We are pondering on "full of grace and truth." We insisted yesterday that the order was right—first grace, then truth. A great many people think Jesus was a moralist imposing a moral code upon humanity—a code for which humanity is badly made. It is an impossible code which humanity, being what it is, cannot fulfill. But Jesus was not a moralist in that sense at all. He was a revealer of the nature of reality. First of God—He said if you want to know what God is like look at me. "He that hath seen me hath seen the Father." We see the Father in the face of His Son. God is like Jesus in character. Transfer every characteristic of character from Jesus to God, and you do not lower your estimate of God—you heighten it. For there is nothing higher for God or man than to be Christlike. Jesus is God simplified, God approachable, God understandable, God lovable. When I say God I think Jesus. And nothing higher can be thought or said! Jesus is the last word that can be said about God.

Then Jesus was a revealer of the laws which underlie the universe. He seldom used the imperative, almost never the subjunctive, almost entirely the indicative. "This is," He said, "and you must come to terms with it, or get hurt." When He finished the Sermon on the Mount "the people were astonished at His teaching for He taught them as one who had authority and not as their Scribes." The Scribes quoted authorities, secondhand teaching—He spoke with authority, firsthand teaching. The term "with authority" could be translated "according to the nature of things." He revealed the nature of things. He was a revealer of the nature of Reality.

So the Christian faith is not a set of propositions to be accepted—it is a Person to be followed. That Person is manifest Reality, so to follow Him is to follow Reality—manifested as the Word become flesh. So to follow Him is not assent to truths, but the acceptance of Truth, embodied in a Person and reembodied in my person.

O Jesus, when Truth walks up to me in Thee, my attitude is assent, not to that truth, but the acceptance of Thee in every portion of my life and with the consent of all my being. It is a life acceptance. Thy Truth is warm, tender and compelling. I follow—singing. Amen.

AFFIRMATION FOR THE DAY: *My code is now a Character, forever beyond me, forever beside me and within me.*

YOU CANNOT DESCRIBE LOVE

We are meditating upon "full of grace and truth" and the fact that "truth" could only be revealed through "grace." I was about to speak on the subject of "The Word became flesh" when a soloist sang very beautifully "O Love of God." It is a moving song describing in vivid terms how, if the sea were an inkwell, and every blade of grass a quill, and every man a scribe by trade, and the sky a parchment upon which to inscribe the love of God, it would drain the ocean dry—would exhaust man's capacity—to describe it. True. For the method used to describe the love of God would be an inadequate method. It would be the Word of love become word. And no matter how vivid the rhetoric may be, it is futile, for it can't be done by that method. You cannot describe love—you have to see it—see it in an act.

I was addressing a mass meeting in a North Carolina city in a public hall. There were probably two hundred pastors on the platform. The Negroes were segregated in the balcony. Before I began speaking the white ministers left the platform, went to the gallery before all, and took their places among the Negroes. I have forgotten what I said about the Christian attitude toward race—perhaps the people have too, but I can never forget that Word of love become flesh in those pastors. They revealed the nature of truth in race relations by a gracious act. The "truth" was revealed through "grace."

But while "grace" is first, "truth" has to be second. This "grace" is not maudlin sentimentality—it is "truth." It works according to the laws of truth, it works within the framework of integrity and truth. Some ex-headhunters of Borneo taught me this very vividly. One of them said to me about his newfound faith in Christ, "Christianity is the only faith where you can't wangle God to get benefits out of Him." He was profoundly right. He was used to a faith where you could cajole, bribe, and wangle your god to get him to do favors. Not so Christ.

O Jesus, my Lord, Thou art truth. We cannot bribe, wangle, or induce Thee. We can come to Thee honestly obeying Thy laws and get everything we need, but we can't come with crooked motives and methods. We are grateful we cannot wangle Thee. I thank Thee. Amen.

AFFIRMATION FOR THE DAY: *I do not attempt to please Christ—I surrender to Him and follow and obey Him. The pleasing takes care of itself—a by-product.*

"AND WE HAVE BEHELD HIS GLORY"

We are studying "And the Word became flesh and dwelt among us, full of grace and truth; we have beheld his glory, glory as of the only Son from the Father." We have considered that "grace" was first and "truth" was second. For the first thing in God is "God is love," and hence the outflowing of that love is grace. If the first thing in God were "God is truth," then the outflowing of that truth would be a statement on how to live life. But that would be the Word become word. God as truth would mean religion as philosophy, but God as love means religion as redemption—God acting in love to save us.

And note it says "full of grace and truth," which would mean that in Jesus there is not a spotty character—grace and ungrace, truth and untruth. There is grace and only grace, truth and only truth. A Hindu put it this way: "We like to listen about a Man who practiced everything He preached." A very important verse is this one: "But now Christ has come, high priest of good things already in being" (Heb. 9:11, NEB). Other versions give the alternate reading of "good things to come." It is both, for Jesus as "the Word become flesh" is the high priest of "good things already in being." He is anticipation and He is realization. When you have Him, you have the present and the future. Jesus is *full* of grace and full of truth so there is no room for the opposite. He is one Character and only one.

And "We have beheld his glory, glory as of the only Son from the Father." "We have beheld his glory"—what would that "glory" be? "Who is he?" I asked a disciple of "a holy man" in India. "He is God, he can tell you anything"—his glory was in his knowledge. Others would reply concerning some other: "He is God, he can perform miracles"—his glory is in what he does. But in Jesus His glory was in what He was—"glory as of the only Son from the Father." It was a glory, not of knowledge and might, but a glory of being. His knowledge and might flowed from His being. Being the "Son" was everything.

O Jesus, I thank Thee for what Thou art. For what Thou art determines everything. And Thou art the only Son. We look on Thee and know, and know that there can be no other like Thee. Thou art the only Son and therefore the only Incarnation. We thank Thee. Amen.

AFFIRMATION FOR THE DAY: *I glory in that I am a child of God—what else do I need?*

ALTERNATIVE INCARNATIONS

We are considering whether there is the one Word become flesh or whether there are many who are the Word become flesh? The answer to that depends on whether this statement is true: "glory as of the only Son from the Father." If He is the "only Son" then there can be only one "Word become flesh"—one Incarnation.

Arnold Toynbe is an able historian, but he missed his step when he said he no longer believed in one Incarnation, that he preferred the attitude of the Hindus who say that Vishnu incarnates himself many times. So he says he has given up an exclusive faith for a more inclusive faith in this regard. But when one looks at the so-called Incarnations of Vishnu, he wonders where Toynbee's sense of history has gone when the list shows: A boar, a tortoise, a fish, a dwarf, a man lion, Parasuram, Rama, Krishna, Buddha. We must dismiss the first six as not worth consideration and look at the last three. Rama was a warrior and a spotty character; the Krishna of history is not only spotty, he is shady, while the Krishna of the Gita is not historical. Buddha would be a strange incarnation of God where he himself did not believe in God. The list is looked on by the Hindus themselves as unsatisfactory, for they are looking for the *Nishkalank Avatar*—the Spotless Incarnation, implying that the others are spotty.

When Krishnamurti, whom Mrs. Besant put forth as the coming messiah, returned from a trip to the West to the college he had founded, the students said to him, "Talk to us about your travels rather than being the Messiah," for they knew he wasn't. And he knew he wasn't, so he has renounced the idea and has dropped out of the picture. I talked with him and heard him swear, "Oh, d— it all," referring to his messiahship. A Hindu put it this way, "There is no one else bidding for the heart of humanity except Jesus. There is no one else on the field." And there isn't. Not only do the Scriptures say "the only Son"—history says the same.

O Jesus, we thank Thee that in the sifting of values, Thy values came out on top. In the sifting of persons Thy Person stands above. To whom else shall we go, for Thou hast the words of eternal life? Having seen Thee we want to see no other. We thank Thee. Amen.

AFFIRMATION FOR THE DAY: *All I have to do is to look in the face of Jesus to decide whether there is any other—there cannot be!*

THE PERFECT BECOMES THE PROGRESSIVE

Since there is an "only Son," then His Incarnation is the only Incarnation. By its very nature the Word became flesh can be only one—and once and for all, for all men. For if humanity is one, and God is one, then there must be one revelation for all humanity. To have more than one would blur the picture of God and what He is like, and blur the picture of man and what he can be like. The Son of God reveals the one God, and the Son of Man reveals the one humanity. The God-Man reveals both God and man.

Does this perfect and final revelation stop progress? No, it begins it. In every realm of life we discover an ultimate which is the beginning of progress. In the realm of mathematics we discovered that two and two makes four. We do not improve on that—it is fixed. Does that fixed ultimate stop progress? No, it begins it, for on this fixed ultimate you build up your vast mathematical calculations. If you were not sure whether two and two made four or six, you would be blocked. The perfect becomes the progressive. In geometry things equal to the same thing are equal to each other. That is fixed. But upon that fixed ultimate you build up vast geometrical calculations. Again the perfect becomes the progressive. In the realm of music we are adding no new notes to the scale, but within that fixed scale there is infinite range—the perfect becomes the progressive.

In the realm of character there has been revealed a Character Ultimate, the Word of Character has become flesh. The adjective Christlike is the highest descriptive adjective of character both for God and man in any language. Beyond that revelation we will never progress. Does that stop character progress? It begins it. For now we know what the Norm is. Now we know where to head in; we know the goal. That fixed Goal is the starting point for infinite progress.

O blessed Redeemer and Savior, how can we thank Thee enough for showing us the Father, showing Him in Thyself? For we could never have known unless we had seen. But having seen, it sufficeth us. We want no other; we want nothing different. We want Thee. Amen.

AFFIRMATION FOR THE DAY: *I see Jesus, and yet I see that there is more to be seen—and so forever!*

THE REAL CHRISTIAN
THE MOST UNIVERSALIZED PERSON

We saw yesterday that the fixed ultimate becomes the beginning point of progress. Until something is fixed, you can never have the progressive. Uncertainty as to the goal means uncertainty as to the way.

So when you become broad and liberal on essentials in the name of universality, you do not become universal; you become hazy and mixed and call it universality. You exchange clarity for fog. In an institution training men and women to go out for Christian service in foreign lands the question of Jesus saying, "I am the Way, the Truth and the Life" was explained by one of the teachers as being "an oriental metaphor, for there are many ways." And the head of the institution said: "Jesus has many names—Mohammed, Krishna, Buddha, Confucius." This is the moral and spiritual fog into which we get when we lose the Norm. The emphasis of the institution was that the representative should go out and love people. But you cannot love people unless you love truth and reality.

Besides we do not know what love is unless you see it in Him who was love. "By this we know love, that he laid down his life for us; and we ought to lay down our lives for the brethren" (I John 3:16). "By this we know love"—we know love when we see it in the cross and that cross inspires us to lay down our lives for the brethren. When we exchange the Word become flesh for the Word become word, it becomes a very sentimental word and fades under realities.

You are not universal when you are less Christian. For the real Christian is the most universalized person on earth. He loves everybody because he loves Christ, for he loves everybody in Christ. When it was said of the early Christians: "Behold how those Christians love one another," it was only partly true. They did not only love one another, they also loved their enemies and they loved the unlovely. When we lose Love we will lose love. And the more you know Love the more you will know love. Without the Word become flesh you will soon have nothing but the Word become word.

O Love that will not let us go into the vague and marginal, save us from the verbal and make us vital with a love that is Thy Love. Let us kindle the flame of our love at the flame of the Love that became flesh. For we know Love only as we see it in Thee. We thank you. Amen.

AFFIRMATION FOR THE DAY: *When I am less Christian I am less universal: when I am more Christian I am more universal.*

CO-REDEEMERS?

There is another phase of the "only Son" which we must consider. The objection is made that Jesus presented God as Father, but not God as Mother, and therefore lacks universality. The difference between mother love and father love as defined by Fromm in *The Art of Loving* is: "Mother's love is unconditional, it is all-protective, all-enveloping; because it is unconditional it can also not be controlled or acquired. Since mother loves her children because they are her children, and not because they are good, obedient, or fulfill her wishes and commands, mother's love is based on equality." On the other hand: "The nature of fatherly love is that he makes demands, establishes principles and laws, and that his love for the child depends on the obedience of the latter to these demands."

In Jesus both of these types of love blend—He is "grace," that is the mother love side, and He is "truth," that is the father love side. In the son the qualities of the mother and father came together. So in Jesus, the Son, the mother-quality of "grace" and the father-quality of "truth" came together and are one. We do not need, therefore, to piece out Jesus, as in Roman Catholicism, to make Him universal by bringing in the mother, Mary. They have lost Jesus as alive—He is usually the dead Christ—so they bring in Mary as more alive, and she is more alive to Roman Catholics than Jesus. They are now about to make Jesus and Mary co-redeemers. Usually it was "The Sacred Heart of Jesus," but I saw a Church called "The Sacred Hearts," and there were two hearts, not one.

But in the living and real Jesus we see the Motherhood of God and the Fatherhood of God, for He is full of grace and truth. "How often I would have gathered you together as a hen gathers her chickens under her wings"—the Motherhood side. "But ye would not. Behold your house is left unto you desolate"—the Fatherhood side. Love and Law meet in Him, for all Love is Law and all Law is Love. In Him they are one. He is tender and terrible—in one hand, grace, in the other hand, judgment.

O Jesus, my Lord, I see Thee as all-inviting, so I come with all my heart. But I see Thee as all-demanding, so I give Thee my whole will and obedience. And I am grateful for both, Thou art my all, for I see All in Thee. And I bring Thee my All. Amen.

AFFIRMATION FOR THE DAY: *The strictness of God is my salvation—He saves me from myself.*

"GRACE UPON GRACE"

We continue to study John 1:14-16. The next portion says: "And from his fulness have we all received, grace upon grace."

There is an objection which Bonhoeffer makes when he speaks of "cheap grace," when grace demands nothing but "faith." It is true that "grace" can be so interpreted as to become "cheap"—"believe and you are saved." But this is a caricature of "grace." Grace has law in it, and the law is the law of self-surrender. The gift of grace is a very expensive gift, for if you take the gift you belong forever to the giver. He binds you to His heart with cords of love that hold you forever, but you wouldn't have it otherwise for worlds. So accepting grace is not a mental assent—it is a life response. He gives all, and you cannot give less in return. It is my all for His all and His all for my all. It is mutuality, but not equality, for His all is infinitely greater than my all. But it is my *all,* therefore not cheap.

And since we know that, we can safely receive "grace upon grace." For my self-surrender is once and for all and yet continuous. So if I am taking grace continuously, I am giving my all continuously. But I know I am getting the better of the bargain continuously. Therefore, it is "amazing grace" that would give so graciously and lavishly. But if lavish giving on His part provokes lavish giving in return on our part, then it is safe giving.

So now He is free to give with both hands. For He is not spoiling us, He is despoiling us! For the more He gives, the more He receives—from us!

This "grace upon grace" actually depicts something that is unexhausted and inexhaustible, and it makes us reach on tiptoe to give and receive more. The Christian life is a life of endless adventure in receiving and giving. We never outgrow Him and we never outgive Him. It is endless mutuality—and effortless mutuality.

O Divine Redeemer, I see and am on tiptoe to see more. I receive and am on tiptoe to receive more. For Thou dost quench thirst and create thirst. The more I receive, the more my heart cries, "More." I am endlessly satisfied and endlessly seeking. I thank Thee. Amen.

AFFIRMATION FOR THE DAY: *My life shall be one vast illustration of "grace upon grace."*

"WE HAVE A LAW"

We continue to look at our passage: "For the law was given through Moses; grace and truth came through Jesus Christ" (John 1:17). Here the essential difference between the Hebrew system and the Christian is shown in one brief sentence. When we speak of the Hebrew-Christian system and hyphenate these two words as if they were a continuation—the Christian growing out of the Hebrew, its prolongation, we err. They are not continuous—they are discontinuous. There is a break—a radical break. This verse puts that break in the "but": "The law was given through Moses, *but* grace and truth came through Jesus Christ." While the Jewish faith was a preparation for Christianity, the Christian faith is also a reversal. It stands in contrast in basic conception. "The Law was given through Moses," that is the Word become word; "but grace and truth came through Jesus Christ," that is the Word become flesh. One is built around an abstract law, the other around a concrete Person. This is not a difference in degree—it is a difference in kind. The end product is different—one produced the Pharisee—correct, legal, proud, separate; the other produced the Christian—humble, receptive, loving, self-giving.

The Jews said: "We have a Law"; we can say, "We have a Person." They add: "We have a law and by that law he ought to die." And we may add: "We have a Person, and by being the Person He is, He will willingly die for man." One ends in retribution—"He ought to die," the other in redemption—"I lay down my life for them."

The Jews of Jerusalem have a saying, according to one of them, "The Messiah will never come, and Ben Gurion will never go." They are right. The kind of Messiah they are looking for—one who will conquer their foes and make *Israel* supreme by physical arms—will never come.

The Jews, I'm told, never read the fifty-third chapter of Isaiah, for there the suffering, self-giving Messiah is shown. He is here—alive.

O Jesus, Thou art "grace and truth." Thou art what we seek in the Godhead and find there. Thou art all I want—and more. For in Thee I seek and find my Heavenly Father and finding Him I want naught beside. For I'm not a subject asking for a Law, but a Son asking for a Father. Amen.

AFFIRMATION FOR THE DAY: *My Law is a Life, my Code is a Character, my obedience is an enabling.*

JESUS WAS THE MESSAGE

We meditate upon the last line of the wonderful passage: "No one has ever seen God; the only Son, who is in the bosom of the Father, he has made him known" (John 1:18). "No one has ever seen God"—that rules out all dogmatic assertions by theologians as to what God is like, all so-called visions of God by mystic dreamers, and it puts a damper on the prophets when they assert that God is this, that, and the other. "No man has seen God"—neither philosopher, nor priest, nor person. "The only Son . . . has made him known." Apart from Jesus we know little or nothing about God the Father, and what we know is wrong.

You see God in the face of Jesus Christ, His Son, or you do not see Him. You may see your imagination of Him, but you do not see Him. That is what Jesus meant when He said: "I am the Way, the Truth and the Life, no man cometh to the Father, but by me." Through Moses you can come to Jehovah and all that conception contains and can give; through Confucius you can come to Heaven and all that conception contains and can give; through Buddha you can come to the Vast Question Mark and all that conception holds and can give; through Shankara you can come to Brahma and all that conception holds and can give; through Krishna you can come to Vishnu and all that conception holds and can give; through the modern philosophers and theologians you can come to the conceptions they hold and can give; but if you come to the Father, the Reality about God, you must come through the Son. For He said: "He that hath seen me hath seen the Father." So if you haven't seen God in the face of Jesus, you have not seen the Father. You have seen something else. The emphasis here is upon "the Father"—you see the Father only in the Son. Note I say, "in the Son," not merely "by" or "through," but "in." " . . . God spoke to our forefathers . . . through the prophets. But in this the final age he has spoken to us in the Son" (Heb. 1:1,2 NEB). Note "through the prophets" and "in the Son." The prophets brought a message; Jesus was the Message. The Gospel was in His Person.

O Jesus, I see the Father in Thee—in what Thou art, in what Thou dost, in what Thou sayest—in everything about Thee. Thou art the silence of eternity interpreted by love. Thou art the language of eternity translated into the speech of time. Thou art my God. Amen.

AFFIRMATION FOR THE DAY: *When Jesus speaks, the eternities listen, for they know their Master's voice.*

WHAT DO I WANT TO KNOW ABOUT GOD?

We continue to meditate on: "No one has ever seen God; the only Son, who is in the bosom of the Father, he has made him known" (John 1:18). "He has made him known." The old version says: "He hath declared him"—"declared Him" would be the Word become word—a verbal revelation of God. This has been tried and has failed. You cannot describe God; you can only show Him, make "Him known." Jesus has made God known in the only way He can be made known, by Life.

What do I want to know about God? His omnipotence? It would scare me to death to see what God can do. His omniscience? How could I, limited as I am, know all that God knows? And what good would it do me if I could know His omnipresence? How could I, limited by a body and confined to a spot in this universe, understand His everywhereness? And His everywhereness all at once? These three things would not help me; they would leave me helpless and prostrate. Then what do I want to know? I want to know what God is like in character. For what He is like in character, I must be like. I cannot be at cross purposes with Reality and not get hurt. So Jesus makes "known" the character of God, makes it known in the only possible way His character can be made known, namely through another character—His own.

And He reveals the central thing in God's character—Love! "Who is in the bosom of the Father"—"the bosom" represents the heart of God. Jesus is not in the arm of the Father—His omnipotence; nor in the mind of the Father—His omniscience. He is in the bosom of the Father—the revelation of His love. So Jesus came, stripping Himself of everything as He came—omnipotence, omniscience, omnipresence—everything except love. "He emptied Himself," emptied Himself of everything except love—His only protection, His only weapon, His only method. And He showed that love is the only omniscience, the only omnipotence.

O Jesus, Thou didst use love and only love, and Thou didst win with love and only love. Now we see into the heart of God, and what we see is very beautiful, so beautiful that we are at Thy feet. And we wouldn't be anywhere else for all the world. Amen.

AFFIRMATION FOR THE DAY: *In some faint way I shall make my Father "known" in everything I do today.*

"NOTHING ELSE MATTERED"

We are still considering, "no one has ever seen God; the only Son, who is in the bosom of the Father, he has made him known." Men of old felt that no one could see God face to face and live. But Jesus is the Divine Transformer who takes the high voltage of the Divine and transforms it into usable form. In Jesus we do see God face to face and do not die, but live. We live by seeing Him face to face—in Jesus. For, as we have said, Jesus puts a face on God. He humanizes God, makes Him approachable.

Idols are an attempt to bring God near. Jesus takes the place of idols, fulfills the need which idols try to meet and, of course, never do. For idols do not represent God; they misrepresent Him. Jesus really represents God. "He is the express image" of God. If you want to know what God is like, look at Jesus.

In the final chapter of the book of Revelation it says: "They shall see him face to face" (NEB). That was the final reward—to see Him "face to face." The whole verse reads this way: "The throne of God and of the Lamb will be there, and his servants shall worship him; they shall see him face to face." The reason they could see God face to face was "the Lamb was there"—Jesus lets us see a lovable, approachable God.

There is a picture of a face of Jesus surrounded by dark clouds. Apart from Jesus there are dark clouds of mystery surrounding God. But in the midst of these clouds I see that one dear Face. We smile at the boy who when asked by his mother what he was doing replied: "I'm drawing a picture of God." "But no one knows what God is like," said the mother. "They will know when I get finished," said the boy with finality. All attempts to tell or draw what God is like are childish. Except one—Jesus! No wonder a young woman in Uruguay who had turned round and round on herself in twenty-one years of futility and mental and emotional agony said with joy: "I looked into the face of Jesus and nothing else mattered." She had looked at herself and her failures for twenty-one years and grew worse; she looked into the face of Jesus and was well.

O Lord and Master, I look at myself and others and everything goes wrong; I look at Thee and everything goes right. I look at Thee and suddenly I know I am not alone and not unloved. I know I can never be alone and can never be unloved. My gratitude is eternal. Amen.

AFFIRMATION FOR THE DAY: *I see Him face to face, and I do not die but live—and how! Till then I'd never lived.*

"REALITY, WHOSE OTHER NAME IS JESUS"

Apart from Jesus, the Word become flesh, men despair of finding Reality. The search ends in nihilism. Lao-tse the Chinese philosopher puts it: "The Tao [way] that can be trodden is not the enduring and unchanging name." Into the midst of this doubt Jesus steps and says: "I am the Way, the truth and the life." He concretes the abstract—puts shoes on the abstract and makes it walk on lowly ways. A white explorer was going through the dense jungles of Africa and as he threaded the trackless labyrinth he said to his African guide: "Is this the way?" And the guide replied: "There is no way—I am the way." And he unwittingly put his finger on a profound truth. The philosophers and moralists could not find the Way, for there is no way by words. The nature of reality cannot be described by words. It becomes something else when the attempt is made to put it into words. There is no way through words—the only Way is the Word become flesh. Reality can only be seen in Reality, in Life.

No wonder Dr. Radhakrishnan, the great philosopher of India and President of the Union of India, said in an Easter morning service at Riverside Church in New York: "May I suggest to you Christians that you emphasize: 'I am the Way, the Truth and the Life,' and 'Ye must be born again.' " The great Hindu philosopher saw that the Way could not be the way of words; it had to be the Way of the Word become flesh—"I am the Way." And the Truth could not be spoken, it had to be embodied; the Life could not be uttered—it had to be lived. The proposition was not the answer—the Person was! Jesus is the Way that can be trodden, for it has been trodden—He trod it. Jesus is the Truth for He is the Truth under life—it rings true there. He is the Life because this Life was lived out and life says: "This is the Life." When reality renders its verdict it says: "There is Reality, whose other name is Jesus."

O Blessed Reality, Thou hast made the complex simple, the hidden known, the unknowable plain. Thou hast come into our lowly doors and in Thy stooping and coming in we see that the Divine Everything has come in. I wonder and am captured forever. Amen.

AFFIRMATION FOR THE DAY: *I go singing down the years, for in Him I live in Eternity—what can the years do to me?*

"I AM THE WAY, THE TRUTH"—RIGHT ORDER?

It is no mere chance that the order: "I am the Way, the Truth, and the Life," is as it is—the Way first. Jesus had to be the Way before He was the Truth and the Life. If "the Truth" had been put first, that would mean that we would have been sent on a quest for verbal truth; Christianity would have become a philosophical system or a theological system.

No, Jesus is the Way before He is the Truth. For truth has to be put under life to see if it is truth.

But note, Jesus did not say, "I am the answer," as we often say in slogans: "Christ is the anwer." No, He is the Way to the answer. If a teacher would give the answer to pupils studying arithmetic, would that help? No, it would weaken. Instead of giving the answer, the teacher gives the way to find the answer. The pupils themselves can find the answer if they know the way. So Jesus does not give us ready-made answers. That would weaken us. Instead He gives us the Way—the Way to find all answers. Take His way and the answers come out of the Way. Apply His method, His Spirit, His Way, to any situation and you've got the answer. So He doesn't give answers, He gives the Way to answers.

And He doesn't give Truth—He gives the Way to find Truth. If you take His Way, you will find the Truth. The Truth isn't something handed to you in a neat bundle tied in a blue ribbon. It is something discovered as you follow the Way. After I was converted I went to the public library and took out a book on the philosophy of religion—I thought this would explain what I had found. I didn't know what it was talking about. I gave it up after some pages and handed it back. I learned that my feet were on the Way and, therefore, I would discover Truth as I followed the Way. So I've been discovering Truth as a Life process. Truth has been and still is an exciting discovery as I follow the Way. It unfolds.

O Lord and Savior, I follow Thy Way, and the Way leads me daily to unfolding Truth as I verify the Way day by day—the Way as Truth. This is an exciting quest, for I see, and the more I see, the more I see there is to be seen. Jesus, my Lord, Thou hast put incitement and excitement in my life. Amen.

AFFIRMATION FOR THE DAY: *I shall know as much as I am willing to practice and no more.*

EXCITED AFTER SIXTY YEARS

We continue our meditation on the Way leading to the Truth and the Life. We insisted that you find the Truth as you follow the Way. Jesus enunciated this principle when He said: "He that is willing to do the will shall know of the teaching." He that is willing to *do* shall *know*. A Hindu said to me, "Is that the price of knowing the truth, being willing to do the will of God? Then I shall not know, for I am not willing to do." He was profoundly right; we know as much of the Truth as we are willing to practice on the Way—and no more! If the Word doesn't become flesh in us, it doesn't remain as the Word, except as a poor ghost.

This finding of the Truth by following the Way makes the finding of Truth an exciting business. A professor of philosophy said wearily: "I'm bored—bored with philosophy, bored with my teaching, bored with my students, bored with life, bored with myself—I'm bored!" He was! His was the quest of propositions, of the Word become word. It was like the little boy who wanted to show his family the roar of Niagara Falls, so he caught some of the water in a bottle and took it home. But when he showed it to the family he said in dismay: "Ah shucks, it's died." Truth taken out of the stream of life is a dead thing. But back in the stream of life it is an exciting thing—the most exciting of things. And you're never bored with it. For sixty years I've thought of one subject, have spoken about that one subject, and have written about that one subject—that one subject, a Person, Jesus Christ. After thinking and talking about one subject for sixty years, one should be bored and should want a moral holiday, want to get away and think of something else. On the contrary, I was never so excited, so exhilarated, so full of surprise as now. Something new breaks out from Him every day, a surprise around every corner, horizons cracking, life popping with novelty and meaning—and value. The Truth is making me free—free to find more Truth and yet more Truth. And so on forever and forever.

O God, my Father, I thank Thee for this gentle excitement, this inner quiver of finding and yet forever seeing the Beyond. The search for the Beyond is not a hopeless quest, for I know I am on the Way. This security bids me follow the Insecure, which, when I practice it, becomes the Secure. I thank Thee. Amen.

AFFIRMATION FOR THE DAY: *From the basis of the Secure I shall today adventure into the Insecure—my life is an adventure with God.*

THE GIFT CREATES INITIATIVE

We continue our meditation on, "I am the way, and the truth and the life." We saw yesterday that we discovered Truth as we followed the Way. You do not find Truth by meditation, but by dedication. You know as much of Truth as you are willing to practice—and no more. So Jesus presents Himself, not first of all as the Truth, but as the Way. And when we take the Way, we find both the Truth and the Life. The only way to find Life is to live it.

I once talked to General Smuts, premier of South Africa and the author of "Holism." He called my attention to something I've never forgotten. He said the word "belief" is literally "by-lief" or "by life." Your belief is your life. And your life is your belief. You believe in a thing enough to act on it, to live it. So you are what you believe, and you believe what you are. Your deed is your creed. And your creed is your deed.

Jesus said: "Not every one that says to me, Lord, Lord, shall enter into the kingdom of heaven, but he that doeth the will of my Father." Not every one who says, "Lord, Lord"—the Word become word; "but he that doeth the will of my Father"—the Word became flesh. You find both the Truth and the Life through the Way.

It is true that Life is a gift—a gift of grace. But it is a gift like the priming of a pump. You pour in water that this poured-in water may be the means of discovering water and producing water from within. Jesus said: "The water that I shall give unto him shall become a well of water springing up to everlasting life"—the water that I shall give shall become a well springing up. The gift creates initiative, spontaneity. He gives you Life, and the Gift creates a thirst for Life and more Life. So you, from then on, find Life by drawing upon it and by living it out. All our questions about Truth and Life are solved by the quest for Truth—Life. As we live it out, all our question marks become exclamation points. "It works, it works," we cry with verified joy.

O Jesus, Thou art verified Truth. We find Thee not at the end of a syllogism, but in the process of following the Way. We find Truth not by taking wings of imagination and soaring, but by putting on shoes and walking the Way. And this Way shines more and more to the perfect day. Amen.

AFFIRMATION FOR THE DAY: *I am not dissatisfied, but forever unsatisfied.*

JESUS FULFILLS THE TOTAL PERSON

We must look again at: "I am the way, the truth, and the life." These three things correspond with the three things that make up the human personality: intellect, feeling, will. "I am the Way"—the will, the organ of acting; "I am the Truth"—the feeling, emotion. Jesus thus fulfills the total personality. And He involves the total personality in His service.

When Jesus was asked what was the greatest commandment in the Law He replied, "Thou shalt love the Lord thy God with all thy heart [the affectional nature], and with all thy soul [the volitional nature], and with all thy mind [the intellectual nature]" (Matt. 22:37). And then He added "with all thy strength." This may be with the strength of the body, but it may be with the strength of all three of these. Some love God with the strength of the mind and the weakness of the emotion. This produces the intellectualist in religion. Some love with the strength of the emotion and the weakness of the mind. This produces the sentimentalist in religion. Some love Him with the strength of the will and the weakness of the emotion. This produces the moral man of iron—ethical, but not very approachable. The really strong person loves Him with the strength of the mind, the strength of the emotion, and the strength of the will.

So the Christian in following Jesus cannot follow Him as the Way-only; or the Truth-only; or the Life-only. It must be all three in one—and at the same time if we are fully Christian. The Hindu has three ways from which you can choose: *Gyana Marg*—the way of knowledge; *Bhakti Marg*—the way of devotion or emotion; *Karma Marg*—the way of works. Jesus is all three ways in one, and when you are in Him you fulfill all three ways. And you fulfill your personality—the whole person—intellect, feeling, which are all loving Him and, hence, fulfilled in Him. He is Life and, therefore, completes all life in Himself.

O Jesus, I want to follow Thee with my whole being—no part left out. For if it is left out, that part will be dark. Everything in Thee is light and only light. "O may it all my powers engage" to do Thy will. For I cannot be less than Thine without being less than myself. Amen.

AFFIRMATION FOR THE DAY: *My all for His all—that is life for me.*

THE MATERIAL WORLD
HAS A MEANING AND DESTINY

We turn now to another phase of "The Word became flesh." We have been empasizing "the Word," but what about the "flesh"? The flesh stands for the organized material—the material organized for the use of the person. It, therefore, stands for the whole material universe. This means that the Divine assumes a material body, not as a temporary garment put on and off at will. The word "dwelt among us" could be translated "tabernacled among us," a permanent dwelling.

This means that the material is not only going to be used for the purpose of the redemption of the spiritual being called man, but the whole person, his body included, and the whole material universe, are going to be redeemed. The material is just as much the subject of redemption as the spiritual.

This plants the faith of Jesus squarely in the midst of human relationships—nothing is alien to it except sin and evil. Anything that concerns life concerns the faith of Jesus, for He is Life and, therefore, includes everything comprehended under the term Life. The fact is that the Christian faith is the most materialistic of religions, the only one that really takes the material seriously. It starts out by saying that when God created the material universe, He "saw it was good"—the material was God-made and God-approved.

When Jesus announced the new order, the Kingdom of God, He said that we were to pray that the Kingdom may come on earth, and come on earth as it is in heaven. The earth was not to be deserted and destroyed, but to be delivered and dedicated, the scene of the Kingdom of God. The earth, therefore, has a goal and a destiny, and its goal is to be added back to heaven from which it fell. "I saw a new heaven and a new earth"—heaven and earth were to be wedded and both were to be new. That puts faith and hope and optimism at the heart of our dealing with this material world. It has a future.

O my Father, I'm glad that Thou dost not despise anything that Thou hast made. Thou hast made it for a purpose and that purpose is redemption. Then everything I touch has destiny in it. So I must touch it with reverence and hope and faith. I thank Thee. Amen.

AFFIRMATION FOR THE DAY: *I shall walk in this material universe as one who walks on holy ground.*

THE CHRISTIAN FAITH NOT A SPIRITUAL
RELIGION BUT A LIFE RELIGION

We continue the emphasis on the importance of "The Word become flesh;" upon the Christian faith and its work in the world. If the Christian faith is the Word become word, then the Christian church is a teaching institution where we try to learn verbal answers to verbal questions. That is exactly what the church has become in Japan where I write this page. The word for church is *"Chaukai,"* literally, "religious teaching institution," and the pastor is called *"Sensei"*—"teacher." There you have the setup—a religious teaching institution with a presiding teacher. Christianity is something to be verbally learned. No wonder the church life of Japan is sterile, in large part. Only where it breaks out from this conception does it become vital. It is founded on the Word become word. No wonder in Japan Barthianism has become the prevailing theology: You proclaim the Word, apart from experience. The proclamation of the Word is supposed to save people. But that Word is not the Person—it is the verbal word. And the more abstruse and abstract that Word is proclaimed, the better the sermon is supposed to be. If it is over the heads of the congregation, they sit entranced. And they go away wondering what it is all about. The Word doesn't take shoes and walk—it takes wings and flies, over their heads! It is transcendental, but not transforming. It is geared into ideas, but not into life. Hence, those interested in living pass it by.

But the Word become flesh puts religion to work in body, mind, spirit, and relationships. "Lo, I come to do Thy will . . . a body Thou hast prepared me." Where was the will to be done? In and through the body and all its relationships. Jesus taught people, healed people, fed people, all as a part of the coming of the Kingdom. "I thought Christianity was a spiritual religion until I heard this emphasis on the Word became flesh. Now I see it is a life religion," said a Japanese pastor. Jesus is Life, hence He transforms life.

O blessed Savior, I need a total Savior for the total Life. I am not a spirit; I'm an embodied person and need to be saved as an embodied person in all my relationships. I am not saved unless I am saved as a total person. Save me. Amen.

AFFIRMATION FOR THE DAY: *My Christian faith shall be a life religion—everything under its control and redemption.*

THE CHRISTIAN FAITH IS SECULAR
THROUGH AND THROUGH

Dr. John Oman says: "The test of a true religion is the extent to which that religion is secular." Startling, but true. The Christian faith is secular without being secularized. It is the spiritual working in and through the material. The sacred is secular and the secular is sacred. Unless our religion functions in material terms, it does not function. We are not ghosts; we are embodied beings and we must function in and through the body or we do not function.

The two blend in Jesus: Even when Jesus insisted on the supremacy of the spiritual, He also insisted on the material as necessary. He said: "I bid you put away anxious thoughts about food to keep you alive and clothes to cover your body. Life is more than food, the body more than clothes. . . . For all these are things for the heathen to run after; but you have a Father who knows that you need them. No, set your mind upon his kingdom, and all the rest will come to you as well" (Luke 12:22,23, 30-31 NEB). While He endeavored to get His hearers to keep their values straight, saying that the spiritual was all-important, He nevertheless put the material in its place as being important—the Father guarantees your physical needs if you seek first the Kingdom of God.

The physical needs were met in the Kingdom of God according to need—not too much, that will burden you; not too little, for that, too, will burden you. Two groups think too much about the material—those who have too much and those who have too little. We need according to our needs—we need just enough of the material so we can forget it and get on with this business of living.

And this is being verified in life. In a school system dealing with problem children, they found the problem children came out of two classes—one where the young people came out of the class which has more than it needs, and the other from the class which has less than it needs.

O heavenly Father, I thank Thee that Thou dost know my needs. Show me the difference, between my wants and my needs. And let me act upon that difference that I may be free to live and live unclogged. In Jesus' name. Amen.

AFFIRMATION FOR THE DAY: *Not wants, but needs shall determine my conduct today.*

THE SIGN WAS A BABE

We are studying the fact that the Christian faith deals with the total life including the material. When the announcement was made that Jesus was born, the angels said to the shepherds: "And this will be a sign for you: you will find a babe." The sign was a babe. The Mohammedans of India claimed they had seen the name of Mohammed written in the clouds—a sign that Mohammed would conquer the world. The sign was a name written in the clouds. This was the Word become word. But the Christian sign was a Babe—the Word become flesh. And that is the difference between the Mohammedan idea of revelation and the Christian. The Koran was dictated by God—and that would be the Word become word. In Jesus the Word was not dictated from heaven—it was lived out on earth—it was the Word become flesh.

When Jesus stood on the Mount of Transfiguration there appeared Moses and Elijah talking with Him. Moses represented the Law, Elijah the Prophets, and Jesus represented the New Revelation. The Jewish heart of Peter wanted to build three tabernacles and keep all three on the same level. But a cloud overshadowed them (a cloud overshadows those who put Jesus on a level with others), and a Voice out of the cloud said: "This is my Son, hear Him." The Law was fulfilled in Him, and the Prophets were fulfilled in Him. But they were not only fulfilled, they were superceded, for the Law and the Prophets were both the Word become word. Jesus was the Word become fiesh. Hence, final. The Voice said, "Hear Him," for when once you've heard the Word become flesh, then the Word become word loses its taste. You've tasted the Real.

Of one modern author it was said: "He wanted to do good in a world of dreams." Jesus was not a dreamer—He was a doer, and a doer amid very real relationships. And you always saw something more than the deed. Through the concrete shone the universal. Through the deed of a Man was revealed the heart of God.

O Jesus, I see Thee and I see more than Thee. Through Thy earthly attitudes and actions shine eternity. I see everything in seeing Thee. Through the earthly lattice of Thy life I see the Face of God, and what I see sets my heart aglow to see more—to see all. I see only glimpses, but I love the Key! Amen.

AFFIRMATION FOR THE DAY: *The signs of my being a Christian will be concrete actions and attitudes.*

THE MATERIAL BECOMES THE MEANINGFUL

The Christian faith accepts the material—and dedicates it. There are passages that seem to say the opposite: "Ye cannot serve God and mammon." True. But it doesn't say, "You cannot serve God with Mammon." If money is dedicated to God along with the soul, then this money is just as sacred as the soul. When Jesus said to the rich young ruler: "Go sell all thou hast and come and follow me," what he lacked was not poverty, but following Jesus, and the riches stood in the way of that following. If he had followed Jesus with his riches in his hands ready to give to human need as it arose, he could have followed Jesus.

The Buddhist monks, disdaining the world, will not touch money—they hold it in a handkerchief so its touch will not pollute them. And when they purchase anything or pay a carfare, the clerk or the car conductor picks out the change necessary. But the material put out at the door comes back by the window. We held an Ashram a few days ago in the Buddhist sacred place of Nara in Japan. It was at Nara that the Japanese emperor became a Buddhist and with him all Japan. It is the holy place of Buddhism. And yet in the three great temples in these sacred places, no religious worship is carried on. They are places for pilgrims and sight-seers to visit and view the huge statues of Buddha—at fifty yen a person! And thousands come every day. Money disdained, now reigns! If you do not dedicate the material, the material will desecrate you!

So when the disciples said to Jesus: "Send the multitudes away so they can buy bread, for they are hungry," Jesus replied: "They need not go away, give ye them to eat." The disciples thought that religion dealt only with the spiritual—let them go to others for the material. But Jesus said to them, and through them to the world: "Religion does have to do with the material—don't wash your hands of the material needs of people, they need not go away, give ye them to eat." So Oman was right; if religion isn't secular, it isn't sacred. It must take in the whole of life—or none.

O Jesus, nothing really human was alien to thee. Life—or none. Thou didst touch everything with sacredness, and Thou didst touch everything. So we touch everything made sacred with Thy touch. We move in a world hallowed by Thy touch and Thy interest. We thank Thee. Amen.

AFFIRMATION FOR THE DAY: *Today I shall turn all the sordid into the sacred by dedication.*

THE INCARNATION UNIVERSALIZED

We said yesterday that Jesus was interested in the poverty of the poor, interested in feeding them. But He was not only interested, He was incarnated in the poverty of the poor. " 'Come, O blessed of my Father, inherit the Kingdom prepared for you . . . for I was hungry and you gave me food, I was thirsty and you gave me drink, I was a stranger and you welcomed me, I was naked and you clothed me, I was sick and you visited me, I was in prison and you came to me.' Then the righteous will answer him, 'Lord, when . . . ?' And the King will answer them, 'Truly, I say to you, as you did it to one of the least of these my brethren, you did it to me' " (Matt. 25:34-40). Here we see something deeper than His own incarnation in His own flesh. He is incarnate on a Universal scale—every man's hunger is His hunger, every man's sickness His sickness, every man's bondage His bondage. To do it to them is to do it to Him. To refuse to do it to them is to refuse to do it to Him.

This broadens and deepens and universalizes the Incarnation. He does not merely have a body that suffers as our bodies suffer—He is suffering in every man's body, hungry in every man's hunger, bound in every man's imprisonment. To suffer in one body—His own—is one thing; to suffer in every man's body is another—and different and breathtaking. It is beyond imagination.

But we could never have known this universal Incarnation if Jesus had not shown it in a particular Incarnation in a particular body. If it had been written in a book that God suffers in every man's suffering, is hungry in every man's hunger, we would have shrugged our shoulders in incredulity. But having seen it in the Word become flesh, we do not shrug our shoulders—we bend the knee. And we mention it in awe and adoration. It is beyond us, but it grips us and we say to ourselves: The God we see in Jesus would do just that.

O Divine Redeemer, we do not understand, but we worship. We worship a God who would love like that. And we love Him too—love Him with a love too deep for words. And we love Thee for revealing Him. May our love be kindled at the flame of Thy love. Amen.

AFFIRMATION FOR THE DAY: *The Africans have a greeting: "Are you well?" and the reply: "I am if you are." Beautiful?*

"HE BECAME SIN FOR US"

We meditated yesterday on the fact that of Jesus said He was hungry in every man's hunger, bound in every man's imprisonment. There was one thing He left out—He could say He was hungry in our hunger, thirsty in our thirst, sick in our sickness, lonely in our being a stranger, bound in our imprisonment, but He could not say He was sinful in our sin. That would be misunderstood. He couldn't *say* that, but He could *do* that. He went to the cross and made the identification with us complete—there He was identified with us at our lowest place—the place of our sin. "He became sin for us." He was crucified between two sinners as one of them. So identified with us in our sin that He cried the cry of dereliction we have to cry when we sin: "My God, my God, why hast Thou forsaken me?" "He bore our sins in His own body on a tree." The identification and, hence, the incarnation were almost complete. He was identified with our sins.

But the identification was not quite complete—sin and death are always connected. So having tasted our sins, He would have to taste our death too. The Author of Life became subject to death. There the incarnation was really complete. But having hit bottom He went up—up to the very Throne.

And we, being identified with Him by surrender and faith, can and do go up with Him. He was identified with us that we might be identified with Him—might partake of His glory. He came down that we might go up.

So the end of the incarnation is not that He should be identified with us, but that we should be identified with Him—that we should be incarnated in Him, become one with His victory and His glory. He stooped to share. And what a stooping and what a sharing! He held nothing back. And there is only one thing left for us to do—hold nothing, absolutely nothing, back. I do just that.

O Savior and Lord, Thy becoming flesh astounds me. Thou didst go further than I dreamed. And now I'm going further in Thee than I've ever dreamed. I feel Thy destiny within my bones. I love its tingle and its beckoning touch. I follow with all my heart. Amen.

AFFIRMATION FOR THE DAY: *"A Christian is one who cares,"* so I'm a Christian to the degree that I care.

A DROP OF WATER ON A LOTUS LEAF—THE SYMBOL FOR US?

If the Center of the Christian faith is not the Word, but the Word become flesh, then the sphere of the operation of that faith is the total Life, including the flesh, the material side of life. For in becoming flesh it meant that the total Life and its relationships would be the sphere of its operation and redemption. This is different from the Buddhist conception which has chosen the lotus as its symbol—the lotus leaf sits on top of the water, and the water does not soak in but rolls around on top of it, unabsorbed. This is an illustration of the religious man on top of the material but unaffected by it. But even the illustration doesn't illustrate, for the lotus has its roots in the material and is made up largely of water in the structure of its being. No more can man reject the material, for he is in large part material.

The Greeks affected to despise "the body as an evil, a prison house to which the soul is shackled, a tomb in which the spirit is confined." And Marcus Aurelius, the Stoic, urged his followers: "Despise the body . . . the whole composition of the body is under corruption." And yet what happened? The Greeks who affected to despise the body glorified it. Never was the human body so glorified in sculpture as among the Greeks.

The Hindus and Buddhists say the material world is illusion—*maya*, like an optical illusion thrown out by a magician. It is *lila*, sport, a Divine Sport thrown out from Itself, but it has no reality. And yet the Burmans, an ardent Buddhist people, are the most pleasure-loving people of the world. The material is denied and then delighted in. The Japanese identify themselves with nature; the Hindus repudiate nature—*maya*; the Christians love nature because they love its Author. "All things were made by Him and for Him." That changes our attitudes.

O blessed Savior and Redeemer, redeem us from wrong attitudes toward the material. For it is here, a part of us. Teach us to live with it. For a part of us is material, and we must know how to get along with that part of us. Teach us to live physically and spiritually as one. Amen.

AFFIRMATION FOR THE DAY: *My body will not be deified, nor despised, but dedicated.*

STRANGE BUT IMPORTANT PASSAGES

We come now to an important question: If the Word became flesh, is the flesh made for the Word? When the Divine Word took flesh, did He take something alien? Is the flesh an alien or an affinity to the spiritual? A Hindu "holy man" said to me: "Teach me to get rid of my body. It is my enemy." Was he right?

There are a number of passages in the New Testament which teach that God created the world through Christ. "Created the world through Christ"—when He appeared only two thousand years ago? What do these strange passages mean? The Christian Church has not taken these passages seriously. But if they are true, they are tremendously true—and meaningful and full of destiny. Here they are:

"All things were made through him [Christ] and without him was not anything made that was made. . . . He was in the world, and the world was made through Him, yet the world knew Him not" (John 1:3, 10). "But in these last days he has spoken to us by a Son, whom he appointed the heir of all things, through whom also he created the world" (Heb. 1:2). "He is the image of the invisible God, . . . for in him all things were created, in heaven and on earth, visible and invisible . . . all things were created through him and for him" (Col. 1:15, 16). "And there is one Lord, Jesus Christ, through whom all things came to be, and we through him" (I Cor. 8:6 NEB). "But it is not true that the body is for lust; it is for the Lord—and the Lord for the body" (I Cor. 6:13 NEB).

What do these strange passages mean? Do they mean that the touch of Christ is upon all creation? And that everything is made in its inner structure to work in His way? And when it works in His way, does it work well, harmoniously, creatively? And if it works some other way, does it work its own ruin? Are we made by Him and for Him? Are we destined by our very makeup to be His? And when we are His, are we then most our own? I believe we can answer "Yes" to all these questions. We are made for Him as the eye is made for light.

O Jesus, my Lord, am I fashioned by Thee and fashioned for Thee? Then that changes the whole picture. For then I can do Thy will with my whole being, knowing that my whole being, including my body, is made for Thee. Thou art its Home and when I'm in Thee I'm at home. Amen.

AFFIRMATION FOR THE DAY: *My body is made for its Maker and finds its life in His Life.*

EVERYTHING MADE TO WORK IN CHRIST'S WAY

We saw yesterday some of the passages in the New Testament which tell us in definite terms that everything has been made "by Christ" and "for Christ." That last phrase "for Christ" is important. It is possible to imagine that Christ would make a universe for purposes other than for Himself—a tentative universe to be made and to be destroyed and replaced by a better one. But this passage is definite in authorship and purpose—the universe is made "by Christ" and "for Christ."

If these passages mean anything, they mean that everything is made to work in its inner structure in Christ's way. If it works in His way, it fulfills the purpose of its creation—it works harmoniously, creatively, and happily. Its very being and the purpose of its being is fulfilled. If it works some other way, it works its own ruin, not by decree from without, but intrinsically; it is ruined by violating the law of its own nature. It is self-destroyed.

I am convinced that we are predestined by the very structure of our beings to be Christian. Note I say "to be Christian," not "to be Christians," for many who are "Christians" in the conventional sense are living against the laws of their being and are thereby being destroyed, maybe slowly, but surely. I believe that predestination is written not in the inscrutable will of God, as was once proclaimed, but written in our nerves, our blood, our tissues, our organs, our makeup. It is not merely written in the texts of Scripture, but into the texture of our beings. We can live against that destiny if we desire, for we are free, but if we do we get hurt—automatically. When Christ made you and me and the universe, He stamped within us a Way—a Way to live. His Way. And if we live according to that Way, we live; if we live some other way, we perish.

O Father of my being, Thou hast wrought into me Thy ways. Help me to make Thy ways my ways. Then my ways will become the Way. If I am on Thy Way, I am a train on the track running harmoniously and smoothly; but off Thy Way, I bump along on the ties. Save me. Amen.

AFFIRMATION FOR THE DAY: *I will decide my destiny according to His predestiny.*

"DOOMED TO BE A SAINT"

We ended yesterday on the affirmation that we are predestined to be Christian. This passage stresses: "Whom He . . . also predestined to be conformed to the image of His Son" (Rom. 8:29). There is an inner predestination to be conformed to the moral and spiritual image of Jesus. That is the purpose and goal of our living. An African chief stood up in a meeting and said: "I'm doomed to be a saint." I think he meant "destined." He saw that there was a destiny in him, and it pointed toward being a "saint"—a Christian.

If what we are saying is true, then the material is made for the spiritual—the "flesh" is made for the Word. And when "the Word became flesh," the Word was coming to His own. "He came into His own and His own received Him not." But whether they received Him or not it was "His own." And not receiving Him meant the doom of the people who did not receive Him. A president of a technical college in Holland in telling about his needs in the "Open Heart" of the Ashram said: "I am the only 'heathen' here—I am not a church member or a Christian." Afterwards, in an interview, I said to him: "You are a marked man. Christ has put His mark upon you. You are His." He said later: "That got me. I knew the mark of Christ was upon me. I felt it in my being, and I knew when I was fighting against Christ I was fighting against myself." When he accepted Christ, it was like a homecoming. He was made the director of the Ashram a few days later. From "heathen" to director in a few days! He was at home in the Kingdom—a natural. It seemed that he had been there all his life. He had been, but he didn't know it! All coming to Jesus Christ has the feeling of a homecoming upon it. All going away from Him has the sense of estrangement upon it. The rich young ruler went away from Jesus "sorrowful." Everybody does. Not only estranged from God, but also estranged from oneself. And the universe! And from Life! You are not at home with life, unless you are at home with Life. And Jesus is Life!

O Life, I dare not ask to fly from Thee. For if I cannot live with Thee, I'll not be able to live with myself nor with life. I'm hemmed in by Grace. And that Grace is Thy love herding me into Thy fold, which turns out to be my home. I'm homesick for Thee. I Thank Thee. Amen.

AFFIRMATION FOR THE DAY: *My soul, forget your name, but don't forget this: You are made for Him.*

THE FLESH MADE BY HIM AND FOR HIM

We now are ready to come to an important conclusion: If the "flesh," standing for the material, was made by Christ and for Christ, then when Jesus Christ came in the flesh He came to His own. The flesh was prepared for His coming. There was a *preparito evangelica*—a preparation for the Gospel in the flesh—the material was prepared by Him and it was prepared for Him. Just as the seed and the soil are made for each other, so the material became the matrix of the new order. It was not a resisting enemy, but a cooperating friend.

The material world responded to Him. It is said in Romans: "For the creation waits with eager longing for the revealing of the sons of God . . . because the creation itself will be set free from its bondage to decay and obtain the glorious liberty of the children of God" (Rom. 8:19, 21). The whole of lower creation with the touch of Christ upon it longs earnestly for the revelation of the sons of God—longs earnestly that men be Christian. For then men will treat nature more justly and more kindly and more creatively. Nature will share the redemption of the sons of God. Therefore, nature "waits with eager longing," literally "on tiptoe" to see the end of its being, namely, to be Christian.

No wonder nature, made by Jesus and for Jesus, was responsive to Him. He used the parable, an earthly happening, to express a heavenly meaning. He walked on the water as if nature were riding its Master on its shoulders as a crowd will carry its hero on its shoulders. He turned water into wine, as if to show in one act what He is doing over an extended period—turning water through the vine into wine. When on the Mount of Transfiguration His face glowed with unearthly splendor as if showing in one moment what takes place on a lesser scale when soul and body accord well. He multiplied the loaves to feed a multitude as if to bring to an instant the process of the multiplying a single grain into a hundred. Nature was sympathetic and pliable in His hand as if listening to its Master's voice.

O Lord of the earth and sky and sea, we thank Thee that Nature heard Thee speak and obeyed instantly, felt Thy touch and knew it was the touch of the Hand that made her. Teach us how to live with the material so that body and soul well in accord will beat out music vaster. Amen.

AFFIRMATION FOR THE DAY: *I have Nature as my Mother, so I shall dedicate and reverence her.*

THE TWO APPROACHES—THE CHRISTIAN AND
THE SCIENTIFIC

Since we have pursued the fact that God created the world through Christ, we are now ready to raise a very big question in religion. The question is based on the fact that there are two great approaches to life: the Christian and the scientific.

The Christian approach works from Revelation down, and the scientific works from the facts up to conclusions. The big question is this: Are these two approaches bringing us out to two conclusions about life, or one? If you work from Revelation down and from the facts up, do you find life coming out at the feet of Christ? Is life rendering a Christian verdict whichever way you approach it—from Revelation down or from the facts up? Are the God of grace and the God of nature two Gods—or one? These are the biggest questions we can ask about our faith and about our world.

We as Christians do not apologize for working from Revelation down. We glory in it. When we speak of Revelation, we mean the life and character of Jesus. We do not believe that the Bible is the Revelation—that would be the Word became printer's ink. But we do believe that the Bible is the inspired record of the Revelation, the Revelation was seen in the face of Jesus Christ—the Word became flesh. We have a starting point for all our thinking and acting. That starting point is a Person. In Him we see what God is like, and we see what we can be like. And, further, we see what life is like. He is our viewpoint. We view all life from the standpoint of Him. And when we do so, and, thus, have the single eye, the whole body is full of light. There is no situation in which He is not Light, and there is no situation in which His absence does not produce darkness. Dr. Huh Shih, the Chinese philosopher, once said to me: "You Christians have a decided advantage in that all your ideas have been embodied in a Person." Yes, not only a decided advantage, but a decisive advantage. In all the others the ideas are the Word become word. Only in Jesus has the Word become flesh. We begin with Him.

O Jesus, Savior and Lord, Thou art our Alpha and our Omega—our Beginning and our End. We do not know what the end will be, but the beginning is good. For we feel that the last word will be with Thee. For Thou art the Christ of the Beginning and the Christ of the Final Word. Amen.

AFFIRMATION FOR THE DAY: *I shall not be afraid of the facts—they will lead me to His feet.*

IS THE CHRISTIAN WAY THE WAY?

We repeat—we do not apologize for working from Revelation down. Jesus is God's authentic self-revelation. "He is the image of the invisible God" "the express image of His Person." In Jesus we have the Key, the Master-Key that unlocks everything in the universe—God, man, life, material, spiritual, individual, and the collective. So we work from Him down to life. In His Life we see life.

But what about this unfolding revelation that comes through science as it works its way through the facts to conclusions? Are these unfolding facts pointing us in a direction different from the Christian direction? Or are these two approaches coming out at the feet of Jesus Christ? The deepest conviction of my life is that if you go far enough with these two approaches you will come out at His feet; that life is rendering a verdict and that verdict is a Christian verdict.

In the Acts of the Apostles the Christian way is called "the Way." So that if he [Saul] found any belonging to the Way, men or women, he might bring them bound to Jerusalem" (Acts 9:2). "But when some were stubborn and disbelieved, speaking evil of the Way . . . " (Acts 19:9). "About this time there arose no little stir concerning the Way" (Acts 19:23). "According to the Way, which they call a sect . . ." (Acts 24:14). "But Felix, having a rather accurate knowledge of the Way . . . " (Acts 24:22). We usually make "the Way" the way of salvation. It is, but it doesn't say so. It says "the Way"—unqualified. Is the Christian way the Way—the way to do everything? To think, to act, to be in every conceivable circumstance, for God and man, in the individual and the collective? Are these just two things in life—the Way and not the way? And is the Christian way always the Way and the unchristian way always not the way? And are there no exceptions? If that is true, then it is the truth of truths.

O Father, we ask that Thou wilt hold us steady as we come to our conclusions. We do not want to be in a paradise if it turns out to be a fool's paradise. We want Reality and only Reality. For there is no refuge save in Reality. Guide us. Amen.

AFFIRMATION FOR THE DAY: *If the Christian Way is the Way, then it must be the Way for me in everything.*

WE HAVE CHRISTIAN STOMACHS!

We are discussing the question of the Christian way as the Way. And we are discussing it as the Way, not by a sovereign decree of God imposed on life, but as something that comes out of life itself—not imposed but exposed—exposed out of the facts themselves. Two and two make four is not imposed on mathematics by decree; it is built into the nature of mathematics. There is a built-in way to live and that way is the Way.

That Way is written in the Bible, supremely in Jesus who said, "I am the Way," but that Way is written into the facts, and they are more and more coming to the surface. Jesus said, "Thou shalt love"; do the facts say the same? A man was shot through the stomach. When the wound healed, an aperture was left open so they could look through this aperture and watch the process of digestion. When he was in a good humor and on good terms with everybody, digestion was normal—the stomach blushed a rosy red, the gastric juices would run down the walls of the stomach like sweat down one's face, and the stomach would go into churning movements. Digestion was normal. But the moment he became angry and out of sorts with others, the color of the stomach would change—the gastric juice would stop and digestion would be at an end. Obviously the stomach is made for good will and not ill will. In other words you have a Christian stomach. Feed the stomach with ill will and it will go back on you; feed it with good will and it will act normally and well.

Jesus said, "Be not anxious." Does the body say the same? I picked up my paper yesterday and read where Roger Maris, striving to hit sixty home runs, found his hair coming out in great chunks. He thought he had an infection. "No," said the doctor, "tense anxiety." So if Jesus said, "Be not anxious," the body, even to the roots of your hair, says the same.

O Son of God, we see Thy footprints everywhere. We see Thee everywhere, for Thou art everywhere. And when Thou dost come to us, Thou dost come to Thy own. And when we come to Thee, we too come to our own. We are at Home—in Thee. Amen.

AFFIRMATION FOR THE DAY: *Life works in His way, or it doesn't work.*

THE KINGDOM OF GOD BUILT INTO BUSINESS

We are looking at the fact of the Christian way as the Way. An ancient papyrus has a supposed saying of Jesus on it: "Raise the stone and thou shalt find Me, cleave the wood and I am there." Uncover the facts of Nature and thou shalt find Him; cleave the tissues of your body and He is there.

In Sweden I quoted from *The Way* the statement of a great surgeon when he said to me, "I've discoverd the kingdom of God at the end of my scalpel—it is in the tissues. The right thing morally, the Christian thing, is always the healthy thing physically." And the comment of a leading economist who said, "I would like to put it this way: 'The right thing morally, the Christian thing, is always the healthy thing economically.' " A Swedish industrial chemist commented, "You're right. In South Africa they put up a chemical plant, investing 100,000,000 pounds in it. They were going to manufacture chemicals and undercut the world in price because they were going to base it on cheap African labor. At the basis of the project was an injustice—an exploitation. In ten years it has never really gotten off the ground—it is fouled up at each turn. It is running afoul a moral law." The wrong thing morally is the unhealthy thing economically. I know that many assume that you can succeed in business if you are crooked. Yes, today and tomorrow, but the third day? No, for the moral universe closes in on the situation and has the last word. I was told by a Japanese businessman that the Japanese have a saying, "Business is like a folding screen—it won't stand unless it is crooked." But he added, "We are finding to our sorrow that is false and we are substituting 'Love your neighbor as you love yourself,' or you cannot get along with him." The improved trade of Japan is based on the improved morality in business.

O Father, we thank Thee that Thou has not left us adrift—Thy laws are our liberties, our protection against self-destruction. So, Father, give us sense, common sense, that we may see Thy ways and walk in them. Then we shall be free—free indeed. Amen.

AFFIRMATION FOR THE DAY: *If the Kingdom of God is "within" it must be in the total me.*

HEAVEN AND HELL ARE PORTABLE

We are studying how morality is written into the nature of things. And when we make morality and Christianity identical, we do it, not dogmatically, but according to the facts. The highest morality seen on this planet is undoubtedly the life and character and teaching of Jesus and illustrated in His own Person. The adjective Christlike is the highest adjective descriptive of character in any language. So we are not amiss when we make Christ and morality synonymous.

But to continue. John Hay, the great statesman said, "After trying the various ways for nations to get along with each other, I've found that the only way for nations to get along is to love your neighbor as you love yourself." "But, John Hay, that's Christian." So clear from the international, down through the sociological, on to the economic, on into the physical, and then to the moral and spiritual—all up and down the whole gamut of life, the right thing morally, the Christian thing, is the healthy thing in every situation.

A girl was deaf and therefore frustrated and unhappy. I talked to her about surrender of herself to Christ. She did it, and joyously exclaimed, "Oh, surrender, why there is nothing else to do. Why didn't I see it before?" It was natural. You don't have to love your neighbor as you love yourself; but if you don't love your neighbor as you love yourself, you can't live with your neighbor and you can't live with yourself. So God has us hooked. You can't revolt against God without revolting against yourself. If you won't live with God, you can't live with yourself. "He who spits against the wind spits in his own face." Romans 1:27 says, "receiving in their own persons the due penalty for their error." The punishment is "in their own persons"—they themselves are the payoff. Again, "God gave them up to a base mind and to improper conduct" (Rom. 1:28). He gave them up—not to outer punishment, but to the punishment of being that kind of person. The punishment was the person, hence inescapable. You can't jump out of your own skin. You are your reward or your punishment.

O blessed Redeemer, redeem me from myself. For I am my own heaven and my own hell. Heaven and hell are both portable. Let me carry around within me nothing but Thee, therefore nothing but heaven. For where Thou art there is nothing but heaven. I thank Thee. Amen.

AFFIRMATION FOR THE DAY: *I shall wear nothing but heaven in my heart today. The choice is mine.*

"ALL THINGS BETRAY THEE WHO BETRAYETH ME"

We pursue the fact that the Christian way is written within us. Therefore morality is not something we can take or leave and nothing happens. Everything happens. Morality is not built up by mores, by custom—it is not built up, but built in. You don't break the moral laws; you break yourself upon them. This is a universe where you get results or you get consequences. If you work with the moral universe, you get results—it will back you, sustain you, and you will have cosmic support for your way of life. But if you go against the moral universe, you get consequences—you'll be up against things, you'll be frustrated. "All things betray thee, who betrayeth Me." Some people go through life getting results; others get consequences. You are free to choose, but you're not free to choose the results or the consequences of your choices. They are in hands not your own.

In India I was talking to a politician, trying to get him to give up a relationship with a woman, for he was snarling up his home and another home—and himself. In order to ward off my appeal he told me of a British general who was challenged by the Oxford Group Movement with its four absolutes: absolute honesty, absolute purity, absolute unselfishness, absolute love. This general was not willing to build his life upon these four absolutes so in order to ward off the appeal said half-humorously and half-seriously that he was going to organize another group movement—the Cambridge Group Movement—and they would have four absolutes, too, but the opposite—absolute dishonesty, absolute impurity, absolute selfishness, and absolute hate. The politician waited for me to laugh, but I looked him straight in the eye and said: "Why don't you organize a movement on absolute dishonesty, absolute impurity, absolute selfishness, and absolute hate? If you believe in evil, why don't you make it absolute? Why are you so tentative in sin? Why don't you sin with the stops out?" He looked at me in surprise and said: "Oh, no, we couldn't do that. You see, it wouldn't work."

O Gracious Father, Thy Way will work, but no other way will. Then bring us back to our senses and let us take Thy Way and only Thy Way. For a mixture of Thy Way and other ways makes a mess and makes us a mess as well. Help me to be all Thine and only Thine. Amen.

AFFIRMATION FOR THE DAY: *Things will go to pieces around me if they go to pieces within me.*

EVIL, A PARASITE UPON THE GOOD

When the politician mentioned yesterday said to me, "Oh, no, we couldn't do that, it wouldn't work," my reply was, "Then you've given away the case. The only way to keep evil going is to throw enough good around it to make it work. For evil is an attempt to live life against itself, and it cannot be done. So evil is not only bad—it is stupid." I challenge you to build a society on absolute dishonesty, no one would trust another; on absolute impurity, it would rot; on absolute selfishness, no one would think in terms of others; on absolute hate, it would be so divisive, so centrifugal, it would not hold together.

Then what conclusion must I come to? This: that every dishonest man is a parasite upon the honesty of some honest man whose honesty holds together that situation long enough for him to be dishonest in it. Every impure man is a parasite upon the purity of some good man whose purity holds together that situation long enough for him to be impure in it. Every selfish man is a parasite upon the unselfishness of some unselfish man whose unselfishness holds together that situation long enough for him to be selfish in it. And every man of hate is a parasite upon the love of some loving man whose love holds together that situation long enough for him to be hateful in it.

The universe is not built for the success of evil—evil sooner or later destroys itself. The Tamils of South India have a saying, "The length of the life of the best concocted lie is just eight days." A projectile is so made that if it misses its target it explodes of its own accord. Life is made like that: if it misses the mark (Jesus), it goes to pieces. So we can say with Passmore:

> When all its work is done
> The lie will rot,
> The Truth is mighty
> And will prevail when none
> Care whether it prevail or not.

The nature of things sees to it that the lie rots and the truth prevails.

O God, we thank Thee that Thou hast made it so. So Thy laws are not planted on us like a stamp, they are implanted within us like the watermark in paper, part and parcel of the paper itself. So we can give ourselves to Thee with all our beings, for our beings are made for Thee. Amen.

AFFIRMATION FOR THE DAY: *The universe backs only the good; therefore, if I am sensible I will be good.*

THREE MATHEMATICAL PRINCIPLES

We are meditating on the fact that the Christian way is written into the constitution of things. A professor of mathematics said to our Ashram group:

I've learned three principles in my study of mathematics: (1) In mathematics you must be completely honest. You cannot play tricks on mathematics if you are to get any results. It demands complete honesty or there is frustration. (2) There are no shortcuts in mathematics. You must work out the problem stage by stage and be completely honest at every stage before you arrive at the answer. (3) The answer is the problem. Because there is a problem there must be the answer or there would have been no problem. The answer is wrapped up in the problem.

These three principles are Christian principles—(1) Complete honesty and truthfulness—"Ananias, why has Satan filled your heart to lie to the Holy Spirit and to keep back part of the proceeds of the land?" (2) Faithfulness in the little—"Well done, good and faithful servant; you have been faithful over a little, I will set you over much." (3) The problem and the answer are bound up together. "And my God will supply every need of yours according to his riches in glory in Christ Jesus."

These principles of the Christian faith are to be found in relationships in industry. A management engineer who specializes in human relations says that when he takes hold of a sick business to put it on its feet again he finds that the sickness is not in the business, but in the persons concerned. They get snarled up with themselves; they can't get along with themselves, so they project those snarls out into their relationships. They cannot get along with others. So cooperation dies, and the business turns sick. He says he cannot straighten out that business until he straightens out the people, so he sits with executives and heads of departments till after midnight. "Yes, we are snarled up within," they say, "but how do we get unsnarled?"

O Father, we thank Thee that questions like these drive us to Thee. They make Thee inevitable. For Thou art the answer to every need of ours whether that need be physical or spiritual or social. We are made for Thee and we are restless until we rest in Thee. Amen.

AFFIRMATION FOR THE DAY: *The little things that come up day by day are the testing ground for the greater.*

TALKED HIMSELF BACK INTO
BEING A CHRISTIAN

We continue to study of the discovery of principles of Christianity in the necessities of business. The management engineer when confronted with the question of how to get unsnarled is compelled by necessity to suggest God—a point of reference and loyalty outside themselves. They are snarled up because they are self-centered and hence self-preoccupied. So there must be some center of loyalty outside themselves to which they can be loyal in order to break the tyranny of self-centered loyalty. That center can only be God. Every other center, being human, will let them down and, hence, is mortal. "Yes," they say, "but how do we get to God?" Then he has to talk about "conversion," "new birth," a change of heart and life. "How do we get a change of heart and life—a new birth?" Then he refers them to a book like *Abundant Living*. Here we find a group of hardheaded men sitting to talk about how to straighten out a business and finding themselves running straight into the necessity of straightening out themselves, of finding a new birth, a conversion. So not merely the pulpit, but production is saying "Ye must be born again."

Dr. Henry Link, the psychologist, threw overboard all his Christian beliefs as he studied psychology—Christianity was outmoded. Then he began to try to straighten out people who were tangled in their lives. He found they were self-centered, tangled in the flypaper of self-preoccupation. He had to talk to them about God—Someone outside themselves to whom they could be loyal. Then he had to talk about conversion and the new birth. Before he knew what was happening, he found he had talked himself back into being a Christian again. Then he wrote two excellent books, *The Return to Religion* and *The Rediscovery of Man*. As he faced life, he found Christianity inescapable—life demanded it. If the Christian faith did not exist, we would have to invent it to meet the demands of human nature.

O Son of the Most High, when Thou didst come into a human body and a human world, Thou didst come to Thy very own. It was waiting for Thee as the eye is waiting for light. So when we see Thee we see that for which we are made—our own. Amen.

AFFIRMATION FOR THE DAY: *Life is taking me by the hand and is bringing me out at the feet of Jesus.*

"I STILL HAVE JESUS"

A Christian woman lost her son and then her daughter and then her husband. And then to cap it all, she lost her eyesight. The doctors said that the eyes were so badly infected that they would have to be taken out and glass eyes put in. A minister sat beside her bed after she got the news. He told her how sorry he was for her. But she replied, "Brother Wilson, don't feel too bad about it. I still have Jesus. They cannot take Him away." Her Christianity was not in what she had around her but what she had in her. It was a part of her—inseparable.

Here was a girl who had bad eyesight. It began with the death of her father. The shock of her father's death made her confused. She couldn't see spiritually, so she transferred the spiritual confusion to a physical symptom, and her eysight went bad; but when she found a conversion, her spiritual eyesight cleared up and the physical insight too. When she worked life in a Christian way, it worked.

I once said to a hardboiled newspaper reporter, "If you don't believe in the Christian way, why don't you put it to the test? Go out and try it out for a week. Think the unchristian thing, say the unchristian thing, act the unchristian thing, and be the unchristian thing in every situation for a week and come back and tell me how you got on." "Shucks," he snorted, "you'd be bumped off before the week was over." If someone didn't bump you off you'd feel like bumping yourself off! Then turn it around. Go out and for a week say the Christian thing, and be the Christian in every situation and come back and tell me how you got on. I'll tell you now. You will come back and say with joy, "This is my homeland. For once I'm at home."

O dear Lord, save me from beating my life out in impossible ways of life. Thou art the Life of my life, the Soul of my soul, my All, my Everything. In Thee I live—live to my fingertips and out of Thee life is not worth living. I know. Amen.

AFFIRMATION FOR THE DAY: *Put to the test, the Christian way stands up, the unchristian way breaks down.*

"THE BODY IS FOR THE LORD AND THE LORD IS FOR THE BODY"

We mentioned the falling out of Roger Maris' hair during the tensions brought on by trying to break the home run record of Babe Ruth. A Japanese beauty parlor operator told me the same thing in Honolulu. She is an ardent Christian and begins to preach the gospel when she sees a bald spot. She asks what the patient is doing for it and is told the physical remedies being used. Then she says the spiritual remedies are the most important, for most falling hair and dandruff comes from inner conflicts and tensions. She tells of a woman who lost her hair in one week. She had been divorced several times. She surrendered her resentments and hate and her hair came back. A child of ten lost her hair and had to wear a skull cap. Her mother was hating her relatives. The mother surrendered her hates, and the child's hair came back.

Sister Lila, a nun and a saint in a Greek Orthodox convent in Jerusalem, was upset and filled with resentments against the police who harried a member of our team unjustly and undeservedly. She immediately got a violent headache. She surrendered her resentments to God, and her headache left her immediately.

When the Scripture says, "The body is for the Lord and the Lord is for the body," life is a verification of that. The body is for the Lord and when it works in His Way it works well, and when it works some other way it works badly. The good is good for us and the bad is bad for us. And the Lord is for the body—He made it and He remakes it whenever it is surrendered to His will. A YMCA secretary was afflicted with blisters on his hands. Long and varied treatments failed to cure him. I asked, "Are you worrying?" He confessed he was tense and anxious. That was causing this skin affliction. He surrendered himself and his worries to God and was well. For that is what happens to the individual—we live in Him, outside Him we perish. "The Lord is for the body"—in Him it is at its best.

O Lord Jesus, Thou art for my body and it is rhythmical and harmonious and alive when I walk Thy ways. When I get out of Thy ways, I limp along a rugged way. All things betray me when I betray Thee. I'm grateful that Thou art for my body. Amen.

AFFIRMATION FOR THE DAY: *If the Lord is for the body and the body is for the Lord, then they are not alien, but affinities.*

"THE DEMANDS OF HUMAN NATURE DROVE ME BACK TO THE CHRISTIAN POSITION"

We are looking at the fact that the Christian way is the Way, and that Way is written in the Scriptures and is supremely and finally shown in Jesus Christ who is the Way. We saw also that the Way is written in us and in the necessities of human living. I have quoted in another book the statement of Dr. Boss, the head of the International Psychoanalytical Association of Europe, when I asked him how he was able to put his psychiatry and his Christianity together, and his reply: "In the beginning I had difficulty, for I was a Freudian. But the demands of human nature drove me back to the Christian position." I sat up and took notice, for I saw that this was probably the most important statement coming out of psychiatry in this generation. I asked him to repeat it, and he did with emphasis. This is of vast importance, for suppose human nature were demanding one thing for its fulfillment, and Christianity were offering another thing; then we as Christians would be in trouble, deep trouble, life trouble. But suppose what human nature is demanding for its fulfillment and what Christianity is offering for that fulfillment are the same, then they fit as hand and glove, then that makes Christianity inevitable. For what Christ commands, human nature demands. His command and our demand are one. So if you work from Revelation down and from the facts up, you come out at the feet of Jesus Christ. "He is the heir of all things"—everything must come out at His feet, or perish.

A biologist heard this exposition for the first time and said excitedly, "This biological predestination to Christianity is the most exciting thing I ever heard." It is exciting—so exciting that I wonder why we don't buttonhole everybody we meet and say, "Have you heard the news? You are predestined, biologically predestined, to be a Christian! Eventually, why not now?" If the Universe had a newspaper to give universal news, it should put out an extra with the above statement as the banner headline!

O Jesus, my Lord, I know that "every tongue shall confess that Jesus Christ is Lord," for Thou art Lord even where that Lordship is neglected or denied. "For my heart and my flesh cry out for Thee." And we cannot stifle that cry forever. Amen.

AFFIRMATION FOR THE DAY: *My biological predestination and my personal choices coincide—I am Christian forever and always.*

"VAST NEUROTIC MISERY . . . A NEUROSIS
OF EMPTINESS"

We ended yesterday in commenting on the statement of Dr. Boss that "the demands of human nature drove him back to the Christian position." He made another statement of real importance when I sent him my book *Conversion.* I thought he would toss it in the corner or write a polite note in reply. But instead he wrote: "This is the kind of book we need. Those psychiatrists who are not superficial have come to the conclusion that the vast neurotic misery of the world could be termed a neurosis of emptiness. People cut themselves off from the root of their being, from God, and therefore life turns sick because it is empty and inane." So life without God is sick because it is empty.

A Harvard doctor said over the radio recently: "The health of this country is being endangered by aimlessness and lack of purpose." Then to be healthy one must have aim and purpose. But without the Christian faith the aims are low aims, and purposes are low purposes. And low aims and purposes also create ill health. So the Christian faith is necessary to health. Paul writes to the Corinthians: "In my letter I wrote that you must have nothing to do with loose livers." Then he explains what a loose liver is: "I now write that you must have nothing to do with any so-called Christian who leads a loose life, or is grasping, or idolatrous, a slanderer, a drunkard, or a swindler" (I Cor. 5:9, 11 NEB). The life of sin is "loose"—it has no cement in it, so it falls to pieces mentally, spiritually, physically, and socially. We speak of a man who is going down hill: "He is going to pieces." He is. Concerning Jesus the Scripture says: "He is before all things, and in him all things hold together" (Col. 1:17). Outside Him all things fly apart, and that "all things" includes the total person. The King James Version says, "All things cohere in Him." Outside of Him all things are incoherent, senseless, aimless, and purposeless. Hence, there is an undermining of health. For we are made by the Purposeful for the purposeful.

O Blessed Father, Thy love has written Thy law not in graven stone but in our flesh. Thy law is a part of us. Therefore we cannot revolt against Thy law without revolting against ourselves. We set organ against organ, and the revolt is chaos. Save us. Amen.

AFFIRMATION FOR THE DAY: *Jesus said: "He who does not gather with me scatters"—life forces break down.*

"IN MY MOUTH SWEET AS HONEY"

We are studying the fact that "the body is for the Lord and the Lord is for the body." So the flesh is His own; when the Word became flesh, He entered His own. This version puts it: "He entered his own realm, and his own would not receive him" (John 1:11 NEB). "He entered his own realm"—so the flesh was "His own realm." And when "the flesh" is in Him, it is in its "own realm," as a fish is in its own realm when in the water. A fish out of water is gasping for life, so men outside Christ gasp for life and do not know they are gasping for Life. There is not a single situation that is not "His own realm" and is at home when in Him and out of home when out of Him.

To put the matter another way: "In my mouth it did taste sweet as honey; but when I swallowed it my stomach turned sour" (Rev. 10:10 NEB). Evil does taste sweet as honey in the mouth, but when you swallow evil and try to assimilate it, the system turns sour. The system rejects it as alien. A woman came to our Ashram with very great skin eruptions on her arms. She had to wear very long sleeves. She had deep resentments against her bullying employer and was worrying over a court case because of an accident. She surrendered her resentments and her worry, and the eruptions cleared up completely. A woman said the doctors had found she had thirty-five allergies, things she couldn't touch or eat. She surrendered to God her resentments against her family, and every one of the allergies dropped away. "Ragweed?" she says, "I can go to bed with it. Peaches? I used to think the acid was in the peaches, then I found out that the acid was in me. Strawberries? I can eat them by the quart." A Japanese doctor in Hiroshima, Japan, said: "The first place wrong emotions and attitudes hit is the stomach. Along about twenty years of age, examinations and uncertainty about the future upset the stomach, and then again about forty—these are the upset ages." On this trip I've eaten in one day squid, octopus, raw fish, two birds, raw egg, and anything else set before me. My digestion will handle almost anything if I am Christian in my attitudes.

O Master of my life, I thank Thee for this freedom in Thee. We are made to live in Thy world. And we are at home in it when we are at one with Thee. We find Thee and find life. And we love life when we love Thee. We are no longer soured with life. I thank Thee. Amen.

AFFIRMATION FOR THE DAY: *Life is all that it can be expected to be—with Jesus.*

"BORN TO THE KINGDOM"

We are considering the fact that the Christian faith and the soul and body are not alien but affinities. Jesus said, "The earth brings forth fruit of itself"—the seed and the earth are affinities, made for each other. So the seed of the Kingdom and the soil of my life are fitted for each other. Another passage speaks of those "born of the kingdom" (Matt. 8:12 NEB). We are born to live in the Kingdom as a child is born to live in this world of ours. When a child is about to be born, we can imagine its fear of being born into a world of this kind—away from the securities of the womb. But everything is awaiting the baby's propensities. If the stomach needs food, it is there; if the brain needs knowledge, it is there for the taking; if the heart needs fellowship, it is awaiting it in the family circle; if the soul needs God, He has been in the whole process. Everything the baby needs is provided for before it arrives. So when we are "born to the Kingdom," everything we need to live by is already provided in that Kingdom. "My God shall supply every need of yours according to his riches in glory in Christ Jesus" (Phil. 4:19).

Jesus said, "My food is to do the will of him who sent me, and to accomplish his work" (John 4:34). Is God's will our food? And is our will, against God's will, our poison? Yes, for our will set against God's will poisons our usefulness, our happiness, ourselves. But when we do God's will, we are fed, we are at our best, we have a sense of well-being, and we are alive all over.

A young minister in Japan said in the Overflowing Heart at one of our Ashrams, "I didn't want to be a holy man—I've wanted to be human. But I've had a brooding sense of emptiness. I didn't want to receive the Holy Spirit, for I was afraid of it—afraid it would make me queer. But last night I surrendered myself to Jesus, and this morning I awoke without my usual sense of gloominess. I felt strange. Now I've been crucified with Christ, and now I share His resurrection. I'm alive—and human."

O Jesus, blessed redeemer, Thou dost make us more human than ever when we are Thine. We walk the earth as though we possess it—and we do! We belong to Thee, and everything that belongs to Thee, including the earth, belongs to us. Glory be! Amen!

AFFIRMATION FOR THE DAY: *God's will is food, my will against God's will is my poison—remember that, O my soul.*

"THE HEALTH OF THE BODY DEPENDS UPON THE SOUL"

We look again at the fact that the "flesh"—the material world— was made by Him and for Him. "These are the words of the Amen, the faithful and true witness, the prime source of all God's creation" (Rev. 3:14 NEB). Jesus is the "Amen"—the last word! Whoever has the first or the intermediate word, Jesus always has the last word. He is the "Alpha"—the Christ of the Beginning, and the "Omega"—the Christ of the Final Word. He is the Amen! And He is "the prime source of God's creation." His touch is upon all creation; everything is made to work in His way and no other way.

> He who formed our frame
> Has made man a whole;
> And how the health of the body
> Depends upon the soul.

There is another passage: "And there is one Lord, Jesus Christ, through whom all things came to be, and we through him" (I Cor. 8:6 NEB). "All things came to be, and we"—"All things" and "we." Things and persons are made to operate in His Way. We have thought that things are neutral, can be used in any direction—good, bad, or indifferent. But they are not. This pregnant line of poetry expresses the fact that things have a bias: "All things betray thee who betrayeth Me," and that bias was put there by "Me"—by "Jesus Christ through whom all things came to be." The Revised Standard Version's "God works in everything for good with those who love Him" is better than the King James, and yet the old had a truth in it: "All things work together for good to those who love Him." "All things work together for good"—there is a bias toward good in all things, put there by their Author. If people cut down forests from the mountains, and ruthlessly and selfishly exploit them, then floods will ruin the valleys where the exploiters live. That law is written in the constitution of things.

O Father God, Thou hast hedged us about to save us from ourselves. Thy laws are Thy love—Thy preventive love to protect us from ruin. The rules in this school of living are hard, but they are redemptive. Help us to have sense and obey them. In Jesus' Name. Amen.

AFFIRMATION FOR THE DAY: *Since Jesus is "The Amen, prime source of God's creation," He shall be the prime source of all my thoughts and acts.*

"MAN IS MADE FOR CONVERSION"

We come this week to something inherent in the Christian faith and inherent in us: conversion, new birth. When the Christian faith says: "Ye must be born again," and "Except ye be converted and become as little children," many think that this "must" and this "except" are imposed from above arbitrarily—God laid down the condition for entrance into His Kingdom, and you can take it or leave it. He as Ruler of the universe has the right and the power to impose those conditions. But as we work from Revelation down and from the facts up, both are saying: "Ye must be born again."

A British psychologist put it in these important words: "Man is made for conversion." The very makeup of his being demands conversion, a new birth. Why? Because man finds himself an incomplete person in an incomplete world. God apparently created the world incomplete. He left it imperfect so man in helping the Creator to complete the creation would help to complete himself in the process. God after creation looked upon the universe which He had created and saw "it was good"—not perfect, but "good" for the purpose He had in creation, namely, to make beings who would grow in His likeness and be perfect as created beings as He is perfect as the Creator God. So to grow into that likeness man would have to be converted—converted from what he is to what he ought to be.

If the necessity of conversion is inherent in the necessity of growth into the Divine Image, that necessity is doubly reinforced by the fact that man has corrupted the raw materials God has put into his hands—including especially himself. He has used the good things and has made them into the bad by using them for wrong ends. He has perverted God's entrustments. He has "sinned and come short of the glory of God." That perversion needs conversion! Conversion is conversion from perversion. It is inherent.

O Father, I know that life is wrong at its center until it is right with Thee. We are bumping ourselves against the system of things until we make peace with Thee. So teach us to live by teaching us how to live with Thee. In Jesus' dear Name. Amen.

AFFIRMATION FOR THE DAY: *If I fight conversion, I fight with the law of my being—I fight myself.*

SIN IS A CANCER

We have quoted the British psychiatrist who said, "Man is made for conversion." This means that until man is converted, he is less than a man, he is beside himself. And yet people have the fear of conversion, lest it make them queer. A pastor said, "Call me a liar, abuse me, but don't call me pious." Piety and being less than a man were synonymous. But a Christian conversion brings you back to the normal, according to the Norm, Jesus, and makes you truly natural.

We are made for change. A doctor who researched in cancer said that cancer cells are cells turned selfish; they refuse to serve the rest and demand that the rest serve them. They have broken the law of loving your neighbor as you love yourself and have loved themselves only. Hence, instead of being constructive they have become cancerous. Sin is a cancer in the personality, hence unnatural. This same doctor told me that there are layers of skin and the lowest layer is constantly dying into the second layer—it loses its life and finds it again. As long as this process of dying to live keeps up, the skin is healthy. But when the lowest layer begins to refuse to surrender its life to the second layer, and saves its life, it begins to die—the first sign of the skin getting old. Thereafter, it is on its way to death. The layer refuses to love its neighbor—loves itself only and loses its life. The law of life is change upward, and when we refuse to change upward, decay and death set in.

Sin is an unnatural intrusion. And yet some think it natural. A passage is quoted: "Among these we all once lived in the passions of our flesh, following the desires of body and mind, and so we were by nature children of wrath" (Eph. 2:3). But note: "And so"—by following the desires of body and mind another nature, a false nature is built up. We produce the unnatural nature. God created us good.

Dear God, save us from building up a false nature and calling it natural. Thou hast created every organ, every tissue, every nerve for Thyself; and when they work in Thy way, they work—they are natural and harmonious and creative. Bring us back to Thyself and hence to ourselves. Amen.

AFFIRMATION FOR THE DAY: *When I sin I am not a man; I am less than a man.*

THE STEPS TO CONVERSION

"Man is made for conversion." These are the stages through which a person gets to conversion. (1) Doubt—fear of change. When the people came and saw the demoniac now "clothed and in his right mind and sitting at the feet of Jesus, they were afraid." Afraid of sanity! We are so accustomed to the insanities of our evils that we are afraid of the sanity of the new. (2) Darkness—the doubt and fear bring on darkness. And that darkness deepens day by day. (3) Despair—as the darkness deepens, despair sets in. We see no way out of this descending spiral. (4) Decision—we decide to try Christ. "If He is a Savior He will save me—I'll try Christ." (5) Dawn—the moment we turn to Him, hope lights up our darkened skies. He is the Dawn. (6) Deliverance—chains fall off, old habits are broken up and remade into new patterns, a new man emerges. (7) Delight—a weak word describing a strong, deep joy which takes possession of the total person—he becomes joy-filled. (8) Development—a desire takes possession of one to grow, to be and do something, become creative.

"Man is made" for these eight steps, and when he takes them he comes to himself, as the prodigal son did. Sometimes these eight steps are telescoped into one creative moment. A man who had been in a high position in government, ran for high office, then became a businessman, then an alcoholic. He set out at four o'clock in the morning to drive the five hundred miles to our Ashram—and set out half-drunk. His wife wondered if he would ever get there. He arrived half-drunk and disturbed the opening meeting. But the next day he was soundly converted. He called up his wife and said, "You'll probably not know me—everybody says I'm so changed, and I am." When I saw him a month later I asked him about the battle with alcohol, and he replied, "The question hasn't ever arisen. It's gone. I have been and am almost deliriously happy." One moment of acceptance of Grace, and he and his entire world were new.

O Lord of Change, make me a totally changed person—me and my world. For when I submit to and accept this change I feel I am submitting to my inner destiny as well as Thy will. So in their coinciding I find life and find it more abundantly. I thank Thee. Amen.

AFFIRMATION FOR THE DAY: *I shall be the word of conversion become flesh.*

A NEW NAME—"AFTER"

"Man is made for conversion." We ended yesterday with the account of an alcoholic coming to himself and his real destiny in conversion. We said that the last step in conversion was development. In conversion there is an awakening of the total person—body, mind, and spirit. One night during the Ashram after the conversion of the alcoholic mentioned yesterday, I asked for volunteers who would offer themselves—first, for full-time Christian ministry; second, for the mission field; third, as full-time workers as laymen, through their regular occupations. He stood up on all three! He explained that he was ready to be a minister, a missionary, or a full-time worker as a layman—and meant it. I urged him not to decide his lifework suddenly, but to circle, say for a year, like a homing pigeon gaining its homeward directions, and then decide. But he has already committed himself to go to a theological seminary to prepare himself for any one of these three. Before his conversion he was "beside himself," another person, now he is himself, fulfilling the destiny of his being.

An African after his conversion took the name "After" as his real name. For "before" he was another type of person, only "after" did he begin to live. Everything happened "after," so he had to have a changed name to express the changed person. The Africans give names to visitors after studying their characteristics. I have been humbled by my new names and have tried to live up to some of them. One they gave, "Reconciler," is the one I love most and am challenged by it most. Another was so overstated that it was the word became word, not "the Word became flesh," for I knew it didn't apply!

But when the soul is converted, he awakens as from a bad dream, a nightmare, as one who has recovered from a dreadful sickness, and worse, from death. The Scripture describes it as a passing "from death to life." Only now you must spell life as Life.

O Jesus, we sit at Thy feet, clothed and in our right minds, and we look into Thy face and know we see the face of our Redeemer. We are startled at the change—so changed, so new, and so altogether unmerited. We will spend our days in telling all around the story of Thy grace. Amen.

AFFIRMATION FOR THE DAY: *Henceforth I shall be an illustration of "after," not "before."*

"WOULDST THOU BE MADE WHOLE?"

"Man is made for conversion." Dr. Starbuck, the psychologist, says, "Every life is stunted unless it receives this metamorphosis called conversion in some form or other. If the Church allows this to fossilize then psychology when it becomes truly biological will preach it." Note: "psychology when it becomes truly biological"—when psychology does not preach conversion, then it is not biological—it has departed from the science of life. It has departed from life. If psychology in not preaching conversion is departing from life, how much more is religion departing from Life when it fails to preach and fails to produce conversion. It has lost its right to be called Christian, or its right to be considered alive, for it has departed from life—hence from Life. It is "twice dead" and shall be "plucked up by the roots." "For every plant which my Father has not planted shall be rooted up." When life is not fulfilling its destiny, it is on its way to death.

But the moment we find conversion we find Life. Withered life begins to live. Take this case:

"I had been working as a social worker when in 1945 I had a severe depression. I saw a psychiatrist, was hospitalized, and had electric shock treatments. I left the hospital with the depression sufficiently lifted enough to eat and sleep, but the days stretched ahead and they appeared endless and futile. I never missed church. Somehow that one hour of the week was more endurable than any other. One day the minister spoke on John 5: "Wouldst thou be made whole?" Something began working in me. Did I want to get well, or did I want to be the object of pity, completely dependent on my patient and loving family? The assurance came that if I wanted to be made "whole" He would supply the power; I gave Him the affirmative answer and the healing began. The next morning I got up so full of energy and purpose I felt ready to burst. I scrubbed, waxed, and polished all day. I read the New Testament. It was new! Now the days were full of adventure and joy. Within a week I was back at my job.

She was herself because His!

O Master of life, Thou hast come to bring life and bring it more abundantly. When we are in Thee, we are automatically in life. Out of Thee we are automatically out of life. In Thee we pulsate with life, alive in every cell and tissue and nerve. Evermore give us This Life. In Thy name. Amen.

AFFIRMATION FOR THE DAY: *The crux of the matter is here: Do I want to be made whole sufficiently to commit myself to wholeness?*

TROUBLEMAKER OR TROUBLESHOOTER?

"Man is made for conversion." Even Freud got a glimpse of this fact and gave this definition of conversion: "The only kind of change in life which means anything, because it transforms everything in its path, is that which changes peoples' thinking, their deepest convictions, that which makes them see the world in a different way. This doesn't happen often." True, it doesn't happen often, not from his premises and from his procedures. Because when he left Christ out, he left out Life. Therefore his method is proving more and more sterile. No wonder Freud was pessimistic about man: "In the depths of my heart, I can't help being convinced that my dear fellow men, with a few exceptions, are worthless." But the Christian never looks on anyone as worthless. He believes in conversion. For instance, in Africa a woman of eighty listened to the Gospel. It awakened her though she was blind and illiterate. She came to the missionary and asked him to underscore John 3:16 in a French Bible. She sat near a school, and when the boys would come out she would ask them to read this passage. Proud of being able to read French, they would gladly do so. Then she would ask them what it meant. When they said they didn't know, she would tell them out of her experience what it meant to her. Forty-four Christian workers came out of her work, most of them assistant lay pastors. This work she did for eight years. She is now known as Madame Dundjee—she was a person!

A beautiful church in Oak Ridge, Tennessee, is made out of bits of waste stone. The Christian church, in general, is made up in large measure of waste material—material that would have been wasted in conflicts and futile living had it not been converted into contributive forms. Here was a wife who was always complaining about everything. Then the light dawned. She was converted. Now instead of complaining she began to take up things as they arose and began to solve them. Then there was nothing to complain about. She is now a troubleshooter instead of a troublemaker.

O Jesus, Thou dost make the nobodies into the somebodies, the waste material into a temple of God. Help me to pick up the broken fragments of my life that nothing be lost and put them into Thy hands. For Thou dost use everything—use even me! Amen.

AFFIRMATION FOR THE DAY: *Outside of Jesus I am wasted, inside of Jesus I am wanted.*

"THE BASIC DIRECTION OF THE ORGANISM
IS FORWARD"

"Man is made for conversion." "Personality tends toward the state we call mental health, handicaps by way of acculturation notwithstanding. The basic direction of the organism is forward." Here Dr. Albert C. Outler says two things about the human personality: it tends toward health and its basic direction is forward. This fits exactly with the statement that "man is made for conversion."

For conversion is a change from sickness to health. The personality in sin is guilty and is unhealthy because of that guilt. So the guilty soul, and consequently the sick soul, tends toward, longs for, health, longs for conversion—conversion back to health. So conversion is the fulfillment of that basic urge toward wholeness, toward health, toward salvation.

If the first tendency is toward health, the second tendency is "forward." If we tend toward ill health and toward retrogression, this is unnatural. So sin is unnatural. Conversion is a movement "forward." The soul gets on by a series of crises. The greatest of the crises is conversion, when the soul rises out of the unnatural ill health and retrogression of sin to the supernaturally natural goodness.

Take the case of a paramount chief in Africa. He had seven wives and could not be baptized because of it. We arranged, with his agreement, that he live with one wife and support the rest, so he was baptized on Easter. His tribe of 1,500,000 was about to go to war with another tribe in the Congo. As a token of reconciliation, the chief sent his best leopard skin to the chief of the other tribe by a missionary. Then he said to his own tribesmen, "If you go to war I will take off my crown and my chieftain robes and will be no longer your chief." It brought peace. Conversion brought total health and a forward urge to his total life.

O Jesus Lord, we thank Thee for this urge within us toward "health" and toward the "forward." We thank Thee for this "upward pull of God in Christ Jesus," this something that will not rest this side of being a changed person. We respond to that pull. Amen.

AFFIRMATION FOR THE DAY: *Sin is the backward look; goodness is the forward look.*

THE SEED AND THE SOIL ARE MADE FOR
EACH OTHER

We have seen how the "flesh," the material part of our personality, has been prepared to receive "the Word." The Word and the flesh are made for each other as the seed and the soil. The seed rejects many things in the soil and selects only those elements akin to its own nature. So the Divine Word selects what is akin to its life in the soil of our lives, but rejects others. The Word rejects unnatural sin and selects only the truly natural good. Conversion is the response of the soil to the invasion of the Divine Seed, the Word. Just as the plant takes hold of elements in the soil akin to its own nature, and transforms them and transfigures them and makes them into the image of the plant, so the Word takes hold of the flesh and spirit and takes them up into the purpose of the Word and makes them into its own likeness.

For instance here is foul, impure mud in a pond. On the bosom of the pond is a lotus flower: one in the mineral kingdom, the other in the plant kingdom—a higher kingdom. How can that lower kingdom get in to the higher? By trying? By lifting itself by its bootstraps? By education about the higher life? By joining a group to study the higher life? No, none of these, except they lead to one thing—surrender! The roots of the lotus flower come down and say to the impure mud: "Do two things: be willing to cease to be mud and surrender your life to my life. Let me have you." And the mud does just that. It surrenders itself to the life of the plant, and it is lifted and transformed into the beauty of the lotus flower. It is born from the above. Except the mineral kingdom be born from above, it cannot see the kingdom of the plant. That mud is made for conversion. If it isn't converted into a higher life, it has missed the end of its being. That is its destiny. It is predestined to the life of the plant. So we are predestined to conversion—predestined to rise from the kingdom of men to the Kingdom of God.

O Divine Word, we are the offspring of Thy purpose. And that purpose reaches down into our flesh. It was fashioned by Thee and for Thee. I feel that destiny pulsating within me, and when I respond I respond to the Homeland pull. I thank Thee. Amen.

AFFIRMATION FOR THE DAY: *All day I shall respond to "the upward pull of God in Christ Jesus."*

THE HIGHEST VALUE—LOVE

We come now to discuss something that goes to the root of the question as to whether the Christian Way is written within us. The highest thing in the Christian faith is undoubtedly love. Is love the deepest thing in man? Is it written into the necessities of his life? In the deepest necessities? So much so that we can say, "No love, no life"?

Is love the highest thing in the Christian way—its chief value emphasis? It was a great moment in the moral and spiritual history of mankind when a lawyer stood up and asked Jesus which was the greatest commandment in the Law. There were over 3,600 commandments to choose from. Would He pick the wrong one, or a marginal one? If He should choose the wrong one, then humanity following His emphasis would go wrong with Him. But if He chose the right one, humanity would go right with Him. The ages held its breath—for it was a breathless moment. The oral and spiritual fate of humanity trembled in the balance. He went unerringly to the highest: "Thou shalt love." He picked out love as the highest value. And He added to the value of that highest value when He defined the supreme and subordinate objects of that love. He replied: "Love the Lord your God with all your heart, with all your soul, with all your mind, and with all your strength. . . . The second is this: 'Love your neighbour as yourself.' There is no commandment greater than these" (Mark 12:29-31 NEB).

First, love to God. And not an occasional, marginal love, but, as we have noted, a love that includes the total being. Love Him with all your heart—the affectional nature; with all your soul—the volitional nature; with all your mind—the intellectual nature; the total man to love God totally. And Mark adds, "with all thy strength"—the strength of the emotion, the strength of the will, the strength of the mind. And the second is: Love man as you love yourself. That is the highest of values: Love to God and love to man.

O Jesus Lord, we thank Thee that Thy divine finger went unerringly to the highest. Nothing higher can be imagined or thought. Here we come to an ultimate in values. We do thank Thee that Thou hast revealed it. Help us to practice it. Amen.

AFFIRMATION FOR THE DAY: *If the highest value is love, then I shall value that highest value above all values.*

THREE GREAT INTERPRETERS TOOK
THE TORCH FROM HIS HAND

We saw yesterday that the Author of our faith put His finger on the highest value as love to God and man. Was that a unique position in the Founder but sidetracked in His followers? For a time it seems as though Paul, His chief interpreter, is going to make faith the supreme value. But when it comes to the crucial choice, he says: "Now abideth faith, hope and love, but the greatest of these is love." So he took the torch from His Master's hand and held love up as the supreme value. John, in his epistles, looks as though, in putting the capstone on Revelation, he will choose knowledge as the supreme value. He did use the word "know" thirty-six times in the epistle, for he was writing against a background of Gnosticism—the so-called knowers. But when he comes to the supreme emphasis, he makes love the supreme emphasis, using the word forty-three times. And he wrote something that had never before been written in human history. And when he was about to write it, all heaven leaned over to see if he really would write it. And when he did, all heaven broke out in applause: "At last they've got it!" And that phrase was: "God is love." Others had said, "God loves," but no one had ever said: "God is love" in His essential nature and cannot do an unloving thing without violating His own nature.

But that could not have been said by John had he not looked in the face of Jesus Christ. Only then could he come to that conclusion. And Peter also takes the torch from His Master's hand when he too makes love supreme in this climax: "Supplement your faith with virtue, virtue with knowledge, knowledge with self-control, self-control with fortitude, fortitude with piety, piety with brotherly kindness, and brotherly kindness with love" (II Pet. 1:5-7 NEB). So the four great interpreters of the Gospel—Jesus, Paul, Peter, and John all make love the supreme value.

Dear Lord and Father, we thank Thee for this revelation of Thy nature as love. Beyond that revelation the human race can never progress. This is it—and forever! And now we know where we head in. Help us to head in with all our beings. Amen.

AFFIRMATION FOR THE DAY: *I shall be in the line of succession of these interpreters and interpret life as love.*

IS SCIENCE COMING OUT TO
THE SUPREMACY OF LOVE?

We have seen that love is the supreme value in the Christian faith—consistently so. So if we work from Revelation down, we come to love as the supreme thing in God and man. That is the verdict of Revelation. What is the verdict as we work up the other way—from the facts up and out to conclusions? Is some other value turning out to be the supreme value as we apply the scientific method of experimentation leading to verified knowledge? Or is scientific investigation leading to the same conclusion that love is the supreme value in human nature?

In one of my books, *Christian Maturity,* I took the position that the human personality is as mature as it is mature in love, and no more. One may be mature in culture and knowledge and in ability, but if he is immature in love he is an immature personality. And the psychologists are increasingly agreeing. Dr. Carl Menninger, head of perhaps the outstanding psychiatric center of America, in Topeka, Kansas, wrote a book on *Love Against Hate.* He took the position that love is the constructive element—love builds up and hate tears down. When he came to the conclusion that people are in his institution because they had not loved or been loved, it was an epoch in his thinking. For psychiatry had been founded on the idea that insight is the cure-all for human personality problems. Give the patient insight as to his troubles, and he is automatically cured. But mental institutions are filled with people who have insight as to what is the matter with them, but they are still there. Insight is not necessarily curative. When the diagnosis shifted, the technique had to shift. These people were there because they hadn't loved or been loved. They must love them into loving.

O Jesus, Lover of my Soul, let me to Thy bosom fly. Love me into loving. If I can't love with my love, let me love with Thy love. Then I will love the unlovely. For Thou didst love the unlovely. Help me to catch Thy spirit. Amen.

AFFIRMATION FOR THE DAY: *As Christ is loving me into loving so I will love others into loving.*

LOVE WAS THE KEY

When Dr. Menninger gained this new insight, he called his staff together and said in essence: These people are here because they haven't loved or been loved. That is their disease. All else is symptom. So we will have to love them into loving, will have to make all our contacts with the patients love contacts, from the top psychiatrist to the caretaker. If you go in to change an electric light bulb in a patient's room, you must make your contacts love contacts. They tried it for six months, and found at the end of that time that the period of hospitalization had been cut in half. The patients were getting well in half the time it took under the old insight technique. Love was the key. And that was important for our quest. For insight is the Word become word, but love is the Word became flesh. You cannot take love as a word; you must take it as an attitude and an act, or you haven't got it. Love makes itself into arms and hands and feet or it isn't love.

When someone asked Dr. Menninger in a forum in Tucson, Arizona: "Doctor, what are you to do if you find a nervous breakdown coming on?" You would have thought that the great psychiatrist would say, "See a psychiatrist," but he didn't. He said instead: "Go to the front door, turn the key in the lock, go across the railway tracks, find someone who needs you and do something for him." For a nervous breakdown is caused by being interested in yourself and no one else. Love breaks that tyranny of self-preoccupation and makes you free.

Another book entitled *Love or Perish*, by another psychiatrist, Dr. Smiley Blanton, emphasizes the same thing. If you don't love you perish—not in hell necessarily, but now as a personality. Nothing will hold the personality together except love. So the title means what it says, "Love or Perish"—now.

O God, we thank Thee that Thou hast made it so that we cannot violate the law of love without violating the law of our own beings. Give me the sense to love and love lavishly upon the worthy and the unworthy. In Jesus' Name. Amen.

AFFIRMATION FOR THE DAY: *Love will be the key to every situation I shall meet today.*

THE DEEPEST THING IN HUMAN NATURE—
TO LOVE AND BE LOVED

Dr. Smiley Blanton, mentioned yesterday, says that "after sitting for forty years in my office and dealing with disrupted people I've come to the conclusion that they are disrupted because they haven't loved or been loved."

When I asked Dr. John Plokker, head of a large mental hospital in Holland, what was the deepest necessity in human nature, he answered without hesitation, "To love and be loved." He said that in his hospital they put on extra nurses to have what they call "Petting Hours"—hours when they give the babies not merely service, but love. In the Bellevue Hospital in New York they found that babies, though given scientific care and feeding, died to the tune of 32 percent the first year of a minor ailment. They decided that the babies were getting everything except love. So they sent out a call for "Love Volunteers"—women who would come in and love babies so many hours a day. Hundreds of women volunteered not only for the sake of the babies but for their own selves. For with their own children gone from the home they wanted and needed someone to love. The superintendent reporting on results said, "We could no more do without these 'love volunteers' than we could do without penicillin. Here is a vitamin, love, without which babies die to the tune of 32 percent the first year of a minor ailment and 22 percent are so damaged that they must be classed as idiots."

An abandoned child, now in a hospital, didn't grow, was underdeveloped. A nurse in her spare time began to love it. The child began to blossom and bloom. On the instruction sheets many doctors write as instruction to nurses: "T.L.C."—"Tender loving care." Chiropractors have as their motto "L.L.L."—"Lather love lavishly." From various angles necessity is taking men by the hand and is leading them to life's deepest necessity—love!

My Gracious Lord, how can I thank Thee enough that the highest is pulling us—pulling us to love, and to accept love? We thank Thee for this transforming pull. We yield ourselves to it and in so doing we find ourselves different. We thank Thee. Amen.

AFFIRMATION FOR THE DAY: *My chief occupation today—to accept love and to give love.*

"I DECIDED TO DO IT JUST FOR THE FUN OF IT"

We continue our study of the sovereign necessity of love in the human personality. For ten years a patient in Sweden lay on her bed, disliked by everybody. For two years she never spoke a word. A Christian nurse decided what she needed was love, and gave it to her. In a few days she spoke for the first time, "How kind you are." In two weeks she was out and well. Today she is well and useful and respected and loved! Her malady was that she did not receive love or give it. So she was an invalid for ten years—love-starved!

A government hospital was set up alongside a mission hospital, obviously to kill it. The government hospital made no charge, the mission hospital did. But the mission hospital is growing by leaps and bounds. The people flock to it, for there they get love. And without love patients get well slowly or not at all.

One would hardly expect this from Bertrand Russell, the skeptical philosopher: "Of all forms of caution, caution in love is perhaps the most fatal to human happiness." He was never more profoundly right. I have quoted at length in *Christian Maturity* what he said before Columbia University when he declared in essence: "What I'm going to suggest is so simple that it sounds absurd. But I see no remedy for the world's ills except love."

A taxi driver was so polite and helpful that a friend asked him about it. He replied, "Well, I heard of a taximan who was kind to a passenger and found that he was remembered in the man's will for $65,000. So I thought I would try it—somebody might leave me something! But after trying it I found it was so much fun that I decided to do it just for the fun of it—reward or no reward." He found he was made for love and when he gave it the reward was in himself.

O Jesus, my Savior and Lord, I thank Thee for the privilege of loving Thee and loving those whom Thou dost love—everybody! Help me this day to form the habit of loving and of loving lavishly. And know that the reward is in myself. Amen.

AFFIRMATION FOR THE DAY: *I shall ask for no reward save the reward of loving.*

"WHAT IS THE NATURE OF LIFE?"

We continue our meditations on love being central in Christianity and central in human nature. In *On Being Human* Ashley Montagu asks: "What is the nature of life? [The answer] can be expressed in one word, cooperation—the interaction between organisms for mutual support in such a way as to confer survival benefits upon each other. Another word for the same thing . . . is love. Without cooperation, without love, it is not possible to live—at best, it is possible only to exist." This is interesting and vastly important, for in asking, "What is the nature of life?" he answers, love. But Jesus picked out love as the highest in God and deepest in man, and scientific investigation echoes Him and says that the highest thing in life is love—no love, no life. So the word of Revelation and the word of scientific investigation are the same—love. Q.E.D. may be added!

But there is this difference: Jesus said, "I give you a new commandment: love one another; as I have loved you, so you are to love one another." (John 13:34 NEB). The phrase that makes the difference is, "as I have loved you." This is the Word of love become flesh. It gives a criterion of what love is—it is to love as Christ loved. That puts content into the word love. Science can call it "cooperation" or "mutual support," but that leaves love thin and undefined. For "cooperation" and "mutual support" may mean cooperation and mutual support in any enterprise supposed to bring benefits upon each other—good, bad, indifferent. But "as I have loved you" gives a standard, sets by example. So no human exhortation to love is sufficient unless it is seen what we mean by love in the Divine Exhibition. The Word made flesh must illuminate the Word become word. Science is earthbound by earth meanings without the Divine Revelation of heavenly meanings.

O Jesus, Thou hast put new meaning into everything earthly by Thy earthly life. Now we see earth in the light of heaven. And what meanings! In and through Thee everything is different. And everything is full of hope. We thank Thee, thank Thee. Amen.

AFFIRMATION FOR THE DAY: *If the word of love becomes flesh in me today I shall be vital.*

"LOVE IS THE ANSWER TO HUMAN LIVING"

We continue to look at love as inherently necessary to human living if that life is to be called life and not tragedy. Here is Dr. Victor Frankl, a psychiatrist, writing in *From Death Camp to Existentialism,* the story of his life in a German war camp. Out of that environment and experience he says: "Then I grasped the greatest secret that human poetry and human thought and belief have to impart: The salvation of man is through love and in love." Here is high intelligence and tragic experience coming to a Christian conclusion, namely, "that salvation is through love and in love." This from a man who is apparently not a Christian. Life is taking everybody by the hand who will be led and leading them to Christian conclusions. Life is rendering a Christian verdict.

Dr. Pitirim Sorokin is an outstanding sociologist at Harvard University and has organized a department of sociology to have research into the effects of love, or "altruism," as they call it, in the affairs of nations and society and individuals. They have produced thirteen books on this subject. He said: "My investigations have led me to the conclusion that love is the answer to human living."

Then we hear this word from Dr. Adler, a famous psychiatrist: "I suppose all the ills of human personality can be traced to not understanding the meaning of the phrase, 'It is more blessed to give than to receive.' " But Jesus said that two thousand years ago, and psychiatry comes along and says, "If you don't understand that, you do not know how to live." And note he said, "all the ills of human personality"—that is sweeping and conclusive. And yet it comes not from a scholar's study, but from a clinic dealing with human ills.

Comte was the author of Positivism, certainly not a Christian movement, and yet the three principles of that movement are: "Love, order, progress." For where there is no love, there is no order and hence no progress.

O Lord and Father, Thy children are learning, through trial and error, that Thy way is their way. Help us to learn it speedily lest we destroy ourselves before we do. We are foolish and break Thy law of love and get hurt in the process. Teach us to be wise and live. Amen.

AFFIRMATION FOR THE DAY: *If love is the answer to human living, then that answer is within my capabilities for I can love.*

"TO GAIN OR REGAIN THE CAPACITY FOR LOVE"

We continue to look at the centrality of love—look at it as the facts of life slowly emerging are pointing to the thing that is central in God and central to the Christian faith and is proving to be central in man. Albert Outler in *Psychotherapy and the Christian Message*, says: "Analytic therapy is essentially an attempt to help the patient gain or regain the capacity for love." Again: "The psychotherapists have come to wide agreement that love is the only force that can cope with libido." "Love is the sovereign specific for human ills; yet love cannot be legislated or evoked at will." "Man can no more generate love by his own powers than he can generate his own true being." "Human love which is not in response to divine love is, therefore, self-erring, self-interested love which enlightenment can direct but cannot reform."

This is interesting and important: "To help the patient gain or regain the capacity for love"—"love is the only force that can cope with the libido"—"Love . . . cannot be legislated or evoked at will"—"Human love which is not in response to divine love is self-erring, self-interested love which enlightenment can direct but cannot reform." So enlightenment, or insight, which has been and is the working hypothesis and power of analytic psychotherapy, is powerless to reform the self-centered libido. That can come only in response to Divine Love. And so we are driven straight into the arms of the Word became flesh—the Divine Love reaching down. But what Divine Love doesn't merely reform—it regenerates! A woman who was having trouble with sex—the libido—went to a pagan psychiarist who said: "Your sex urge is too heavily loaded—distribute the load, take up smoking and drinking and that will lighten the load of sex." She did and was more frustrated than ever. She saw the utter and complete bankruptcy of this suggestion, surrendered herself to Christ and was delivered from all three bondages: cigarettes, liquor, and sex!

O Jesus, my Lord, Thou art the sovereign remedy for all our ills, for Thou art Love and only Love. Thou canst expel the drive of the libido toward the lower and convert it into the higher, into Love itself. Then we are free—free indeed. I thank Thee. Amen.

AFFIRMATION FOR THE DAY: *Where there is no love there is no life—only death.*

BARREN INTELLECTUALISM

We are studying the supremacy of love in human nature and the supremacy of the Divine Love in changing human nature. A man who was widely experienced in dealing with alcoholism said that he had never seen a case of alcoholism cured by purely psychiatric methods. Unless psychiatry can introduce the patient to the redeeming grace of God-in-Christ, it leaves the patient helped at the edges perhaps, but unredeemed at the Center—the self-preoccupied libido holds the center. That center must be surrendered to something beyond itself—to God, through Christ. Love for Christ expels the lower love—the lower love is converted from eros, self-regarding love, to agape, the other-regarding love. You cannot get rid of one desire except to replace it by a higher desire. Psychiatry with its barren intellectualism, when it offers insight as the remedy, finds itself giving light on life, but powerless to give life to life. It lacks the God-in-Christ reference and the God-in-Christ power to change love, and therefore, life. It is moonlight, not sunlight.

A psychological counselor teaching counseling in a Christian institution said he was going to get a divorce from his wife on the ground that he had grown up and was mature and she had not grown up and was immature. But he was personally disrupted and constantly took tranquilizers. Dependence on tranquilizers was a sign of his maturity! Tranquilizers are the refuge of bankrupt psychiatry and bankrupt medicine when they know no God-in-Christ.

A nurse of thirty-eight years' experience said: "This country is being turned into imbecility and dullness by tranquilizers, taken because of any national crisis or any personal trouble." The love of Christ is not a tranquilizer, an opiate; it is a stimulus—"By all the stimulus of Christ." He converts all our desires to higher ends—stimulates them with His own love and power. Then we are so taken up with the love of Christ that the expulsive power of a new affection drives out the lower. And that works to the degree that we make it work. This is emerging as "the sovereign remedy." There is no other on the field.

"O Love that will not let me go, I rest my weary soul in Thee." Where else should I go? Thou hast the words of eternal life. And those words can become flesh in me. I can love with Thy love when I cannot love with mine. So I turn to Thee to be filled—filled with love. Amen.

AFFIRMATION FOR THE DAY: *"The sovereign remedy"—love—is so simple, so at hand, so available that we marvel that everyone doesn't use it.*

"I'VE FOUND MY FATHER AGAIN"

We have been studying love as the deepest thing in man and the sovereign remedy for all our ills. Dr. Eric Fromm, who in his personal view of life leaves God out, nevertheless says, "Love is the answer to the problems of existence." The weakness of his position is that love has no cosmic backing—it is not rooted in God, hence it is a frail flower growing out of human soil. Even with that handicap Fromm, as a psychiatrist, sees that "love is the answer to the problems of existence." Take some very tangled problems and see how the skillful hands of love untangle them.

Estelle Carver tells of a very intelligent and beautiful girl who was filled with hate for her father. She hadn't spoken to him for five years. "I could gladly kill him." Estelle Carver said, "Will you go home and pray the prayer: 'God bless Daddy?' "I couldn't," she replied. But she did. One day he stood with his back to the fire. Obeying an impulse she ran and threw her arms around him. They wept in each other's arms. "I've found my father again. I'm so happy and so is he," she wrote. A note from the father: "I understand you have been the instrument of our reconciliation. I thank you." Restrained, but it told worlds. There was simply no way out of that tangle except one way—love. A human love, buried, was brought to life by a divine love through prayer.

Here was a woman ill for fifteen years, twenty-eight hospitalizations. She was full of resentments, but she gave them up and was cured and is well. A lack of love wrought havoc. Love cured her. Here was a wife who was very suspicious of her husband. But she found she was wrong about him. She went to him and confessed it on her knees. They went into each other's arms. He has never touched liquor since. Love cured him—and her—and them!

In one of our Ashrams a little boy of six and a little girl of five came across the dining room hand in hand and said, "Brother Stanley, may we ask you a question? What is the Christian attitude?" I could scarcely believe my ears! But I replied: "To love everybody, everywhere." They said "Thank you" and walked back hand in hand.

O God, forgive me that I use infected hands in dealing with human problems—infected by methods other than love. Wash my hands, my heart, my life in the disinfectant of love that I may be healing in every situation I touch. Wash me thoroughly. Amen.

AFFIRMATION FOR THE DAY: *Washed, I shall wash every situation today with the disinfectant of my love.*

"I'LL BE THE BETTER FOR GIVING IT"

We are looking at the effects of love in human relation and personal lives. A young pastor in Obihiro, Japan, was obviously a man of deep devotion to Christ and possessed a rich personal experience of God. He had lost his own mother and had a stepmother against whom he revolted in resentments. Someone got him as a non-Christian to go to church to see some slides. As he entered, the first slide he saw was "God is Love" in Japanese. It struck him deeply. "God is love"—and would forgive him? This haunted him and led him to be a Christian. He decided to go into the Christian ministry and entered a theological seminary. He read books on philosophy and found his faith undermined. He thought of suicide. So he left the seminary to go to the slums where Dr. Kagawa had lived and worked and suffered. Here he saw alcoholics, drug addicts, the down-and-outs transformed and made into new persons by the power of the love of Christ. His faith came back again, and now he is radiant and on fire. He lost his faith through the Word become word, the philosophies, but regained it through the Word become flesh—transformed human lives.

A cultured and refined woman came up to me after an address on love, the deepest thing in human nature, and said, "Your message touched something in my heart this morning and awakened something within me. I'm going home and love h— out of my husband. If he responds, good, but if he doesn't respond it will still be good, for I'll be the better for giving it!"

In general, one out of four families in America breaks up in divorce. Among church members, one out of fifty. When they both read the Bible and pray, one out of five hundred. Obviously to expose ourself to the Bible with its revelation of God in Christ awakens love and maintains love and helps hold the family together. A woman said she couldn't go back to her husband. Her doctor said, "Don't try to make your husband good. Make yourself good—be the best wife, mother, daughter-in-law. Love them all." She did, and won her husband and saved the marriage.

O Savior, save me from the worst sin of all—the sin of not loving. And save me from the sin of loving only those who love me. Give me a love unlimited. But I can only do this as I love with Thy love. My love is limited and breaks down. Give me Thine—abundantly. Amen.

AFFIRMATION FOR THE DAY: *"Love them all"—no exceptions, and no limitations.*

"OBSERVE THE GOLDEN RULE IN DRIVING"

The policy and practice and attitude of love is the only thing in this universe that can't lose. For if the one loved responds, well and good; if that person doesn't respond, it is still good—for you are the better for having given the love. Jesus said: "Let your peace rest upon a city and if a son of peace is there he will receive it, but if he doesn't receive it then let your peace return to you again." "Let your peace return to you again"—you are more peaceful for having given the peace. So give out love and only love, for you are born of the qualities you habitually give out. If you give out hate, you become hateful; give out criticism and you become critical. Give out love and you become loving. The payoff is in the person.

A woman was about to have her home broken up by another woman. But she was converted and began to pray for this woman. This woman called her on the phone, and she was weeping: "Can you help me? I know you must hate me." "No, I don't. I'm praying for you," she replied, "Do come to see me." And she did again and again. Her husband had walked out on her and had gone to another woman. In that tangled situation, the whole thing a mess, there was only one person who was whole and intact—the one who had surrendered herself to Christ and had loved—had loved even the woman who had wronged her. She had the victory even in defeat. But she was not defeated personally for she is radiant and happy.

If love of others is the way out personally, it is the way out in tangled social relations. The Sociology Society in Lucknow, made up of non-Christians, for the most part, has as its motto: "Do unto others as you would that men do to you." On the back of buses in Cleveland, Ohio, is the sign: "Observe the Golden Rule in Driving." So whether it is tangled relations in family life, or in the sociological relationships on a wider scale, or in the snarled traffic of a city, the rule of love is the rule of life, and there is no way out except the love way. And this from experimentation.

O Christ of the Galilean Road, Thou are fast becoming the Christ of every road. For on every road we meet Thee and everywhere Thou art authoritative. It is Thy way or chaos. And the alternatives are sharpened year by year. Life is leading us to Thy feet. We thank Thee. Amen.

AFFIRMATION FOR THE DAY: *Today I shall put myself in the other man's place and treat him as I would like to be treated if I were in his place.*

PRINCIPLES WITHOUT THE PERSON—EMPTY

We are looking at the fact that if you work from Revelation down and the facts up you come out at the same place—at the feet of Jesus Christ. Life is rendering one verdict—the Christian verdict. While many thoughtful persons would agree to the fact that "we come out at the same place," they question the interpretation that the same place means "at the feet of Jesus Christ." They would say we come out to the same principles, but not to the same Person. There is a disposition to accept the principles apart from the Person.

For instance, Fromm, in *The Art of Loving,* says: "To love God, if he were going to use that word would mean, then, to long for the attainment of the full capacity to love, for the realization of that which 'God' stands for in oneself." Again: "Having spoken of the love of God, I want to make it clear that I myself do not think in terms of a theistic concept, and that to me the concept of God is only a historically conditioned one, in which man has expressed his experience of his higher powers, his longing for truth and for unity at a given historical period." God is then only a concept mediated through oneself, his experience of his own personal higher powers, his longing for truth and a desire for unity. Man puts his own content into "God" and is the mediator of God to himself. God then is all he sees in himself, writ large, when he says, "God." No wonder then, that Fromm has a chapter entitled, "Love—Disintegration in Western Society." For the moment any idea or principle gets away from Jesus Christ, it disintegrates. And love is an illustration. If you don't take the content of your love from Jesus Christ, you will probably take it from Hollywood. So principles of ideas are bound to get their content from the sons of men or from the Son of Man. And if they get the content from the sons of men, they degenerate. If from the Son of Man, they are regenerated. So to take the principles apart from the Person is to take degenerated principles.

O Jesus Lord, Thou art our personal Savior, but Thou art the Savior of principles and ideas, for Thou dost put into them a new content, the content of Thy divine illustration. We see everything different when we see Thee. For Thou art different. Amen.

AFFIRMATION FOR THE DAY: *This is the new crucifixion of Jesus—to take His principles and reject the Person.*

"HUMANITY SEEKS THE IDEAL . . . IN A PERSON"

We saw yesterday that persons, words, concepts, and principles have to be constantly reclaimed and regenerated by contact with a Higher Illustration, by the Highest Illustration, by the Word become flesh. "As literature can never rise higher than life," so words and principles can never rise higher than the life that surrounds the literature. For persons, words, concepts, and principles sink to the level of surrounding life and get their content from that surrounding life, unless renewed by contact with and surrender to Higher Life.

As Ernest Renan says: "Humanity seeks the ideal, but it seeks it in a Person, and not in an abstraction. A Man, the incarnation of the ideal, whose biography might serve as a frame for the aspirations of the time, is what the religious mind sought." The only one who fits that is Jesus Christ, the Word become flesh. He turns the abstract into the concrete, the ideal into the real, the Word into flesh.

The word "love" is an illustration. Jesus redeemed the word, put the content of His own love into that word. So much so that the early Christians had to reject the ordinary word for love, "eros," for it meant sex love, and chose "agape," into which was poured the love that Jesus illustrated and taught. Here in Japan, where I write, my interpreter in speaking before non-Christian audiences hesitated to use the Japanese word for love, for it meant only sex love. The word had not been in contact with Jesus and hence was unredeemed.

We in the West have to go back to the Greek word "agape" to get the meaning of the word "love" redeemed by Jesus. Jesus redeemed the word "agape" by putting into it His own illustration of its meaning—agape love is Christlike love. For He puts universal meanings in it. Dr. F. R. Barry has said: "Jesus did not do everything good that can be done. He revealed the nature of goodness." Jesus did not do every loving thing possible, but in His acts and attitudes and words reveals the very nature of love. Look at Him, listen to Him, live with Him, and you know what love is.

O Jesus Lord and Example, we look at Thee and now we see a universe in a word, the whole meaning of life in a sentence. We look at Thy life and we see Life! We listen to Thy truths and we see Truth! We watch Thy ways and see the Way! We are prostrate at Thy feet. We thank Thee. Amen.

AFFIRMATION FOR THE DAY: *Close to Him today all my eros will be converted into agape.*

EROS AND AGAPE CONTRASTED

We are studying a word and are discovering a universe—that redeemed word "agape." Mygren has shown us in his analysis of the difference between eros and agape how one word in contact with contemporary life sank to the low level of man and the other word in contact with Life arose to the highest level to which a word has ever risen. Eros is acquisitive desire and longing. Agape is sacrificial giving. Eros is an upward movement. Agape comes down. Eros is man's way to God. Agape is God's way to man. Eros is man's effort—it assumes that salvation is his own work. Agape is God's grace—salvation is the work of Divine Love. Eros is egocentric love, a form of self-assertion of the highest, noblest kind. Agape is unselfish love, it seeketh not its own, it gives itself away. Eros seeks to gain its life, a divine immortalized life. Agape lives the life of God, therefore dares to lose it. Eros is the will to get and possess, which depends on want and need. Agape is freedom in giving, which depends on wealth and plenty. Eros is primarily man's love—God is the object of eros. Even when it is attributed to God, eros is patterned on human love. Agape is primarily God's love; God is Agape. Even when it is attributed to man agape, is patterned on Divine love. Eros is determined by the quality, the beauty, the worth of its object; it is not spontaneous, but evoked, motivated. Agape is sovereign in relation to its object and is directed both to the evil and the good; it is spontaneous, overflowing, unmotivated. Eros recognizes value in its object and loves it. Agape loves and creates value in its object.

That difference between eros and agape could never have been described by philosophy or moralism or art or poetry. It had to be seen. Agape had to become flesh. There and then only could it be known what agape really is. Until then it would have been a surmise instead of a Surprise, a dream instead of a Deed, an imagination instead of an Illustration. Now we see—and fall at His feet!

O Jesus, Son of God, my heart bursts with gratitude that once the curtains of mystery have been rolled back and we see through the heart of God the meaning of the universe, the key to our own living. In Thee we see Everything. And we love It and Thee. We thank Thee. Amen.

AFFIRMATION FOR THE DAY: *I offer all my eros loves to Christ to be redeemed into His Agape.*

"YOU THINK AS MEN THINK"

We have been studying the redemption of the word love—redemption from eros to agape. So far we have come to the edges of that redemption. Now we look into its depths—we look at the cross. Only at the cross do we see the true nature of agape.

When Jesus spoke to His disciples about His going to the cross, Peter took Him by the arm and began to rebuke Him: "Heaven forbid! . . . No, Lord, this shall never happen to you." Then Jesus turned and said to Peter: "Away with you, Satan; you are a stumbling-block to me. You think as men think, not as God thinks" (Matt. 16:22-23, NEB). Peter was thinking in eros terms—save yourself. Jesus was thinking in agape terms—give yourself. Jesus said that Peter was thinking as men think—save thyself, and not in terms as God thinks—give thyself. For eros is love primarily interested in one's self.

The same division comes out at the Cross. Five classes converge upon one thing: "Save yourself, come down from the cross and we will believe in you." "The passers-by," "the chief priests with the lawyers and elders" (Matt. 27:39-43 NEB), "the rulers," "the soldiers," and "one of the criminals" (Luke 23:35-39 NEB)—all take the same position: Save yourself. Peter for the moment thought as men thought. Only one, the penitent thief, saw through the mystery of things, saw that He was saving others therefore He could not save Himself, and said: "Lord, save me." He passed from the eros conception to the agape conception—the single exception in all that crowd. And he passed from perdition to paradise the moment he did. He knew little, but he knew Everything when he saw this Divine Self-giving Love. He saw into the very heart of Reality. For the Cross throws back the curtains and lets us see the heart of God.

O Savior, save us from not seeing This. For This that we see in the Cross is Reality. If we see This we see Everything—if we miss This we miss Everything. Then help us to walk softly and have eyes that see and hearts that love. Amen.

AFFIRMATION FOR THE DAY: *I look within and see eros, around me and I see eros, I look at Jesus and see agape.*

IS THE CROSS AN AFTERTHOUGHT?

We are meditating upon the cross as the supreme manifestation of agape love. Is the redemption by the cross an afterthought, read back into the account to rescue it from being a stark tragedy? Or is the cross the very revelation of the love that will not let us go? Through the cross do we see God's Heart?

It all depends on who Jesus is. If He was a good man and just a good man, then His death is a martyrdom—a martyrdom for a cause. Lincoln's death was a martyrdom and so was Mahatma Gandhi's, for they were both good men dying for a cause. But suppose Jesus was the Incarnate God, then significance would be attached to His death by that very fact. And Jesus was very particular that men should get a right view of who He was. He said to His disciples, "Who do men say that the Son of man is? . . . Who do you say I am?" (Matt. 16:13, 15). If He were only a man, why should He raise that question? It was the one and important question.

When He stood silent before the High Priest, He was asked, "By the living God, I charge you to tell us: Are you the Messiah, the Son of God?" Jesus replied, "The words are yours" (Matt. 26:63 NEB). Or as Bishop Christopher Wordsworth puts it, "You have really said it"—the strongest affirmation. Then when Pilate asked Him: "Are you the king of the Jews?" Jesus replied, "The words are yours." Or the marginal reading, "It is as you say" (Matt. 27:11, 12 NEB). And when one of His disciples said, "Lord, show us the Father and we ask no more," Jesus replied, "Any one who has seen me has seen the Father" (John 14:8, 9 NEB). So the idea of a martyr dying on a cross for a cause is ruled out. The background forbids it.

O Jesus, Lord and Savior, we dare not minimize the meaning of Thy Cross and make it into a martyrdom. That would be the new crucifixion. Toning it down to a martyr's death would put Thee on a new cross forever. Save us from that sin. Amen.

AFFIRMATION FOR THE DAY: *There is no middle ground—if Jesus was not God, he was not good.*

LIFE LEADS US TO THE CROSS

If the cross is more than a martyr's death, just what does it mean? A Japanese minister was a communist while a student in the university. All his "comrades" had been sent to jail. It was the cross that brought him back to Christianity—one dying on the cross for a cause. He started there and then was led to the very core of its meaning and became a Christian. Some of the followers of Gandhi, during the days of struggle for independence when many were going to jail as nonviolent non-cooperators, said to me: "Now we know what you Christians mean by the cross, for we are carrying it." Many went from that to the real thing—went from martyrdom to atonement. But many stopped at martyrdom, failed to get to the Real and fell away. For the cross of martyrdom holds your admiration, but not your allegiance. It gets your mind and emotion but not your committed will. If you say, "There is a man on a cross," you may run to see the morbid sight. But if you say, "There is a God on a cross," then you kneel in wonder, or like the centurion, smite your breast in contrition.

He could not die in a room, confined to four walls. He had to die under the open skies, with the universe looking on and the whole earth shaking in a cosmic shudder. For the cross had the marks of a cosmic struggle—God dying for man.

And the cross brings to light, full light intimations here and there of a God who would die for men. The Aztec gods were seated around a fire, creating the universe. To create the sun was too big a task until one god threw himself into the fire and the sun came into being. A pelican will pull out her feathers with the blood and give it to her young in times of drought and scarcity.

O Jesus Lord, all these words of sacrifice become the Word of Sacrifice made flesh in Thee. Thou didst gather up these broken lights and at the cross made them into the Light of the World in Thyself. They were candles; Thou art the sunrise. We thank Thee. Amen.

AFFIRMATION FOR THE DAY: *I shall bear the cross as my attitude, then I shall know the cross as my affirmation.*

GOD NEVER INTENDED JESUS TO BE CRUCIFIED?

The cross is not an afterthought, an expedient to turn a tragedy into supposed triumph. One prominent minister thinks it was: "God never intended Jesus to be crucified. He intended that He should be followed." Or as Dr. Albert Schweitzer puts it, in essence: "Jesus expected the Kingdom to come at Jerusalem. And when it didn't He died on the cross of a broken heart, crying 'My God, my God why hast thou forsaken me?' But in dying He left an ethic of love." And that's all. And it would have been *all*, if that were all there were to it. The movement would have died with His death. A life movement cannot live upon a dead Christ.

Instead of the cross being an afterthought, something read back into the account by loving hearts to save it, I am persuaded that the cross is written into the texture of our own beings. It is, as someone has said, "the ground plan of the universe." Life is built upon it—the sacrifice of the one for the other.

Not long ago I was at the place in Japan where they showed me a mirror used during the persecution of the Christians. Since Christian worship was forbidden, the Christians would sit in a room and let the sun shine upon this mirror, and it would throw the outline of Jesus hanging on the cross upon the ceiling or wall. The cross was wrought into the structure of the mirror. If a strange person came in they simply turned the mirror over. As we throw the light of investigation upon the facts of nature, do we find the cross coming out as the very ground plan of the universe? Yes! The cross is in our blood. The white corpuscles circulate through the blood looking for infection. When they find it they absorb it, if possible. If not, they throw themselves against the infection and die that the rest of the body might live. The pus that comes off is the corpses of the white corpuscles which have died that the rest might live. The principle and practice of the cross is in our blood.

O Son of the Most High, Thou art revealing the Most High through the most low—revealing Him through the cross. We look up through the cross and see what Thou art like and see through Thee what our Father is like. And what we see sends us to our knees. Amen.

AFFIRMATION FOR THE DAY: *If the cross is in my blood, it will be in my will.*

CROSS IMPOSED OR INHERENT?

We are asking whether the cross is imposed or inherent, If the cross is in our blood, then it, as Mrs. Herrmann says "is writ large in the universe. It is the ground plan of the universe.'—When you face life, the cross is inescapable. There is a Bengali film entitled "An Astonishing World," written by a non-Christian. It is the story of a converted pickpocket who ends up kneeling at the foot of the cross and is forgiven and converted. Why did this Hindu author have the pickpocket end up at the foot of the cross? There was simply no other place for him to come out except the cross. Neither Hinduism nor Mohammedanism nor any other faith could provide a place of forgiveness and redemption. The cross was inevitable.

When Jesus was hanging on the cross, the crowd around the cross cried: "He saved others, himself he cannot save." Unwittingly they put their finger upon the deepest thing in life—He was saving others, therefore He could not save himself. That is the deepest law of the universe: those who save others cannot save themselves trouble, pain, suffering, or death. A mother and father bird grow lean in foraging for food for their little ones. And if a serpent makes its treacherous way up the tree, the mother bird will throw herelf into the open jaws of the serpent. She is saving her family; herself she cannot save. A mother goes down to the valley of the shadow of death to bring a child into the world. She is saving another; herself she cannot save. Ants crossing a stream will make a bridge of their dead bodies, clinging together in death that the rest might walk across their dead bodies to safety. They are saving others; themselves they cannot save. The cross is inherent. It is not merely written in the Scriptures; it is plowed into the facts of life.

O Father God, the universe is not alone the work of Thy hands. It is the work of Thy heart as well. Thy heart is written into it. We see it exposed again and again, and we stand in awe and we worship. For everywhere we see Thy cross of love. Amen.

AFFIRMATION FOR THE DAY: *The Cross is the most important spot in the universe.*

THEY WERE SAVING OTHERS; THEMSELVES
THEY COULD NOT SAVE

We are looking at the cross as it is written into life. Recently I went by large ferry from the island of Honshu to Hokkaido, the northernmost island of Japan. A few years ago during a typhoon there was a lull, and it seemed that it was over. So the ferry started across, but the lull proved to be the treacherous calm of the center of the typhoon, and the ferry was caught in open waters by its full fury. Obviously it was going to sink. A Canadian missionary went around helping people put on the life belts. He found a young man without a belt, and there were no more—the supply had been exhausted. He took off his own belt, put it on the young man saying: "You are young, take my belt, grow up to be a good man and serve Japan." Fourteen hundred people perished, among them the misssionary. Useless sacrifice? No, he had to. He was saving another; himself he could not save. He was a Christian, and he had to fulfill that law. The sequel was this: the young man told this story to a group of college students, then disappeared and was never heard of again, ashamed that a foreigner would die for him. Don't be too hard on the young man, but remember when you, perhaps, and so many among us, are ashamed to witness that Christ died for us. We merge ourselves into the crowd of anonymity and try to forget that we are persons "for whom Christ died."

A student sat by the seaside studying for an examination. A lad came down to go into the sea to swim. The student warned him not to, that the currents were treacherous. But the lad paid no attention. Then there was a cry far out at sea. The boy was struggling with the currents. The student ran to the shore, got a plank, and because he was a good swimmer got to him and put him on the plank. The boy fell off and again the student got him on and pushed him toward the shore—saved. But the student's strength was exhausted, and he sank.

O God, Father, Thou who hast put this impulse to sacrifice oneself for the sake of another into the hearts of the best of men, will this be absent from Thee? Will the noblest of men rise higher than Thee? We cannot believe it, we will not believe it, we do not believe it. For Thou art saying, "O heart I made, a Heart beats here." We thank Thee. Amen.

AFFIRMATION FOR THE DAY: *In some small way let me step this day between someone and disaster—no matter the cost.*

WHY DID GOD CREATE MAN FREE?

We continue our meditations on the cross as the revelation of the Heart of Reality.

I have often wondered why God dared to create man and to create man free. It was a risky business for Him and the creatures created. To make man free would mean that God would have to limit Himself. He would have to step back and allow that free will to operate. He could not coerce it, for if He did the will would not be free. And the will would have to be free in both directions—it must be free to choose evil as well as good or it would not be free. To be able to choose in one direction only is not freedom. But suppose that will should go wrong—it would break its own heart and the heart of God too. For God would have to live alongside that straying, rebellious will as love. And it is the nature of love to insinuate itself into the sins and sorrows of the loved one and make them its own. If love stays out of the sins and sorrows of the loved one, it is no longer love. But if it gets in it bleeds. All love has the doom of bleeding upon it as long as there is sin in the loved one.

God, the all-knowing, must have kown this. Then why did He create? Well, why do parents create children? It is a risky business on their part to bring into the world children who might go astray and break their own hearts and the hearts of the parents. Then why do parents create? Simply because it is the nature of love to create objects of love upon which it can lavish love and be loved in return. Love by its very nature is bound to create. But the parents say, consciously or subconsciously, "If anything falls on that child, it will fall on us. Its joys will be our joys, its sorrows our sorrows, its sins our sins." Was it different in God, our Father? Not if He were love. God saw the risk and took it on one condition, that anything that falls on man would fall on God Himself. He would bear the sin and sorrow of man in His own body.

O God, my Father, when I think of Thee doing this, my heart is bowed in the deepest gratitude and the profoundest awe. I wonder at such love that would take such risks and carry through though it meant the cross. That love has me forever and forever. Amen.

AFFIRMATION FOR THE DAY: *Since God took the risk of creating me free, I'll not let down His trust in me.*

THE UNSEEN CROSS ON THE HEART OF GOD

We ended yesterday on the thought that God being love would create objects of love upon whom He could lavish His love and be loved in return. But God would be responsible for man's sin by making man free! Yes, and God accepted that responsibility and discharged it upon a cross.

That is what the passage means in the book of Revelation where it speaks of "the Lamb slain from the foundation of the world." But the Gospel accounts say that He was slain two thousand years ago! No, the cross began the moment man sinned. There was an unseen cross upon the heart of God the moment man began to sin. The Lamb was slain from the foundation of the world. But how would we know there is a cross upon the heart of God? He is Spirit. How would we know there is an unseen cross upon the heart of an Eternal Spirit? We could not know unless He showed this inner cross through an outer cross. The outer cross lifted up in history shows the inner cross upon the heart of God.

Amy Wilson Carmichael, a saint in India, had a Home with three hundred girls in it, most of them rescued from prostitution. But through her wonderful spirit and the Spirit of God these girls were changed and radiant. But one girl resisted the whole spirit of the home, was hard and rebellious. Miss Carmichael did everything to get the girl to change. No result. One day she took the girl into her home, bared her arm, took a needle, and told the girl that she was going to thrust the needle into her arm. The girl objected: "This will hurt you." "Yes it will, but it will hurt me nothing to what you are doing is hurting me." When she thrust the needle into her arm and the blood began to trickle down, the girl threw her arms around her neck and wept as if her heart would break: "I didn't know you loved me like that," she cried. From that moment she was changed.

O Father God, we know our sins hurt Thee, but we never saw it before we saw it in the cross. Now we know what our sins cost Thee. They cost a cross. When we really see that, we are changed. We thank Thee, thank Thee for the cross. Amen.

AFFIRMATION FOR THE DAY: *I am a child of God's love, also the result of my freedom—the love will win.*

"GOD WAS IN CHRIST RECONCILING"

We ended yesterday with the girl saying to Miss Carmichael: "I didn't know you loved me like that." And from that moment she was changed. She looked up through the blood and saw past the blood the unseen cross upon the heart of the one who loved her and was saved, as it were, through that blood. Did something like that happen in human history? I look up through the blood of Christ, past His wounds back into the soul of God, and see there the unseen cross. But I could never have seen it had it not been for the outer cross lifted up in human history. The cross lights up the nature of God as redemptive love.

An Italian painter has painted the nails going through the hands of Jesus, through the wood into the hands of God back in the shadows. "God was in Christ reconciling the world unto Himself." "God was in Christ"—in His suffering, in His "bearing our sins in His own body on a tree." He isn't laying our sins on Jesus to appease His own anger—He took it on Himself.

If there isn't a God like that in the universe, there ought to be one. Would the highest in man rise higher than the highest in God? "Would I suffer for one I love? So wouldst Thou, so wilt Thou," says Browning. The Psalmist asks: "He that made the eye will He not see? He that made the ear will He not hear?" And we may ask, He that made love, will He not love? And He who put the impulse to sacrifice themselves into the souls of the highest men, will He not sacrifice? Will man rise higher than his Maker? An old Chinese scholar who heard for the first time the story of the Redeeming God ran his fingers through his hair, turned to his neighbors, and said: "Didn't I tell you there ought to be a God like that?"

O God, our Heavenly Father, we are now at the heart of things. For if we are right here we are right everywhere. Take us by the hand and take us into this Divine mystery—this Open Secret of the Universe. Open our minds, hearts, wills to it. Amen.

AFFIRMATION FOR THE DAY: *God has shown me The Way—that Way a cross. I follow blindly, if necessary.*

KARMA AND THE CROSS

If love is in God, if God is love, then what about the law side of things? Is law also in God? It is certainly in nature. A scientist has said: "Christianity is God's method with man, and evolution is God's method in nature." Can these two come together? Do love and law meet in Jesus?

The Hindus stress the law of sowing and reaping—the law of karma. They believe there can be no forgiveness. "As a calf will find its mother among a thousand cows so your deeds will find you out among a thousand rebirths," say the Hindus. Whatever suffering you are undergoing is just. You are reaping what you have sown. This law of sowing and reaping, apart from the corollary of rebirth which is brought in to explain the inequalities of life, which can be explained on a better basis, nevertheless has a truth in it. Christianity also has this law of sowing and reaping: "Be not deceived; God is not mocked, for whatsoever a man soweth that shall he also reap." This is a universe where you get results or you get consequences. If you work with the moral universe, you get results—you will have cosmic backing for your way of life. But if you go against the moral universe, you will be up against it—you will get consequences. You will reap what you sow. This is a halftruth, however. You alone do not reap what you sow—other people reap what you sow, for good or evil. A good father does not alone reap the good fruit of his good life and actions; others reap it too—his family, his friends, his community, and, faintly, the world. A bad father, on the other hand, does not alone reap the bad harvest of his life and actions; others reap it too—his family, his friends, his community, and, faintly, the world. This vicarious passing on to others the results of your karma has far-reaching consequences—very far.

O God our Father and our God, Thou art not alone bound up with our sin and our sorrow; we are bound up with one another for good or ill. This opens the way for Thy Everything. Give us eyes to see and hearts to accept this stupendous possibility for our redemption. Amen.

AFFIRMATION FOR THE DAY: *This is a moral universe and I must come to terms with it—I reap what I sow.*

"AS IF THE DAY SUDDENLY BRAKE"

We finished yesterday with the thought that other people reap what we sow, for good or ill. We can pass on to others the fruit of our karma. And the greater the person the more far-reaching the effects of that passing on. Gandhi and Lincoln touch the world with the effects of their lives and acts. Suppose there were one who stood at the center of life as the Son of Man and the Son of God, a part of God and a part of every man, could He not pass on to every child of the race the effects of His life and acts—His karma? And could we reap, not what we sow, but what He sowed? That is, if we identify ourselves with Him by surrender and obedience? If we are "in Him," do we not reap what He sowed—His victory our victory, His love our love, His purity our purity?

At the cross we find God Incarnate sowing Himself in sacrifice for His creatures. So that the statement of the Rig Veda becomes true by the substitution of a name: "Prajapati, Lord of creatures gave himself for them—He became their sacrifice."That was the word of sacrifice become word—no reality in history, but it does become the Word become flesh when you read it, "Jesus Christ, Lord of Creatures, gave Himself for them—He became their sacrifice." Now every creature need not reap what he sowed, but reap what He sowed—redemption! That is not a philosophy—the word became word; it is a fact—the Word became flesh. It is not good views—it is Good News!

"O Father Latimer," cried one, "I prithee hear me, when I read in the New Testment Christ Jesus came into the world to save sinners, it is as if the day suddenly brake." When you discover a truth in philosophy or moralism, it is a candle, a torch; but when you get hold of this Truth and it gets hold of you, then the day breaks! The Sun is up!

O Jesus Lord and Savior, Thou art a sunrise! When we look at Thee—at Thee upon the cross, all our half-truths become flickering candles. Thou art the Sun, And when we see Thee we say from the depths: "This is It! Our quest is over! Now we belong to Reality forever." We thank Thee. Amen.

AFFIRMATION FOR THE DAY: *Jesus is my Daybreak. And the cross is the reddening sky announcing the Daybreak.*

TWO METHODS OF GOD—IN LOWER
NATURE AND MAN

We come now to the task of gathering up the threads of what we have been saying. We have been writing about the two approaches to life—the Christian approach from Revelation down and the scientific approach from the facts up and out to conclusions. We have been saying that if you take either of these approaches, or both, you will come out to the fact of Christ. "He is the heir of all things"—all things come to His feet. And the last emphasis is important. We have said that a scientist comes to the conclusion that "Christianity is the method of God with man, and evolution is the method of God with nature." But note that he says that both are "the methods of God." In this discussion we are saying that they are not two distinct methods; they are two sides of one method—the method of redemption. God is redeeming from weakness and incapacity through evolution and from sin and incapacity through Grace. They are both redemption.

Jesus puts these two processes together. He gives the parable of the pounds (Luke 19:12-27). To each servant was given a pound, and they were told to develop it. The first had developed the pound into ten and was made ruler of ten cities; another had gained five and was made ruler over five cities; and one buried his pound—he did nothing with it. So it was taken away and given to the man who had ten. "To every one who has will more be given; but from him who has not"—does not develop what he has—"even what he has will be taken away." This is the hard school of the survival of the fittest and the elimination of the unfit. And Jesus, as the Author of nature, accepts that and applies it to human conduct. Develop or decay is the stern dictum. This is hard, but the alternative would be harder—the race would never progress. Softness would mean decay and death.

O Father, Thou art our Father and Thy sternness is our salvation. Thou art pressing the hard facts upon us, but always pressing us forward. Thy pressures are Thy redemption. Thou wilt not let us rest this side of our highest possibilities—in Thee. We thank Thee. Amen.

AFFIRMATION FOR THE DAY: *Soul of mine, listen to this: develop or decay.*

THE CROSS CANCELS OUR KARMA

We said yesterday that Jesus gave the parable of the pounds, which said in essence: Develop or decay. This sounds like the law of karma, as interpreted by the Hindus. There is no forgiveness—you reap what you sow. But the next verse after the parable of the pounds says this: "And when he had said this, he went on ahead, going up to Jerusalem" (Luke 19:28). Why was He going up to Jerusalem? To lay down His life in sacrifice. So if the preceding verses teach karma, this verse teaches the cross—the sacrifice of the Fit for the unfit. So if the preceeding verses teach the survival of the fittest, this verse teaches the revival of the unfit in terms of the redemption of the sinful and weak.

Here it is revealed that God does not leave us to the inexorable consequences of our sins and weaknesses. He provides in His own self-giving at the cross redemption from our sins and strength for our weaknesses. This is not only a way out of our dilemma—it is a way up!

I have lived among a people—the Indian people—who are burdened with fatalism. The Hindu gets into trouble, and he blames it on his karma—deeds—of a previous birth. The Mohammeden when he gets into trouble taps his forehead and says, "My kismet [fate] is bad." So they both turn over their hands and say, *Ham kya karen?*—"What can I do?" On the other hand the real Christian gets into trouble and says, "In Him who strengthens me, I am able for anything" (Phil. 4:13 Moffatt). This verse is revealing: "It follows, my friends, that our lower nature has no claim upon us; we are not obliged to live on that level" (Rom. 8:12 NEB). The tyranny of sin and fate is broken. So Jesus cancels your karma by His, cancels it by forgiveness and regeneration—from above.

O Father, Thou has lifted me out of the inexorable consequences of my sins. Thou has borne them Thyself in Thy own body on a tree. I accept Thy grace, Thy offer. And lo, I'm free, free in Thee—free to live, free to develop, free to be what Thou dost want me to be. Amen.

AFFIRMATION FOR THE DAY: *Soul of mine listen to this: You can have a new heredity from above—take it!*

THE FITTEST TO SURVIVE

We are looking at the fact that the truth in karma is fulfilled in Jesus when He gives His life for us and lets us reap what He sowed. This opens the door upward for us. We become reborn men as different from the ordinary man as the ordinary man is different from the animal. A new type of being comes into existence. This new type of being represents the revival of the unfit, now turned into the survival of the fittest. The Christian type of personality is turning out to be fittest to survive in the future. The Christian represents the serving type. He becomes the greatest of all because he is the servant of all. The serving meek will inherit the earth—the fittest to survive.

A Hindu governor of a state in India said to a Hindu doctor attending lepers: "You are doing a real bit of Christian service here. Thank you." A Hindu telling a Hindu that he was doing a Christian service! The type of service represented by the truly Christian servant is turning out to be the standard. Among values the Christian type is turning out to be the highest value. The truly Christian person loses his life in lowly service and finds it again as the head of the procession in the upward march of man. An American officer wounded by a mine left after the war found himself in a German hospital, lovingly attended by a German doctor and his wife. "Why do you do this?" he inquired. And the reply, "Oh, I see you are not a Christian, or you would know." It led to his conversion, for he saw the most beautiful service he had ever seen—Christian service. Some Quakers were feeding people in Poland. A Polish woman asked: "You feed everybody?" "Yes." "Germans?" "Yes." "Russians?" "Yes." "Jews, Atheists, Communists?" "Yes." She thoughtfully replied: "Well, I thought there ought to be people like that in the world, but I didn't know there were." That type is the survival type—the fittest.

O Lord and Savior, we thank Thee that Thou, the lowly Galilean, art now at the right hand of final authority. Thou hast proven that Thy type is the type that is fittest to rule. For Thou art the Servant of all. Give us Thy spirit of lowly service this day. Amen.

AFFIRMATION FOR THE DAY: *Soul of mine listen to this: You will be great only as you greatly give yourself.*

THE MEEK DOGS, CATS INHERIT THE EARTH

As we look at the question of the type that will survive, we must face the question of the survival of the types in evolution. We have been taught that nature is red in tooth and claw and that the fiercest or the most cunning survive. That conclusion seems to cut across the Christian conception that it is "the meek" which "will inherit the earth." But a closer look at the process shows that this very thing is happening—the meek do inherit the earth.

They tell us that all dogs were once wolves. Somewhere along the line a wolf came around behind man and said: "I'll not fight you; I'll serve you." The fierce wolf became the serving dog. Result? The fierce wolves are being slowly but surely exterminated everywhere in the world while the meek serving dogs are inheriting the earth—everywhere! And how!

All cats were once wildcats and survived by fierceness. But somewhere along the line one of those fierce cats came behind man—and woman!—and said: "I'll serve you; I'll be your friend and companion and I'll rid your house of pests." Result? The fierce cats—the tiger and the leopard, and wildcats in general are slowly but surely being exterminated while the meek cats are inheriting the earth—taking over our hearths and our hearts.

And where there is no probability or possibility to serve man, those types are being exterminated by the advance of science—mosquitos, disease germs, cobras, poisonous vines, and weeds. The poisonous types are being eliminated, and the serving types are inheriting the earth—wheat, rice, oats, corn, flowers.

In the hard school of evolution it is the meek, serving types which are surviving, while the red-in-tooth-and-claw types, which are nonserving, are slowly but surely being pushed to the wall—exterminated.

O God, we thank Thee that Thy laws are one, whether in nature or human nature—the servant of all becomes the greatest of all. Help us then to apply Thy law to every day and in every way—help us to be the servant of all in every situation. In Thy name. Amen.

AFFIRMATION FOR THE DAY: *If I am meek enough to receive, I will be great enough to survive.*

AN UNFINISHED WORLD A GOOD WORLD

Another question remains: If the laws of God are the same whether in nature and human nature, and the God of Grace and the God of nature are the same God, then why did he create mosquitos, disease germs, cobras, typhoons, earthquakes? What function do they perform? Of course we do not know the final plans which the all-wise Creator has in mind for the redemption of man and nature. But we can see through the chinks in the lattice of nature the trend of things which helps us chart His final purpose.

The purpose of God, our Father, seems to be to produce character in His children. Not their ease, nor their happiness except as a by-product, but their character. This means that this life would seem to be a vale of character-making. If this be the end, then He could not create a perfect environment. For character is produced out of overcoming oppositions, obstacles, impediments. So God had to create a world unfinished. His purpose seems to have been to leave creation unfinished so that we could help Him finish it. He left just enough opposition on which to sharpen our wits and our characters. If He had made us perfect beings in a perfect world, we would never have developed—nothing to sharpen us on. Perfect beings in a perfect world would lack one thing—growth!

But in leaving this universe open to completion, He allowed for the possibility of helping Him complete His creation and completing ourselves in the process. Scientific men would never have come into being were there no disease germs to study and overcome. Engineers are produced by the need of making earthquake-proof houses, bridging raging rivers, and building dams to beneficently distribute wasted waters. Character is produced by intelligence, directed effort, and good will. This world is exactly the kind of world to produce the most precious thing in the universe—character.

O Loving Father, Thy love has set us hard tasks, but Thy purpose has also set us wonderful goals. So we take the hard tasks for we see the goal, "Give us not tasks equal to our powers, but powers equal to our tasks." Give us Grace and more Grace. Amen.

AFFIRMATION FOR THE DAY: *I shall match my redeemed powers against unredeemed nature.*

THE SELFISH PERISH—THE UNSELFISH SURVIVE

The view of creation of an imperfect universe which we can help God finish, and so complete ourselves in the process, fits in with the declared purpose of creation: "So God created man in his own image . . . and God said to them, 'Be fruitful and multiply, and fill the earth and subdue it' " (Gen. 1:27, 28). "Subdue it" would imply that the earth is not perfect—it is recalcitrant, resistant, needs to be subdued to the higher purposes of God and man. But "God saw it was good"—not perfect, but "good" for His purposes to make character in man.

The research medical man, mentioned before, after his own conversion said: "I'm going back to my laboratory to convert the worst pagans in the world—cancer cells. They are my mission field." Cancer cells are cells turned selfish. They do not serve the rest, they make the rest serve them. They are basic enemies of nature's process: "Serve or be eliminated." Everything in nature and human nature is pagan—alien to God and His creation—when they serve themselves and refuse to serve the rest. They are on their way to death and destruction. The universe eliminates them. They are breaking the deepest law of the universe: "He that saveth his life shall lose it, and he that loseth it shall find it." That law is the same in lower nature and among men. So the God of Grace and the God of nature has written one law in both nature and man: "The servant of all becomes the greatest of all. The servant of itself alone perishes." Note "servant of all"—the catch is in the word "all." You may be willing to be the servant of some—your race, your class, your family, your religion. That service doesn't make you great—only a great snob! Only the servant of all becomes the greatest of all.

O Father God, we thank Thee for the revelation of Thy purposes—Thy purposes of redemption. Thou art redeeming us and the mold in which we live—nature. Thou hast long-range purposes and we follow breathlessly their unfolding. We thank Thee. Amen.

AFFIRMATION FOR THE DAY: *Everything that happens to me—good, bad, indifferent—can be used for my redemption.*

THE FLESH MADE BY HIM IS MADE FOR HIM

We are now in a position to gather up on this last day of the week our conclusions regarding the working from Revelation down—the Christian approach—and from the facts up—the scientific.

The Christian approach from Revelation, from Christ down, reveals the nature of God and the nature of His purposes for man—God is Christlike, and He intends that we be Christlike in character. "It does not yet appear what we shall be, but we know that when he appears we shall be like him, for we shall see him as he is" (I John 3:2). That "is the Way." But His way is also written in our physical nature and in lower nature. We see the outcroppings of His purposes there. And it is the same—to serve as He served and to give His life a ransom. The principle of atonement is in lower nature.

So "the creation waits with eager longing [literally, "on tiptoe"] for the revealing of the sons of God . . . because the creation itself will be set free from its bondage to decay and obtain the glorious liberty of the children of God" (Rom. 8:19, 21). So it, too, is coming out at the feet of Christ.

So when Jesus became "the Word became flesh," He was not coming to an alien element, the flesh, He was coming to His own—"He entered his own realm" (John 1:11 NEB)—the flesh, the material, was "His own realm." It was made by Him and for Him. It works well in His way and badly in some other way. Just as He purified all foods, "making all foods clean," so He purified our ideas about the material. It is not an alien element, to be hated and rejected and fought. It is something to be accepted and dedicated to the purposes of God. This makes the Christian faith at home in the world. It is its field of operation. The natural order is a *preparito evangelica*—a preparation for the Gospel. The flesh is made for the Gospel as soil and seed. They are affinities.

O Lord Jesus Christ, we thank Thee that Thy gospel is not an alien importation—it is inherent. And when we come to Thee we come to our own, come to that for which we are made, our Homeland. We thank Thee for the blessed at-homeness in Thee. Amen.

AFFIRMATION FOR THE DAY: *My flesh and I are partners in a common service to Him.*

THIS SETS THE CHRISTIAN FAITH APART

We saw last week Jesus was the Supernatural, but He was naturalized in the natural, for the natural was made by the Supernatural and for the Supernatural. This sets the Christian faith apart. In *The Mystery Religions and Christianity,* Samuel Angus says:

The Logos of the Stoics was a pure abstraction, the inspiration of which would touch only the enlightened, and of their ideal Wise Man Plutarch declared, "He is nowhere on earth, nor ever has been." The Logos of Philo was merely a Hypostasis [something imposed on the situation] or, at best, never stepped beyond the limits of personification. But for Christians "the Logos became flesh and tabernacled among us, and we beheld His glory," an advantage which Augustine declares he could not find in any of the competitors of Christianity.

Since the Word became flesh now flesh has become Word. Nature speaks of Him:

> I see His blood upon the rose,
>   And in the stars the glory of His eyes,
> His body gleams amid the eternal snows,
>   His tears fall from the skies.
> I see His face in every flower,
>   The thunder and the singing of the birds
> Are but His voice; and carven by His power
>   Rocks are His written words,
> All pathways by His feet are worn
>   His strong heart stirs the ever-beating sea,
> His crown of thorns is twined with every thorn,
>   His cross is every tree.
>
> —Joseph M. Plunkett

We quoted an ancient papyrus on which was a supposed saying of Jesus: "Raise the stone and thou shalt find me; cleave the wood and I am there." And we may add: Raise the facts of nature and you will find Him there; cleave your tissues and you will find His laws written there; consult your nerves, your organs, the laws of your relationships, and they will tell of Him. The Lord of life is in all life as its life, when it departs from Him it dies—it lives when it lives in Him.

O Jesus Lord and Master, we see Thee in Galilee and by the Ganges; see Thee on the Mount of Tranfiguration and on Mount Fuji; we find Thee wherever human need is found, and when we serve them we serve Thee. I reach out to touch Thee and reach too far—Thou art within. Amen.

AFFIRMATION FOR THE DAY: *Since I see Thee everywhere I shall take Thee everywhere, to everything.*

THE CROSS EVERYWHERE

Yesterday we quoted, "I see His blood upon the rose," and I see His blood everywhere. The Africans have a greeting, "Are you well?" And the other replies, "I am if you are." This simple and beautiful greeting touches deep cords within us, for it reminds us of Him "who bore our sickness"—He is well if we are, but He is sick in our sickness and sinful in our sin—His by identification with us.

A missionary woman was giving an examination to an Indian Bible student. She was asked to tell what she knew about the crucifixion of Jesus. She started in, and soon she forgot about this being an examination, and, as she described the cross where her dear Lord died, she burst into tears, threw her arms around the missionary's neck, and soon they were rocking in each other's arms weeping together at the foot of the cross. This was no examination—it was redemption; reality took over from formality.

It is a far cry from that scene to another: Dr. Radhakrishnan, President of India and a leading philosopher of India, was speaking in the Mormon Temple in Utah on "Were you there when they crucified my Lord?" He said in essence that we are not merely to remember the cross, we are to realize the cross. We are to be there—going through ourselves what He went through, identifying ourselves with Him in His sufferings. The philosopher went back past the words of philosophy to the Word of Suffering made flesh.

The leading Christian of India, when he was a Brahmin student, heard the Gospel of the Cross for the first time and said to himself, "If that isn't true, it ought to be true."

O Jesus, Revealer of the Heart of God and revealer of the purpose and goal of creation, we turn to Thee to find something of Thy spirit. For if Thy Spirit is within us we are in line with the meaning of the universe—its very key. Teach us Thy cross. Amen.

AFFIRMATION FOR THE DAY: *I shall find a situation today in which I will take it on myself to save another.*

"THE CHRISTIAN FAITH IS GOD TAKING HIS OWN MEDICINE"

We have seen that the cross is the highest thing in God and the deepest thing in man, for it is the highest manifestation of the highest thing in God—love—and the deepest thing in man—love. The cross is not therefore an afterthought of God—it is inherent in the nature of things. God being what He is—love—and we being what we are—sin—the cross was inevitable. The cross is the price God pays to get to us in spite of our sins. Dorothy Sayre says, "The Christian faith is God taking His own medicine." If the medicine which man takes as a result of his sins is bitter, and God made it so, then at the cross God does take His own medicine. And it was bitter for "the sin and sorrow of the world was forced through the channel of a single heart." And that heart broke—on the cross.

But someone objects, "If God suffers then He is unhappy, if He is unhappy He is imperfect, and if He is imperfect He isn't God." But this is based on a misunderstanding. The law of happiness in this universe seems to be this: The happiest people in the world are the people who deliberately take on themselves sorrow and pain in behalf of others. Their hearts sing in the midst of the suffering—sing with a strange, quiet joy. On the other hand the most miserable people of the world are the people who think of nothing and do nothing except for themselves. They are the center of misery—automatically. A God who would sit in awful isolation, apart from the tragedy of pain and sin in the world, and contemplate His own perfection would be a miserable, unhappy God. But the God of the cross—the God who deliberately takes on Himself man's sin and sorrow at deep cost to Himself—would be a God of infinite joy, the joy of saving others at cost to Himself—the deepest joy this universe knows.

O God, my Father, Thou didst drink the poison of my sin that I might ambrosia taste. Let me put to my lips the cup of others this day that I may taste their sorrow and at the same moment taste Thy Joy—the Joy of redemption. Amen.

AFFIRMATION FOR THE DAY: *My joys will be not what happens to me, but what happens through me.*

WAS THE RESURRECTION OF JESUS
A SPIRITUAL RESURRECTION?

If there is a cross in God, is there also a Resurrection in God? Bultmann says that "at the cross Jesus came to peace with Himself in His self-surrender to death. In the Resurrection He came to triumph in Himself." But this is too much "in Himself." At the cross there is the sense of a cosmic struggle. He could not die in a room confined to four walls—only the open canopy of heaven with the blue sky for a dome would be befitting for such a death, for it affected the universe. The earth smote its breast in a vast shudder, like to an earthquake; nature felt it—the veil of the temple was rent in twain; religion felt it—the centurion smote his breast, pagan though he was and cried, "Truly this was a Son of God"; the Roman empire felt it—the sky drew a dark veil over the tragedy; heaven felt it; God felt it, for it was His own heart wrapped in flesh and blood that was breaking on a cross.

Jesus was the cosmic God incarnate—the cosmic God offering Himself for His cosmos. "God was in Christ reconciling the world unto Himself"—note, "the world," not just coming to peace with Himself and not just redeeming man, but reconciling the whole creation unto Himself. If Jesus at the cross bears our sins in His own body and we are crucified with His crucifixion, then if He arises from the dead we arise with Him. We and the whole cosomos come up with Him. We are alive in His resurrected Life—provided we identify ourselves with Him.

But did He just arise from the dead spiritually? If so, then only the spiritual is redeemed—the physical is left out of redemption, for it is left out of Resurrection. If the Word became flesh is the center of the Christian faith, is the flesh left out of the final victory? Then the material world is left out of redemption—a part of Incarnation but not of Resurrection.

Dear Lord and Savior, didst Thou leave out the material as too hard a proposition in rising from the dead? The material was in the Alpha, but not in the Omega. We cannot believe it. For having created the material Thou art redeeming it too. Amen.

AFFIRMATION FOR THE DAY: *In my flesh I shall see God, for I have seen God incarnate in flesh.*

HIS TWISTED BODY A VAST QUESTION MARK

If the cross is inherent, is the Resurrection also inherent? Or is it the attempt of loving hearts to read back into the tragedy of the Cross a resurrection from the dead so that the tragedy becomes triumph? Or does the Resurrection fulfill something that is seeking to come to birth everywhere in nature and in us?

Tagore, the great Indian poet and philosopher, said, "Everything from the lowest cell to the highest man is lifting up strong hands after perfection." The religious urge is this life urge turned qualitative. We want to live, but we also want to live better, more fully. So as long as men want to live better, we will be religious, incurably so. But apart from the Resurrection death puts an end to all this upward longing and striving. But with the Resurrection this striving and longing is fulfilled, gloriously so.

But, objects someone, why the physical resurrection? If He were raised in the spirit, that would be sufficient. Would it? All the problems Jesus raised were raised while He was the Incarnate, while in the body. When He hung upon the cross, His twisted body against the skyline seemed like a vast question mark against the heavens. And in His cry of agony, "My God, why?" He seemed to gather up all the agony of the ages—agony that makes men cry, "My God, why?" He raised in His tortured body all the questions that have haunted men's minds and raised them in an acute form—in His own body. It wasn't a philosopher's discourse on the why of unmerited suffering—that would be the Word become word. This was the Word of haunting questions become flesh. Suppose He had raised these questions in the flesh and then answered them in the spirit by a spiritual resurrection, would that be an answer? No, He raised them in the flesh and must answer them in the flesh.

O Jesus, Thou art not an evader, a bypasser of our problems. Thou didst face everything, yes, everything, including death. And Thou didst go through death, not around it. Thou didst conquer death—death spiritual, death physical. We thank Thee. Amen.

AFFIRMATION FOR THE DAY: *Let me not be one who evades or just gets by with things—let me go through them victoriously.*

SOME QUESTIONS JESUS RAISES IN HIS BODY

We saw yesterday that Jesus raised at the cross all the problems that haunt the mind of man—and raised them in His own body. The Word of Question became flesh. "My son, the world is dark with griefs and graves, so dark that men cry out against the heavens." In His orphaned cry He gathered up on His parched lips everything that makes men "cry out against the heavens." What were some of those questions He raised in His body?

How far can evil go in a world of this kind? How far can force go? How far can lies and clever manipulation go? How far can you cover up the designs of evil in the cloak of good and religion? The answer is that evil can go a long, long way—it can put the Son of God, the Creator of creation, on a wooden cross—wood which He created. That's a long, long way. How far can force go? It can nail the Creator's hands upon the cross. And it can lift it up for all men to see what force can do. How far can lies and clever manipulation go? It can twist the truth of Him who was the Truth and make it into a falsehood and can thus crucify Him on misquotations. How far can evil designs be wrapped in the cloak of religion and good? It can go a long way—it can make evil seem good—they crucified Jesus in the name of God, His Father. They made it appear that they were protecting the sacred name of God. "You have heard the blasphemy!" they cried. Evil, force, lies, perverted religion can go a long way in a world of this kind.

They can do these things today and tomorrow, but the third day? No! For Jesus gathers all these questions in His body and answers them in His resurrected body and spirit the third day!

O Jesus, Thou art the Omega, the Christ of the Final Word. For Thou didst let men have their word, and Thy answer was Silence—Silence until the final victorious word of the blessed Resurrection. We thank Thee, thank Thee, dear Lord. Amen.

AFFIRMATION FOR THE DAY: *If He conquered in the flesh so can I—by His grace.*

DEBATE ENDS AND DEDICATION BEGINS

Suppose Jesus had answered all these questions verbally as philosophers and theologians do. It would have all ended in a debate and question marks. But when He answers them in the Resurrection, debate ends and dedication begins. Our question marks are straightened out into exclamation points! Our questions now become a quest—a quest "to know Him and the power of His resurrection."

Evil is self-defeating. The universe is not made for the triumph of evil. For the word evil is the word live spelled backwards—an attempt to live life against itself. Only as you throw enough good around evil is it able to survive—for a time. Force can go a long way—it can fill the earth with wars and devastation. But force is now shown to be bankrupt—shown on a world scale. God is saying to humanity, "You have used force through the ages to settle your disputes, now I'll let you see force." And He uncovered the heart of an atom. When we saw it we turned pale, for God also said, "But if you use it again, both sides will be ruined irretrievably." That is the utter bankruptcy of a method, the end of the rake's progress: Use it again and everybody concerned is ruined. This took two thousand years of experimentation to prove itself. But Jesus exposed the impotence of force when in the presence of the Resurrected One "the keepers were like dead men"—the custodians of force helpless in the presence of this New Power. Men wouldn't take that Embodied Answer, so two thousand years of agony and pain have ensued, and the Great Fear is over our heads and in our hearts. God has two hands. We wouldn't take the answer from the hand of Grace, so we had to take it from the hand of Judgment.

O Divine Redeemer, Redeem us from our illusions—illusions which are costing us deeply. Save us by Thy Truth. Wisdom is in Thy nail-pierced hands, not in the hands that loose atom bombs. Save us—from ourselves. Amen.

AFFIRMATION FOR THE DAY: *It will save me a lot of costly experimentation if I find the answers in Christ.*

"IN THE ABSENCE OF THE MULTITUDE"

How far can lies and clever manipulation go? The soldiers were given money as a bribe and were told to say that His disciples came and stole away the body of Jesus. That lie is the most exposed lie ever told. The world knows it was a lie. And to stop the movement by money—by bribery? How much money do you think it would take to stop the Christian movement now? Judas took thirty pieces of silver to sell his Lord. I have one of those thirty pieces of silver, or one like them, bought for me by the coin collector of the Chase National Bank at a coin auction. I have also two other coins—one the widow's mite, the same kind of coin the widow threw into the treasury, and a copper coin with its melted edges taken out of the ruins of Hiroshima where the first atomic bomb fell. One I call the Coin of Desecration; the second, the Coin of Consecration; and the third, the Coin of Destruction. But Judas took the money on condition he would betray Him "in the absence of the multitude." "In the absence of the multitude"— and it became the best advertised fact in history, and the most execrated.

Jesus raised all these questions in His body and spirit and answered them in His risen body and spirit. Had He raised them in His body and spirit and had answered them in His spirit, only by a spiritual resurrection, that would have been no answer. They were raised in a material world, and they had to be answered in a material world. And He was very careful that they should not take Him for a disembodied spirit: "Then He said to Thomas, 'Reach your finger here and put it into my side.' " "Have you anything here to eat?" They offered Him a piece of fish they had cooked which He took and ate before their eyes.

So the Word of victory became flesh—became manifested flesh.

O Jesus Lord, Thou art the Open Manifest Victory. Thou didst quietly rise from the dead and lo, darkness turned to light, questions turned into hallelujahs, and complete defeat turned into complete Victory. Nothing could be more decisive. We thank Thee. Amen.

AFFIRMATION FOR THE DAY: *My victories shall be manifest victories.*

"I HAVE OVERCOME THE WORLD"

So the Word of Victory is not the word of victory become word—an idea, a doctrine, a hope, an expectation—it is the Word of Victory become flesh, an accomplished Fact.

Jesus summed it up in these graphic and important words: "In the world you have tribulation; but be of good cheer, I have overcome the world" (John 16:33). "In the world you have tribulation"—realism, a courageous facing of the hard facts; "but be of good cheer"—an optimism won out of those hard facts. "I have overcome the world"—"I have overcome"—not will, but "have." We are dealing with accomplished Fact. So when temptation, difficulties, sins, and problems confront me to bully me, I say to all of them, "Bend your neck." And when they do, I point in triumph: "There, I knew it, the footprint of the Son of God is upon your neck." So I overcome in His overcoming; I am pure in His purity; I am victorious in His victory. I work out from His Wrought-Out Victory to my being wrought-out victory.

I identify myself with Him, with His victory, by surrender and obedience, and my faith then is largely receptivity and response. Receptivity and response are the alternate beats of the Christian heart. Not all receptivity, not all response. It is both. I face a defeated foe, not here and there, but in every realm of human living—"I have overcome the world"—"the world" with all its problems and pains and sins—all included. I accept His accomplishment and work it out with Him. This is not quietism—it is dynamism. For Jesus is alive and at work. I join Him in His cosmic re-creation. I am a part of an exciting movement—exciting because I know the outcome. The outcome has already come—"I have overcome the world."

O Jesus Lord, I thank Thee that I see the end, for I see Thee. Thou art the Omega—the Christ of the Final Word. Therefore I live in Thee with a sense of security and adventure. I know that my Redeemer liveth and because He lives I live also. Amen.

AFFIRMATION FOR THE DAY: *I live on Accomplishment, so I accomplish.*

"I HEAR JESUS IS A DEAD JEW"

This whole matter of the Resurrection and its sweeping Victory is summed up in this story: A Mohammedan was converted. It upset, of course, his relatives and friends. They said, "Why have you bcome a Christian?" And the convert answered, "It is this way: If I were going down a road and came to a fork in the road and didn't know which way to take, and if there were two persons there—one alive and the other dead—from which do you think I would ask the way?" That story is sweeping in its implications. We cannot ask the way from those who are dead—their philosophy broke down at the place of their victory over death—death reaped them all. All, except One. Only One has gone down through death and has come out the other side alive for evermore. "Fear not, I am the first and the last, and the living one; I died, and behold I am alive for evermore, and I have the keys of Death and Hades" (Rev. 1:17). Only He who has the keys of Death and Hades has the keys of life.

A young philosopher went to perhaps the leading Hindu philosopher of India and said to him, "Please become my *guru* [guide], let me become your *chela*" [disciple]. "No," said the philosopher, "I am not worthy to become your *guru*." "Then who is?" asked the young philosopher. "There is only One who is worthy to be your *guru*—Jesus." "But," said the young man, "I hear Jesus is a dead Jew." "No," said the philosopher, "His followers believe Him to be alive." "Where can I get in touch with Him?" "Read the New Testament." He did and out of the pages came this Person, alive, redemptive. He opened his heart to Him, was transformed, and is now a flaming evangelist of the Good News.

Catherine of Sienna at thity-three lay dying, and she said, "This hour for which I have been living has now come. And you are with me." Living or dying He is with us, so life is Life and death is Life.

O Jesus, Lord of life and Lord of death, we thank Thee for Thy aliveness. In Thy presence death seems unbelievably unreal. For in Thee we stand possessed of Life, therefore death has no hold upon us. We are free in life; we will be free in death—I thank Thee. Amen.

AFFIRMATION FOR THE DAY: *Life and death are the same to me, for they are both life.*

"THROUGH THE AGES ONE WORD"

We have been studying how the main facts of the Christian faith—the Incarnation, the creation of the world through Christ, the *preparita evangelica* in the body, the redemption through the Cross and the Resurrection of Jesus—all are founded in and illustrated as the Word became flesh. We must now turn to see if the New Testament scriptures in general support this thesis. Are these outstanding facts standing above, unsupported by the rest of the New Testament? Or is the whole of the New Testament a whole? And is there one message running through the whole—the message of the Word became flesh? One modern commentator says, "After the one statement in John about the Word becoming flesh the rest of the New Testment dismisses it, so we can dismiss it." Can we? If you dismiss it, do you dismiss the very genius of the Christian faith and turn that faith into a philosophy or moralism—man's search for God—instead of a redemptive invasion of us—God's search for man? If so, then the Christian faith takes its place as one of the religions of the world—a philosophy of good views, but with no Good News.

I was in China on the twenty-fifth anniversary of my landing in India as a missionary. The Chinese cook brought in a cake with a quotation written on it from the Chinese classics, which applied to a local situation: "Through the ages one word." Meaning that through the years I had had one Word—the Word made flesh—Jesus Christ is my theme. Does the New Testament through the whole have one Word—the Word made flesh? Or does it begin with the Word became flesh and end with the word become word—a degeneration? I am persuaded that the Christian faith is one word—the Word became flesh, and that it runs consistently through the whole.

O Jesus, my Lord, Thou didst not begin with the Word became flesh and peter out into the Word become word, though very often Thy disciples have crucified Thee on the Cross of the Word become idealism. Save us from this. And confront us anew with Thy redemptive Realism. In Thy name. Amen.

AFFIRMATION FOR THE DAY: *Let me not start with the Word became flesh and taper off into idealism—the Word become word.*

A SIGN? THE WORD BECOME FLESH!

As we begin to study the solid mass of evidence that the New Testament is primarily and basically the Word became flesh, we are confronted with this: "And this will be a sign for you: you will find a babe" (Luke 2:12). The "sign" of the Christian faith was a Babe, an Incarnate Fact. Not a teacher teaching religious truth, a philosophy of life, the word become word. In China a missionary interpreted for me to help a Chinese woman get rid of a resentment. In her eagerness to get the Chinese woman to shed her resentment, she uncovered one of her own—a resentment against an older missionary. Both of them got rid of their resentment—a double cure. The sign was not a schoolroom dealing with questions—they were on a quest.

This turning from speculation to fact, as represented in the Babe, is now becoming a world trend. The intellectual climate of the world is no longer philosophical—it is scientific. India has been the home of philosophy, and yet the students are deserting courses on philosophy and turning to science. Philosophy is based on speculations; science is based on specifications. The Christian faith is based on the specific, on the Word become flesh. So it is at home in the world of science. It is its native air. It brings the spiritual out of the hazy into the happenings, out of mystery into mastery.

The Jews of Jesus' day asked Him for a "sign." And Jesus replied, "This is a wicked generation. It demands a sign, and the only sign that will be given to it is the sign of Jonah . . . and what is here is greater than Solomon . . . and what is here is greater than Jonah" (Luke 11:29-32 NEB). He was there! And He was the Sign. The Babe had now become the world's Redeemer. And there is no other "sign." The signs of table rappings, the signs of unintelligible sounds, the signs of non-decaying bodies after death have claimed followers of Hindu swamies—all these and others are the Word become magic. The Word that is the Word is the Word become flesh.

O Jesus Lord, we ask for no "sign" but Thee. For we see in Thee the beauty and redemption of the Lord our God. We see in Thy face the Divine Everything. In Thee we have seen the Father and it sufficeth us. We ask no more. Our hearts are at rest. Amen.

AFFIRMATION FOR THE DAY: *The sign of my being a Christian will be the sign written in my acts and attitudes.*

THE THINGS THAT HAVE HAPPENED

In Luke 1:1 the writer says: "Many writers have undertaken to draw up an account of the events that have happened among us" (NEB), or "have been accomplished among us" (RSV). The latter is perhaps more accurate—these events hadn't just "happened," they were "accomplished"—He accomplished them—His impact upon people, and upon surroundings "accomplished" these "events."

So the Christian faith is not primarily a set of rules and regulations, a set of principles and practices; it is not a code of morals to be adopted, nor a teaching to be believed. It is primarily something "accomplished"—something accomplished from the side of God—God's redemptive invasion of us. The New Testament is not the revelation of God, for that would be the Word become word, but it is the inspired record of the Revelation—the Revelation was seen in the face of Jesus Christ—the Word become flesh.

The word "accomplish" is used in the Transfiguration scene: "And behold, two men talked with him, Moses and Elijah, who appeared in glory and spoke of his departure, which he was to accomplish at Jerusalem" (Luke 9:30, 31). Note the word "accomplish." Most deaths are an acquiescence. His was an accomplishment. He invaded death and took it captive. Death is no longer a bugaboo but a blessing; no longer an end but a beginning—it is a gateway into eternal life. It is no longer a sunset, but sunrise—it is an accomplishment. And the whole purpose of His life is fulfilled in His last words: "It is finished," not "I am finished and done for"—but "it"—the thing which He came to do, namely the redemption of a race—"It is finished," an "accomplished" fact.

O Jesus, Lord and Savior, Thou art the Great Accomplisher. Thou art the Creator and the Re-creator. We rest in Thy finished work and find a great new beginning. The rest becomes a restlessness to awake in Thy likeness. For having seen Thee, we want to see ourselves like Thee. Amen.

AFFIRMATION FOR THE DAY: *Life shall be not an acquiescence but an accomplishment; and death shall not be an acquiescence but an accomplishment.*

"EYEWITNESSES AND MINISTERS"

This fact that the Gospel is an accomplishment and not a mere system of ideas determines the manner in which that accomplishment is to be passed on and the qualifications of the person presenting it. The next verse after the one we considered yesterday says: "Just as they were delivered to us by those who from the beginning were eyewitnesses and ministers of the word" (Luke 1:2). "Eyewitnesses and ministers"—they have seen something and therefore proclaim something. So the Gospel is not something to be heard from mouth to ear, but something to be seen from Face to face. That seeing was a physical seeing, as in the case of the apostles, or it might be a spiritual seeing of Him, as in the case of Paul—"Am I not an apostle? Have I not seen Jesus our Lord?" Though he had not seen Jesus in the flesh—nevertheless, he had *seen* Him!

This seeing of Jesus after the manner of Paul is perhaps the more important seeing of Jesus. For if He is seen in the flesh, or seen in a vision, there will always be the turning back to that sight of Him—in remembrance. But if you see Him as your Savior and Lord—really see Him as a daily, hourly, moment-by-moment Companion and Guide—then you do not remember Jesus, you realize Him. And the realization is worth far more than the remembrance. Remembrance turns back; realization turns in and around and ahead.

And unless we are thus "eyewitnesses," we will never be "ministers." We can never say, "We cannot but speak the things which we have *seen* and heard"—note "seen." You can transmit knowledge about Him if you have "heard," but you cannot transmit Him unless you have "seen" and realize Him.

O Blessed Face, when I see Thee all else fades into insignificance. For I know that when I see that Face I see a Universe, and God and Everything. I could conceive of nothing higher; I could be content with nothing less. I thank Thee. Amen.

AFFIRMATION FOR THE DAY: *My motto: To know Him—to help others to know Him.*

"THE TRUTH CONCERNING THE THINGS"

We turn now from Luke's Gospel to Luke's Acts of the Apostles. In the Gospel he begins by saying: "It seemed good to me also, having followed all things closely . . . to write an orderly account . . . that you may know the truth concerning the things of which you have been informed" (Luke 1:3, 4). Here the Gospel account is described, not as truths expounded, but as Truth exposed—"followed all things"—the truth concerning "the things." Here the Gospel is not an academic discussion of truth—a set of doctrines about life, but an interpretation of "things," not ideas, but "things" that have happened—better, "accomplished." Some "things" had happened on this earth that had never happened before—our planet has been invaded by God—redemptively invaded. That is the biggest and most decisive "thing" that has ever happened or can happen on this planet. Our feverish and well-advertised efforts to land on the moon, or Mars, are passing events even if accomplished, for what would we have to bring to these satellites and planets? The good news that we are about to blow our planet to pieces, come and join us?

This is all massive child's play. But this is worthy of our Heavenly Father, Creator of worlds, to go and personally redeem a race that has lost its way. This is cosmic news—the Good News, that will make every planet, every cell, every thing dance with joy at the wonder of it. Of all the things that have happened, or could happen this is *the thing*. But it is a *thing*, not an idea, not a teaching, not a proclamation—it is the Central Cosmic Fact: God appeared on a little planet to take us by the hand and put us back on the Way. This is news—Good News—comparatively speaking, the only Good News that ever reached our planet.

O Father God, we thank Thee, thank Thee for the heart of love that could not rest until it found this one lost sheep, this planet of ours. Thou didst leave the ninety and nine in heaven to find us, to find me. Read my gratitude and my love. Amen.

AFFIRMATION FOR THE DAY: *I shall be a demonstration of this "thing" and not merely a declarer of this idea.*

"EMPHASIZE CHRIST . . . NOT JESUS"?

In the Acts, Luke begins the refrain of the Word become flesh: "In the first book, O Theophilus, I have dealt with all that Jesus began to do and teach." (Acts 1:1.) Note the order "Jesus began to do and teach." First "Jesus," the Gospel begins with Jesus, not with Christ—Jesus the Incarnate, not Christ the Designate. Christ is a title—"the Messiah, the Anointed Coming One," but Jesus is the Savior—"Thou shalt call his name Jesus: for he shall save his people from their sins" (Matt. 1:21 KJV). Jesus, the Savior—that is not a designation, it is a Deed.

Tillich, the theologian, after visiting the Far East said on return: "We should emphasize Christ, in the interest of universality, not Jesus." That is a serious misconception. It is Christ who limits Jesus. The idea of Jesus being the Jewish Messiah has cramped Jesus—the Incarnation of the Universal God. He was the Jewish Messiah, but He was very much more—and very different from the Jewish conception. You cannot say "Christ" until you have first said "Jesus," for Jesus puts His own character content into Christ. And breaks the Jewish mold and universalizes Christ. Paul could proclaim the universal Christ because he had hold of the universal Jesus first.

Jesus is the Universal Particular—He is what Luccock calls "the Everywhere now coming into the Here." You cannot know the Universal unless you see it in the Particular. For apart from the particular you put your own thought particular into the universal and make it less than Universal. You limit it to your conception. But Jesus is God putting His own Universal into the Particular. And the Universal God is the only One who knows the Universal. Jesus is the Universal revealing that Universal in understandable terms—human terms.

O Jesus Lord, we see Thee and seeing Thee we see all that lies behind. Not "all," but glimpses, and what we see makes our hearts dance with joy. We glimpse Eternity and that Eternity has Thee at its Center. We ask no more. Amen.

AFFIRMATION FOR THE DAY: *I shall be the Universal illustrated in the particular—in me.*

"FIFTEEN BOOKS TO EXPLAIN NOTHINGNESS"

Concerning the universal Christ you can speculate interminably, but concerning the historic Jesus you are confined to the facts. The books on theology are innumerable; the Gospels are just four brief accounts. Shankara, the great Hindu philosopher, wrote fifteen books to explain Maya, or Illusion. And he came out to *neti*—not that! When asked to define Maya simply, he replied, "Maya is a son of a barren woman." When you give yourself to words you must say in the end, *Neti*. But when you speak of Jesus, you may say, "Yes. This."

It is interesting and illuminating that all the so-called messiahs who have come through the ages have said that they were "another Christ," not another Jesus. For into the "Christ" they could put their own imaginative content and that content would not be Jesus, for Jesus died to redeem a race and none of the so-called messiahs have been ready to undertake that role. There they were the Word become word, not the Word become flesh.

Sir Edwin Hodkyns asks:

Can you study a word and discover a universe; can you learn a language and awake to the truth; can you lose yourself in a lexicon and arise in the presence of God?

Yes, if that "word" is the Word made flesh; if that "language" is the Language of Eternity translated into the Speech of Time—the one Name before which every knee shall bow; and if that "lexicon" is not a lexicon but a Life. For in the presence of that Life you are in the presence of God.

So we begin with Jesus and from Him we work out to God and from Him we work down to man. In His life we see Light.

O Jesus, Thou art so near—so near that if I reach out to touch Thee, I reach too far. For "Thou art nearer than breathing and closer than hands and feet." Thou art the Life of my life, the Joy of my joy. Thou art my glorious universe. Amen.

AFFIRMATION FOR THE DAY: *If men should cut open my heart, would they find the name of Christ engraved there? Yes!*

ALL THE IDEAS ARE GUARANTEED BY THE FACT OF JESUS

We linger another day upon beginning with Jesus—the Incarnate. To soften the emphasis on Jesus in the interests of universality is to soften God's Particular, which is God's universal, and substitute our own eclectic particulars. This is to abandon God's universal in favor of our universals, which are not universal. They are a revelation of us instead of a revelation of God.

A principle without a concrete illustration is a person without feet—it gets nowhere. I don't know whether a principle is true until it is put under life to see whether life will approve of it. A principle is only a hypothesis until it is verified by life. All the principles of the Christian faith have been verified in the life of Jesus—they work and have produced the character of Jesus. And "in any battle of ideas the victory will go to those ideas guaranteed by the facts." In the Christian faith all its ideas have been guaranteed by the fact of Jesus. So the final victory goes to Him. For you will never get better ideas than Jesus held until you live a better life than Jesus lived. That can't be done. He is standard.

"When we hear him present Christ," said a Hindu chairman, "we feel, we hear the notes of Buddha, the ancient sages, the notes of Positivism, of Humanism—all seem to sound and blend in his message." And yet I had mentioned none of these; I had only presented Christ.

Someone asked Dr. Malik how the American University at Beirut was lost to the Christian Church, and he replied, "The curse of Christianity in the Middle East has been and is syncretism." They try to be broad and only succeed in becoming shallow, sometimes succeed in becoming a swamp. The difference between a swamp and a river: a river has banks, a swamp spreads over everything.

O understandable God, O adorable God, O approachable God, O Jesus—we come to Thee to see through the aperture of the little happenings of Thy life, the universal laws and the universal Love of God. We thank Thee for being Thee. In Thy name. Amen.

AFFIRMATION FOR THE DAY: *I shall be universal today because I shall be Christian.*

FOUR SUGGESTIONS FROM GANDHI

We pause today to look at what the greatest Hindu of modern times says to the Christians about their faith. I asked Mahatma Gandhi, in the early days when he had just come from South Africa to begin his work of gaining freedom for India, "What would you suggest to us as Christians that we do to make Christianity more naturalized in India, not a foreign thing, identified with a foreign people and a foreign government, but a part of the life of the people and making its contribution to the remaking of India?" He replied without a moment's hesitation:

I would suggest four things: First, that all of you Christians, missionaries and all,—must begin to live more like Jesus Christ. [He needn't have said anything more!] Second, I would suggest that you practice your religion without adulterating it or toning it down—practice it as it is. Third, I would suggest that you emphasize love and make it your working force, for love is central in Christianity. Fourth, I suggest that you study the non-Christian faiths more sympathetically to find a more sympathetic approach to the people.

Here was the leading Hindu telling the Christians that they should live more like Jesus Christ—the central Figure of our faith; to practice our faith without adulterating it or toning it down. A representative of the most syncretic religion in the world, Hinduism, suggests that we be Christians in the deepest sense of that word, that will make us universal. That we use love as our working force, for Jesus came armed with no weapons save the weapon of love. And that we discover any truths in the old faiths we can, for he implied that that will lead you on then to the Truth—the Incarnate Truth. A great commission from a great Hindu.

O Savior and Lord, we thank Thee that but to see Thee is to see what the ages have longed to see. So we can say to our eyes: "Blessed are you for you see what the best of men everywhere have longed to see." Thank Thee, thank Thee. Amen.

AFFIRMATION FOR THE DAY: *Let these four things be incarnate in all I do and say today.*

THE DEED AND THE DEEDS

We now turn again to the passage in Acts: "In the first book, O Theophilis, I dealt with all that Jesus began to do and teach" (1:1). Note the order—"began to do and teach." The Christian is first a doing and then a teaching. It began in a Deed—the Deed of deeds—the Deed of God's coming to us in the Incarnation. No Deed can be imagined greater than that. Suppose you try to imagine the coming Incarnation. Someone has put it thus: "The attempt to impose divine qualities on the framework of human nature has always resulted in a monstrosity, except in the case of Jesus." Jesus is infinite sanity, infinite balance, supernatural naturalness. Pilate cried, "Behold the Man!" We don't look as the Hindus do for a spotless incarnation—we have Him. And He has us. When Jesus asked His disciples as they turned back from Him, "Will you also go away?" Peter replied, "Lord, to whom else can we go, for Thou hast the words of eternal life?" And the ages echo the question, "Yes, Lord, to whom else can we go?" There is nothing else on the horizon. It is Thou or nothing. Thy coming is the Deed of deeds.

Now this Incarnate Deed was interpreted "by all that Jesus began to do"—the Deed was illustrated and interpreted by what Jesus did—the Deed was revealed by deeds. Many of those deeds were small, but every deed revealed something more than itself—the small interpreted the Big, the Universal behind the limited. In watching Jesus you see more than you see, you hear more than you hear, for the little has become great with meaning; the trivial becomes the tremendous. The shell of the outer deed cracks, and you see the kernel of Eternal meanings. And never once did His deeds cut across the Deed—the whole is a consistent whole. The deeds and the Deed fit, revealing one thing—God.

O Lord, Christ, we thank Thee Thou didst not miss Thy step. Thou didst show us the Father and nothing but the Father. There are no blurs, no canceling out of one statement or deed by a contradictory statement or deed. We thank Thee. Amen.

AFFIRMATION FOR THE DAY: *I cannot be a spotless follower of the Spotless Incarnation, but my love can be single.*

JESUS GOES BEYOND OUR DREAMS

We ended yesterday by saying that the Deed and the deeds were one in Jesus. This has not always been true in the attempt to create a divine figure. "Do these frescoes on the walls, the doings of your gods, help you in your worship?" I asked a man in charge of a temple. He replied: "You have to be very strong if you come to this temple, otherwise you will go off and do what the gods do." Revealing. We feel that we will never be as good as our Savior. And in Him we feel that these divine qualities are not imposed on Him—they are exposed out of Him. They come from within. And we can detect at once what is imposed on Him by later centuries and what is exposed out of Him. One is artificial, the other artesian. For instance, the Gospel of Thomas, discovered in Ethiopia and recently translated the "Gospel," closes with words like these: Peter says to Jesus, "Send Mary away, for it is not befitting that a woman should inherit eternal life along with the men." "No," said Jesus, "she need not go away. I will turn her into a male and she can therefore inherit eternal life." That is what man will do when he imposes divine qualities—he produces a monstrosity. This kind of thing makes me feel more than ever the wonder of the inspired record in the New Testament.

If ignorant fishermen created Jesus out of their imagination, put suitable and deathless words to His life, suitable deeds revealed through His life, and made the whole into the most beautiful character that ever lived—well, if the fishermen did that then the creators would be more astonishing characters than the hero. Bad men could not have created Him, and good men would not have created Him.

"All that Jesus began to do"—His doing is exactly what we would expect God to do, except that it is beyond our imagination, goes beyond our fondest dreams. Our surmise has become a surprise!

O Lord Jesus, we thought great things of God, our Heavenly Father, but we never thought This—This that we see in Thee. You surprise us by the wonder of it all—we are lost in wonder, love, and praise. Blessed, blessed, Jesus, Jesus—that is all we can say! Amen.

AFFIRMATION FOR THE DAY: *When I stand before Jesus I know He is not my creation, but my Creator and Re-creator.*

"ALL THAT JESUS BEGAN TO DO AND TEACH"

We come now to the other side of "all that Jesus began to do and teach." It was first doing and then teaching. That is not a chance order—doing and then teaching—it was the center of the Christian faith—the Word became flesh before the flesh became word. He talked what He lived and lived what He taught. In all other teachers it was the opposite: "Follow my truth, but not me." Jesus says, "Follow Me and ye shall know the truth." The truth He shared was operative fact—operative in His own experience. So the truth He uttered came with authority—deep spake to deep. When Jesus finished the Sermon on the Mount, the people were astonished at His teaching, for "He spoke with authority and not as their Scribes." They quoted authorities—He spoke with authority, the authority of doing and then teaching. All His teaching was an exposition of His doing.

A pastor said in the Hour of the Open Heart at an Ashram in Japan, "My wife sent me to this Ashram, for, she said, 'When you stand up and preach you sound like a radio announcer—parroting news that doesn't concern you.'" It didn't come from the heart, hence it didn't reach the heart. A Sikh driver for a missionary in India became interested in the village preaching and said to the missionary, "Sahib, let me preach to these people." "What would you preach about?" asked the missionary. "Oh, I would preach against liquor and tobacco," said the Sikh. "But," said the missionary, "you use both." "Yes, I do, but these people don't know that." But actually the people do know, "for there is nothing covered that shall not be revealed," and the people sense reality as they sense beauty and harmony. So when Jesus spoke, Reality spoke. The people knew that His teaching was not the exposition of a text, but the exposure of the texture of His being.

O Jesus, in Thee I feel the feel of consistency. Thy words and Thy deeds have a consistency—they hold together, for they are two sides of one reality. Therefore speak to us, for everything within us listens, for everything in Thee speaks when Thou dost speak. So we listen. Amen.

AFFIRMATION FOR THE DAY: *My doing and my teaching must be one—or I do not teach.*

THE NAZARETH MANIFESTO

We come now to a key passage which reveals the whole Christian Gospel as the Word became flesh. Not only in the initial incarnation in human flesh, but as a continuing incarnation—as a method and attitude in everything connected with that Gospel—it was all an application of the principle of the Word become flesh, the principle become practice. As Jesus stood up to read in the Synagogue at Nazareth, He announced His program and purpose: "The Spirit of the Lord is upon me, because he has anointed me to preach good news to the poor [the economically disinherited]. He has sent me to proclaim release to the captives [the socially and politically disinherited] and recovering of sight to the blind [the physically disinherited], to set at liberty those who are oppressed [the morally and spiritually disinherited], to proclaim the acceptable year of the Lord [a fresh world beginning—the corporately disinherited]" (Luke 4:18-21). He closed the Book and began to say to them: "Today this Scripture has been fulfilled in your hearing"—today this word of Scripture becomes flesh, in me. And it did!

In His own Person He embodied this fivefold redemptive impact upon life and started movements which then and now are leading to the emancipation of the poor from economic bondage, the downtrodden masses from social and political captivity, the physically disabled from their disabilities, the morally and spiritually bruised from their guilts, the world from total bondages in the total life. The program became the Person and the Person became the program—they were one. The text became clothed in flesh and blood. No wonder "they were surprised that words of such grace should fall from his lips" (NEB). It was the grace of embodied fact—the grace of being and doing.

O Jesus, in Thee what we hear we see—the hearing and the seeing are intertwined like the words and music of a song. We are enthralled by the wonder of it. Now Reality has a face and hands and feet, and a heart. We bow in the presence—the blessed presence of the Embodied. Amen.

AFFIRMATION FOR THE DAY: *All my programs will be the interpretation of my person, for I must preach only what I produce.*

"HAS COME TRUE"

We pause another day upon the scene in the synagogue. The marginal reading says, "Today, he said, this text which you have just heard has come true" (Luke 4:21 NEB). That phrase "has come true" can now be written across all the best longings and prayers and yearnings of all the ages—they have come true—come true in Jesus. And all the promises of the Old Testament have "come true" in Jesus. "The Desire of the ages" has been fulfilled in Him.

But the utter realism of this coming "true" was never more vividly seen than in this synagogue incident. "They all wondered at the words of grace that fell from His lips," but He would not go on a misunderstanding. He would let them know how far He intended to go with this new order, the Kingdom of God. As long as the hearers thought that Jesus was a Jew leading a Jewish movement for the uplift of the Jewish people, and for them alone, the sailing was smooth. But the moment Jesus revealed how far He intended to go, the weather turned rough—very rough. When He said that there were many widows in Israel but Elijah was sent only to a Gentile woman, and there were many lepers in Israel but none were cleansed except Naaman, also a Gentile—"When they heard this, all in the synagogue were filled with wrath." Straight off He put His finger on the biggest barrier to the coming of the Kingdom—race pride and consequent race prejudice. The pious Jew every day thanked God he was "not born a woman, a leper or a Gentile." And here Jesus showed God cared especially for Gentiles, especially for a woman, and especially for a leper. Their boasting prayer was shattered.

So they took Him to the brow of the hill "to cast Him down headlong." "But passing through the midst of them He went His way"—His way, not theirs. And "His way" is the way of looking upon all persons as "persons for whom Christ died." A man was a man before God and man.

O Jesus, Thou didst start a world revolution in a sentence. The walls of exclusive standing began to crumble with the impact of these words—these words which are now leveling the high walls created between man and man. We thank Thee, thank Thee. Amen.

AFFIRMATION FOR THE DAY: *If Jesus demolished all their snobberies He has demolished mine—mine more subtle and more hidden.*

"ALL GREAT LITERATURE IS AUTOBIOGRAPHY"

We must linger another day on the keynote address given at the very opening of the campaign in launching the greatest movement that ever touched our planet—the Kingdom of God. The Spirit of the Lord was upon Him to launch a Kingdom which would touch the whole of life—economic, social and political, the physical, the moral and spiritual, and the collective. It was marvelous as a program, but the program took flesh and blood—the program became a Person. The program as program would have died, as many paper utopias have died through the ages, but this program was no word become word—it was the Word of the Kingdom became flesh. "This text . . . has come true."

This set the pattern for preaching—it was witnessing out of experience. As "all great literature is autobiography," so all great preaching is testimony. "When they had testified and preached"—note the order—first, testimony. That preaching which is not primarily testimony is the Word become word, or as a theologian, Dr. Adolph Keller, put it, "the Word became theology."

Bishop Pakhenham-Walsh, an Anglican saint, once heard me speak in India on the Kingdom, and he asked, "Where do we begin?" And I replied, "I suppose the way to begin is to go out and act as though the Kingdom were already here, and it will be as far as we are concerned." "Then," said the bishop to himself, "I will act as though the Kingdom were already here." So he went and established an Ashram among the Jacobite Syrians of Travancore who had had a court case on for many years which left the church divided. He gave his life for the healing of that division, lived a life of utter sacrifice and self-giving love. And the division was healed, and a court case of over forty years canceled by agreement. The kingdom had come as far as the saintly bishop was concerned—had come in him.

O Jesus Lord, Thou hast become the pattern for our preaching. In Thee message and man were one. So much so that Thou didst become the Message. Help me, Lord, so to identify myself with Thee that in me people may see the message—the message in a man. Amen.

AFFIRMATION FOR THE DAY: *My words will reveal me today. By my words I shall be judged.*

"I'VE BEEN PERJURING MYSELF"

We continue yesterday's discussion of preaching as testimony. I write this in Japan where Barthianism has taken hold of the ministers. But it is the old Barthianism, not the new. The old Barth would have nothing to do with experience—it savored of mysticism, which was anathema. The word of God was to be given as the pure word of God uncorrupted by man's experience. It was apart from and beyond experience. Barth was asked by Harnack, "Have you ever thought of the humanity of God?" and Barth replied decisively, *Nein*—No! So the Gospel according to Barth became the Pure Word become pure word. Then Barth saw his mistake and wrote a book in 1956 on the humanity of God—the Word became flesh. But most of Barth's followers are following the Barth of the Word became word with its resultant words which have lost contact with reality and hence their vitality.

A famous Hindu swami wrote in a book for a friend, "I am pure, I am humble, I am mighty, I am charitable, I have orphanages and dispensaries." When the friend objected, the Hindu said: "Didn't Jesus say, I am the light of the world, I am the way? I, too, am God and I can say it." The difference? One was the Word become word and the other was the Word become flesh.

A theological student came to a friend of mine and said, "I've been perjuring myself. I've been preaching things not operative within me. I'm through with this unreality. I'll give God till Sunday to do something for me. And if He doesn't do something for me before Sunday, someone else can preach. I won't." He took Saturday off as a day of retreat. God met him, was waiting for him. He went into the pulpit a new man. The congregation filed in to listen to the old words. They got the shock of their lives. They had a new minister. The whole congregation found themselves seeking what their young minister had found. The Word had become flesh.

O Blessed Redeemer, redeem me from words out of which the content has dropped. Give me reality, Thy kind of reality, and thus may my words and my life be one! I thank Thee, thank Thee for this blessed conversion. Amen.

AFFIRMATION FOR THE DAY: *I am prisoner of a vocabulary. Give me a new vocabulary to express a new vitality.*

"JESUS HAS GOT INTO YOUR BLOOD"

We linger on the preaching which is essentially witnessing. That which is to reach the heart must come from the heart. Deep must speak to deep.

A student came to me one day in India and said, "Sir, tell me how to find God." I took the Bible and began to go through it pointing out the passages which pointed the way to find God. In the midst of it he leaned over, closed the book in my hand, and said, "Now, sir, you tell me how you found God." It was a real challenge, so I told him how I found God, or rather how God had found me and my response. At the close he said, "Thank you, that's what I want." Of course, we cannot close the Bible, for from its pages is revealed Him who is the Way—the Way to the Father. But unless the truth in the Bible becomes truth in the blood, it is bloodless truth, anemic and ineffective.

"Jesus has got into your blood, hasn't He?" said a Hindu one day to me. "Yes," I said, "and I hope He has raised my temperature." Another Hindu said to me: "I've read the Acts of the Apostles, and there seems to be a strange power at work in the lives of the people there—have you got that power in your life?" That was a good question and legitimate, for he wanted to know if the word of the Acts had become flesh in me. The account says that "the high priest then questioned Jesus about his disciples and his teaching" (John 18:19). Note the order—disciples first and teaching second. The first inquiry is about the disciples—has the word He is teaching become flesh in them? We are the first Bibles people read. If they like the samples, they go on to the real thing. "One seeing is worth a hundred hearings," is an Eastern proverb.

O God, Thou who didst show Thyself through Thy only Son in Whom the Word became flesh, wilt Thou make one of the least of Thy sons, even me, in some real way the Word become flesh again? For having seen it I seek it. Amen.

AFFIRMATION FOR THE DAY: *Hindu observation: "Christians are ordinary people making extraordinary claims." Am I one?*

WOULD NOT PREACH ANYTHING NOT OPERATIVE

This speaking out of experience and its power was illustrated by a minister who decided that he would not preach anything that was not operative within himself. He began to preach with power. His range was less, but his power in what he did say was greater. He claimed less, but reclaimed more—more people wanted what he had.

Bishop Oldham, before he became a bishop, was pastor of a church in Singapore. One day he preached on the Holy Spirit and at the end said frankly, "I haven't got what I have preached. But I want the Holy Spirit. I am going to this altar to surrender myself and to pray for the Holy Spirit. Those who would like to join me in this seeking may come." Nearly the whole congregation surged forward to seek what their pastor was seeking. No wonder the church elected him a bishop and no wonder a saintly life underlay all his activities, inside and outside the pulpit and platform.

When the Japanese had taken over Manchuria from the Chinese, some Chinese pastors said to me, "Don't preach to us to love our enemies, preach to us spiritually." They wanted the Gospel as spirituality, and not the Gospel as the word of spirituality become flesh in loving one's enemies. Those in our churches who are without sin in this regard may cast the first stone. Not many stones will be cast! "There is nothing covered that shall not be revealed"—revealed, whether it is reality or unreality. For reality steals into the words of the real and unreality steals into the words of the unreal. And the people sense it intuitively. "There is nothing covered"—good or bad. So all our inner thoughts became words and the words become flesh—good or bad.

O Jesus, Author and Finisher of Reality, may everything about me be real today. May the thoughts of my mind, the meditations of my heart, and the acts of my will be acceptable in Thy sight. And then and then only will I be real. Amen.

AFFIRMATION FOR THE DAY: *May all my spirituality take shoes and walk this day.*

"THE COLDNESS OF A BODILESS INFINITY"

We continue to look at the passages which tell us of the Word become flesh. "Behold a virgin shall conceive and bear a Son and his name shall be called Emmanuel (which means, God with us)" (Matt. 1:23). He had to be with us, bone of our bone, flesh of our flesh, and yet He would be "God" with us. Like us and unlike us. He could not redeem us seated in awful grandeur apart from the tragedy and pain of the world—He had to come Himself. He had to show us His heart or we would never have believed it.

This quotation is from a Hindu religious journal:

Now the home was empty—bereft of light, music, laughter and love. He was alone with his own thinking self and God—God that Mighty, Unknown Power to Whom for millions of ages Creation has cried and prayed and wept—God, that majestic Silence which is never disturbed for all the clamour of men—which creates and kills at a breath, and no reason given—which is Light and Darkness, Gladness and Sorrow, Love and Hate in one—and which we instinctively worship in all creeds, not so much because we Will but because we Must. . . . But it is natural to weak man to prefer the warm tenderness of a woman's arms about him to the coldness of a bodiless Infinity, no matter how full of exquisite promise and suggestion that Infinity may be.

Note: "the coldness of a bodiless Infinity." That is the view of God when there is no face on God. As we have said the Incarnation puts a face on God—God visiting and redeeming His people. The God without a face is the God without worshipers. You cannot say your prayers to the multiplication table, nor to the law of gravitation, however true they may be.

O Jesus, Thou art God approachable, God lovable, God simplified, God with a Face. I thank Thee, Blessed One, that in Thee we worship not "the coldness of a bodiless Infinity," but the warm tender Finite—Infinite. Amen.

AFFIRMATION FOR THE DAY: *In Jesus the Holy becomes the approachable, even by the unholy. So I can come.*

"EMPTIED HIMSELF"

We have meditated on, "He has visited and redeemed His people." How deeply did the Divine Visitor penetrate the life of His people? Was it the momentary visit of a Sovereign to a slum—a few words of greeting, a smile or two, and then back to the palace of royalty? In Jesus did God go aslumming? No, His visit was identification—and what an identification! "Have this mind among yourselves, which you have in Christ Jesus, who, though he was in the form of God, did not count equality with God a thing to be grasped, but emptied himself, taking the form of a servant, being born in the likeness of men. And being found in human form he humbled himself and became obedient unto death, even death on a cross" (Phil. 2:5-9). That is what "visited" meant to Jesus. The steps down were seven: First, He inwardly renounced the security of being equal with God. Second, He emptied Himself of everything, except love. Third, He would love not as a superior from above, but as a servant from below. Fourth, He was willing, though God, to be a man,—not a man at the top, but man at the bottom. Fifth, He humbled Himself as a man—became the lowest man—sinful man. Sixth, He took man's heritage, death, as His own. Seventh, He took man's sin as His own and died as a malefactor on a cross.

The visitation meant identification, and the identification meant not identification with man at the top, becoming the best of men, but becoming the worst of men—a sinner, dying between sinners. "He became sin for us."

That identification was gradual, beginning at inner renunciation of being equal with God, coming in a Virgin's womb, and going deeper at every step until He hit rock bottom on a cross: "My God, why hast Thou forsaken me?"

O Divine Redeemer, we can never understand the mystery of the Thy self-giving, but we can worship at the shrine of it. And we do worship with a deepening reverence that passes into awe and that passes into complete surrender. We thank Thee. Amen.

AFFIRMATION FOR THE DAY: *I am a missionary—is my being a missionary a visitation or an identification?*

"THE CHILD IS NOT WAKED"

We left off yesterday at the thought of the gradual identification with man as Jesus more and more became incarnate in man as sinful man. It couldn't be done all at once—born of a Virgin—finished! It began in a Virgin's womb and ended in a tomb, and between the two there was a deeper and deeper identification, step by step. For thirty years He was identified with the Ordinary—a growing boy, a carpenter's bench, a narrow village life, the pettiness of surrounding life. For thirty years He was baptized into the world's toil. Then He began to be baptized into the world's sin.

The account says that when "all people were baptized, and when Jesus also was baptized" (Luke 3:21). That means that Jesus entered a repenting stream of people coming to be baptized with a baptism of repentance—He entered as one of them. He who wore a stainless conscience took a baptism of repentance as though He too were a penitent sinner. John objected, but Jesus replied: "Let it be so now; for thus it is fitting for us to fulfill all righteousness" (Matt. 3:15). Here was a new kind of "righteousness." The Pharisee was righteous by apartness from sinners, but Jesus showed the righteousness of identification, of being a part of sinners that sinners might be a part of Him and His redemption.

In the account of Elisha and the Shunamite's son lying dead in her home, Elisha sent a servant with a staff telling the servant to lay it on the face of the dead child. But the servant returned saying, "The child is not waked." Then Elisha himself went and put his face to the face of the child—eyes to eyes, mouth to mouth, he stretched himself upon the child. And the child came to life. Many prophets and philosophers had laid the stick of sermons and philosophical systems upon the face of a dead sinful humanity, but the dead soul of humanity was not waked.

O Jesus, we thank Thee that Thou didst lay mouth to mouth, eyes to eyes, and soul to soul. The warmth of Thy love has awakened us. Thou hast done what no one else could do—Thou hast brought us life—life from Thy life. We thank Thee. Amen.

AFFIRMATION FOR THE DAY: *My identification shall not be a name identification, but a life identification.*

"IT DOESN'T PUT ITS ARMS AROUND MY NECK"

We ended yesterday with the episode of Elisha sending a servant with a dead staff to lay upon the face of a dead child, and saw the fruitlessness of that method. Only when life in Elisha touched death in the child did the child come to life. Before the Incarnation of Jesus many servants came with their dead staffs of precepts and teachings and exhortations and philosophies and moralisms to lay on the face of the dead humanity, but the verdict was and is: "The child is not waked." So Jesus came personally and laid His lips to our lips, His eyes to our eyes, and His soul to our soul—and humanity came to life. It was the only way—"He hath visited and redeemed His people." And the "visited" turned out to be more than a visit or a visitation—it turned out as identification. He was baptized between sinners as one of them and died between two thieves as one of them.

A father told the story of the three bears every night to his children. "This is silly," he said to himself. "Why not have it recorded and played for them." He did. Then he sat and read his paper in peace. But after listening to the recording the little boy came downstairs and climbed into the father's lap. The father, surprised, said, "Son, didn't you hear the story, and wasn't it my voice?" "Yes," said the boy, "but it doesn't put its arms around my neck." Any faith which lacks the Incarnation is a faith whose God doesn't put his arms around the neck of His children. On the veranda where I write there are wooden sticks hanging by strings. When the wind blows the sticks hit upon one another and utter noises that sound like the chirping of birds. But it is no substitute for the song of birds. It is wooden music.

O Jesus, Thou didst stoop to share, but how far Thou didst stoop we shall never know, but we shall explore forever. And in that exploration we shall be lost in wonder, love, and praise. We see enough to send us to our knees. Amen.

AFFIRMATION FOR THE DAY: *Without real love, I shall be a tinkling stick—wooden music.*

HE VISITS US IN OUR SIN

We are considering the passage, "God hath visited and redeemed His people." That visitation was the most thoroughgoing ever seen or heard of on this or any other planet. The mother who put her picture in a house of prostitution for her wayward daughter to see, "visited" her daughter. Jesus, in the story of Dostoevski, when told by a church dignitary that He could go back to heaven, that He was an embarrassment to them as they managed His affairs on earth, then leaned over and kissed the ashen lips of the ecclesiast, "visited" His church. The mother who requested the body of her son from the jail authorities executed for crime and was refused, then requested that she be buried alongside her son in the jail yard, "visited" her boy.

But these, deep as they are, are not as deep as this visitation of God in visiting and redeeming His people. For His visitation meant identification, not with one chosen person in his sin, but with all the human race in their sin. "All the desperate tides of the world's sin and woe were forced through the channel of a single heart." And that heart broke upon the cross.

It is true that the Hindu scriptures say that the All-God is the goodness of the good and "the gambling of the cheat," but this pantheism—God is all, sin-included. There is no choice—His allness includes all sin. But here in Jesus the Holy God chooses to be identified in love with all the sin of all men—chooses it, for being love He must choose it.

And when He chose to be identified with their sin, He chose to be identified with their death, for sin and death are one. And further, sin and death and hell are one—so "He descended into Hell."

O Love Divine that stooped to share—how deep that sharing is we shall never know. But we know enough so that it makes us tremble—and rejoice with joy unspeakable and full of glory. It is all beyond us, but deeply in us. It has us. Amen.

AFFIRMATION FOR THE DAY: *If God had not come to me I could never have gotten to Him.*

"I AM JESUS WHOM YOU ARE PERSECUTING"

There is one more thought that must be added if we are to see and feel the full impact of "God hath visited and redeemed His people." Was it a momentary visitation of thirty-three years, and when it was all over did God say, "Well, that's that. I'm glad that is all over. Now I can rest in a job well-done. But it is past." No, the Christian Incarnation is deeper than that. It is a continuing Incarnation.

When Paul was upon the Damascus Road, he heard a voice: "Saul, Saul, why do you persecute me?" And he said, "Who are you, Lord?" And he said, "I am Jesus whom you are persecuting." Jesus, after He had gone to heaven was still being persecuted in the persecution of His followers. Whatever fell on them fell on Him. So the identification and hence the incarnation continues, and will continue until the human race is redeemed. At least until all who want to be redeemed are redeemed—the rest perish.

So the Incarnation continues, for Love continues. And Love being love must by its very nature insinuate itself into the sin and sorrow of the loved ones. So while there is no outer cross on Calvary's hill, there is the inner cross upon the heart of Calvary's God. For God rules from a cross. "And I if I be lifted up will draw all men unto me." He draws men—He doesn't drive them. "Isn't this coercion," I asked Mahatma Gandhi in jail, "when you fast to make men give up untouchability?" "Yes," he replied, "the same kind of coercion Jesus exercises upon you from the cross." It is coercion, but the coercion of Love—we are free to resist it, but Love narrows down the freedom to the point that if we resist it we are bad. And we know we are bad. And we reject ourselves in that choice.

O Blessed Savior and Redeemer, we now see that in sinning we sin not only against impersonal moral law—we sin against Love—the Personal Love of our Redeemer. That makes sin dreadfully sinful. Do save me from sinning. Amen.

AFFIRMATION FOR THE DAY: *Every act and attitude I take today to anybody will be an act and attitude toward Jesus.*

IS HE THE GOD OF THE PERMANENT SCARS?

We saw yesterday that the Incarnation continues—continues in the fact that Jesus is still persecuted in the persecution of His own, still suffering in the sins and sorrows of the sinful. So the Incarnation continues in that whatever falls on us falls on Him. But there is a further step: The Incarnation means that our manhood is taken up into God. So Browning cries: "It's weakness in strength that I cry for! My flesh, that I seek in the Godhead! I seek and I find it!" Is our flesh now in the Godhead? Is our humanity now a part of the Godhead? I see God in the stars, but do I see Him more deeply in the Scars—the scars in the nail-pierced Hands? Certainly it is not flesh and blood. For flesh and blood cannot inherit the Kingdom of God so certainly will not inherit the Godhead. But in some real way are we not now represented in the Godhead—our humanity a part of God in the Incarnation became a part of us?

Jesus after His resurrection showed His pierced hands and side—these marks were in a resurrected body—a body which could pass through closed doors and could rise from the earth and be caught away into heaven. Did He ever divest Himself of those signs, or are they still there? The church has always believed that this is true—and rightly. For if He became part of us in the Incarnation then in that same Incarnation we became a part of Him. These scars are pledges that we belong to Him and He will await His own. And we will come seeking our Homeland.

So the Incarnation was not like an insect at evening time diving from the air and skimming the surface of the lake and in doing so laying its eggs and then going back to its flying in the sky. No, "the word became flesh and dwelt among us"—dwelt among us and made us His own and took our humanity back with Him. So we are permanently *there.* So when we come to Him we come to our own because we are His own.

O Savior, we are saved in no light fashion. "He loved His own and loved them to the end"—and that "end" is forever. Because of this we are not Thy passing interest—we are graven on Thy hands and our destiny is in Thy wound prints—there is where we belong forever. Amen.

AFFIRMATION FOR THE DAY: *My flesh taken up into Him? Yes, today and forever.*

SERMON ON THE MOUNT UNREALISTIC?

We saw how deeply God in Christ "visited and redeemed His people." We turn now to a portion of the biblical account which many regard as idealistic teaching and not meant for actual practice. They thereby suggest that Jesus is teaching by the method of the Word become word and not the Word become flesh. The Sermon on the Mount is looked on as impractical idealism—the Word become word and not practical realism—the Word become flesh.

The Sermon on the Mount is beyond most of us, but it is not thereby idealism. What we are trying to live is an inverted realism—a realism that is a bad idealism that won't work—it lands us in a mess. Nothing sustains it except our own unrealistic wills. The universe doesn't sustain it, hence to live some way other than the Sermon on the Mount turns out badly—turns out to be the kind of mess we are now in, individually and collectively.

But the Sermon on the Mount is realism. First of all, it is a portrait of Jesus Himself. He put into words the principles and attitudes He himself was acting upon. This Sermon is not preaching but revelation—a revelation of the inner life and character of Jesus. It is the Word become flesh in relationships. Jesus is here not imposing an impossible code on human nature, a code for which humanity is badly made. He is lifting up principles underlying the universe. When He finished speaking, "The people were astonished at His teaching for He taught them, not as their Scribes but as one having authority." The phrase as "one having authority" could be translated "according to the nature of things." He lifted up out of reality the principles that were according to "the nature of things." The people who heard Him felt the "authority" of what He was saying. It hit them with an inner thud. Impossible idealism doesn't do that. It arouses you emotionally, but it doesn't come with authority.

O Jesus Lord and Master, this is Thy new crucifixion, that we take this portraiture of Thyself and say it is unrealistic, when these principles produced Thee. And Thou art One whose "authority" does not lessen, but grows from age to age. Forgive us our stupidity. Amen.

AFFIRMATION FOR THE DAY: *The Sermon on the Mount is my Code, for Jesus is my Character.*

CHRISTIAN FAITH IDEALISM?

We are considering the Sermon on the Mount as realism. I was seated in a train with a Russian actress. She said, "I suppose you are a religious man? You are religious because you are weak. You want someone to hold your hand. You want God to comfort you." I replied, "You are wrong really. I don't want religion as comfort, but as adequacy. I don't want God to hold my hand, I want Him to strengthen my arm that I might reach out a helping hand to others. I don't want God to wipe away my tears, I want Him to give me a handkerchief so I can wipe away the tears of others." Seeing she was on the wrong track, she said, "I suppose you are an idealist?" I replied, hesitatingly, "Yes, I suppose I am." *"Au revoir,"* she replied, "I'm a realist." This set me to thinking. I came to the conclusion that if I'm a Christian, then I must be a realist. For Christianity is not the Word become idea but the Word become flesh. It resulted in my writing the book, *Is the Kingdom of God Realism?* Since then my conviction has deepened, and I find myself writing this book on the same theme with a slightly different slant.

The Sermon on the Mount seems to undercut this—it seems a sermon and sermons are usually classed as idealism. But this Sermon on the Mount was a Sermon for the Mart—it was a revelation of the principles underlying the universe, therefore workable anywhere. And not one word did He utter that was a mere word—it was the Word become flesh in Himself. Here, as everywhere, His words were deeds and His deeds were words. And you can't tell where His words end and His deeds begin—it was two sides of one reality. It was harmony—the highest harmony, moral and spiritual harmony. It was a revelation of life—His inner life.

O Divine Son of God, I thank Thee for this inner revelation. We are in awe at the wonder of it and yet the awe doesn't repel us—it draws us—draws us to emulate. So open to us this Sermon and open us to the Sermon. Amen.

AFFIRMATION FOR THE DAY: *If I am a Christian, I am a realist—an out-and-out realist.*

THROWS A DART AT SELF-SUFFICIENCY

The Sermon opens with the Beatitudes. It is the Be-attitudes, not the Do-attitudes. In this Jesus was realistic, for the doing comes out of the being. A good tree brings forth good fruit. This is not the attempt to get human nature to do good apart from being good which is the basic unrealism of moralism. "Out of the abundance of the heart the mouth speaketh." So He goes straight to the fountain knowing if that is pure the stream will be pure.

His first beatitude is "Blessed are the poor in spirit, for theirs is the kingdom of heaven." The word for "poor" is *anav*, a chosen poverty. It could be translated, "So poor that you are willing to receive and became the receptive in spirit." The two ideas put together could mean—the surrendered and receptive in spirit.

Here He strikes the keynote of the Christian faith. All other faiths are a struggle upward, a whipping up of the will. You try to climb the ladder to God to find Him at the topmost rung of worthiness. This is the egocentric attempt to find God—man lifting himself by the bootstrap method. This says that salvation can be earned by what we do—the system of merit. Every single approach to God, including the Jewish, must be classified under this category of self-salvation—it is what we do that procures it. And every single one ends in self-stultification. Every single one centers you on you—saves its life and loses it. This includes modern character-development. The concentration of your own character, even to develop it, is self-defeating. It leaves you self-preoccupied, leaves you self-defeated by the very nature of the quest. Jesus threw a dart in His opening sentence at the very heart of this off-the-track attempt.

O Jesus Lord, we do thank Thee for this opening sentence. We don't have to be good—we have to be open to Goodness. For Thy Goodness is a seeking goodness. Make me receptive to that Goodness. Then I shall be good—unconsciously good. Amen.

AFFIRMATION FOR THE DAY: *I commit myself to God—sufficiency, not self-sufficiency—God is my sufficiency.*

SCIENCE TEACHES SURRENDER
TO THE WILL OF GOD

We are considering the opening sentence of the Sermon on the Mount: "Blessed are the poor in spirit for theirs is the kingdom of heaven," or "Blessed are those poor enough to be receptive in spirit."

Is this an outmoded attitude belonging to the ages of self-repudiation, a denial of the will to live? No, this is as up-to-date as tomorrow. Huxley once wrote to Kingsley: "Science seems to me to teach in the most unmistakable way the Christian conception of entire surrender to the will of God. Science says: 'Sit down before the facts as a little child, be willing to give up every preconceived notion, be willing to follow to whatever end nature will lead you or you will know nothing.' " Every great scientist must be a humble, receptive man or he couldn't be a great scientist. The proud, self-sufficient, unreceptive are automatically excluded from the kingdom of science.

And here Jesus laid down the first law of the Kingdom, a law that is the first law of science—be surrendered, be receptive, or you will get nowhere. But on the other hand, if you are surrendered and receptive you will get everywhere; everything is open to you—the Kingdom of heaven is yours, it belongs to you. Note it doesn't say that you belong to the Kingdom of Heaven; you do, of course, but it says the breathtaking opposite—the Kingdom and all its resources and power belong to you. It is all at your disposal. This opens up moral and spiritual wealth beyond our dreams. The Kingdom of God is the ultimate Order, the Ultimate Authority, the Ultimate Good. All this is open to those humble enough, surrendered enough, to receive it. That leaves you centered on another, on Jesus, on the Kingdom of God—and when you seek first the Kingdom, all these things, including yourself, are added to you.

O Blessed Redeemer, we are in awe at Thy truth. It sends us to our knees. But it also makes us stretch out our hands to take, to take Thy Everything. Having seen, we seek. And in the seeking find, for we find Thee seeking. Amen.

AFFIRMATION FOR THE DAY: *I am scientific, as well as Christian, if I follow Jesus in His emphasis on receptivity.*

THE ULTIMATE IN IDEALISM:
"BE YE . . . PERFECT"?

We would like to take up each statement of the Beatitudes and each subsequent statement in this opening chapter of the Sermon on the Mount and show how each statement is realism—a realism so far ahead of us that we think them idealism. But let us skip over to the last statement of the chapter: "Be ye therefore perfect, even as your Father . . . is perfect" (Matt. 5:48 KJV). This seems the ultimate in idealism. In fact it is the most matter-of-fact realism. For we are made in the inner structure of our being for just this—perfection and for this kind of perfection referred to.

We are made for perfection—the perfect God made us for perfection. And this striving after perfection is written unto the whole process of living. From the lowest cell to the highest man there is a striving for a fuller, more abundant life. If the Bible says: "Be ye therefore perfect," then everything within me says the same: "Be ye perfect." Man's striving after perfection is simply the culmination of a process we see in all nature. In everything there is a cry for life, more abundant life. In the Christian this cry for life has turned qualitative—it is the cry for a particular type of life—the life we have seen in Jesus. We can be satisfied with no other type of life. He has spoiled us for any other type—it is this or nothing. In Him we have seen the ultimate. He says here we are to be perfect as the Father is perfect, but really He was saying, "Be perfect as you have seen perfection in me, for he that has seen me has seen the Father." He couldn't say that. So He refers us to the Father as the pattern. But it is the stronger for the silence—a silence which speaks in the sentence more strongly than through utterance.

O Jesus, we have seen Thee and having seen Thee we cannot stop this side of being made into Thy likeness. This divine urge is the saving thing within us. It keeps us from sinking back into the fatalities of lower nature. Stir it, stir it within us. Amen.

AFFIRMATION FOR THE DAY: *The Divine Urge to be like Christ is upon me—may I feed and lead that Urge.*

THE CONTEXT SAYS: "BE PERFECT IN LOVE"

The statement "Be ye therefore perfect, even as your Father . . . is perfect," means at first sight idealism, but it is realism since we are made by our very makeup for perfection. Perfection is our life prayer, our deepest life urge. As a British psychiatrist, mentioned before, says, "Man is made for conversion," so man is made for perfection. But to put it that way is to take it out of its setting and to put the emphasis on isolated perfection, which would make the perfection self-conscious and tend toward Pharisaism. This perfection here is perfection "as your heavenly Father is perfect"—it is perfection related to the heavenly Father. And the perfection of the heavenly Father is interpreted by the life and character of Jesus. It is not perfection in power and wisdom, it is perfection in love. That is the heart of the revelation of the Father as seen in Jesus Christ. It culminated in the statement: "God is love."

The word "therefore" corroborates this: "Be ye therefore perfect." The "therefore" points back to the preceding verses where it speaks of loving your enemies, turning the other cheek and going the second mile. Since God makes His sun to rise on the evil and the good and send His rain on the just and unjust, you are to treat your enemies the same. And if you do you are fulfilling this command: "Be ye therefore perfect."

The word "as" does not mean "as" perfect as God is perfect, but it could be translated "since"—"since" your Heavenly Father is perfect as God, so you are to be sons of your Father, perfect as sons in love as the Father is perfect as God in love. That is possible, for it is possible to have a perfect attitude of love though not perfect in the manifestation of that attitude.

O Jesus, we thank Thee that we can be perfect in love, for we can love with Thy love and that love is perfect. When it gets through the stream of our lives it may not be perfect manifestation, but the love is perfect for it is Thine. We thank Thee. Amen.

AFFIRMATION FOR THE DAY: *It is always open to me to love with the love of Christ when I cannot love with my own.*

THIS CHRISTIAN PERFECTION SAVES
FROM PERFECTIONISM

We are meditating upon the statement: "Be ye therefore perfect, even as your Father . . . is perfect." Is this idealism—an impossible idealism—or is it stark realism? We have seen that an urge after perfection is inherent in man—is inherent in everything from the lowest cell to the highest man. So the urge upward is met by an offer downward; God the Father offers in Christ Jesus what our inner urges reach for—perfection. This is realism. Apart from this the whole process would be the word become word—an upward cry but no answer from God. But this offer of God makes the word of striving become possible—the word of perfection becomes flesh.

At the very time, it saves this striving after perfection from perfectionism. Perfectionism is the striving after perfection turned in upon itself, becoming self-conscious and therefore uninviting and repulsive. A girl came to one of our Ashrams bent on her own perfection. She used everybody to further her ends toward perfection. As a result her perfectionism became obnoxious self-centeredness. Her fiancé had to break off the engagement, for he saw that the marriage relationship was going to be used to further her self-conscious aims. So perfectionism turned into imperfect relationships. "Lilies that fester smell worse than weeds."

This offer from above saves us from another type of perfectionism—telling people they are to recognize themselves as already perfect, and working out from that as a hypothesis. The same worm of self-centeredness is eating at the heart of that hypothesis. But this perfection Jesus offers does not begin in us. It begins in a relationship with the perfect God, and all our perfection then is a gift of grace—Christ-conscious instead of self-conscious. It is also outgoing, instead of in-growing—it is love for enemies. It is wholesome, for it makes you whole.

O Jesus, Thou dost redeem our highest urge as well as our lowest urges. We are grateful that we can now give vent to our highest longings, for they are now turned into redemptive channels—for us and others. We are in awe at Thy redemption. Amen.

AFFIRMATION FOR THE DAY: *I'm looking away from my imperfect self to the perfect God as seen in the face of Jesus. He has my attention, therefore has me.*

THE UNDIVIDED IN HEART SEE GOD

Instead of being idealism the Sermon on the Mount is stark realism—it emphasizes all the way through that the outer and inner must be one—the words of religion must become flesh, or else it all becomes hypocrisy, playacting.

After laying down the central Beatitude: "Blessed are the pure [undivided] in heart, for they shall see God" (Matt. 5:8), Jesus proceeded to point out the areas of inner division which plague and paralyze the life of the religions and keep them from seeing God continuously. The first thing He points out is that anger is murder, setting the sin back beyond the deed to the hatred (Matt. 5:21, 22). Then He closes the gap between worship and human relations—"If you are offering your gift at the altar, and there remember that your brother has something against you, leave your gift there before the altar." Note—"before the altar," not on it, for God cannot accept the gift until the relationship with the brother is right (Matt. 5:23, 24). Here right relationships with your brother has precedence over worship—the worship is worthless unless it issues in right relationships. The word of worship is the word become word unless it becomes flesh in right relationships.

Then Jesus emphasizes the necessity of closing the gap betwen the deed of adultery and the looking with lust at a woman—they are the same, said He. The lustful look and the deed are one (Matt. 5:27, 28). Then He made the legal and the moral one. Men thought themselves good if they were legal—give a certificate of divorce to your wife and that makes you good, because it's legal. But Jesus puts divorce on the moral alone—unchastity by its very nature dissolves the bond between husband and wife and for that reason and for that reason alone divorce is legitimate. The legal had to be moral or it wasn't legal. In every situation life had to be one—the Word must become flesh.

O Jesus, Lord and Teacher, Thou dost penetrate to our depths. But Thy penetration is not mere probing—it is healing. For our inner divisions are our inner diseases. So probe on until we become inwardly one. For we would be well and whole. Amen.

AFFIRMATION FOR THE DAY: *I can choose to be one, for I can choose to be won—won by Him wholly.*

UNLIMITED, LIMITED, NO REVENGE

We continue to look at the Sermon on the Mount as realism. It is the most amazing account of the attempt of Jesus to get men to give up the paralyzing dualisms in their characters and conduct.

He goes on to urge us to stop the dualisms in our speech. You try to be impressive in speech by adding oaths, He said, but the very attempt to be impressive by adding oaths to your statement weakens those statements, for it reveals your own inner insecurity. "Let what you say be simply 'Yes' or 'No'; anything more than this comes from evil" (Matt. 5:33-37). Here He would purify our speech from the dualism which would need binding oaths to hold it together. Be so one that your speech is one, needing no outer props to make it stand.

His next emphasis was upon getting rid of limited revenge—one eye for one eye and one tooth for one tooth—replacing it by no revenge at all (Matt. 5:38-42). Before the Jewish Law came in revenge was unlimited—if a man knocks out one tooth of yours knock out as many as you can of his. The law limited the revenge to its exact equivalent—one eye for one eye. Jesus abolished revenge. For the simple reason that if you act upon revenge you allow the other person to determine your conduct—you react to his act. That makes him decide what you do. Work out from your own principles regardless of what the other man does, Jesus said. If he strikes you on one cheek, then seize the initiative and turn the other cheek. That puts you in control of the situation, on the moral and spiritual offensive. It also disarms the other man—he strikes you on the cheek, and you strike him on the heart. He doesn't know what to do with this new and unexpected weapon—the weapon of love. But the weapon must be one weapon not two—now love and now force—which would cancel the effectiveness of love.

O Lord Jesus, we thank Thee that Thou didst come to our world with no other weapon save the weapon of love. Thou didst conquer us by love and by love alone. Help us to be single-minded and single-weaponed. In Thy name. Amen.

AFFIRMATION FOR THE DAY: *If I take revenge I sink to the other man's level.*

LOVE WITH LOVE UNLIMITED

Jesus breaks down another division—the division of dividing love—loving your neighbor and hating your enemy. And also the loving of those who love you and hating those who hate you. It must be Love Unlimited. He reminded them that that is the way God loves—He makes the sun to rise on the evil and the good and sends His rain on the just and unjust. God loves with Love Unlimited, and if you love that way only "so can you be children of your heavenly Father."

This going down to the bedrock of undivided and undiscriminating love hits at the central division in human personality—loving only those who return love. For this discriminating love is not even love for it has a worm of self-interest eating at its heart. So it is self-defeating. You have to love with Love Unlimited or you don't love. For limited love is Unlimited Selfishness. For one who loves only those who love him really does not love the other person—all he loves is what he gets back from the other person, which is in essence, self-love, not love but selfishness.

And this kind of love Jesus expounds is not an imposition upon life from a high-sounding Sage or Potentate seated on a dictating throne of the universe—it is the actual revelation of God's character and conduct. That is what God is and does. And this kind of love in God and man is the only kind that will save the world. Admiral Sato, commander of the submarine fleet at Pearl Harbor said to me, "This verse got me. I couldn't get into the Kingdom of God because I was good, but I could get in if God loves like that—He makes the sun rise on the evil. That opened the door for me."

O Jesus Lord and Savior, we thank Thee for this healing word—healing us at the place of our central sickness. For if our love turns sick, because it is turned into essential selfishness, then we are sick indeed. Heal us at this place. Amen.

AFFIRMATION FOR THE DAY: *When God takes away my limitations in love, He takes away my limitations.*

GOD IS NOT A COSMIC SIGNPOST

This whole fifth chapter of Matthew is not a collection of sayings, but a connected and organic whole, beginning at the sounding of the standard note, "Blessed are the pure [or undivided] in heart for they shall see God," and ending in the final crescendo, "Be ye therefore perfect as your heavenly Father is perfect." If you are undivided in heart, then you not only see God, you become like God, perfect in character and life as a son of God, as God is perfect as God. Nothing could be more ethically and spiritually sound than this. Our code of conduct is not based on ethical principles—the Word become word—nor upon the will of God—again the Word become word—but upon the very character and conduct of God—the Word become flesh. The universe is not only a physical universe, or a multiverse, but a moral and spiritual universe—a consistent whole. There is not one set of principles for God and another for man. The Head of the Universe acts basically on the same principles He requires of us. He is not a cosmic signpost pointing the way to live—He is the Way. That Way had to be revealed through an act—Jesus, the Act of God.

> By all that God requires of me,
> I know that He Himself must be.

In one Christian group Jesus is called "the Way-shower"—He shows the way. But He not only shows the way—He is the Way. Through the trackless jungles of human life there is no abstract way, a cosmic map; there is the glorious fact of the Creator and Sustainer of the Universe as the Way—the Way revealed in the Person of Jesus Christ!

And the central point of that revelation is God's perfection in love—"God is Love," and the central point of our maturity in character—we must be loving. We are mature or perfect as we are mature or perfect in love.

O Jesus, Revealer and Redeemer, Thou has thrown back the curtain from the Character of God the Father and what we see in just Thyself, universalized. And what we see sends us on a quest to be like Thee. We thank Thee, thank Thee. Amen.

AFFIRMATION FOR THE DAY: *I shall not be a signpost pointing the way; I shall be a shepherd—showing the way.*

"BEWARE OF THE LEAVEN OF THE PHARISEES"—
OUTWARDISM

After coming to a climax in the amazing revelation of the destiny of His followers: "Be ye therefore perfect, even as your Father . . . is perfect," Jesus then goes on to strike at the things which hinder the realization of this perfection. He mentions three phases of the same thing—outwardism. Outwardism is the tribute that hypocrisy pays to goodness. Hypocrisy says, I am not good, but this is what I would like to appear to be.

He puts His finger on three religious acts where outwardism asserts itself. First, outwardism in doing charitable things: "Be careful not to make a show of your religion. . . . Thus, when you do some act of charity, do not announce it with a flourish of trumpets, as the hypocrites do in the synagogue and in the streets to win admiration from men" (Matt. 6:1, 2 NEB). This tendency to do charitable acts to win favor from God and applause from man is as old as yesterday, new as tomorrow, and as present as today. Collections in churches are often doubled when bags are replaced by plates! "Erected to the Glory of God and to the memory of So and So." And the last emphasis is always the emphatic emphasis!

A motto on the Sat Tal Ashram in India says, "There is no limit to the good you can do if you do not desire any credit for it." It is the desire to get credit that cancels the good we do. For the self-regarding motive is the real motivating motive—the rest is playacting with yourself as the central character. An actress said to her actor husband, "Darling, I'm afraid you play too big a part in your life." The self-display motive plays too big a part in much of our charity. "Beware of the leaven of the Pharisees," said Jesus to His disciples. It is valid today, for outwardism destroys the inward, makes it hollow.

O Father God, Thou dost work in such hidden ways, so hidden that men doubt Thy existence. Thou dost feed us, clothe us, and by the very strength of that care we ask where Thou art. Thy humility sends us to our knees. In Jesus' Name. Amen.

AFFIRMATION FOR THE DAY: *There is no limit to the good I can do today if I ask no credit.*

"SPEECHES BY WAY OF PRAYERS"

Jesus pointed to another outwardism: "Again, when you pray, do not be like the hypocrites; they love to say their prayers standing up in the synagogue and at the streetcorners, for everyone to see them. I tell you this: they have their reward already" (Matt. 6:5-6 NEB). Praying to God to be heard of men! A newspaper reports: "Dr. So and So prayed one of the most eloquent prayers ever delivered to a Boston audience." And it *was* delivered to a Boston audience—that was its intended destination. In India a Hindu, Mohammedan, and a Christian were to pray at a public function, and the program announced it thus: "Speeches by way of prayers." That was more frank than usual!

Then He goes on and says: "In your prayers do not go babbling on like the heathen, who imagine that the more they say the more likely they are to be heard" (Matt. 6:7). I saw widows in a certain institution repeating the name of one of the gods for six solid hours continuously, and I never saw such blank faces on any group of human beings. The "babbling" produced no bubbling as real prayer does.

Jesus then gave the Lord's Prayer, which is prayer reduced to its simplest and profoundest form—all adjectives squeezed out, and the words and reality coincide and are one. The self-regarding emphasis is precluded by the first word, "Our." So the prayer is self-purifying by its very nature.

And to remind His disciples of the very necessity of making the prayer an embodiment of attitudes toward others, Jesus turned back and said, "But if you do not forgive others, then the wrongs you have done will not be forgiven by your Father" (Matt. 6:15). Prayer is the word of request become flesh, or it is mere words. So real prayer to God is a revelation of our attitudes toward others.

Dear Savior, Thou dost save us by purifying our very prayers. Thou dost show us how to pray for answerable things. So our prayers become Thy prayers, hence all answerable. Thou dost redeem our lowest moments and our highest. We thank Thee. Amen.

AFFIRMATION FOR THE DAY: *"At forty a man's face reveals what his life prayer is."*

LIGHT TURNED TO DARKNESS

The third place of the danger of outwardism is fastings or the place of renunciations: "So too when you fast, do not look gloomy like the hypocrites: they make their faces unsightly so that other people may see that they are fasting. I tell you this: they have their reward already" (Matt. 6:16 NEB). This amounts to calling attention to the self-renunciation by displaying the supposedly renounced self as heroic. Which means, of course, that you use the renunciation to display the unrenounced self—which is self-defeating. You have your reward. You wanted the praise of men, and having received it you have nothing beyond that.

So the very light in giving charity, in prayer and in fasting, turns to darkness. And how great is that darkness—self-deceived by self-display. You save your life and you lose it.

So this verse sums up the necessity for inward and outward sincerity of purpose and intention: "The eye is the lamp of the body. So, if your eye is sound, your whole body will be full of light; but if your eye is not sound, your whole body will be full of darkness. If then the light in you is darkness, how great is the darkness!" (Matt. 6:22, 23 RSV). This is penetrating in that it reveals that your highest things, giving charity, prayer, fasting, have become your lowest things—your very light has become darkness, if not accompanied by the single eye, namely, that you do these things for God and not for your unsurrendered self, for self-display.

Preaching the Gospel is good, but that good can be and is turned to bad if at the close we wait for and invite compliments and are disappointed if they don't come. A famous preacher was the first speaker on a program and didn't do too well; he was followed by a less famous preacher who did better. After that he would not speak to the man who outdid him. His light was darkness.

O Savior, save us at our highest moments as well as our lowest moments. For walking the high places if we lose our footing and stumble, then we fall far. So keep our hand lest we lose our heads at dizzy heights. Save us at the heights and at the depths. Amen.

AFFIRMATION FOR THE DAY: *If I twist doing good into doing good for myself, then my light has turned to darkness.*

CAN A CHRISTIAN LAY UP TREASURE
UPON EARTH?

In looking at the Sermon on the Mount we discover its essential realism—it is the Word become flesh.

But this passage seems idealism: "Do not store up for yourselves treasure on earth, where it grows rusty and moth-eaten, and thieves break in to steal it. Store up treasure in heaven, where there is no moth and no rust to spoil it, no thieves to break in and steal. For where your wealth is, there your heart will be also" (Matt. 6:19-21 NEB). This sounds as though it means that no treasure is to be stored up on earth. But it doesn't say that; it says, "Do not store up for yourselves treasure on earth." The emphasis is on "for yourselves." If the emphasis is there, then that means that you can store up treasure if it is for others.

Now the Christian basis is that one has a right to as much of the material as will make him mentally, spiritually, and physically fit for the purposes of the Kingdom of God. That means he gets according to his needs. The rest belongs to the needs of others. Then a person has a right and duty to as much as he needs for his needs, and in this is included the needs of his family now and for his own old age. That is not an easy line to draw. And no rule is given. A man's conscience and the guidance of God should determine it. After the needs of himself and those dependent on him are met, then all the rest belongs to the needs of others. He can lay up for others treasures upon earth. But "others" doesn't mean selfish relatives who are not included in "the needs of others." The needs of others must be those "in need."

The idea that we have a right to pile up for ourselves and for others regardless of need is canceled by this principle. But it affirms the right to meet our needs and the needs of others dependent on us.

O Jesus Lord, Thou art putting Thy finger upon the sensitive nerve of possessions. We know that we must possess our possessions, and they must not possess us. Help us then to listen to Thee—to listen to need and not greed. In Thy Name. Amen.

AFFIRMATION FOR THE DAY: *I will go over my possessions and classify them into "Need" and "Not Need."*

SERVE GOD AND MAMMON, OR SERVE GOD WITH MAMMON?

We come now to a central verse in the consideration of inner division: "No one can serve two masters; for either he will hate the one and love the other, or he will be devoted to the one and despise the other. You cannot serve God and mammon" (Matt. 6:24). This verse touches the nerve center of the spiritual problem of the Christian. We live in a society where to have is to be. And to have not is to be not. It is the atmosphere we breathe from childhood to old age. It is our native air. No wonder this verse sounds strangely foreign. And yet how realistic, for if anything is plain in the actual working out of life it is this: Things and their possession do not guarantee, or even produce, happiness. A man stood up in one of our Ashrams at the time of the Open Heart and said, "I am a businessman, successful, but unhappy and confused." He had everything and nothing. For if you have everything on the outside and nothing within, you have nothing. "I've learned how to make money, but I've not yet learned how to live," said a sad millionaire after a musician performed on a huge pipe organ he had installed in his palace of a home. The music temporarily lifted him out of his depression. Finally he put a pistol to his head and blew out his brains.

And yet the pursuit of happiness through mammon goes on from disillusioned age to age. And the voice of Jesus keeps saying, "You cannot serve God and mammon." And yet people try—and fail inevitably. The only people who can deal with mammon are the people who serve God with mammon. It is in their hands and not in their hearts. They set mammon to work in service. Then mammon becomes an instrument of the Kingdom. The only way to deal with mammon is to take out of it what you really need and dedicate the rest for the needs of others. Then mammon is no longer mammon—it is converted mammon.

O Lord Jesus, I offer to Thee all I am and all I possess. Cleanse both from selfishness and dedicate both to Thee and Thy Kingdom, and to Thee and Thy Kingdom alone. For I would be mastered by nothing but Thee. For Thy mastery is freedom. Amen.

AFFIRMATION FOR THE DAY: *I can possess my possessions or my possessions will possess me. I make the choice.*

THERE IS NOTHING BEHIND MAMMON
EXCEPT MAMMON

Jesus goes on in the process of closing the gaps that grow up in the spiritual life and in so doing unified the life. The last one was the gap between God and mammon. God is the Lord of the spiritual and the material, and when we truly serve Him they become one. Now an illuminating passage comes in: "Therefore I tell you, do not be anxious about your life, what you shall eat or what you shall drink, nor about your body, what you shall put on. . . . Your heavenly Father knows that you need them all. But seek first his kingdom and his righteousness, and all these things shall be yours as well" (Matt. 6:25, 32-33). The word "therefore" is important. It points back to the attempt to serve God and mammon. And the moment you try to serve both, you thereby serve one—mammon. And the moment you begin to serve mammon, anxiety about your material needs sets in, hence the word "therefore." It points back to "mammon." The moment you make mammon central, anxiety possesses you. For there is nothing behind mammon except mammon. You and your mammon have to hold your world together. If mammon goes, your world of security goes.

But if you seek first the kingdom of God, then all that you need of material things is guaranteed—everything is behind you—you have a cosmic guarantee for your way of life. Anxiety drops away. You are basically secure.

Anxiety over material things is the most devastating thing in the spiritual life. Jesus says so: "And others are the ones sown among thorns; they are those who hear the word, but the cares of world, and the delight in riches, and the desire for other things, enter in and choke the word, and it proves unfruitful" (Mark 4:18, 19). It is the sin of otherwise good people. Anxiety is more devastating than adultery, because it is more widespread.

O Jesus Lord, Thou art the Master Surgeon. Thou dost put Thy finger on our sore spots and sayest, "Thou art ailing here and here." And Thy finger is upon our anxiety. Save us from this most corroding of ailments. For if Thou art within, anxiety is not; but if anxiety is within, Thou art not. Save us. Amen.

AFFIRMATION FOR THE DAY: *"Have no anxiety about anything, but in everything by prayer and supplication with thanksgiving, let your requests be made known unto God."*

"LIVE IN DAY-TIGHT COMPARTMENTS"

Jesus puts in another "therefore" in His teaching about anxiety: "Therefore do not be anxious about tomorrow, for tomorrow will be anxious for itself. Let the day's own trouble be sufficient for the day" (Matt. 6:34). Here He closes the gap between today and yesterday and today and tomorrow. Concentrate on today, He says. Be a today man, not a yesterday man, nor a tomorrow man. Live today. For if you try to live three ways at once—living in worry over the mistakes of yesterday, living tensely about tomorrow, and hence living ineffectively today—you will not be Mr. Facing-Both-Ways, but Mr. Facing-Three-Ways, and you will be a blur.

If you allow the anxieties of yesterday, and the anxieties of tomorrow, plus the anxieties of today, to gang up on you, it will break the strongest spirit. Live today today. Dr. Osler, the famous surgeon of Johns Hopkins, urged men to "live in day-tight compartments"—shutting off yesterday and shutting off tomorrow and living today today. Then you will deal with things once—today. But if you don't do this you meet everything three times—yesterday, tomorrow, and today. So you are exhausted by over-attention to your problems. Meet them once—today—settle them, and then dismiss them and go on to the next thing today.

Anxiety is the advance interest you pay on tomorrow's troubles. And some people go bankrupt paying interest on troubles that never come. Some do come and if you meet them today, one by one, by the grace and power of God you can conquer and solve them. Someone asked me how I manage to keep fresh day by day. I replied, "I clip off my engagements like coupons. After I've given an address, or have made a decision, I dismiss it. I do my best and leave the rest." Simple? Very, but effective. Useless regret over the past and useless anxiety over tomorrow make a useless person.

O Jesus, Thy forgiveness covers my mistakes and sins of yesterday. Thy grace will be sufficient for tomorrow; Thy power is available for today. So I go forth with Thee knowing that all I need for today is adequate. Help me to draw heavily on Thee, today. Amen.

AFFIRMATION FOR THE DAY: *Anxiety is a tri-headed parasite, eating into yesterday and tomorrow and making me ineffective today.*

"JUDGE NOT, THAT YOU BE NOT JUDGED"

Jesus continues to put His finger on the divisions in human character which corrupt and cancel the good. He saves to the last the most important emphasis—the emphasis on the danger of the good becoming the critical, and hence no longer the good. "Judge not, that you be not judged. For with the judgment you pronounce you will be judged, and the measure you give will be the measure you get" (Matt. 7:1, 2). Here Jesus puts His emphasis on the greatest danger to the divided person—the divided person compensates for his own inner inconsistencies by pointing out the inconsistencies of his brother man.

The man who buried his talent turned upon his master and said, "I knew you to be a hard man, reaping where you did not sow . . . and I went and hid your talent" (Matt. 25:25). He blamed his master for his own delinquency. The critical and the faultfinding are invariably the guilty—the guilty who are suppressing their guilt by pointing out the guilt of others. "Look how bad he is" means "Look how good I am—good, because I can point out his bad." It is a vivid illustration of the Word becoming word and not the Word becoming flesh.

The good do judge, but it is not verbal—it is the word of judgment become flesh, the silent judgment of superior living. A good man sat in a train, and a man in flashy clothes sitting nearby said very seriously, "If there were more men like him there would be less men like me." A social worker lectured the slum children about their dirty faces, and it did no good. Then she brought a clean-faced child with clean clothes and she played with the dirty-faced. And soon the dirty-faced children went off one by one and washed their faces. Criticism by cleanliness was effective.

O Jesus Savior, we look on Thy face—then we want to wash ours. We see Thy deeds and abhor ours. We are judged most deeply and redemptively at Thy cross. For there Thou dost confront everything we are by everything Thou art. And we are at Thy feet. Amen.

AFFIRMATION FOR THE DAY: *It has been well said: "If I point one finger at another I point three at myself."*

THE PAYOFF IS IN THE PERSON

In the closing words of the Sermon on the Mount Jesus sums up the whole outcome of this inner division: "Thus you will know them by their fruits" (Matt. 7:20). The outcome is the criterion. Life renders its verdict and the verdict is the outcome—the fruit, the finished product. "Beware of false prohets, who come to you in sheep's clothing [the Word become word] but inwardly are ravenous wolves [not the Word become flesh]. You will know them by their fruits. Are grapes gathered from thorns, or figs from thistles? So, every sound tree bears good fruit, but the bad tree bears evil fruit" (Matt. 7:15-17). The good ends in good and the bad in bad. The judgments are inherent, not imposed. They come out of the nature of reality. They are inescapable.

"I am two persons," said the vice-principal of a great educational institution—"one when I am with you, and another when I am with a crooked political group." The end was suicide. The end of a divided personality is just that—suicide, slow or sudden. The personality is destroyed by the very inner division. The good is good for us and the bad is bad for us. The outcome of the good is good, and the outcome of the bad is bad. And there are no exceptions.

Jesus is simply lifting up the laws underlying the universe. He was pronouncing their judgments. His and theirs were the same. For He made those laws.

"It's all right to do these things," said a woman in regard to sex license, "provided you can get away with it." I replied, "That 'provided' is a very big word. Nobody gets away with anything. For the payoff is in the person. The results are registered in the person. You become what you do." And psychiatry, when it is honest, would say "Amen" to the above. For life says it.

O Jesus, we write our own sentence of judgment and we are writing it day by day. And some day we will say with Pilate: "What I have written I have written." Save us, dear Lord, from writing the wrong thing before it is too late. Amen.

AFFIRMATION FOR THE DAY: *I am what I am, because I have chosen as I have chosen.*

"AS ONE WHO HAD AUTHORITY"

We come now to the last meditation on the Sermon on the Mount in which Jesus draws the net to the shore and lets us see the catch, the final outcome. "Not everyone who says to me 'Lord, Lord,' shall enter the kingdom of heaven, but he who does the will of my Father who is in heaven" (Matt. 7:21). Saying "Lord, Lord" is the Word of allegiance become word, but doing "the will of my Father" is the Word become flesh. Nothing could be clearer than that the Christian faith is a sound and solid realism and not idealism at all.

And Jesus gives a final illustration of the parables of the two men—one who built his house upon a rock and the other who built his house on the sand. One stood when the storm struck, and the other collapsed. Why was one on rock and the other on sand? This is rock: "Every one then who hears these words of mine and does them will be like a wise man who built his house on the rock." "Hears these words of mine and does them"—this is the Word become flesh. This is sand: "And everyone who hears these words of mine and does not do them will be like a foolish man who built his house upon the sand" (Matt. 7:24, 26). This is the word become word—"hears but does not do them."

So the greatest sermon that was ever preached was not a sermon at all—it was a revelation of reality. And the people heard it as such: "The crowds were astonished at his teaching, for he taught them as one who had authority, and not as their scribes" (Matt. 7:28, 29). As we have said, the phrase "as one who had authority" could be translated "as one who spoke according to the nature of things." The Greek word is *exousia*—"out of life," literally. So Jesus was a Revealer of the Nature of Reality. And the one who obeys Him is "wise," not only "good" but "wise"; and the one who does not obey Him is foolish, not only "bad" but "foolish." The Christian faith is not only goodness—it is wisdom. And you are a fool if you don't take it.

O Jesus, Teacher and Lord, Thy teaching is Deep speaking to deep. It finds our depths. We cannot argue—we can only obey and be saved, or refuse and be damned, self-damned. Save us from ourselves and our foolisness. In Thy dear and precious name we ask. Amen.

AFFIRMATION FOR THE DAY: *If I am wise I will say "Lord, Lord," with my life and lips.*

"JESUS IGNORED THE REMARK"

We now turn from the Sermon on the Mount in our study of the realism of Jesus to a happening where He seems not to be realistic. When Jesus was on the way to the healing of the daughter of Jairus, word was brought to the father that the child was dead: "Your daughter is dead. Why trouble the teacher to come any further? Instantly Jesus ignored the remark" (Mark 5:36 Moffatt). But the remark was a fact—the child was dead—why did Jesus ignore reality? Did not this prove Him unrealistic?

No, for He was realistic on a higher level—the Kingdom level. The lower set of facts said, "The child is dead." And the higher set of facts said, "The child can live." Jesus chose to be realistic on the higher level. There are two levels of reality: the lower level, life around you, and the higher level, life above you. Some people are realistic on the lower level. Whatever the facts around them declare, they decide. They are this—worldly realistic. But Jesus was more conscious of the Kingdom set of facts than He was of the lower set. The lower set of facts did not decide things for Him—the higher set did.

And the higher set of facts—the Kingdom facts—were realistic; the child lived. The last word was not with death but with life. The so-called realists are realists on too low a level. They are earthbound and earth-fact-bound. They are only half-realists. But Jesus was a total realist. He didn't deny the lower set of facts—He simply "ignored" them. For He was more conscious of the higher set. He lived and moved in the reality of the Kingdom. Some live and move in the half-reality of the lower: "The church is dead"; "Nothing can be done here"; "This generation of young people is impossible"; "War is inevitable"; "Things are hopeless." But the Kingdom realism says, "Yes, I admit the lower set, but apply the higher set. Life is stranger than death." It is!

Blessed Jesus, we are so grateful that the two worlds were Thy home. And yet Thou didst know that the ultimate reality was in the Higher—and the last word there too. Teach me to live in both these worlds, especially the Higher. Amen.

AFFIRMATION FOR THE DAY: *Today I shall live in two sets of facts—may I draw on the higher to change the lower.*

DISEASE ROOTED IN GUILT

We saw yesterday that Jesus was at home in two worlds but knew that ultimate and finally authoritative word was with the higher world, the Kingdom of God. This is seen in another incident in His life:

And behold, they brought to him a paralytic, lying on his bed; and when Jesus saw their faith he said to the paralytic, "Take heart, my son; your sins are forgiven." And behold, some of the scribes said to themselves, "This man is blaspheming." But Jesus, knowing their thoughts, said, "Why do you think evil in your hearts? For which is easier, to say, 'Your sins are forgiven,' or to say, 'Rise and walk'? But that you may know that the Son of man has authority on earth to forgive sins"—he then said to the paralytic—"Rise, take up your bed and go home." And he rose and went home (Matt. 9:2-7).

Jesus saw that the man's sin and his disease were connected, and to cure him physically and leave him uncured spiritually would have done little or nothing for the man. For the man would probably have created another symptom in his body if the guilt had not been cleansed by forgiveness. He had to be cured of the guilt before he could be cured of the paralysis, for the guilt was the root of the paralysis.

This is the basic fallacy of Freudianism. It says that the basis of neurosis is guilt feelings. Get rid of the guilt feelings and you get rid of the neurosis. The truth is, as Mowrer says, that not guilt feelings, but guilt is at the basis of the neurosis. Here Mowrer is in line with Jesus, and Freud departs from Him. And here Freud is fruitless—and worse—he creates more neuroses by trying to get rid of standards which create guilt feelings. Jesus gets rid of the guilt by forgiveness, and the paralysis no longer paralyzes. The man is free to carry the bed that carried him. This is the Word of forgiveness become flesh.

Dear Jesus, we thank Thee that Thou dost go to the root of our malady—our sin. We thank Thee for forgiveness of sin—a forgiveness that cost Thee dearly, a forgiveness that heals us completely—body, mind, and spirit. We thank Thee for making us well and whole. Amen.

AFFIRMATION FOR THE DAY: *Quacks treat symptoms, doctors treat diseases. I shall deal with diseases, not symptoms.*

"A NEW KIND OF TEACHING! HE SPEAKS
WITH AUTHORITY"

This distinctive thing in the Christian faith, namely the Word became flesh, instead of the Word became word, is seen in this passage:

Now there was a man in the synagogue possessed by an unclean spirit. He shrieked: "What do you want with us, Jesus of Nazareth? Have you come to destroy us? I know who you are—the Holy One of God." Jesus rebuked him: "Be silent," he said, "and come out of him." And the unclean spirit threw the man into convulsions and with a loud cry left him. They were all dumbfounded and began to ask one another, "What is this? A new kind of teaching! He speaks with authority. When he gives orders, even the unclean spirits submit" (Mark 1:23 NEB).

Note, Jesus would not allow evil spirits to confess His Messiahship. Why? It was valuable testimony! Yes, but it was given by those who had no intention of obeying Him, so it was the Word of confession of His Messiahship become word. It was out of line with what He was doing. The Messiahship confession would have to wait till it became the Word become flesh—confessed by man who would embody it. To Jesus it was reality or nothing. Had He been a self-seeker, He would have grasped at this: "Look, the devils know me." But He was a Redeemer and redemption can come only through Reality.

And the people saw this difference: "What is this? A new kind of teaching! He speaks with authority." The authority of embodied fact and not of mere words. His teaching hit people with an inner thud—it was "a new kind of teaching," a teaching that was interpretation of lived-out life. It was a teaching you could not argue with, as with a verbal proposition; it was fact you had to accept or reject. And those who did reject it knew it was to their doom. The evil spirits felt this reality too and they obeyed—often reluctantly, but they obeyed.

Dear Redeemer, Thy authority reaches to the world of evil spirits. Then it will reach to my inner world too. Thou canst command where I cannot command—the subconscious. Speak the authoritative word there and make me free—conscious and subconscious. Amen.

AFFIRMATION FOR THE DAY: *I will accept no backing save the backing of Reality.*

Acts 4:13, 14 Week 24—WEDNESDAY

"TELL JOHN WHAT YOU HAVE SEEN AND HEARD"

Here is another important word regarding the nature of the Gospel. John sent messengers with this inquiry:

"Are you the one who is to come, or are we to expect some other?" There and then he cured many sufferers from diseases, plagues, and evil spirits; and on many blind people he bestowed sight. Then he gave them this answer: "Go," he said, "and tell John what you have seen and heard: how the blind recover their sight, the lame walk, the lepers are clean, the deaf hear, the dead are raised to life, the poor are hearing the good news—and happy is the man who does not find me a stumbling-block" (Luke 7:18-23 NEB).

Here we come to a vital issue: What is the nature of the evidences for the truth of the Christian faith? We have in Christian theology a branch called "apologetics." The dictionary says: "Apologetics—systematic argumentative discourse in defense, esp. of the divine origin and authority of Christianity." That definition is taken out of a conception of Christianity as the Word become word. But it does not fit the conception Jesus had—His was that evidence was the Word become flesh. "Tell John what you have seen and heard." Note, it was "seen" first. The sight was redeemed people—redeemed from disease and demonic domination and from inner conflicts and guilts. The evidence was redeemed people. The evidence for Christianity is the Christian. "The poor are hearing the good news"—that "poor" meant the materially poor, but it embraced the poor rich—rich in goods and poor in inner resources—the empty.

Elijah on Mount Carmel said, "The God that answers by fire, let Him be God"—the God that answers by a sign and wonder, a portent. We would now say, "The God that answers by healed, changed men, let Him be God." The evidence is a person, not a proposition, not a verbal argument, but a vital alteration—something you have "seen." The evidence for Christianity is not found on Mars Hill where they debated new ideas, but in the marketplace where new men are "seen."

O Savior, Thou dost save. The evidence for Thy salvation is not a true proposition but a true Christian. Make me that kind of evidence today. When they have "seen," may they say "Now we have seen and heard"—it works and is at work. In Thy Name. Amen.

AFFIRMATION FOR THE DAY: *May my evidence for the Christian faith be me—a changed me.*

183

AMAZING: "HAPPY IS THE MAN WHO IS REPELLED BY NOTHING IN ME"

We pause for an additional comment on yesterday's passage: "And happy is the man who does not find me a stumbling block," or as Moffatt puts it, "who is repelled by nothing in me," or, "who finds nothing in me by which he is offended" (Luke 7:23). That is amazing. We usually think the other way round: "Blessed am I if people find nothing to be offended by in me." Here He says the opposite: "Blessed are you if you find nothing in me regarding which you can take exception." For I am the Standard, and if you fit that Standard you are a blessed and happy person. Here is supreme arrogance or supreme authority speaking. And the ages have decided that it is supreme authority, for every departure from Him turns out badly—always has and always will.

A passage along the same line is this one: "Then turning to the disciples he said privately, 'Blessed are the eyes which see what you see! For I tell you that many prophets and kings desired to see what you see, and did not see it, and to hear what you hear, and did not hear it' " (Luke 10:23, 24). Here He says that your eyes are blessed to see what you see. Your eyes have looked on the desire of the ages! We can say the same to ourselves. I do! I say to my eyes, "You are blessed eyes—you have looked on your Redeemer." And to my feet, "You are blessed for you have walked with Him for sixty years and have never found a misstep in Him." And to my heart, "You are blessed for you have known a love that does not disappoint." And to my whole being, "You are blessed, for you have given yourself to One who knows you absolutely and yet loves you completely." And I can say to the future, "Blessed are you, for you hold Him and I cannot drift beyond His care. I don't know what the future holds, but I know who holds the future." Blessed be life, for He makes it blessed! Everything is blessed, for He is Everything. Everything is blessed when it is seen and held in Him.

O Jesus, my Everything, I hug myself in gratitude that I had sense enough to open to Thee when Thou didst knock and wisdom enough to see amid the fog of things that this is It! My only regret is that I haven't walked in all the Light I've seen. Forgive me. Amen.

AFFIRMATION FOR THE DAY: *May no one be repelled by anything they see in me today!*

TEACH THE WORD, OR BE THE WORD?

We come now to an incident which was crucial—the coming of the Greeks:

They went to Philip . . . and appealed to him, saying, "Sir, we want to see Jesus." . . . And Jesus answered, "The hour has come for the Son of man to be glorified. Truly, truly I tell you, unless a grain of wheat falls into the earth and dies, it remains a single grain; but if it dies, it bears rich fruit. He who loves his life loses it, and he who cares not for his life in this world will preserve it for eternal life. . . . *My soul is now disquieted.* What am I to say? 'Father, save me from this hour'? Nay, it is something else that has brought me to this hour: I will say, 'Father, glorify Thy name.' " Then came a voice from heaven, "I have glorified it, and I will glorify it again." . . . "Now is this world to be judged; now shall the Prince of this world be expelled. But I, when I am lifted up from the earth, will draw all men to myself" (John 12:20-32 Moffatt).

Why this commotion in the soul of Jesus over the coming of the Greeks? This was obviously a real life crisis. Was it not this? The Greeks seeing the impending storm about to break upon the head of Jesus came to invite Him to come to Greece and be their teacher. "You can put your message into the center of the world's thought—Athens—and from there it can spread throughout the world. The Greeks are responsive and will accept your teaching. The Jews are narrow and rebellious. Come to Greece and be our honored and loved Teacher." The issue was: Athens or Jerusalem? Athens, an honored Teacher; Jerusalem, a crucified Redeemer. The one was the Word become word; the other the Word become flesh.

He stated the issue: "Unless a grain of wheat falls into the earth and dies, it remains a single grain; but if it dies, it bears rich fruit." "You ask me to be the Word become Word—a teacher; I must be the Word become flesh—a Redeemer."

O Jesus, Thou dost here go through the temptation that we all go through who begin to follow Thee: Shall I proclaim the Word, or shall I be the word? Shall I withdraw myself and be a single grain, or sow myself and die? Jesus, save me from this temptation. Amen.

AFFIRMATION FOR THE DAY: *The issue: Shall I be the saved grain, abiding by itself alone, or the sown grain, bearing much fruit?*

SAVED FROM, OR SAVED THROUGH?

We continue yesterday's meditation. The issue: Shall it be Athens—the Word become word, or Jerusalem—the Word become flesh? Shall I go to Athens and live long and teach, or shall I go to Jerusalem and live briefly and sow myself upon a hill and die to redeem?

No wonder He said, "Now is my soul disquieted." And no wonder He asked, "What am I to say? Father, save me from this hour?" For the most part Christendom has said just that—"Save from," not, "Save through." For Christendom has said Athens instead of Jerusalem. The Christian faith has been turned into something to be taught, something to be preached from pulpits—the word become word—a philosophy, a moralism. Not the Word become flesh—something to be embodied, acted on, died for. We have asked that the Kingdom come *through,* us, not *as* us.

So we have turned the Gospel into a verbalism—something to be mentally accepted, instead of a vitalism—something to be embodied and died for in our Jerusalem. And because we have taken the verbal instead of the vital we are not able to say, "Now is this world to be judged; now is the Prince of this world expelled." We lack moral and spiritual authority, for our authority is verbal, as our Gospel is verbal. And the prince of this world sits tight at the center of world authority.

And our Gospel lacks not only expelling power—it also lacks compelling power. "But I, when I am lifted up from the earth will draw all men unto myself." Athens without a cross is Athens, a final ruin—a museum piece. But this Man on His cross is the magnet drawing all men to Himself—the center of Power. But we, choosing Athens, are centers of powwow.

O Lord Jesus, every day is a day of decision between the easy Athens way or the hard Jerusalem way. Save us from asking that we be saved from. Help us to ask that we be matched against this hour. In Thy dear Name. Amen.

AFFIRMATION FOR THE DAY: *In every decision there is hidden this issue: the broad, easy way, or the straight and narrow way.*

"YOUR LORD AND TEACHER"

We note an order of statement which is very important: "When he had washed their feet, and taken his garments, and resumed his place, he said to them, 'Do you know what I have done to you? You call me Teacher and Lord; and you are right, for so I am. If I then, your Lord and Teacher, have washed your feet, you also ought to wash one another's feet. For I have given you an example, that you should do as I have done to you'" (John 13:12-15).

This correction He made has far-reaching influence: "You call me Teacher and Lord; and you are right, for so I am. If I then, your Lord and Teacher. . . ." Why did He reverse that order? The destiny of His movement hung upon that order. Would His impact be primarily that of a Teacher and secondarily a Lord? Or would it be primarily Lord and secondarily a Teacher? If His order—first Lord and then Teacher—then the Gospel is something to be obeyed, then understood. But if it is the disciples' order—first Teacher, then Lord—then the Gospel is something to be understood then obeyed. On the face of it the latter seems sensible. But only on the face of it, for Jesus was profoundly right—it is first Lord and then Teacher—first obey and then you will understand. For the fact is that you know only as much as you are willing to practice: "If any man's will is to do his will, he shall know whether the teaching is from God or whether I am speaking on my own authority" (John 7:17). Here the order is that if you are willing to do the will of God you shall know. But you cannot know if you are not willing to do. So knowledge is through obedience. We know as much as we are willing to practice and no more. The modern dictum of "learning by doing" is in line with this. But modern religious education is out of line: "Know and then you will do." The Word has to become flesh or it will not even be the word.

Dear Lord and Savior, we thank Thee for Thy saving us from the barren intellectualism that makes itself the end. Help us to be willing to do so we can know. For "this is life eternal that we may know Thee"—as Lord first and foremost. Amen.

AFFIRMATION FOR THE DAY: *It is easier to act yourself into right thinking than to think yourself into right acting.*

"DO THAT AND YOU WILL LIVE"

A very telling passage on the Word become flesh is this one: "A lawyer came forward to put this test question to him: 'Master, what must I do to inherit eternal life?' Jesus said, 'What is written in the Law? What is your reading of it? He replied, 'Love the Lord your God with all your heart, and all your soul, with all your strength, and with all your mind; and your neighbor as yourself.' 'That is the right answer,' said Jesus, 'do that and you will live'·" (Luke 10:25-28 NEB).

Note that Jesus did not say, "Believe that and you will live." He did say, "Do that and you will live." The belief had to become an act, or it wouldn't remain a belief. Your creed is what you believe in enough to act upon. So your creed is your deed.

And then comes the vivid illustration of love becoming flesh in the parable of the Good Samaritan. The priest and the Levite were both religious. They would have both said, "We believe every word of the Law." But it was the word of belief become word. They were both probably on religious missions—on missions where they would interpret the Law, verbally. But they were too busy with the verbalism to respond to human need—they fulfilled the letter of the Law, but not the life of the Law. So they both stand forever as symbols of barren, unrelated religion. The Samaritan is now nearly always called "The Good Samaritan," though in the parable he is just "a Samaritan"—the ages have judged him "good." For he was the Word of love become flesh. The other two were the word of love become word. And the ages have judged the word become flesh "good," and the word become word "bad." That silent judgment is going on, and that is the reason the Christian faith, embodied in Jesus, the Word became flesh, will be chosen as a world choice and the Word became word rejected. It is inevitable.

O Lord and Savior, we thank Thee that the final judgment of acceptance will fall on Thee. It is slowly but surely taking place. For it is in the destiny of things. Men are choosing and they are choosing Thee. If not, they choose their doom. Blessed Redeemer. Amen.

AFFIRMATION FOR THE DAY: *Verbalism says: "Believe this and you will live", vitalism says: "Believe and do this and you will live."*

THE WORD BECAME OUTER PORTENT

We now turn back and look at the temptation in the wilderness in the light of our study. It stands out as a master strategy on the part of the Adversary—it was an attempt to get Jesus to adopt the Word become word—not the Word become flesh. He resisted the temptation; we have fallen into it. It did not succeed with Him—it has succeeded with us.

The Tempter said when He was hungry, "If you are the Son of God, tell these stones to become bread." The proof of His being the Son of God would be that He could perform miracles—turn bread into stones. That is the Word become miracle. The second said, "If you are the Son of God throw yourself down" from the pinnacle of the temple. This was the Word become presumption, making God toe the line. The third said, after showing Jesus the kingdoms of the world, "All these I will give you, if you will only fall down and do me homage." This is the Word become worldly wisdom—get to your ends by any method, or means.

Not one of these suggested the Word become flesh. For if the Tempter had suggested that, it would not have been a temptation—it would have been fulfillment.

Jesus went straight from the wilderness to the little synagogue and announced His program:

> The spirit of the Lord is upon me . . .
> To announce good news . . . ,
> To proclaim release . . . recovery of sight . . . ;
> To let the broken victims go free,
> To proclaim the year of the Lord's favour.

And then after rolling up the scroll, He said: "Today, in your very hearing this text has come true" (Luke 4:18-21 NEB). In other words, "This word of Scripture has become flesh. The program is in me and not in outer dazzling miracles which startle, but do not save." The choice was made. If Jesus had succumbed to the temptation to make the Word become word, we would never have heard of Him again.

O Lord, Savior, Thy steps did not falter. Thy heart was true. So we cannot forget Thee. And the kingdoms of the world will become the Kingdom of our Lord and Savior just because Thou wouldst not try to get them by wrong means. We thank Thee. Amen.

AFFIRMATION FOR THE DAY: *Wrong means will get me to wrong ends—inevitably.*

DELEGATED AUTHORITY, OR AUTHORITY WON?

According to Matthew, the last temptation which the Tempter presented to Jesus was this, after showing Him the kingdoms of the world: "To you I will give all this authority and their glory; for it has been delivered to me, and I give it to whom I will" (Luke 4:5, 6). The authority was to be granted from the outside by the will of another—"I will give it to whom I will." That was a delegated authority—it was the word of authority become word—it was not authority won from within, not the Word become flesh.

That was rejected. Then this at the very end of Jesus' life: "Full authority in heaven and on earth has been committed to me" (Matt. 28:18 NEB). This "authority" included heaven as well as earth—it was universal. That kind of authority could not be delegated—it had to be inherent, from within. It could not be the word of authority become word—someone else's word, even God's word. It had to become flesh, from within, or it wouldn't be authority.

Jesus won that authority by His alignment with the will of God and by His being what He was—it was both inherent and won, because of what He was and because of what He did. And because He was God and because He became man and obeyed all the laws of the universe, He therefore won the backing of those laws. The servant of all became the greatest of all. He lost His life and found it again. "Therefore God has highly exalted Him and bestowed on him the name which is above every name, that at the name of Jesus every knee should bow, in heaven and on earth and under the earth, and every tongue confess that Jesus Christ is Lord." This authority included heaven, earth, and under the earth—Satan's abode! He refused earthly authority and gained all worlds.

O Jesus Christ, Thou art Lord—Lord with a Lordship that is the Word of Lordship become flesh—it is real and not imposed. So we bow to that Lordship with a glad, free heart. In winning Thy Lordship Thou hast won us. We love Thee. Amen.

AFFIRMATION FOR THE DAY: *I will not ask that authority be given me, but will ask for an opportunity to earn authority.*

"WHO CAN PRODUCE FROM HIS STORE"

Another telling passage: "When, therefore, a teacher of the law"—the Word become word—"has become a learner in the kingdom of Heaven"—the Word become flesh—"he is like a householder who can produce from his store"—from within himself, from the Word become flesh—"both the new and the old" (Matt. 13:52 NEB).

This is penetrating: "A teacher of the law"—a scribe, who merely quoted what others wrote, a dry-as-dust teacher of written law, now becomes "a learner" or "disciple to the kingdom of God" (Moffatt), or "trained for the kingdom of God (RSV) becomes committed to the kingdom of God, so becomes vital. He can "produce from his store." He is not quoting from others—He has something within and can produce from his own store. He is creative. He is the Word become flesh. That is transformation—the quoter becomes the creator.

This is what the transition from the Word become word to the Word become flesh produces. It turns the non-creative into the creative. "Life for me began at seventy-two," said an Anglican bishop in India. Up to seventy-two he had been a dry-as-dust ecclesiast, quoting the past, its rules and regulations, and living in that quoted past. He was an ecclesiastical mummy, bound by the graveclothes of yesterday. Then he made his surrender to Christ—the Word became flesh. Now he was creative. He did more in the next ten years than in the previous seventy-two.

This new man "trained for the Kingdom of God" now produces "from his store"—from the depths of his sub-conscious "both the new and old." He doesn't repudiate the old—he makes it alive in the present. But his primary emphasis is on the new—the new is first. He is primarily a voice, not an echo.

O Jesus, if I've been a quoter instead of a creator, forgive me. But not only forgive me—fire me with the kingdom. May it absorb me, possess me. In vital contact with the Creative make me creative. In Thy Name, Amen.

AFFIRMATION FOR THE DAY: *"The kingdom of heaven is within you," therefore, I have an abundant store for everything I need.*

FAITH THAT RIGHT ENDS WITH RIGHT MEANS
WILL BRING RIGHT RESULTS

As we draw near the halfway point in our study of the Word become flesh, primarily in the Scriptures, we now give a passage which sums up everything we have been saying: "And yet God's wisdom is proved right by its results" (Matt. 11:19 NEB).

This passage is an important conclusion—put the supposed wisdom under life and see if it is proved right by its results. If it is right, it will have right results; if it is wrong, it will have wrong results. In other words you cannot prove a thing by a syllogism—that would be the Word become word. It must be put under life to see what life will do to it. If it is wisdom, wise results will follow. This is the Word of wisdom become flesh, and when it becomes flesh then it verifies itself as wisdom by being lived out, and thus producing wise results.

The outcome is the criterion. This is a courageous statement of belief that the whole universe of reality is behind the word of wisdom become flesh. Put it under life and right results will follow. In other words, wisdom with right means will bring right results. This is a supreme faith that the sum total of reality is behind the Way, and the sum total of reality is against not-the-Way.

Test it, put it under life, says Jesus, and, as sure as sure it will turn out right, will bring right results. And everybody who has ever tried it has come to the conclusion that it works. If, as we have quoted, "All things betray thee who betrayeth Me," then conversely, "All things back thee who backeth Me." Life is behind Life. It is a dependable universe and can be depended on to bring right results if the thing itself is right.

O blessed Redeemer, we thank Thee for this assurance. For we need to know that if we sow ourselves as grain in Thy will, rich fruit will follow, maybe not today or tomorrow, but the third day, yes! We thank Thee, thank Thee. Amen.

AFFIRMATION FOR THE DAY: *I should not ask about results. I should ask only if my ends and my means are right.*

"THE GOOD SEED MEANS THE SONS OF
THE KINGDOM"

We are on the last day of the halfway week in our quest, and we sum up our studies with two passages: "Hear then the parable of the sower. When one hears the word of the kingdom . . ." (Matt. 13:18, 19). "He who sows the good seed is the Son of man; the field is the world, and the good seed means the sons of the kingdom" (Matt. 13:37, 38). Note in one place "the word of the kingdom" is the "seed"; in the other "the sons of the kingdom" are the "seed." In one place it seems that a verbal proclaiming of the word of the Kingdom is the seed, and in the other the Word of the Kingdom has become flesh in the sons of the Kingdom. The sons are the seed.

So I do not sow a message apart from myself—I must be the message, embodied. Proclaiming a message apart from experience is the Word become word. It must be out of experience if it is to be the authentic Christian message. It must be the sharing of a fact operative within me if it is to be Christian.

Then "preaching the Word" is not preaching words out of the Bible—it is preaching the Word become flesh in Jesus and the Word become flesh in the proclaimer.

A theological student was troubled that he was proclaiming something not operative within himself. But he said he was comforted and relieved when he took a course in a theology which said that proclaiming the Word had nothing to do with yourself, that it was proclaiming the Word entirely apart from yourself—it was from the Bible to people and not mediated through one's own experience. Yes, he was "comforted and relieved," but it was apart from salvation, for it was apart from the Christian faith—it was the Word become word and not the Word become flesh.

O Lord Jesus, sow my life as seed. I consent to be buried in the furrows of Thy will and purpose. I am ready to die. For I know that I won't really die—I shall live. For Thy resurrection power will live within me. I thank Thee. Amen.

AFFIRMATION FOR THE DAY: *I am a son of the Kingdom, therefore seed to be sown anywhere He wills.*

THE WORD CONTINUES TO BE FLESH

We have now begun on the second half of our year's pilgrimage and we also begin on the second part of our study of the Word become flesh. We have looked at this Word become flesh as revealed in the four Gospels, in Jesus the Person. Did it stop there with Him? Is this Word become flesh a once-and-for-all event, never repeated? Or is it a continuing principle inherent in the Christian faith? Does it pass over into the lives of the followers of Jesus as continuing fact? Did they become the Word become flesh? Imperfectly, of course, but nevertheless, was it the Divine Intention that they be a continuing incarnation of the life and spirit of Jesus? And did that happen? And does it happen now when we are in line with the reality of the Christian faith?

I am persuaded that the Word became flesh is not only an event in time of Jesus—it is a continuing principle—a fact that is inherent in the Christian faith. And this is seen and realized in the coming of the Holy Spirit. The coming of the Holy Spirit was the Word become flesh in receptive and obedient believers. Here the historical passed into the experimental. The Word became flesh, not only in "the body of Christ"—the church—but in the bodies of believers as individuals and persons. There was a collective manifestation of the Word become flesh in the new community and an individual manifestation in the new person.

The pattern of the Word become flesh was fixed in Jesus—in His character and life, and that forever fixes for us our type of reproduction of the Word become flesh—it will be Christlike character and life. Nothing higher in heaven and on earth. This is It! The transition from the pattern to the reproduction was through the coming of the Holy Spirit—the most important event in human history.

O Jesus Lord, Thou didst come and didst provide for Thy deeper coming within us by the coming of the Holy Spirit. In the Holy Spirit we are in the line of succession of the Word became flesh. May that be in me today in thought, word, and deed. Amen.

AFFIRMATION FOR THE DAY: *In some real way I shall be an extension of the Incarnation.*

THE HOLY SPIRIT IS THE SUCCESSOR OF JESUS

We saw yesterday that the link between the Word become flesh—Jesus—and the Word become flesh in the disciples was and is the Holy Spirit. Jesus provided for no successor except the Holy Spirit. By the very nature of things the successor of Jesus had to be a divine successor. To appoint a human successor, a collection of human beings, or a church as the successor would spoil the whole thing. So when it was taught in a New York cathedral that the Roman Catholic Church, as the successor of Christ, "is really Christ on earth," we shudder. We know it is blasphemy. The first great temptation of the Tempter was, "Ye shall be like God," and man fell into it—tried to be God and became corrupted man. The second great temptation of the Tempter was to the Church: "Ye shall be Christ," and the church fell for it and became a corrupted institution.

"Nevertheless I tell you the truth: it is to your advantage that I go away, for if I do not go away, the Counselor will not come to you; but if I go, I will send him to you. . . . When the Spirit of truth comes, he will guide you into all the truth; for he will not speak on his own authority, but whatever he hears he will speak, and he will declare to you the things that are to come. He will glorify me, for he will take what is mine and declare it to you" (John 16:17, 13-14). The Holy Spirit was to continue the work of Jesus—His Successor. But as a Successor who will not replace Jesus, but who will reveal Jesus and glorify Him. He will unfold what was infolded in Jesus. His revelation will not be different, but simply more of the same. For Jesus was the ultimate.

And this revelation of Jesus by the Holy Spirit was not to be from the outside—but from within. "I will pray the Father, and he will give you another Counselor, to be with you for ever, even the Spirit of truth . . . for he dwells with you, and will be in you" (John 14:16, 17). The Holy Spirit is the applied edge of redemption.

O Holy Spirit, reveal Jesus to me. For I thirst to know Him better, follow Him more perfectly, and to show Him more clearly. I have seen Him and my soul can be satisfied with nothing—absolutely nothing—other than Him. Teach me. I listen, I obey. Amen.

AFFIRMATION FOR THE DAY: *I can extend the Incarnation only as the Holy Spirit lives in me.*

THE HISTORICAL BECOMES THE EXPERIMENTAL

Luke was the one writer who chronicled for us the account of the Word become flesh in his Gospel, and then the Word become flesh in the Acts of the Apostles. The Word became flesh in Him, and then the Word became flesh in them. He saw and interpreted the connection, and it was not a literary connection—it was a life connection. The Acts was an extension of the Incarnation, of the Word become flesh. For if it had ended with Jesus, it would have ended. It had to be universalized or it wouldn't have been universal.

So Luke in the first five verses of Acts sums up what he had spread out through twenty-four chapters in his Gospel, and the five verses are these:

In the first book, O Theophilus, I have dealt with all that Jesus began to do and teach, until the day when he was taken up, after he had given commandment through the Holy Spirit to the apostles whom he had chosen. To them he presented himself alive after his passion by many proofs, appearing to them during forty days, and speaking of the kingdom of God. And while studying with them he charged them not to depart from Jerusalem, but to wait for the promise of the Father . . . you shall be baptized with the Holy Spirit (Acts 1:1-5).

These verses are the pivot upon which the Jesus of history becomes the Christ of experience—the historical becomes the experimental. And before Luke describes the fact of that transition, he pauses and sums up the essential facts involved in that redemptive impact.

The first was the Word become flesh—"all that Jesus began." The Gospel begins with Jesus, the Incarnate. If you don't begin with Jesus you don't begin—you don't begin anything except roads with dead ends. We know little or nothing about God, and what we know is wrong, unless you begin with Jesus. If you do not see God in the face of Jesus, you see something other than God—and different.

O Lord Jesus, Thou art the express image of the Father, and unless we see the Father in and through Thee, the Son, we see a caricature. We can be satisfied with no caricature—we want to see the Father. We thank Thee that we do—in Thee. Amen.

AFFIRMATION FOR THE DAY: *If the Historical became the Experimental in the Apostles, am I not an apostle, one sent?*

FIRST A DEED THEN A DESCRIPTION

We are looking at Luke's summing up of the Divine Redemptive Impact in the Word become flesh.

We saw that the Gospel begins with the Person—Jesus. He didn't come to bring the good news—He was the Good News. The Gospel lies in His Person.

This Gospel does not begin with a philosophy about life, nor a moralism to regulate life—it was a revelation of Life itself. "I am . . . the Life." He is the revelation of Reality. He uncovered the nature of Being. And when He does, it is so beautiful that we want to be like that Being. If we don't, we cease to be—we wither into non-being; we perish.

And this revelation of Life was not a description of Life—it was a demonstration of Life. "Of all that Jesus began to do and teach." It was first a deed, then a description—He "began to do"—a deed and then "teach"—a description. We reverse this; we begin to teach and then hope that our doing will catch up with our teaching. A student said to a famous theologian, "Dr. N., you are always saying that all human doing is touched and corrupted by human pride. We find you an illustration of that, for you are full of pride yourself—proud that you can expose human pride." And the theologian replied: "I am the illustration of that pride, not its cure." But it was different with Jesus—He taught out of His doing. His teaching was an interpretation of His doing. Everything He taught was operative within Himself. A Hindu was impressed by this difference and said, "We are glad to hear about a Man who illustrated what He said." In Jesus you can't tell where His words end and His deeds begin and where His deeds begin and His words end, for His deeds were words and His words were deeds. They were one and a part of one Reality. So His teaching was sunlight—firsthand, not moonlight—secondhand. You don't argue with Him. He commands and you either obey, or go away—sadly.

O Jesus, Savior and Lord, Thou art not a Divine Signpost pointing the way. Thou art the Way, for Thou art walking the Way ahead of us. So we follow—gladly, for we see the outcome and the end—in Thee. How wonderful Thou art. Amen.

AFFIRMATION FOR THE DAY: *May the order be for me this day: Do and teach.*

"ALL THAT JESUS BEGAN"

We are studying Luke's opening statement in the Acts about the Word become flesh. "All that Jesus began." This is important, for it means that the Word becoming flesh in a given point of time was not a closed chapter. It was a beginning: "All that Jesus began." If it were a closed episode in human history, then that changes the nature of the Christian faith. It is a recollection, not a realization; it is historical, but not experimental. It would be something to ponder, but not to practice.

But the statement that it was something He "began" implies that He was beginning an amazing possibility. This new Life of His would be a redemptive reinforcement open to all men. It was the opening of an Era. A young man in Latin America, hearing for the first time about the new creation, and the new birth, said in astonishment, "When did this new creation begin?" It sounded too good to be true—a new beginning, a new birth! A new and astonishing possibility had come into life. Well, it began with Jesus and was imparted to everyone who came into contact with Him—saving contact. "Now when they saw the boldness of Peter and John, and perceived that they were uneducated, common men, they wondered; and they recognized that they had been with Jesus" (Acts 4:13). This New Life was capable of being imparted into life. It was contagious and communicable. Had it failed at this place, it would have failed. And Jesus would have been a religious mummy embalmed in history. A Greek saint, Sister Lila, and a Hindu doctor toured the sites of famous Gurus in India and came back with this report: "It is the twilight of the Gurus. They have failed their devotees. They are non-contagious. They are revered but not realized. They haven't what it takes—contagion." But Jesus did have it. He did greater things in His followers and through them than He had done Himself alone.

O Jesus Lord, we thank Thee that we do not merely remember Thee; we realize Thee. We are in line, direct and immediate, with the most Redemptive Fact of the universe. That Fact is a fact within us. We thank Thee. Amen.

AFFIRMATION FOR THE DAY: *If Jesus' life was just a beginning, then my life, at whatever age, is just a beginning.*

"SOMEONE HAD TO SUFFER TO REDEEM ME"

We saw yesterday that the Word became Continuous. The Incarnation became reincarnation in His followers. They never became Christs. There would be only one Christ, but they partook of His life, carried on His work, and were filled with His Spirit. He was not merely with them as a recollection—He was in them as a realization. The bridge was made between the Word become flesh and the Word become flesh in other flesh.

We came to the next step: The Word became Sacrifice—"after his death" (vs. 3). It was not enough that the Word become flesh, that the Word became guidance, became continuous—the Word had to redeem us. And there was no way for the Word to redeem us except to die for us. For when that Love came in contact with our sin, it crimsoned into sacrifice. For whenever love meets sin in the loved one—it bleeds. A young woman was an alcoholic. Her father, a doctor, began a fast unto death. I saw her after this had happened. She was changed. Alcohol was gone. I asked her how it happened! "Someone had to suffer to redeem me!" she replied.

We spoke of something unique in Holland: The chimes of a church were in a cross! The chimes of redemption's song can only come from a cross. Apart from a cross there is no song—no redemption song. The heart refuses to sing unless it can sing the song of redemption, of forgiveness, of reconciliation. I once had a canary that would not sing until it had its bath. Then it would sing deliriously. My soul is like that—it refuses to sing unless it is washed from guilt, conflict. And yours too! The "Song of Moses" is good—the song of deliverance from outer bondage; but the "Song of the Lamb" is better, for it sings of deliverance from inner bondage and outer habit. It sings of total freedom—it sings of freedom.

O Lord Jesus, Lamb of God that taketh away the sins of the world, redeem our surrendered souls from every chain and every strand of bondage. We bring nothing in our hands to buy it. Simply to Thy cross we cling—we receive it by grace. Amen.

AFFIRMATION FOR THE DAY: *If I am redeemed by blood, then this redemption must get into my blood.*

"HE PRESENTED HIMSELF ALIVE"

We continue to look at the summing up of Luke in Acts 1:1-5 of the whole of the Divine Impact. Yesterday we saw the Word became Sacrificial at the cross. We now look at "the Word become alive"—"To them he presented himself alive after his passion" (vs. 3). God's last word is not the cross—it is the Resurrection. The Resurrection is God's seal of approval on the Cross. It is God saying: "Well done, come up higher." And He went to the right hand of final power.

Without the resurrection of Jesus we would come out at the place of Dr. Schweitzer's conclusion: Jesus expected the kingdom to come at Jerusalem. It didn't come. "Jesus therefore died of a broken heart on the cross. 'My God, my God, why hast Thou forsaken me?' His dream collapsed, but He left an ethic of love to live by." And that is all. If that were all, then the Christian faith is the Word become word—the word of promise unfulfilled, the word of final victory become the word of final defeat. If so, then there is no Word of Victory become flesh.

But with the Resurrection the Word of Victory is flesh. It is not a Word of Victory become promise, but the Word of Victory become performance.

A Muslim Moulvi was questioning a Christian preacher in a bazaar in India and said: "Padre Sahib, we have a proof in our faith which you haven't in yours. When we go to Medina we can find the tomb of Mohammed, but when you go to Jerusalem you cannot be sure of the tomb of Jesus. So we have a proof that you haven't." "Yes," replied the preacher, "we have no tomb in our faith because we have no corpse." Of a certain swami it was said that after his death his body remained intact, free from decay for several days. But it decayed! Of Jesus it was said: "Thou will not suffer Thy Holy One to see corruption." "He showed Himself alive."

O Lord Jesus, I thank Thee for the embodied victory—not the embalmed victory. Everybody else's victory ends with the grave—Thine really begins there. The grave is the beginning, not the end with Thee. Now the Victory has nail-pierced hands! Amen.

AFFIRMATION FOR THE DAY: *Today in every situation I shall present myself alive—alive with light and life.*

"UNTIL THE DAY WHEN HE WAS TAKEN UP"

We continue this week to look at the outstanding elements of the Divine Impact. We saw yesterday that the Word became Alive. But suppose the Word had become alive in that particular situation and suppose the Victory had been a local victory in a local situation and suppose He had been finally taken by death—would that have been the answer? It would have been interesting, but irrelevant. It would have belonged to the past, but not to the present and the future. The next step covers that—"until the day when he was taken up" (Acts 1:2). He was "taken up," and Peter explains what that "taken up" meant: "This Jesus God raised up, and of that we are all witnesses. Being therefore exalted at the right hand of God, and having received from the Father the promise of the Holy Spirit, he has poured out this which you see and hear" (Acts 2:32, 33). So the Word became Final Authority and Final Power.

It was not enough for the Word to rise from the dead. The rising from the dead in a particular situation must have cosmic significance. It has. A nail-pierced hand holds the scepter of the Universe. Goodness—Sacrificial Goodness—is at the place of Final Authority and will have the last word in human affairs; whoever has the first or the intermediate word, he has the last word. He is "the Alpha"—the Christ of the Beginning; He is also "the Omega," the Christ of the final word.

This is not only Good News—it is Universal Good News. Were He not at the place of Final Authority this could not have been said: "Therefore God has highly exalted him and bestowed on him the name which is above every name, that at the name of Jesus every knee should bow, in heaven and on earth and under the earth, and every tongue confess that Jesus Christ is Lord, to the glory of God the Father" (Phil. 2:9-11). This is sweeping—"every knee should bow . . . every tongue confess." And we may add: "And everything made shall acknowledge its Maker"—Jesus is Lord!

O Jesus, Thou art Lord! Men are not acknowledging it; but if they don't, life goes badly. But with Thee as Lord life goes singing down the years. If we do not confess Thee as Lord we have to confess ourselves as beaten. We thank Thee. Amen.

AFFIRMATION FOR THE DAY: *I rule in His ruling; He invites me to His Throne!*

"GIVEN COMMANDMENT THROUGH
THE HOLY SPIRIT"

We are looking at the next Divine Impact. We saw that the Word became Final—final authority, power. There is another step: The Word became Within. "After he had given commandment through the Holy Spirit to the apostles" (Acts 1:2). "And while staying with them he charged them not to depart from Jerusalem, but to wait for the promise of the Father, which, he said, 'you heard from me, for John baptized with water, but before many days you shall be baptized with the Holy Spirit' " (Acts 1:4, 5). Up to this point in our study of the Word become flesh it has all been on the outside—in history. Here at this step the Word becomes Within. Note: "After he had given commandment through the Holy Spirit." The commandments were from this time on from within —"through the Holy Spirit." The authority over us was being transferred from the without to the within.

And that is important. For authority to be real authority must come from within. As long as authority is from without, not identified with us, it cannot be real authority. It must speak from within if it is to be final authority. As long as authority is from without, it is autocracy. When it is within, it is autocracy with autonomy—a blending of the two.

This is most amazing. When Jesus comes to final authority at the right hand of the Father, He deliberately chooses to exercise it from within. That means that He speaks from within and awaits our inner consent before it becomes manifest as final lordship. For Divine Wisdom knows that only as we willingly and gladly consent to cooperate with the Word, will that Word become flesh in us. If we are only governed from without, we are not governed—we are coerced. Only when the government is identified with us by consent is it the government of free men. What a Lord!

O Jesus Lord, we stand amazed at the humility of Thy authority. Thou art not willing to exercise it from without entirely; only from within dost Thou rule in Thy final rule. We are at the feet of such Humility—the Word of Humility become flesh. Amen.

AFFIRMATION FOR THE DAY: *Jesus does not govern me by bluster, nor by blister—He does it quietly and calmly from within.*

"TAUGHT THEM ABOUT THE KINGDOM OF GOD"

We come to our last item in the Divine Impact. The Word became Total Program: "Over a period of forty days he appeared to them and taught them about the kingdom of God" (Acts 1:3 NEB). This is the climax. He was not out merely to come and dwell within individuals and rule them from within; He is a total Redeemer of the total life—individual and collective. The Kingdom of God is God's total answer to man's total need.

This emphasis of the Kingdom was Jesus' first emphasis, and now it was the last. "And he went about all Galilee, teaching in their synagogues and preaching the gospel of the kingdom" (Matt. 4:23). "The gospel of the kingdom" is the only thing He ever called His gospel. And now it was His final emphasis.

The Kingdom was important. It was the overall and in-all framework of the movement Jesus was inaugurating. He began by saying, "Repent for the Kingdom of heaven is at hand." Repentance was in the framework of the Kingdom. You were not to repent because you will get to heaven, or escape hell, or to join a group—the Church, but repentance was in reference to the Kingdom. The Kingdom was the ultimate order with the ultimate claim upon the follower of Jesus. "Seek first the kingdom of God and His righteousness and all these things will be added unto you." You were not to seek first heaven, nor the Church, nor correct faith in creeds—you were to seek first the Kingdom—all else subsidiary to it. A motto on our Ashram walls at Sal Tat, India, says,

> Nothing above the Kingdom,
> Nothing outside the Kingdom,
> Nothing against the Kingdom,
> Nothing less than the Kingdom,
> Everything within the Kingdom.

An Indian doctor came to me to surrender himself to Christ. He said, "As the ship was leaving Hong Kong a non-Christian Parsee called to me from the dock: 'Seek first the Kingdom of God.' That has haunted me. I want to make my surrender." He did.

O Jesus Lord of the Kingdom, we have tried to take Thee, the King, without the Kingdom. And we are in danger of losing both. Save us—save us to Thy Kingdom. For without Thy total reign we are in total ruin. Save us, we perish. Amen.

AFFIRMATION FOR THE DAY: *I come into a Kingdom which is total in meaning and total in possession.*

EIGHT STEPS IN THE DIVINE IMPACT

We recapitulate the elements in the Divine Impact:

1. The Word became flesh: "I have dealt with all that Jesus began" (Acts 1:1). The Gospel begins with Jesus, the Incarnate, the Particular, not with Christ, the universal. You cannot get to the universal except through the particular. When you want to jump to the universal without any particular, you find a contentless universal. The only content in that universal is the one you read into it, which is false.

2. The Word became Guidance: "All that Jesus began to do and teach . . ." (vs. 1). It was first "do" and then "teach"; His teaching was a revelation of His doing. He practiced before He preached, and His preaching was an unfolding of that practice. Therefore, His preaching was the Word become flesh.

3. The Word became Continuous: "All that Jesus began." His doing and teaching was not an end—it was a beginning. The Incarnation was to be continuous in His followers. The Word became flesh was to become flesh in them.

4. The Word became Redemptive: "After His passion . . ." (vs. 3). When this Word came into contact with human sin it crimsoned into sacrifice—the cross. Had the Gospel been a philosophy or a moralism, this would not have happened. But since the Gospel was a Person it bled.

5. The Word became alive: "He presented Himself alive" (vs. 3). The Word was alive when it came into contact with human sin, and it was more alive after the offering of Himself at the cross.

6. The Word became Final Power: "Until the day He was taken up . . ." (vs. 2). This man on a cross becomes the Son of Man on a throne of final authority—at the right hand of God.

7. The Word becomes Within: "Given commandment through the Holy Spirit . . . you shall be baptized with the Holy Spirit" (vss. 2, 5). The Word becomes authority within.

8. The Word becomes Total Program: "[He] taught them about the kingdom of God" (Acts 1:3 NEB). A total answer to the total need.

O Lord Jesus, we thank Thee for this Divine Impact. It could not be more wonderful or more complete. It takes in everything and redeems everything. Are we grateful? Read the gratitude on our hearts. May we be the extension of the Word. Amen.

AFFIRMATION FOR THE DAY: *If God made these eight steps toward me, how many steps will I make toward Him today?*

"A RESOLUTIONARY CONFERENCE"

We have seen Luke's amazing summing up of the essential elements in the Word become flesh Impact and we now turn to implementation of that Impact. It is revealed in the Acts of the Apostles.

Note that it is called "The *Acts* of the Apostles." Had the Gospel been a philosophy or a moralism, the title would have been "The Teaching of the Apostles." It would have been the Word become word. But because the Gospel is the Word become flesh the transition of the Gospel from Him to them is by its very nature, "The *Acts* of the Apostles." Because the Gospel was a Deed in Him, it became deeds in them. They interpreted the Deed in Him and the deeds in themselves, and the result was not merely a revelation but a revolution. They turned that ancient "world upside down."

But the tendency was then, and is now, to turn the Gospel of the Word become flesh into a Word become word. So in the third century there appeared "A Teaching of the Twelve." The "Acts" had become a "Teaching"—a dogma instead of a deed. This substitution of the creed for the deed has turned Christianity into something to be believed instead of something to be acted on.

I have come to believe that the excoriation of the Scribes and Pharisees in Matthew 23 was the most cleansing wind that ever blew through the pages of any Scripture. It blew away the chaff of outwardism and left the wheat—which was little. It was redemptive—very. Someone describing a religious conference said, "It was a very resolutionary conference," but he meant "revolutionary"! Our conferences are resolutionary because they are based on verbal answers to verbal questions. So they are resolutionary and not revolutionary—the Word become word and not the Word become flesh. A little girl said, "I tell you, Dorothy, that the Bible does not end in Timothy, it ends in Revolutions." It does. And the Acts of the Apostles was the opening chapter of that Revolution. It is a continuing world Revolution.

O God, our Father, we thank Thee for this Revolution. It is revolutionizing us from darkness to light, from defeat to victory, from our self-idolatry to bowing the knee to Thee. We thank Thee for Thy Son. In His name. Amen.

AFFIRMATION FOR THE DAY: *The Gospel within me is one continuing revolution.*

THE ACTS OF THE CHRISTIANS

We saw yesterday that the link between the Word become flesh in Him and the Word become flesh in them was entitled "The *Acts* of the Apostles"—"The Acts" and not the Teaching. The teaching was an interpretation of the acting—the acts of Him and of them.

But another twist is given to turn this Acts of the Apostles into something to be contemplated instead of something to be emulated. It is made into the "Acts of the *Apostles*"—and the Apostles is confined to the Twelve. Originally it wasn't. Every disciple became an apostle—one taught became one sent. For instance, Paul says that "Andronicus and Junias . . . are eminent among the apostles, and they were Christians before I was" (Rom. 16:7 NEB). They were "apostles," but they didn't belong to the "Twelve." And Paul was an apostle, but he didn't belong to the Twelve. He says, "Am I not an apostle? Have I not seen Jesus our Lord? Are not you my workmanship in the Lord? If to others I am not an apostle, at least I am to you; for you are the seal of my apostleship in the Lord" (I Cor. 9:1, 2). Here Paul's credentials were changed people—"*You* are the seal of my apostleship"; you are my credentials. Paul was more concerned over apostolic success than apostolic succession. Paul was not in that so-called line of apostolic succession. A layman, "Ananias a disciple," laid his hands on Paul that he might receive his sight and be filled with the Holy Spirit. A guide in Jerusalem was showing people around and said, "This hen is a direct descendant of the cock that crowed at Peter's denial." A man from Texas replied, "I'm not interested in her pedigree, I want to know if she lays eggs and how many."

This "Acts of the Apostles" means the Acts of Disciples who had turned Apostles, whether they were of the Twelve or not. Every learner, a disciple, became an apostle—one sent. So the Acts of the Apostles was really the Acts of the Christians. This is important—very.

O Lord and Savior, save us from confining Thy manifestations to a chosen few, thus excusing ourselves from being a part of Thy redemptive movement. There must be no mental barriers to keep me from feeling Thy full impact—none. Amen.

AFFIRMATION FOR THE DAY: *I as a Christian will write a new chapter of the Acts today.*

THE CENTER OF SPIRITUAL POWER SHIFTS FROM
THE TWELVE TO THE SEVEN

In this transition from the Word become flesh in Him to the Word become flesh in every follower, the barriers are all down. This was not handed down to a chosen few. The fact is that the Twelve drop out of the account after the first few chapters of the Acts, and the so-called lay movement takes over—and for a reason.

In the sixth chapter of Acts is an account where the Twelve called together the main body of believers and said that it was not befitting that they should forsake the word of God and serve tables, that they would give themselves "to prayer and to the ministry of the Word," and they would turn over the serving of tables, distribution of food, to the Seven. That seemed like a highly spiritual and sound thing to do. But I'm persuaded it was a disastrous thing to do, and it has resulted in much unnecessary conflict through the ages. They put asunder what God had joined in the Incarnation. In the Incarnation the spiritual and the material were one—the Word became flesh. The Divine Word was to function in and through the material. They were two sides of one reality. Life was one.

But they drove a wedge between the material and the spiritual and that wedge persists until today. The spiritual was separated from material manifestations and left unrelated; the material was separated from the spiritual and was thus unredeemed. That disastrous dichotomy sterilizes both the spiritual and the material.

Then what happened? Those who kept life together, the spiritual and the material, the Seven, became the center of spiritual power. It shifted from the Twelve to the Seven. The Twelve for the most part drop out and the Seven take over. It was Stephen the leader of the Seven who precipitated the revival in Jerusalem and brought on his martyrdom. It was Philip, another member of the Seven, who brought the Gospel to Samaria and all Samaria turned to Christ.

O Lord God, Thou hast made us one—help us to act as one. Help us to show the spiritual in every material relationship so that life will be one and its manifestation one. I would be united with a united service. Amen.

AFFIRMATION FOR THE DAY: *All my material contacts spiritualized and all my spiritual contacts materialized.*

STEPHEN, PHILIP, PAUL LEAD THIS
LAY MOVEMENT

We saw yesterday that the spiritual initiative shifted from the twelve to the Seven. The Seven kept life together—the spiritual and the material were two sides of one reality. They were not disembodied spirits floating above the material lest they be entangled and contaminated by contact with it. Their spiritual lives functioned in and through the material. So God tipped His power in the direction of the Seven. When Philip was going to turn all Samaria to Christ, the Twelve sent down John and Peter to regularize what they couldn't produce. They laid hands on the Samaritans that they might receive the Holy Spirit.

Philip also first preached to an Ethiopian and led him to Christ, thus founding the Ethiopian church which persists to this day. He also established the ministry of women since he had four unmarried daughters who prophesied, and prophesy here was not foretelling human events, it was forth-telling the Good News. And he also was the only person in the New Testament who was called an evangelist—"Philip the evangelist," and yet he was set aside to serve tables and the Twelve were to be the evangelists, a reversal.

Again, those who were scattered under the persecution of Stephen—this lay group—went to Antioch and preached the Gospel not only to Jews but to Greeks as well and "the strong hand of the Lord was upon them." They founded the Antiochian Church. And it was out of Antioch that Paul and Barnabas were sent on their great missionary journeys to Asia and Europe. Antioch, founded by a lay group and constituted as a lay group, sent forth Barnabas and Paul, also laymen. From then on laymen headed by Paul became the center of spiritual contagion. The Christian movement was emphasizing what God had emphasized in the Incarnation—the Word had become flesh. In the Twelve the Word had largely become word.

O God, our Father, we thank Thee for this emphasis. We thank Thee that men, just ordinary men, touched by thy extraordinary grace and power did extraordinary things. We thank Thee that this is open to ordinary men today. Amen.

AFFIRMATION FOR THE DAY: *I am a follower of Christ, as such everything is open to me which is open to a follower of Christ.*

"SCATTERED . . . EXCEPT THE APOSTLES"

We pause to note something seldom noted. This: "And on that day a great persecution arose against the church in Jerusalem; and they were all scattered throughout the region of Judea and Samaria, except the apostles" (Acts 8:1). That phrase, "except the apostles," is interesting and revealing. Why was this lay group "scattered" and not the apostles? Were they more brave than the lay group? Hardly, for the lay group went out not to hide from danger, but to get into more danger through the bold preaching of the Word: "Now those who were scattered went about preaching the word" (Acts 8:4).

Did the people who opposed the Christian movement in Jerusalem have a real discernment that the lay group were the truly dangerous ones—dangerous because their revolution was a revolution of the total life, spiritual and material? And did they see that the apostles, confining themselves to the spiritual, were thereby not dangerous to their society? For by their action to confine themselves to the spiritual, they were the Word become word. But these laymen who were a total commitment—spiritual and material—well, that was different! They challenged the spiritual and material basis of life and therefore challenged their position as rulers of the spiritual and material. They were the Word become flesh. They were in head-on conflict. So they kicked back in persecution—against these laymen. But they let the apostles alone.

A South African Dutch minister after being with me in several cities said, "You preach a very troublesome Gospel. We preach a Kingdom in heaven and that doesn't upset anything now. You preach a Kingdom on earth and that upsets everything." The Kingdom in heaven Gospel has left South Africa the unhappiest spot on earth. For if you don't bring a Kingdom on earth Gospel, you'll soon have a kingdom of hell on earth.

O Savior, save us from confining Thy Gospel to certain areas of life, for if we confine it we cripple it. And if we cripple the Gospel, we are crippled ourselves. Give us, we pray Thee, an all-out commitment to Thee and Thy Kingdom. Amen.

AFFIRMATION FOR THE DAY: *I will not be a compartmentalized Christian, I will be a Christian unlimited.*

"AT THE FOOT OF THE CROSS
THE GROUND IS LEVEL"

We are now considering the fact that this word "apostles" applied to every Christian. Every "disciple," a learner, became an "apostle," one sent. So the Acts of the Apostles were not the acts of the Twelve, but of the total body of believers.

This outcome in Acts was inherent in the fact that the total body of believers received the Holy Spirit on the day of Pentecost. An able Bible teacher said that he thought just the Twelve received the Holy Spirit. If that were true, it would change the whole nature of the Gospel. There would be a specially sacred group with a special standing and pull with God. That would undermine the whole conception of the equal standing of every one before God. "At the foot of the cross the ground is level." And it would not fulfill the promise:

> And in the last days it shall be, God declares,
> that I will pour out my Spirit upon all flesh,
> and your sons and your daughters shall prophesy,
> and your young men shall see visions,
> and your old men shall dream dreams;
> yea, and on my menservants and my maidservants in those days
> I will pour out my Spirit; and they shall prophesy (Acts 2:17-18).

Now note: "I will pour out my Spirit upon all flesh"—the "all flesh" could mean "all humanity." But it could also mean that the Spirit was to be poured out on all "flesh," in contrast to "all spirits," or "all souls." The "flesh" could mean and does mean that this coming of the Holy Spirit was a continuation of the Incarnation. The Word become flesh. They were not spirits filled with the Spirit—they were persons filled with the Spirit, and the persons were made up of body, mind, and spirit. The total person was totally filled. Life was one and was to be redeemed as one and lived as one. Just as the flesh was taken up into the Godhead in the Incarnation in Him so the flesh was taken up into Redemption in us.

O Blessed Lord, Thou art the Lord of all life, of us, of spirit and flesh. So we cannot compartmentalize Thee lest we cancel Thee. Come into us totally and possess us totally and redeem us totally, so we can manifest Thee totally. Amen.

AFFIRMATION FOR THE DAY: *I expect the Spirit to be poured upon me—body, mind, and spirit—and to be operative in the total me.*

AND THE GROUND WAS LEVEL FOR THE
WOMEN TOO

We noted yesterday that the Holy Spirit was to be poured out upon all flesh, with the emphasis on the "flesh"—the total embodied person. Then the prophecy goes further and says, "Your sons and daughters shall prophesy." If "flesh" wipes out the distinction between the material and the spiritual, this portion wipes out the distinction of standing between the sexes—the women and the men should proclaim the Good News.

The Holy Spirit came not only upon the Twelve but upon the hundred and twenty. The addition of the cipher to the Twelve was one of the most important things in history. Man as man, and not man as priest or prophet, received the Holy Spirit. The highest gift of God was open to a person as a person. This equal standing before God makes an equal standing before man.

But this gift of the Holy Spirit was not only open to man as man, but was open to women as women—"with the women." In Islam, which proclaims its democracy and equality, women are not even allowed in the mosque for public prayers. Among the Buddhists, women cannot attain Nirvana as women; they must be reborn as men before this can happen. But here were women taken into the very center of privilege and opportunity. Women received the highest gift of God, the Holy Spirit. That opened everything down the line. At Pentecost women not only received the Holy Spirit on the same basis as men, but they proclaimed that Gospel on the same basis as men—"your sons and daughters shall prophesy." There were equality of standing before God and equality of opportunty before men—there was equality! And that equality of opportunity extended to Mary, the mother of Jesus. The last thing we see of Mary is that she was praying for the Holy Spirit on the same basis as the rest. She was a supplicant and not a co-Redeemer with Jesus, as we have noted that the Roman Church is about to make her. She was in her place along with the rest.

O Lord and Savior, we thank Thee that the highest gift, the gift of the Holy Spirit, is open to the lowest. Here we all stand equal—persons for whom Christ died. This makes our hearts tingle and our souls exult with expectancy. We thank Thee. Amen.

AFFIRMATION FOR THE DAY: *Under the impact of Thy Spirit all my walls of special privilege and separation are crumbling.*

THE TWO GENERATIONS NO LONGER AT CROSS-PURPOSES

We are studying the prophecy of Joel which Peter quoted as fulfilled with the coming of the Holy Spirit. We saw that the distinctions between flesh and spirit, man and man, man and woman were broken down in the coming of the Spirit. Another barrier went down—the barrier between ages: "Your young men shall see visions, and your old men shall dream dreams" (Acts 2:17). Youth and old age would be together in a fellowship of the Spirit, sharing the forward look—seeing visions and dreaming dreams—both feeling the tingle of the new creation in them and in the world. This shows the two generations united, no longer at loggerheads with youth representing radicalism and old age representing conservatism, but a radical-conservatism emerged. And we need both, for if we were all conservative we would dry up, and if we were all radical we would break up! But between the pull back of the conservative and the pull ahead of the radical we make progress in a middle direction. This tension between the generations has been here for ages—it is not a modern phenomenon, it is ancient. One of the oldest bits of writing in the world is found in a Constantinople (now Istanbul) museum. On it is written, "Alas, times are not what they used to be. Children no longer obey their parents and everyone wants to write a book." Sounds modern! But under the new creation of the Spirit the two generations were one—one in creative outlook and action.

I was to speak in a university convocation, but it was "Sadie Hawkins Day" and these ceremonies of rube costumes and horseplay had to be gone through with before I spoke. It seemed impossible to speak on a serious religious subject after all this rollicking fun. But to my surprise, and to everyone else's, that great student body settled down and in five minutes were giving rapt attention. At the close several hundred stayed for personal surrender to Christ. That group of youth was sound down underneath. The older generation was proud of them.

O Holy Spirit, Thou art harnessing the generations to produce the Regeneration—a new world order. Save us from futile recriminations between the age groups—help us to harness the energy of youth and experience of age to our world tasks. Amen.

AFFIRMATION FOR THE DAY: *A wise radicalism is true conservatism.*

"I WILL ENDUE EVEN MY SLAVES . . . WITH . . . MY SPIRIT"

There is another item in Peter's interpretation of what had happened with the coming of the Holy Spirit: "Yes, I will endue even my slaves, both men and women, with a portion of my spirit, and they shall prophesy" (Acts 2:18 NEB). (Why the English translators should reduce "Spirit"—the Holy Spirit—to "spirit" is a mystery, and cannot be explained except as a tendency to tone down our faith. For here Peter was talking about the coming of the Holy Spirit!)

But the point to be noted is this: the coming of the Holy Spirit broke down the social and economic cleavage between slaves and free men, "I will endue my slaves, both men and women, with a portion of my Spirit and they shall prophesy." The slave was not only on the basis of equality in receiving the Holy Spirit, but in opportunity of forthtelling the Good News. That quiet happening spelled the doom of slavery. For a member of the House of Lords once said, "There is no power for reform so great as this: if alongside of a corrupt practice you lay an incompatible principle, then that incompatible principle will slowly but surely overthrow that corrupt practice. In this way the Christian principle of equality before God was placed alongside the corrupt practice of slavery and silently worked its overthrow." And how! For the sons of those slaves are now taking over the governments in Africa and more—are standing in the United Nations and are helping in the government of the world. All in five years! A major revolution! And Dr. Ralph Bunche, a descendant of slaves, is the representative of the U.N. in the most troubled spot of Africa, the Congo, to unite them.

A Negro friend told me how he was in a German train and when a white woman got on he gave her his seat. He stood up for three hours. The German woman wanted to thank him, but she knew no English and he no German. So she took a piece of paper and wrote on it Isa. 58:11. White and colored were united around a common loyalty to God through the Bible.

O Jesus Redeemer, Thou art slowly but surely redeeming this race of ours. We are in the birth throes of that redemption. Help us not to be afraid of it. For if we are afraid of it we are afraid of sanity. We welcome Thy redemption. In Thy name. Amen.

AFFIRMATION FOR THE DAY: *In my eyes every man shall be, not a problem, but a possibility.*

"FOR WHITES ONLY"–IN THE DUSTBIN

For centuries these principles of the Christian faith have lain alongside corrupt customs and practices. The full impact of them has not been felt. Why? Because the Christian faith has been emphasized as the Word become word. It worked by implication, not by application. Its effect was indirect, not direct. Now we are more and more seeing that the Christian faith is not a faith but a fiction unless applied—unless it is the Word become flesh.

And the moment it becomes flesh it means revolution. One African pastor said this after one of my addresses: "A child before it is born begins to kick. Africa wants to be born so Africa is kicking." And kicking means upset. But upset had to come to set things up on a higher level, God's level of equality for all.

I saw in a newspaper a picture of signs which had been taken down and were now in an ash can. They read, "For Whites Only." We are fast dumping such signs in the ash cans. That is where they belong—they belong to a discarded and outgrown past.

Another sign which is slowly but surely doomed for the ash can is, "For the Rich Only." That sign is not a visible sign in our civilization, but it is no less potent because it is invisible. Slowly but surely we are seeing the need to distribute wealth widely to have a healthy society. For wealth is like manure, gathered in one pile it is a stinking mess, but scattered across the fields it becomes a golden harvest. We are scattering our wealth across the world, partly through fear of Communism and partly through our Christian principles that we must share with human need. But we are scattering it, and if it is wisely done it will result in a golden harvest of a free and uplifted humanity. And we will lift ourselves in the process. For only the servants of all become the greatest of all. The Word is becoming flesh!

O Blessed Father, Thou art putting Thy helping, saving arms under the dispossessed of the world and Thou art lifting them. Help us to co-operate with Thee. For if we do not cooperate with Thee we belong to the dustbin. Save us. Amen.

AFFIRMATION FOR THE DAY: *I shall throw into the dustbin every vestige of old and dying snobberies.*

"GUIDE YOU INTO ALL THE TRUTH"

We are at the transition stage in our quest, where we are passing from the Word made flesh in Jesus to the Word made flesh in His followers. The Holy Spirit is the Agent of the Transition for He is the applied edge of Redemption—He is Operation–Redemption. Jesus said: "When the Spirit of truth comes, he will guide you into all the truth" (John 16:13). Note this does not say that the Holy Spirit will expound to you the truth—that would be the Word become word. But it does say, "He will guide you into all the truth"—He will guide you into the possession of the Truth and into the Truth possessing you—a life possession. He guides you into being the Truth becoming flesh.

If Christianity had been only a set of doctrines to be believed it would have said, "He shall teach you about the truth." But that would have been the Word become word. And it would have been less than, and other than, the Christian Gospel. The translators of the new versions slipped into the Word become word conception when they called the "Comforter" in the King James Version "the Counselor"—Counselor, one who counsels you, gives verbal advice. But the Holy Spirit is neither just "Comforter," nor just "Counselor"—He is the *paraclete,* literally, *para,* beside and *kaleo* to call—the One called alongside you, the Guide who guides you into all truth. He is not a "Counselor" to help you with your lessons, but a guide who meets you on the quest and guides you into the very possession of the Truth. This takes the setting out of the lecture room or school room and puts it on the Way—you are not dealing with questions—you are on a quest—a life quest. The Holy Spirit takes you by the hand and leads you right into the life-possession of the Truth. He makes the Word become flesh—in you. He makes the Blood get into your blood—become you!

O Holy Spirit, take me by the hand today and guide me into the Truth in every situation. For I want to live in the Truth, and become the Truth in some little but real way. Make me so truthful that I will become truth by identification. Only grace can do that. Amen.

AFFIRMATION FOR THE DAY: *The Holy Spirit will reveal to me as much truth as I am willing to practice and no more.*

THE "THIS-NESS" OF THE GOSPEL

The Holy Spirit did exactly what Jesus said He would do—He guided them into all Truth. For ten days—the ten days which shook and shaped the world—they were guided to surrender this, that, and the other until they came to themselves and they surrendered that last barrier. And the Holy Spirit, the Spirit of Truth, flooded them as if He had been pent up for ages. This was the Moment. God was to rule men from within, by man's consent, according to a pattern fixed in Jesus and according to a power supplied by the Holy Spirit—from within.

This was the greatest leap forward in the moral and spiritual history of humanity. The Divine Word was becoming flesh in ordinary humanity, very ordinary humanity. Infinite possibilities opened to anybody, everybody, provided they surrendered and cooperated with this Divine Process. And it was not to be imparted to the learned, but to the willing. That opened the gates to all. No one barred, except the unwilling.

Peter announced the coming of this astonishing fact in these words: "This Jesus God raised up, and of that we all are witnesses. Being therefore exalted at the right hand of God, and having received from the Father the promise of the Holy Spirit, he has poured out this which you see and hear" (Acts 2:33, 34). Note that last phrase: "This which you see and hear." It was "this," not "that," or "yonder"—it was *this,* a present incarnate fact. The center of emphasis had been taken out of the past and out of the future and put into the present. The "this-ness" was unique. The longing had become life, the search had become arrival, the Way had become the Truth and the Life. It was here—and available. The Desire of the Ages had become the Possession of the Present. And you could "see" it. The Word had become flesh in them. It was primarily seeing and secondarily hearing. The flesh had become Word and the flesh was proclaiming that Word. Seeing was believing.

O Blessed Father, we thank Thee for this moment. And we thank Thee that the Moment is not past, it is Now. It is available Now. All we have to do is reach forth willing hands and take It. And there are no favorites. We thank Thee, thank Thee. Amen.

AFFIRMATION FOR THE DAY: *I live in the Eternal Now, in the Eternal Here, with the Eternal.*

"THIS IS THAT"

We ended yesterday on the "This-ness" of the Christian movement. If the emphasis had been on "that," it would have been outside them in history; if the emphasis had been on "yonder," it would have been ahead in the future. But the Movement glanced at the past and glanced at the future, but it gloried in the present. Peter exclaimed after the Holy Spirit had come, "This is that which was spoken"—note "This is that"— the "that" of the past and "yonder" of the future had become the "this" of the present. The Word has become flesh again.

Note Peter said, "This Jesus . . . has poured out this." Jesus was alive and present and He made them alive in the present. The "this-ness" of the Gospel comes to its climax in John's Epistle where the word "this" is used twenty-one times. "By *this* we know love, that he laid down this life for us; and we ought to lay down our lives for the brethren" (I John 3:16). John 3:16 was a revelation of the Word become flesh; this I John 3:16 is a revelation of that Word become flesh in us—"we ought to lay down our lives for the brethren." We emphasize the first John 3:16 and overlook the second I John 3:16! "By *this* we shall know that we are of the truth, and reassure our hearts before him" (I John 3:19). "And by *this* we know that he abides in us, by the Spirit which he has given us" (I John 3:24). "In *this* is love, not that we loved God but that he loved us and sent his Son to be the expiation for our sins" (I John 4:10). "By *this* we know that we abide in him and he in us, because he has given us of his own Spirit" (I John 4:13). "In *this* is love perfected with us, that we may have confidence for the day of judgment, because as he is so are we in this world" (I John 4:17). "And *this* is the testimony, that God gave us eternal life, and this life is in his Son" (I John 5:11). This "this-ness" is characteristic only of the Christian Gospel. All others are wistful, but not witnesses. Here promise has become performance—the Word become flesh.

O Holy Father, how can we thank Thee enough that Jesus is the Way—the way to finding, to realization. We are not like "the hart panting after the waterbrooks"—we drink. And we drink now. And are satisfied now. Amen.

AFFIRMATION FOR THE DAY: *I shall be not a man of the past, nor a man of the future, but a man of the now.*

"I ADJURE YOU BY THE JESUS WHOM
PAUL PREACHES"

This "this-ness" sets the pattern of the proclamation of the Christian gospel by its very nature. If the experience was the Word become flesh, the expression would also be the Word become flesh—it would be a witness, and Jesus said it would be: "But you shall receive power when the Holy Spirit has come upon you; and you shall be my witnesses" (Acts 1:8). "My witnesses"—not "my lawyers" to argue my case, but "my witnesses" to tell what has happened to you, of what you've "seen and heard." This made the proclaiming of the Gospel not secondhand, but firsthand. That was one of the secrets of its power. If "all great literature is autobiography," so all great preaching is witnessing.

A rector was fifty-eight years in the same parish in England, and in those years he had never preached an original sermon. The only original thing about the rector and his parish was that there was nothing original. I watched the fish in a Japanese pond crowding near the place where fresh water flowed in. They deserted the murky waters for the fresh. Congregations will gather around a pulpit from which living water is flowing. "Then some of the itinerant Jewish exorcists undertook to pronounce the name of the Lord Jesus over those who had evil spirits, saying, 'I adjure you by the Jesus whom Paul preaches.' Seven sons of a Jewish high priest named Sceva were doing this. But the evil spirit answered them, 'Jesus I know, and Paul I know; but who are you?' And the man in whom the evil spirit was leaped on them, mastered all of them, overpowered them, so they fled out of the house naked and wounded" (Acts 19:11-16). This was secondhand preaching: "I adjure you by the Jesus whom Paul preaches." Its modern counterpart would be, "I adjure by the Jesus whom Barth, or Fosdick preaches, come out." But the evil spirits don't come out by quotations or secondhand preaching. We must be witnesses, sharing facts which have happened in us and to us and not mere lawyers quoting laws or evidence from others. It must be the Word become flesh.

O Lord Jesus, brush from my heart secondhand accumulations. Let me speak out of the simplicity of experience. May my heart be a fountain of joy—gratitude ready to overflow at the slightest invitation or opportunity. In Thy Name. Amen.

AFFIRMATION FOR THE DAY: *I am not a secondhander—I am a firsthander, by His Grace.*

"THINGS WE HAVE SEEN AND HEARD"

The "this-ness" is the keynote of the Christian Gospel. When the Jewish authorities tried to silence the apostles with this, "They then called them in and ordered them to refrain from all public speaking and teaching in the name of Jesus" (Acts 4:18 NEB). They thought it was simply a "public speaking" and "teaching"—the Word become word. But Peter and John set them right: "We cannot possibly give up speaking of things we have seen and heard" (vss. 19, 20). Note "seen," first in Jesus and then "seen" in themselves. "Seeing is believing," and they had "seen." When the attempt was made over again to repress the apostles, they replied, "We must obey God rather than man . . . and we are witnesses to all this, and so is the Holy Spirit given by God to those who are obedient to him" (Acts 5:30, 32). "We are witnesses . . . and so is the Holy Spirit"—we have seen it with our eyes and we have known it in our hearts by the Holy Spirit who is within. We witness and the Holy Spirit witnesses to the same thing—the human and Divine blending in the witness. This fulfilled the promise of Jesus: "But when your Advocate has come, whom I will send you from the Father—he will bear witness to me. And you also are my witnesses" (John 15:26, 27). Here was the double witness: "He will bear witness to me. And you also are my witnesses." It was a double witness, and yet one and the same witness—the witness of the Word become flesh.

The Jewish authorities might have suppressed teaching—the Word become word, but they ran against the rock of testimony—the Word become flesh, and it confounded them. They didn't know what to do with it. It was rooted in Reality and not in mere idea. The Christian faith was a realism and just "teaching" was no match for it. Testimony reaches the heart—and mind. Teaching reaches the mind—maybe.

O God, our Father, we thank Thee for this blessed Realism. It is the Rock upon which we can and do build. And the gates of hell and the storms of life cannot prevail against it. Help us to be real in the Realism. In Jesus' Name. Amen.

AFFIRMATION FOR THE DAY: *No fear of anything shall keep me from witnessing to what I've seen and heard.*

"TESTIFIED AND SPOKEN THE WORD OF THE LORD"

We are emphasizing the fact that the New Testament was the Word become flesh. This verse is to the point: "Now when they [Peter and John] had testified and spoken the word of the Lord, they returned to Jerusalem" (Acts 8:25). Suppose it had read, "Now when they had spoken the word of the Lord." It would have been the Word become word—something outside themselves. But when the passage reads, "They had testified and spoken the word of the Lord," it was definitely the Word become flesh. And because testimony dropped out of our preaching, power has also dropped out. Note, we are not witnessing to ourselves, but witnessing to what a great Redeemer has done. The pastor who determined that he was not going to preach anything that was not operative in his own life found his preaching taking on power. "That which is to reach the heart must come from the heart."

Leontyne Price, the singer, before a concert would say, "Now, dear Jesus, You got me into this. You get me out." And when criticism comes she says, "Well, they say I have a good voice. If I have, then I can learn the rest." Basically she was sound, the word of song become flesh. She could add the rest. If there is a basic soundness in people, we can put up with not-too-perfect trimmings. But if the center is the word become word no amount of put-on trimmings will atone. Something tells every man's heart: "This is reality speaking" or "This is unreality speaking."

So New Testament preaching was the expression of an experience, the interpretation of a fact at work in the preachers. It did not come out of texts of scripture only, but out of the texture of their lives. It was deep speaking to deep. Hence power. A young man sat down on a bus beside a radiant Christian and said, "I thought when I saw you that you had a face that had visited someone you loved." She had. For she was visiting with Jesus all the time.

O Lord Jesus, as we hear Thee we do not hear words—we hear Thee. We feel that the essential Person is speaking. And we listen with bated breath. For Thou hast the words of eternal life. For Thou art Eternal Life. We thank Thee. Amen.

AFFIRMATION FOR THE DAY: *All my preaching shall be a witness—the word of preaching become flesh.*

"ANY WORD OF EXHORTATION"

This word become flesh emphasis is seen in contrast to the Jewish conception in this incident. In Antioch in Pisidia the rulers of the synagogue said to Paul and Silas: "Brethren, if you have any word of exhortation for the people, say it" (Acts 13:15). They expected "a word of exhortation," something to whip up peoples' wills to make them try a little harder, to be a little better. It was the Word become word—word of exhortation. But Paul stood up and replied, "And we bring you the good news . . . that through this man forgiveness of sins is proclaimed to you" (13:32,38).

The rulers of the synagogue expected them to bring a word of exhortation—good views, a philosophy or moralism. Instead of bringing good views, Paul brought them Good News! Good News that through "this man" forgiveness of sins could be found and experienced here and now. It was *this* Man" offering *this* experience. It was not the Word become word—an exhortation—it was the Word become flesh—an exhibition. It could be seen and felt and experienced. It was not words attempting to whip up the jaded wills of men; it was an offer of redemption to those jaded wills, so they would be no longer jaded—they would be joyous and spontaneous. This was Good News!

So the account says, "As they went out, the people begged that these things might be told them the next sabbath" (vs. 42). Asked that the same sermon be repeated the next sabbath! With us now that isn't done! People ask that the next sabbath they hear something new and different. For to them the Word becomes word—good views. But here the Word was so fresh out of the heart of Reality that they wanted it over again. So the account further reads: "The next sabbath almost the whole city gathered together to hear the word of God" (vs. 44). People will not listen to the Word become word over and over again—they demand novelty. But if the sermons are not sermons, but the Word become flesh, then it is new by its very nature. Hence the demand to hear it over again!

O Jesus, we never tire of Thy words. We have repeated them for a lifetime. Yet they are always fresh—new depths, new meanings, new everything. Eternal newness presents itself in Thee. And yet eternal oldness too. We thank Thee, thank Thee. Amen.

AFFIRMATION FOR THE DAY: *My life shall not be good views—clever; it shall be Good News—converted!*

"EVERYONE"

Here is a vivid illustration of the word of equal standing before God and man become flesh. The Christian faith could have proclaimed the doctrine of equal standing before God and man, but it would have left little dent on the prejudiced minds and hearts of men. The prejudices were taken in with the mother's milk and were part and parcel of them. So preaching against them would have been shrugged off as mere words—Word become word. But an amazing happening took place—the Gentiles received the gift of the Holy Spirit—God's highest gift—on the same basis exactly as the Jews.

Peter was speaking to the assembled Gentiles in the house of Cornelius. Peter began by reminding his hearers: "I need not tell you that a Jew is forbidden by his religion to visit or associate with a man of another race" (Acts 10:28 NEB). Patronizing. But Peter began the preaching of his gospel, and it carried him beyond himself and he uttered a word which God was looking for: "It is to him that all the prophets testify, declaring that everyone who rests in him receives forgiveness of sins through his name." And when he uttered that word "everyone" through that word God poured the Holy Spirit. "While Peter was still saying this, the Holy Spirit fell on all who heard the word" (RSV) (Acts 10:43, 44). Note the "this"—the "this" was "everyone." The moment Peter gave God an opening through that word the Holy Spirit fell—"fell on all who heard the word." "Everyone" was Peter's invitation; the Holy Spirit "on all" was God's reply, and the greatest gulf between racial groups was bridged—bridged not by a word, but by the Word of equal standing before God and man become flesh. God had given His highest gift to a person as a person and not to a person as a Jew. That was the most leveling-up fact that ever occurred in human history.

O God, our Father, we thank Thee for this happening—the coming of the Holy Spirit. And we thank Thee that this Gift was given to "everyone." And that opens the gate of this possibility to me. Give me the Holy Spirit for I'm a person for whom Christ died. Amen.

AFFIRMATION FOR THE DAY: *Prejudices and circumstances press me to say, "Some," but Jesus presses me to say, "Everyone."*

"EVEN ON THE GENTILES"

We saw yesterday that the deepest chasm between man and man—the chasm of race prejudice—was bridged in the moral history of mankind, even wiped out, by a simple method—the Word of equality become flesh. The despised and hated Gentiles received the gift of the Holy Spirit, God's highest gift, on the same basis as the Jews. That was decisive—and breathtaking. No argument or exhortation could have accomplished this. The account says: "And the believers from among the circumcised who came with Peter were amazed, because the gift of the Holy Spirit had been poured out even on the Gentiles" (Acts 10:45). Note: "*even* on the Gentiles." To fight with this equality of standing was to fight with God. For God did it.

The same thing happened when Peter reported the happening in the Jerusalem assembly: "If then God gave the same gift to them as he gave to us when we believed in the Lord Jesus Christ who was I that I could withstand God? When they heard this they were silenced. And they glorified God, saying, 'Then to the Gentiles also God has granted repentance unto life' " (Acts 11:17, 18).

This method of solving a deep-rooted prejudice by the simple expedient of letting people see what God thought of it, by a simple act of God, did more to root out that prejudice than all the disquisitions of philosophers and the exhortation of moralists put together. The problem wasn't solved, it was dissolved. Race prejudice melted before this tender act of God's acceptance of the despised ones. At the height of the clash of color, C. F. Andrews on board ship went over and picked up a black baby from its mother's arms and fondled it. When he came back to the white group, clouds were on their faces. "That isn't done in South Africa, you know." That simple act divided the group—the scowling white men belonged to the past; Andrews belonged to the future.

O Blessed God, Thou didst do just that. Thou didst take into Thy arms every child of the race in forgiveness and restoration, and as we see it our hearts melt and our lips are silent. We see it; we see it and are forever different. Amen.

AFFIRMATION FOR THE DAY: *I shall look today for an opportunity of doing some act which will dissolve race prejudice.*

"UNDISCIPLINED VERBIAGE"

We see in this passage the difference between the Christian Gospel and other ways: "Paul was just about to speak when Gallio said to them, 'If it had been a question of crime or grave misdemeanour, I should, of course, have given you Jews a patient hearing, but if it is some bickering about words and names and your Jewish law, you may see to it yourselves; I have no mind to be a judge of these matters. And he had them ejected from the court" (Acts 18:14-16 NEB).

Here was a proud Roman official, fed up with the bandying of words and legal wrangles at court, who dismissed the Christian faith with a wave of his hand, for he thought it was just another philosohy, or moralism, or legalism—another instance of the Word become word. And he represents the attitude of the sophisticated modern man; he too dismisses Christianity as a juggling of words about words. But suppose this is not words, but the Word become flesh? Suppose this is the eternal God visiting and redeeming us in understandable form, then this is different—startlingly different. You can't wave this aside with a sophisticated gesture. This is God confronting you—inescapably confronting you. You cannot drive this away from your judgment seat, for you are at the Judgment Seat of This. Something happens when you drive This away—something within you and to you. You are self-damned automatically. When This confronts you, it is the most decisive moment of existence—all past, present, and future are packed in that momentous moment.

Because Christianity has actually become in many quarters, a bickering about words, Dr. Mowrer, a psychologist, could say, "The prime reason for this state of affairs is the fact that theology, i.e., the science and art in which many of our ministers are trained, is undisciplined verbiage." The Word become word.

O Lord Jesus, save us from "undisciplined verbiage." Give us the fresh fountain of Thy reality. That and that alone will suffice us. For when we touch Thee we know we touch Life. And we can be satisfied with nothing less than Life. Amen.

AFFIRMATION FOR THE DAY: *Not "undisciplined verbiage," but disciplined Life will be the spring of action today.*

"PROCLAIMING THE RESURRECTION FROM THE
DEAD—THE RESURRECTION OF JESUS"

This passage reveals the Word become flesh: "They were still addressing the people when the chief priests came upon them, together with the Controller of the Temple and the Sadducees, exasperated at their teaching the people and proclaiming the resurrection from the dead—the resurrection of Jesus" (Acts 4:1, 2 NEB). Note "proclaiming the resurrection from the dead"—that would have been innocuous—a doctrine, a philosophy, an abstract idea. But when they added "proclaiming the resurrection from the dead—the resurrection of Jesus"—that made the teaching concerning the resurrection become flesh. In the resurrection of Jesus they were confronted, not with a philosophy, but with a fact—the greatest fact of history.

No wonder they reacted, not verbally, but violently: "They were arrested and put in prison for the night" (vs. 3). You have to take sides with a proposition like this for it is not a proposition—it is a Person, alive and inescapable. Some threw them into prison, but some threw open their hearts and received this glorious fact: "But many of those who heard the message became believers. The number of men now reached about five thousand" (vs. 4).

Here was a Gospel that wasn't a subject of discussion, but of decision. God had acted and men were compelled to react, one way or the other. No place for indifference. Today's preaching is mainly the Word become word, so you need not decide anything. You can like it or dislike it, but nothing vital happens. You can treat it as you do a commercial on TV, "Oh, yeah!" But you don't treat the real Jesus with, "Oh, yeah!" You go away sorrowful or you are at His feet. This kind of preaching brings prison or conversion.

O God, forgive us that we preach the resurrection of the dead—a doctrine, instead of the Resurrection of Jesus—a fact. Save us from the gospel of the turned edge—turned toward an idea, instead of the Gospel of the cutting edge. Amen.

AFFIRMATION FOR THE DAY: *My gospel shall lead, not to comment, but to conversion.*

"TAKE HEED TO YOURSELF AND
TO YOUR TEACHING"

The interest of men is in this Word become flesh. In one of our Ashrams a lady stood empty-handed at our table and asked, "Does anyone want more coffee?" I replied, "No, thank you." But when another woman came in with a coffee pot in her hand and asked, "Anyone want more coffee?" I replied, "Yes, thank you." The difference? The first woman presented the word of coffee become word, the second the word of coffee become flesh! We have to see the reality, then we seek it. "One loving heart sets another afire."

Paul emphasized this to the young minister, Timothy, "Take heed to yourself and to your teaching" (I Tim. 4:16). Take heed to the Word become flesh and then the Word become word will be the Word become flesh too, for behind the word will be the Word become flesh. For what you are gets into what you say and puts a plus or minus to it. Two people can say the same thing—one falls on the soul dead, the other falls upon the soul with quickening, converting power. Why? Well, in one case it is the Word become word—dead truth; in the other case it is the Word become flesh—Spirit-quickened truth, hence, converting truth.

When Paul called the Ephesian elders he said, "Take heed to yourselves and to all the flock" (Acts 20:28). Note the order "to yourselves" and "to all the flock"—first yourselves that the Word become flesh in you, that you embody what you pass on to the body of believers.

Dr. Oscar Buck came out to India to spend a Sabbatical year with me in evangelistic work. After two weeks he said, "I can teach theology, but this is demanding something of spiritual experience I haven't got. I'm going out on the bank of the river and not come back till something happens." A few hours later he came back, "I went out to get my gasoline tank filled but I come back with a new engine." The Word had become flesh.

O Lord Christ, if my words have become words out of which the Word has dropped, come in, O Word, and make my words live again by Thy Presence. For without Thee I may have a body of truth but no soul of truth. In Thy Name. Amen.

AFFIRMATION FOR THE DAY: *I am the first and only Bible some people will ever read.*

TAKE HEED TO YOUR REACTIONS

There are several other passages which emphasize this taking "heed to yourself"—the emphasis of beginning with yourself, making the word become flesh in yourself before you go out to your brother.

First, "Take heed to yourselves; if your brother sins, rebuke him, and if he repents, forgive him" (Luke 17:3). The emphasis here is upon the reactions, what you do when your brother sins against you. For your reaction may color and corrode your whole life. The temptation will be to note and emphasize your brother's action—his sinning against you. But Jesus said your reactions are more important to you than your brother's action. Your reactions can harm you, but his actions cannot harm you unless you let them. So the reactions are more important than the brother's action. Be the Word of forgiveness and reconciliation become flesh and you are unhurt by his actions.

Again, another passage: "But take heed to yourselves; for they will deliver you up to councils; and you will be beaten in synagogues; and you will stand before governors and kings for my sake, to bear testimony before them" (Mark 13:9). Here the emphasis is upon yourselves—upon yourselves at the moment of deep, unmerited injustice and suffering; be sure that through this injustice you bear witness! This is an important word, for it clarifies the whole attitude toward unmerited suffering. It was the passage upon which my whole attitude toward unmerited suffering turned. I saw you could not merely bear it—you could use it. Every injustice was opportunity, every wrong an open door—an opportunity and an open door to witness. Not to preach at others about their wrongs but to witness by your rightness of demeanor and your deeds that the Word has become flesh in you. Don't bear evil, use it!

Dear Lord and Father, when we are in Thee we always have an open door—the door of witness. Help us always to be so acute that we can see that door—and enter it. For we have "come for a witness"—that is our life purpose. In Jesus' Name. Amen.

AFFIRMATION FOR THE DAY: *In Jesus everything is opportunity—opportunity to witness.*

"WEIGHED DOWN WITH . . . CARES OF THIS LIFE"

We come to look at the final "take heed." "But take heed to yourselves lest your heart be weighed down with dissipation and drunkenness and cares of this life" (Luke 21:34). This was in the light of the "standing before the son of man," that Great Crisis. But it could be applied to the lesser crises of life when we are called on suddenly to face an issue. What we are then will determine what we do. The Word become flesh, whatever it is, will be the word revealed. So Jesus was saying, Don't be off-color, unprepared, when the crisis turns unto you for a testimony. And He named the sins of the flesh—"dissipation and drunkenness," and also the sins of the disposition—"cares of this life." And of the two the probabilities are that the sins of the disposition cause the greater weighing down of spirit, because affecting more people including otherwise good people.

"The cares of this life" may range from the Negro maid who said to her mistress that she was resigning, "because life here is so daily." She felt the "cares of this life" added up to monotony. Or it may reach to the woman who said, "I don't have to work, but I work to keep from committing suicide. And my husband doesn't have to work, but he works to run away from himself." They were both weighed down with the oppressive inner feeling that there is no goal, no meaning to this thing called life. We can stand anything, provided there is meaning and goal and purpose in the things. Emptiness becomes the heaviest of burdens and weighs us down. And the burdened spirit is unfitted to be a witness—the Word become flesh. We are so weighed down by that which is around us that we cannot witness to that which is above us.

O Lord God, keep us fit every moment so that if we are called on by men or circumstances we may be razor-edge sharp to seize the opportunity and be ready witnesses for Thee. May we be minutemen—ready every minute. Amen.

AFFIRMATION FOR THE DAY: *May my inner strength be strong enough to not allow the cares of this life to weigh me down.*

A BUILT-IN REPAIR SHOP

As we look through the Scriptures and life around us to see the Word become flesh, we are struck with the fact of Paul as the Word of physical vitality become flesh: "They stoned Paul and dragged him out of the city, supposing he was dead. But when the disciples gathered about him, he rose up and entered the city; and on the next day he went on with Barnabas to Derbe" (Acts 14:19, 20). Paul was dragged out of the city like a dead dog, and when they stood around him he rose up and went on his own steam into the city. Note he didn't go away into hiding to lick his wounds, he went straight back into the city where he had been stoned, really asking for more. Someone has defined faith as "the attitude that asks for the hardest job and then asks for more." Then Paul had faith to the nth degree.

He must have been terribly bruised from the stoning and the dragging, and yet without complaint he walks back into the city and asks for more! And to prove it was no bravado the account says: "And the next day he went on with Barnabas to Derbe" (Acts 14:20). And Derbe was about twenty-five miles away— a twenty-five mile walk after a day of stoning! That is the word of vitality became bruised flesh. And the bruises were healed by the built-in health of the man.

Signs on the expressways say, "No stopping except for repairs." But Paul didn't even stop for repairs. For evidently he had a built-in repair shop—the Holy Spirit. The Holy Spirit was quickening his mortal body: "The Spirit of him who raised Jesus from the dead dwells in you, he who raised Christ Jesus from the dead will give life to your mortal bodies" (Rom. 8:11). This is repairing as you go. Dr. Cannon, the great physiologist, says, "All the healing forces are laid up within the body ready to go into operation when needed." That happens spiritually and physically. No need to lay up long periods for repairs, for the Spirit quickens the mortal body as you go. You have a built-in repair shop, giving instant service when needed.

O Holy Spirit, I thank Thee that Thou art within and within for immediate help and healing. I thank Thee that even before I know my need Thou art healing and Thou art saving and Thou art energizing. How can I thank Thee enough? Amen.

AFFIRMATION FOR THE DAY: *I shall depend not on recreation, but re-creation to repair me daily and hourly.*

"I AM NEVER TIRED IN MY WORK"

We saw yesterday that Paul had a built-in reactivator. But Wesley had it too. At eighty-two he declared: "Mr. Henry said 'I bless God that I am never tired *of* my work, yet I am often tired *in* my work.' By the blessing of God, I can say more: I am never tired *in* my work. From the beginning of the day or the week or the year to the end I do not know what weariness means. I am never weary of writing or preaching, or travelling; but am just as fresh at the end as at the beginning. Thus it is with me today, and I take no thought of to-morrow."

That passage was open for me on my desk, opened by my son-in-law, Bishop J. K. Mathews, when I returned from a six-month evangelistic tour abroad. He said he opened it for me, for it reminded him of me, that I could say that too. I could, humbly and gratefully. I have been speaking from two to five times a day, sometimes more, for half a century, and taking no vacations except to write on a book, and yet, at seventy-eight I find no sense of tiredness at all. At this writing I am in Cochin, India, having just come out of the Mar Thoma Convention, where for a week the crowds would go up to fifty thousand, and beyond; and yet, speaking to them up to four times a day, I find no sense of weariness at the close at all. After speaking to the crowds you do not walk away from them—they crowd your veranda, peep through the curtains, and throng around you everywhere. But no strain, no drain! There is the built-in reactivator, the Holy Spirit, source of life and strength and renewal.

The Holy Spirit within makes actual what Jesus made possible. He is the applied edge of redemption—redemption to body, mind, and spirit, to the total person. Without the Holy Spirit you are the victim of your circumstances; with the Holy Spirit within you are on top of your circumstances. The principle and power of renewal is working within you every moment.

O Blessed Holy Spirit, Thou has made what is implicit in Jesus, explicit in us. Thou dost not only take the things of Christ and show them unto us, Thou dost make them available for us. Make His Everything available to me today! Amen.

AFFIRMATION FOR THE DAY: *I will live today in Regeneration, Recuperation, Renewal, Revival.*

"EXCEPT THESE CHAINS"

Perhaps the most beautiful and touching illustration of this word of victory become flesh is the scene of Paul before King Agrippa and "an array of military tribunes and prominent men of the city." Agrippa said to Paul, "In a short time you think to make me a Christian!" And Paul said, "Whether short or long, I would to God that not only you but all who hear me this day might become as I am—except for these chains" (Acts 26:28, 29). Here was a lone prisoner, deserted by his own people, on his way to be tried before a foreign tribunal, the emperor at Rome, and yet standing there as master of circumstances and men and wanting nothing more than that those who heard him should be as he was! No self-pity, no envy of those around him—he stood there the epitome of everything good he could think of. He stood there the Word of life—satisfaction become flesh. And the people who heard him didn't laugh—they knew instinctively that he had everything and they had nothing—nothing in comparison.

And then the gentle courtesy, "except for these chains." These chains are your gift, I want you to have everything about me except the thing you gave me—chains. It was a gentle courtesy and yet a gentle thrust. He revealed what he was and what they were in one gentle sentence. He stands there as the incarnate revelation of free and victorious manhood—free and victorious in spite of!

The leading Communist of India came to our Ashram in India at Sat Tal and he told a friend afterwards, "The thing that struck me about these Christians was that they expected to get me." We do—we expect to get everybody as Paul did—"that not only you but all who hear me might be as I am." That is the Christian—he is so satisfied in God, so altogether happy, so altogether grateful that he wants everybody to be as he is! He is not at the Goal, but He is on the Way! And knows that this is the Way!

Dear Redeemer, Thou art redeeming me from all self-pity, all envy of others, all wanting of this, that, and the other. I have Thee and having Thee I have Everything. Why should I long for the things of life when I have Life? The stream when I have the Source? I thank Thee. Amen.

AFFIRMATION FOR THE DAY: *Can I say to everyone today, "I want you to be as I am, except possibly this marginal thing"?*

"THESE . . . SERVANTS OF THE MOST HIGH GOD . . . PROCLAIM . . . SALVATION"

The complete realism of Paul was never more clearly seen than in this passage:

> As we were going to the place of prayer, we were met by a slave girl who had a spirit of divination and brought her owners much gain by soothsaying. She followed Paul, and us, crying, "These men are servants of the Most High God, who proclaim to you the way of salvation." And this she did for many days. But Paul was annoyed, and turned and said to the spirit, "I charge you in the name of Jesus Christ to come out of her." And it came out that very hour. But when her owners saw that their hope of gain was gone, they seized Paul and Silas and dragged them . . . before the rulers . . . and magistrates (Acts 16:16-20).

And then the riots, the beatings and imprisonment.

Why did Paul refuse to accept the witness of this soothsaying slave girl? What she told was the truth: "These men are servants of the Most High God, who proclaim to you the way of salvation." It was the truth—they were servants of the Most High God, and they were proclaiming the way of salvation. Then why didn't Paul gratefully accept this auxiliary witness? Well, for one thing—it wasn't a witness—the girl was not accepting it for herself. She was telling others to accept it, but she left herself out of it. It was the Word become word, and not the Word become flesh. So Paul stopped this unreality though it was seemingly in his favor.

Suppose we would stop all this unreal support of our churches and our Christian movement—unreal because it is only verbal, not vital, giving lip praise and not life support—what would happen? Trouble, upset, maybe resentment would become imprisonment. But Christianity would learn to sing again as Paul and Silas did at midnight in prison, and we would have power to convert jailers and the movement would be true to itself. And hence full of power. The Word should become flesh or be silent! That would be a cleansing attitude for the Christian movement to take!

O Lord Jesus, Thou didst show reality and require it. Save us from unreal words that come from no depths of reality and hence reach no depth of reality in others. Make us real in thought, word, and deed. In Thy dear Name we ask it. Amen.

AFFIRMATION FOR THE DAY: *No wrong source witness for me, however true.*

"YOUR FUTURE IN YOUR HAND"

We must pause another day on accepting anything less than the Word become flesh in support of the Christian Gospel and the Christian movement. The girl mentioned yesterday was a soothsayer, a teller of fortunes. We need not argue the truth or falsity of telling fortunes. True or false it represents the Word become word—your fortune is a verbal statement of what is going to happen to you. It makes no attempt to derive the fortune through you, depending on what you do to decide your own fortune. That sends life on the wrong track and anyone who takes that method of deciding his fortune will decay—decay by the very method. Your fortune is decided by the way you decide and act and in no other way.

A palmist in India said, "I want to read your fortune in your hand." "Yes," I replied, "my destiny is in my hand, but not the way you think. My destiny is in the way I grasp the situations I meet around me—it is in the grasp of my hand, not in the lines of my hand."

Take spiritualism. The spiritualists bring in materialization as a proof of the reality of spiritualism—table rapping, falling plates. Suppose they could be proved to be true, what good would that do? What moral quality is in table rapping, and flying plates? This materialization is a false instance of the Word become flesh. The embodiment is not in moral living, the Word become flesh, it is in magical happenings—the word become the wand.

Astrology is in the same category. India is in the aftermath of a recovery from an orgy of fear and panic over the doom predicted by the astrologers because of the universal position of the planets. Nothing happened—nothing except that a people were let down and weakened by trying to read their destiny in their stars instead of in their decisions. The Word that becomes flesh only in lumps of matter floating in space is a false word become flesh—it is pure materialism.

O Lord Jesus, we thank Thee for the cleansing sanity of the Word becoming flesh. It saves us from all signs and wonders and pseudomaterializations and concentrates our attention and love upon the fact of Thy Incarnation. That is enough. We thank Thee. Amen.

AFFIRMATION FOR THE DAY: *My destiny is my decisions and nothing can change that destiny except my choices.*

"THE KINGDOM . . . NOT . . . TALK BUT . . . POWER"

Nothing could be more to the point than this verse: "For the kingdom of God does not consist in talk but in power" (I Cor. 4:20). This plants the Christian Gospel in the Word become flesh and not in the Word become word.

And yet the whole of the Christian setup is around the Kingdom of God consisting in talk. Our "services" are sermons, with a padding of hymns and prayers—they are "talk," lip services instead of life services. We don't go out of these "services" asking, "What do I do next?" but commenting, "It was a good sermon. I enjoyed it." You are supposed to react in comment and not in commitment.

But the Kingdom of God is "in power"—power to change lives, power to remake character, power to start movements, power to lift horizons and nerve men to live, power to turn inner and outer defeat into victory, power to break chains and make men free, power to enable men to do what they cannot do—power!

A pastor said in the Morning of the Open Heart in one of our Ashrams: "I am more and more convinced of the truth of the foolishness of preaching—my preaching is foolishness." And it was, for it was the Word become word. But he surrendered himself to Christ and was made into a new man. On the last day he said, "Now my preaching won't be foolishness. I'm going to be a witness to what Christ has done for me." Now it was no longer the Word become word—it was the Word become flesh, hence power.

A young pastor beaten and discouraged saw a sign on a very vital church: "Jesus Christ is in this place, anything can happen here." It struck him. He went in and found it was true. He poured out his emptiness and defeat and arose a new man. He went in one type of person, he came out another. And now he himself has made over a church, the center of contagion and power.

O Son of God, when we listen to Thee we hear more than Thou dost say—we hear Thy life and love speaking silently through Thy words. And Thy words thus have a strange power over us. They send us to our knees in gratitude. Amen.

AFFIRMATION FOR THE DAY: *The Kingdom of God shall be manifested in me today as power—power to change myself and others.*

"IT WAS NOT ON TALES ARTFULLY SPUN"

This passage puts clearly the essential character of the Christian Gospel as the Word become flesh: "It was not on tales artfully spun that we relied when we told you of the power of our Lord Jesus Christ and his coming; we saw him with our own eyes in majesty, when at the hands of God the Father he was invested with honour and glory, and there came to him from the sublime Presence a voice which said: 'This is my Son, my Beloved, on whom my favour rests.' This voice from heaven we ourselves heard; when it came, we were with him on the sacred mountain" (II Pet. 1:16-18 NEB).

And then the writer adds: "All this only confirms for us the message of the prophets, to which you will do well to attend, because it is like a lamp shining in a murky place, until the day breaks and the morning star rises to illuminate your minds" (II Pet. 1:19). Here the prophets were likened to "a lamp shining in a murky place" and Jesus like the daybreak. The difference? The prophets were the Word become word—hence a lamp; Jesus was the Word become flesh—hence a sunrise!

And those on the mount saw this Word become flesh—become glorified flesh—He was transfigured before their eyes. Now the flesh had become Word and spoke of His glory and majesty. So the flesh is not just a temporary instrument, it is a permanent part of redemption—it too can be glorified. "It's my flesh in the Godhead that I see." So the despised, lowly flesh becomes redeemed as it redeems.

We saw in another reference that Moses and Elijah talked with Jesus "about his departure which he was to accomplish at Jerusalem." His death an accomplishment! Here we see that it was not only an accomplishment but it was God-approved: "This is my Son, my Beloved, on whom my favour rests." God, the Sum Total of Reality, is behind the Word become flesh! He cannot be behind anything else.

O Lord Jesus, we thank Thee that Thou art the fully approved of God and Thou art man and more, becoming fully approved of man. For the Word become word is waning but Thou art waxing, for Thou art the Word become flesh. Amen.

AFFIRMATION FOR THE DAY: *This flesh of mine must become word and reveal the soul's supreme loyalty.*

"THE SPIRIT OF ANTICHRIST"

In the light of what we have been interpreting we are now ready to understand an otherwise startling passage: "By this you know the Spirit of God: every spirit which confesses that Jesus Christ has come in the flesh is of God, and every spirit which does not confess Jesus is not of God. This is the spirit of antichrist, of which you heard that it was coming and now it is in the world already" (I John 4:2, 3).

The immediate reference here was to the Gnostics. They were "the knowers"—they knew by immediate intuition apart from the Incarnation of Jesus. They bypassed the Incarnation and said they could know immediately within by intuition. They affected to regard the flesh as impure and the spirit alone as pure—so they could know God and life apart from Jesus coming in the flesh. This, John brands as antichrist. His words sound severe, but he was profoundly right, for it was the substituting of the Word become word, for the Word become flesh. Man has the answers in himself instead of finding the answers in the Incarnate Jesus. In other words, man makes himself the medium of revelation instead of taking the Son of God as the medium—man makes himself God.

No words are too sharp at this point, for the division is sharp—this is antichrist. This cuts the root of the whole of the Christian revelation and substitutes man's wisdom. And yet the descendants of the Gnostics are many and are with us now and have many followers.

Those who turn the Christian faith into a philosophy or moralism are descendants—distant descendants of the Gonostics—for philosophies came from philosophers and moralism came from moralists. Man's ideas tinged with Christian nomenclature, but man's ideas are still earthborn. The Gospel produces philosophies, but it is not a philosophy—it is a Fact—the Fact of Jesus Christ. Philosophies are man's ideas about God, Jesus is God's idea about Himself—the Word become flesh.

O Lord Jesus, we turn to Thee. To whom else can we go, for Thou hast the words of eternal life, for Thou art the Word of Eternal Life become Flesh? In Thee we see and we find our Heavenly Father. And seeing and finding Him sufficeth us. We thank Thee. Amen.

AFFIRMATION FOR THE DAY: *The answers are not in me—they are in Him, not self-reference but Christ-reference.*

"NO DIFFERENCE . . . IF JESUS NEVER LIVED"

We are looking at those who bypass the Incarnation as the antichrists. Why does the non-Christian prefer that we preach principles and not the Person? It is simple: The Person demands decision and commitment—Follow me. The principles demand study and weighing, but no life commitment. Principles demand no more than mental assent, but Jesus, the Person, demands us as persons—the total person, not mental assent, but life decision and dedication. The difference is profound. Another Hindu said to me, "We are all interested in the universal Christ." And when I asked him, "Not in the Incarnate Jesus?" he replied, "No, we are only interested in the universal Christ." The reason was obvious: Into the universal Christ—the Christ, not rooted in history, they could put any content, even a Hindu content. But you cannot put any content you want into Jesus, the Incarnate, for He has put His own content, the content of His life and teaching lived out in history. He is in history, though now universal, and demands that we follow Him in history, in our own day-by-day lives.

Bultmann has a large modern following. He told a friend of mine, head of a theological college, that "it would make no difference to my theology if Jesus never lived." He has accepted the Word become word, but not the Word become flesh, so it is something other than the Christian Gospel.

But if Jesus never lived, then His teaching had no historical backing, no illustrative content. Moreover, we have no idea of the truth of a proposition or idea until it is put under life to see what life will do to it. "In any battle of ideas the victory must go to those ideas which are guaranteed by the facts." The ideas of the Gospel are guaranteed by the fact of Jesus. Cut out that guarantee and your ideas have no guarantee. They are the Word become word.

O Jesus blessed One, Thou art the Guarantee to all that we hold. In Thee we hold steady, for in Thee "all things consist," or hold together. Thou art the cement that holds life from flying apart at the seams under pressure. We thank Thee for Thyself. Amen.

AFFIRMATION FOR THE DAY: *If Jesus never lived, then the words apart from Jesus have a human content in them.*

DAMNING OTHERS INSTEAD OF RESCUING
THE DAMNED

We continue to look at the persons and systems which bypass the Incarnation. Any movement which suggests guidance from God without reference to the revelation of God in Jesus Christ is bypassing the Incarnation. Apart from Jesus we know little about God and what we know is wrong. You see the Father in the son, or you don't see Him. You substitute your ideas of God for God's revelation of Himself, and thus make yourself and your ideas the mediator. "There is one Mediator between God and man, himself man, Jesus Christ." You don't go directly to God if you bypass Jesus; you substitute yourself and your ideas as the mediator. That, says John, is antichrist.

Perhaps the most serious tendency, because it is the most widespread, is the tendency of the emphasis of finding guidance from God within. If you do not have the corrective of the revelation of God in Jesus Christ, you are liable to listen to the voice of the subconscious and call it God's guidance. One man said, "I heard God say, 'Your relationships with S. (his wife) are dissolved, and I am giving you new ones.'" On the strength of that he got a divorce and has become a spiritual wreck.

Existentialism would seem to be an ally with the Word became flesh since it demands that life be faced as it exists. But existentialism seems to be now becoming a cult which shocks by verbal paradoxes. Instead of shocking people into change by loving examples, it seems bent on shocking by verbal invective. In other words, it is the word of shock become word, not the word of shock become flesh.

And often evangelicalism itself, instead of propagating itself by evangelism and producing changed lives, makes its stock in trade, criticism, not conversion; damning others instead of rescuing the damned. It is all a species of the Word become word. It is bypassing the Word become flesh.

O Jesus, Savior and Revealer, open my eyes that I may be saved from substituting words for the Word become flesh. For words are so easy, so cheap, but, oh, so deadly. Save me from them. For they become dry river beds—no water. I thirst for Thee. Amen.

AFFIRMATION FOR THE DAY: *I am committed to the Word become flesh; let me be an illustration of my committal.*

ECUMENICITY IN SHOES

We are looking at the bypassing of the Incarnation, some of it conscious and deliberate and some of it unconscious. Take the word, the blessed word "ecumenical"—we've actually learned to pronounce it, but not produce it. Halford Luccock says that "the word ecumenical does not come out of the everywhere into the here." And it is only when it becomes the "here" that it becomes power. It is refreshing to turn from the endless discussions on ecumenicity, going round in circles, getting nowhere, to a quiet experiment, an illustration of the word of ecumenicity become flesh.

In Lunenburg, Massachusetts, there were two churches in a town of 2,500, just struggling to keep their heads above water. They heard of the principle of Federal Union and decided to try it, to put it in shoes. They decided to have one church—"The Church of Jesus Christ in Lunenburg," but under it two branches—the Congregational Branch and the Methodist Branch, each with its pastor and each with its emphasis. Over those branches they put "The United Parish," a body made of representatives of the two Branches. In this "United Parish," they began to do things together. Soon they were doing twelve things, the last, a united budget. The Congregational Branch was the stronger of the two, so they said to the Methodist Branch, "You have only a student pastor, put enough in your budget to get a full-time pastor and a good one, and we will go out to the community together to get it." They did. The Congregational Branch increased its income 48 percent and the Methodist Branch 128 percent. They went out to the community in visitation evangelism, two by two, one from each Branch, to strengthen both Branches, for now they belonged to one church and the strength of each was the strength of all. Each Branch doubled its constituency. Then there were those who did not belong to either of these Branches, and they were allowed to join "The United Parish" without losing their denominational loyalties. This took in all the church people of the town. The pastors were paid partly by their Branches and partly by the "United Parish" and were thus pastors of a total community.

O Father God, gather us into one flock. We may not necessarily be in the same fold, but we can and do belong to the same flock. Help us to feel and act upon our oneness. For in Christ we are one. Help us to act like it. Amen.

AFFIRMATION FOR THE DAY: *Every one who belongs to Christ belongs to every one who belongs to Christ.*

CHURCH UNION LED TO COMMUNITY UNION

We continue our consideration of ecumenicity become flesh in the town of Lunenburg, Massachusetts. The union there was a federal union made up of the Congregationalist Branch, the Methodist Branch and the various people, not Congregationalist or Methodist who were brought in as members of the United Parish. When they saw they had church union they went a step further and planned community union—they united the community around the United Church. They went out and raised $130,000 to put up a parish house which would be a center for church and community activities. The two Branches had separate church services, but one Sunday school in the parish house, thus saving each Branch from building a separate educational plant. The young couples could now do community and church service as one. They did not have to choose between them.

The tenth anniversary celebration brought out the fact that the churches and town had found real unity. And were they enthusiastic! At a panel discussion of achievements the Methodist pastor said, "Before the coming of this union it was not respectable to be a Methodist in this town. Now it is. Before, I was the pastor of a segment of the town—the Methodists; now with my brother pastor I'm the pastor of a whole town, we are both in on everything."

The Methodist and Congregationalist district superintendents were at the celebration and backing the plan, for the two Branches were still members of the Methodist and Congregational wider fellowships and sent their benevolences to them. Yet they were really united at the local level.

And now the plan is being inaugurated in a hundred localities across the country with the Lunenberg group giving their witness to what has happened. Dr. Pat McConnell, a rural-life expert, said, "This is the best answer on the local level we have." But this is Federal Union at the grass roots, ecumenicity in shoes, the word of church union become flesh.

O God, our Father, as we have seen these possibilities help us to act upon them and put them into operation. For Thy prayer that we may be one must be answered. Help us to answer it by planting these demonstration centers everywhere. In Jesus' Name. Amen.

AFFIRMATION FOR THE DAY: *I will demonstrate the ecumenical spirit by being a brother to all my brothers in Christ.*

"WHEN YOU SPEAK, GOD SPEAKS"

As we have been discussing the Word become flesh, in specific situations, I am reminded that I am in a section of India, Kerala, where an Indian Christian judge used to arise at 4:00 A.M. and have an hour of devotion and prayer, and then still kneeling he would write the judgments of the day. He would thus take the justice of God and translate it into courtroom justice—the word of Justice become flesh. No wonder his judgments were permeated with something beyond human wisdom. A Brahmin lawyer got out of hand one day in the court and the judge said, "I'm sorry, but I'll have to fine you for contempt of court." The lawyer straightened up and said, "Your Honor, if you fine me I will take it as the very judgment of God, for when you speak God speaks." The word of justice had become flesh.

Another step further was taken by Supreme Court Judge Youngdahl of Minnesota, who heard me say that Christian men should go into politics with the same sense of dedication as a man going into the ministry and that services of commission and consecration should be had for them just as we have ordination services for those going into the ministry. It went home: "Why shouldn't I give up the securities of the Supreme Bench and go into politics to help clean up the State?" He did, was reelected three times Governor and did just that—he helped clean corruption from the state. He was the word of justice become flesh where it counts—at the place of putting laws into effect.

Tucson, Arizona, was fast becoming disreputable, another Las Vegas, a Reno. One hundred citizens, banded together by a common purpose—to clean up Tucson—went to work and did just that. And now Tucson is one of the most respectable and progressive cities in America. The word of public sentiment became flesh in a hundred men. And the Word become flesh became power.

O God, our Father, today I shall meet situations which will need action—dedicated, determined action. Help me this day to meet everything with a prayer and a purpose to turn every opportunity into obligation and every obligation into operation. In Jesus' Name. Amen.

AFFIRMATION FOR THE DAY: *I shall be at the disposal of God today to make by His grace all my Christian attitudes into Christian actions.*

"THEN WE GO OUT AND DO SOMETHING ABOUT IT"

Someone asked George Williams, the founder of the YMCA, what was the secret of the success of the movement and he replied, "Well, if there is any secret it may be found in this: We see a need, we pray about it and then we go out and do something about it." That last was the Word become flesh—hence power. Without that last they would have been like the well-fed geese who made as though they were going to take off and fly, marched up and down, flapped their wings a few times, and then returned to their feeding.

Some rich Hindus were sent off with bands and banners from Hyderabad to walk on a pilgrimage to Banaras. They got the send-off, walked out about ten miles, returned at nightfall, took the train in comfort to Banaras! It was the word of foot pilgrimage become word.

Another Hindu promised before his god in the presence of his wife that he would give half the crop if the god would give a good crop. His wife shook him by the shoulder and whispered, "That's too much." The husband replied by sticking out his tongue and wiggling it—the sign: "I don't mean it!" The word of promise become word. We do that too. We promise God our "all" and it turns out to be "some." Or we are like the youth who prayed, "Tell me, O God, what you want me to do and I'll do it." And then added: "I hope it will be in an advisory capacity!" Or we pray the prayer of Isaiah, thus, "Here am I, Lord, send him!"

On the other hand, there are those who like "Brother Bryan" of Birmingham, Alabama, the patron saint of that city, who listened to a speaker telling how to win people to Christ, stood it as long as he could, left the meeting, went across the street, sat down with a workman who was eating his lunch and led him to Christ. The word of soul-winning became flesh. The Scripture says, "Behold a sower went out to sow. And as he sowed . . . " he did what he came out to do—he sowed. Some preachers go into the ministry to win souls and stay in to win applause and commendation.

O Blessed Redeemer, redeem me from an intoxication of words that stop me this side of putting them into action. May I be long on deeds and short on words. And may all my words that are true become true through action. Amen.

AFFIRMATION FOR THE DAY: *My life motto: See a need, pray about it, do something about it.*

WHERE IS THE PLACE OF AUTHORITY IN THE CHRISTIAN FAITH?

The question of where the place of authority rests in the Christian faith is acute in the Christian world today. I am writing this in a section of India where churches are being torn apart by it. Perhaps this viewpoint of Christianity as being the Word become flesh can throw light on it.

To this question of where authority resides in the Christian faith three great historic answers have been given. One group says, The Infallible Bible; the second, The Infallible Christian Experience; the third, The Infallible Church.

Each of these holds a kernel of truth, with a wrapping of less than truth. The Bible is infallible—vitally infallible. If you take the way it shows you, you will infallibly find God. For it shows you Jesus and Jesus is that Way. Jesus is the Way from God and therefore the Way to God. The rays of the sun are the way of the sun to us, so they are the way to the sun. If you substitute in place of Jesus your thoughts about God, your techniques on how to find God, then you become the way to the Father. That makes you the mediator between God and man. But there is only one Mediator between God and man—Jesus, and the Bible leads you to Him.

The Bible is inspired because it is inspiring. It is a revelation because it reveals. God has gone into it, for God comes out of it—the God-man comes out of it. It is the inspired record of Him. The Bible is not the revelation of God; that would be the Word become printer's ink. But the Bible is the inspired Record of Revelation—the Revelation is seen in the face of Jesus Christ; the Word become flesh. He is the final and perfect Revelation of God.

O Blessed Revealer of God our Father, we are in awe at the Revelation. For it is all beyond our fondest hopes and imaginations. But not beyond our grasp by faith and appreciation. It is too good to be true. But it is true. I've found it so. Amen.

AFFIRMATION FOR THE DAY: *I love the Bible, for these words take me beyond the words to the Word—the Word made flesh.*

THREE SUGGESTED PLACES—THE BIBLE, CHRISTIAN EXPERIENCE, THE CHURCH

We saw yesterday that the truth in the infallibility of the Bible is that if we take the Way it shows—Jesus as the Way—then we infallibly find God. This is vital infallibility.

The second answer is that the place of authority is in infallible Christian experience. There is a great truth here, for "he who says experience says science." That which has gone through one's own experience is firsthand and incontrovertible. One knows that he knows and is sure that he is sure. In "The Inner Light" Frederick Myers said:

> Whoso has felt the Spirit of the Highest
> Cannot confound nor doubt Him nor deny
> Yea, with one voice, O world, though thou deniest
> Stand thou on that side, for on this side am I.

One who knows Him "cannot but speak the things which he has seen and heard." So there is a real infallibility in Christian experience.

The third place of authority is claimed to be the infallible church. There is only one church that claims that infallibility. To be infallible this church claims to be Christ. This view expounded in the pulpit of St. Patrick's Cathedral, New York, by the Rev. Bernard P. Donachie says, "The Catholic Church claims to be Christ. She acts like Christ and she can prove from the Scriptures that she is Christ." The answer to that is simple: A Hindu on board a British ship claimed to be Christ. The bluff British captain listened to his claim and commented, "Well, if you're Christ then I'm going to change my religion." If the Roman Catholic Church acts like Christ, is Christ, then I too would have to change my religion!

However, there is a truth in the infallibility of the church. But it is not the truth of an infallible pope, or the church being Christ Himself. We hope to find that truth.

O Father God, guide us amid the maze of claims and counterclaims and let us see Thy face—Thy face in the face of Thy Son. For any other likeness is unlikeness and any other Face on Thee means that Thou art defaced. Save us. Amen.

AFFIRMATION FOR THE DAY: *I can let my full weight down only on the Divine—no human authority will suffice.*

REALITY DIVIDED INTO OBJECTIVE AND
SUBJECTIVE REALITY

We must now gather up the truth in each of these strands of truth to see if we can come nearer the truth.

Someone has said that reality is divided into objective and subjective reality. Objective reality is that which has occurred in history; subjective reality is that which has occurred in our experience. Each kind of reality can be proved to a high degree of certainty. But the highest degree of certainty is where the objective becomes the subjective—the historical becomes the experimental—and corroborate each other.

In the Christian faith there is the historical Jesus—the Word become flesh. But that historical Jesus becomes the Christ of experience—the Word becomes flesh in us, in an imperfect way, of course, but in a real way. The experimental corroborates the historical. So the two kinds of reality come together and become one. This brings a high degree of certainty—objective and subjective reality verify each other. Christ lived—He lives in me. Myths cannot produce reality, for like produces like. Only if Christ is real in history can He be real in experience.

So Paul says, "If Christ has not been raised, then our preaching is in vain and your faith is in vain" (I Cor. 15:14). And it may be added, "Your experience is a myth, for it was founded on a myth." So those who cut the historical from under Christianity use a two-edged sword—they cut both the historical and the experimental at the same time. They make Christianity the Word become word and, at the same time, make experience the Word become word. And that word is myth. The Word cannot be saved from becoming myth unless that Word becomes flesh in history and flesh in us. So the Christian faith stands or falls upon the Word became flesh.

But it stands, for the history is corroborated by experience. "You ask me how I know He lived? He lives, He lives within my heart." The person who has experienced the living Christ is certain with an invincible certainty—it is an immediate underived certainty.

O Blessed Redeemer, Thou has redeemed me from resting on question marks. Thou has turned all my question marks into exclamation points. I know Thee better than I know anyone else. Thou art more intimate than breathing. Amen.

AFFIRMATION FOR THE DAY: *I know Him without in history, I know Him within in experience—I know Him.*

HISTORICAL AND EXPERIMENTAL
CORROBORATED BY THE COLLECTIVE

We are studying the place of authority in Christianity, and we have seen that two kinds of reality—the historical and the experimental—corroborate each other. This brings a very high degree of certainty. But there is one weak spot in this—it rests too much on the individual experience, and the individual may be deceived—he may be suffering from a hallucination. That weak spot can only be corrected when the individual experience is corroborated by collective experience.

And the Church supplies the collective experience. The claim of the Church to be infallible is, of course, silly, beneath contempt. But what the Church supplies is the collective corroboration of the individual experience. In all ages, in all climes, among all classes of people, young and old, male and female, this experience of the living Christ within has been experienced as the central reality of life. When I was a young Christian I met with a man, very argumentative and very clever. He could run circles around me when it came to an argument. So finally I said, "Well, one thing I do know that whereas I was blind, now I see." He was silent. His arguments couldn't touch that.

People do not speak of experiencing Buddha—they worship him in an image. Experiencing him? No. People do not speak of realizing within the Virgin Mary—it is always an "appearance," "a vision," never an experience. The Hindus take long pilgrimages to get the "darshan" of the god—the "meeting" with the deity in the person of the idol—it is not an experiencing within. But the real and simple Christian does experience Him within. He discounts "appearances" and "visions" of Jesus. His attitude: "I do not need or want such 'appearances' or 'visions'—I have Him within. He discounts "appearances" and "visions" of Jesus. His attitude: "I do not need or want such 'appearances' or 'visions'—I have Him within—all the time. 'Lo, I am with you always' is fact. I need no fading visions, I have the unfading Fact. I am never alone, hence never lonely." And the reality of that Fact is seen in the fruits of changed character and attitudes. Christian experience is a Solid Reality.

O Lord Jesus, I do not ask Thee to come down from heaven in vision or dream, for that would be betrayal—betrayal of this blessed Fact within. Thou hast brought heaven to me. I ask no heavenly Vision. I have Him. Thou art my Heaven—now. Amen.

AFFIRMATION FOR THE DAY: *If I rest on a "vision" I have to look back; if I rest on the present living Christ I look within.*

THE PLACE OF AUTHORITY: AT THE JUNCTION
WHERE THE HISTORICAL BECOMES THE
EXPERIMENTAL AND IS CORROBORATED
BY THE COLLECTIVE

We have been insisting on the fact of Christian experience. It is a fact—a corroborated fact among all races—I've found it so. I've heard the people of all languages speaking the same language—the language of a common experience. This is the corroborating witness of the Church. So the individual does not stand alone in his sole and unique experience—he shares it with every real Christian of every age.

This impressive collective verification of individual experience seals the individual experience as true. It works whenever tried and is as well verified as any verified scientific fact.

So the threefold strands come together—the Historical, the Experimental, and the Collective—and they verify the same thing. Where then is the place of authority in the Christian faith? It is at the junction where the Historical becomes the Experimental and is verified by the Collective Experience. That Junction is the Place of Authority.

So the Christian faith does not rest on the historical alone, nor the experimental alone, nor the collective alone. Each one alone would be weak. But all coming together and witnessing to the same thing brings the highest certainty that the human being can know. It is a Threefold Cord that cannot be broken; all other authority compared to this is weak.

And this authority is the Word become flesh at all three stages—the Historical is the Word become flesh, the Experimental is the Word become flesh, and the Collective is the Word become flesh. The place of authority is not an impersonal junction, for at that junction is "Jesus is Lord"—the Word become flesh. So He is the Word become flesh, verified by experiments in making the Word become flesh in personal and collective experience. So the place of authority is not in councils, or popes, or conventions—it is in the Person—the Word become flesh—and verified by persons in whom that Word has become flesh in experience.

O Lord Jesus, my Redeemer and my Authority, I rest in Thee, for Thou art the manifested God. I can let my full weight down knowing that I cannot and I will not be let down. And this blessed Authority is written within me—I want to obey it. Amen.

AFFIRMATION FOR THE DAY: *I am held by a threefold Cord which cannot be broken.*

FRUIT OF THE INNER LIFE
NOT MAGICAL BUT MORAL

If the place of authority is the experimentally corroborated Word become flesh, then the center of our propagating of this Gospel must be the Word become flesh in us. The center of the propagation is not a proposition—it is a Person, or persons, in whom the Word has become flesh. One of the parables speaks of the seed as "when anyone hears the word of the kingdom," and then adds, "The good seed means the sons of the kingdom" (Matt. 13:19, 38). So "the Word of the Kingdom is "the sons of the kingdom"—the Word of the Kingdom made flesh. Propaganda must be through a Person, or persons.

This determines whether some methods are in line with the Christian faith and whether some have departed from it—the word become flesh is in line, and the Word become word is a departure. Take these two accounts of what constitutes the outcome of the Holy Spirit within. One passage says: "And these signs will accompany those who believe: in my name they will cast out demons; they will speak in new tongues; they will pick up serpents, and if they drink any deadly thing, it will not hurt them; they will lay their hands on the sick, and they will recover" (Mark 16:17). Now note these "signs" of the believer in Christ. Not one of them is a moral quality embodied in the character and life of the believer—every one a magical power exerted apart from his character and life. If these had been the signs of a Christian we would never have heard of Christianity—it would have died along with the wonder cults. Man filled out this list, for all the translations say that the Gospel of Mark was lost from the eighth verse on and this was a second or third-century attempt to fill it out. And when man, unaided in inspiration, makes out a list of qualities of a Christian he almost invariably endows man with magical rather than moral qualities—as here. It is the word become magic rather than the Word become flesh. It tries to coerce the minds of men by signs and wonders instead of converting the minds of men by moral and spiritual living.

O Jesus my Lord, I thank Thee that Thy revelation was moral not magical—out of life, not imposed on life. We gaze at Thee and see not a desire to impress us but a desire to redeem us. Save us from twisting that revelation into our image, not Thine. Amen.

AFFIRMATION FOR THE DAY: *If I am always trying to impress people by my powers it leaves me self-conscious.*

THE FRUIT OF THE SPIRIT—ALL MORAL

We saw yesterday the uninspired list of qualities of a Christian believer. It was the Word become magic. Now look at an inspired list where the Word has become flesh: "But the fruit of the Spirit is love, joy, peace, patience, kindness, goodness, faithfulness, gentleness, self-control" (Gal. 5:22). Every one of these is a moral quality and a Christian moral quality. These qualities begin with "love"—the highest Christian characteristic—and end in "self-control"—a self controlled by love. Not one of these can be manifested except through character and life, by the Word becoming flesh.

If you deal in signs and wonders as the authentication of a faith you run into this Indian newspaper clipping in yesterday's paper:

Nine pandits went on hunger strike yesterday to protest against nonpayment of remuneration to 800 priests who were engaged in a ceremony, or Great Sacrifice, started a month ago to appease the conjunction of eight planets. The principal organizer of the Yagna, or sacrifice, who is himself a pandit, was kept confined in a room by the priests as the former refused to pay the remuneration due on the plea that the feared deluge did not occur. Police arrived and rescued him. According to the hunger strikers the remuneration worked out to a hundred thousand rupees.

That is the aftermath of religion based on outwardism, on magic.

The Christian faith keeps its weapons clean. It wins by being winsome; it saves by exhibiting salvation; it converts by being converted.

And these fruits of the Spirit are not something of which you can have too much. They are universal and for all men in all situations. You cannot have too much of love—it can be Love, Unlimited, as it was in the Master. He masters us by being morally and spiritually masterful. The Word of mastery becomes flesh.

Blessed Lord, Thou art all Thou claimest to be and more. For when we look at Thee we see more than what we see. We see the unrevealed and hear the unspoken. We are in awe—lost in wonder, love and praise. We thank Thee. Amen.

AFFIRMATION FOR THE DAY: *I want no "signs" save the signs of Thy moral and spiritual character within me.*

"IDEAS ARE POOR GHOSTS"

It is only as the Word becomes flesh that the Word becomes power. "What you are speaks so loud I cannot hear what you say." For whatever is embodied has the final word in any life. George Eliot puts it this way: "Ideas are poor ghosts until they become incarnate. Then those ideas look out at us with compassionate eyes, touch us with warm, redemptive hands, then they shake us like a passion."

The idea of freedom in India was a poor ghost until it took flesh in Mahatma Gandhi. It existed in resolutions drawn up by the Indian National Congress. They became stronger and stronger as the years came and went, but the British sat tight, for these resolutions were the word become word. Then something happened. The Word of freedom became flesh in a person—Mahatma Gandhi appeared. I have told in *Christian Maturity* the story of his being in a first-class compartment with a first-class ticket on a South African train when a white man got in and objected to riding with a man of color. The guard was called and Gandhi was ejected. This turned out to be the most expensive expulsion in modern history, for it meant the expulsion of the white man from the whole of the sovereignty of the East and of Africa. As he walked the station platform at midnight he conceived the idea of nonviolent, non-cooperation. Reduced to its essence it was this: "I won't hate you, but I won't obey you. Do what you like. I will match my capacity to suffer against your capacity to inflict the suffering—my soul force against your physical force, and I'll wear you down by good will." That idea took flesh in the little man. Freedom became embodied in him—looked out at us with compassionate eyes, touched us with redemptive hands and shook India and the world like a passion. He won the freedom of 400,000,000 people. A new power had been loosed in the world—the power of nonviolent soul force.

O Father, we thank Thee for this gentle power of love. We have seen it supremely in Thy Son and when reflected in the sons of men it grips us to our depths. Help us to embody this gentle power in all we do and say this day. Amen.

AFFIRMATION FOR THE DAY: *All my ideas will remain poor ghosts until they become embodied in me.*

THE RISING TIDE OF FREEDOM

When India gained her freedom it started a chain reaction—Burma was next, then Ceylon, Indonesia, Indochina, Malaya, Singapore. Then it leaped over to Africa, and when Ghana got her freedom that too started a chain reaction. Thirty-three nations have found their freedom in the short space of three years and most of them are in the United Nations determining the destiny of the world—an international miracle.

In the early days in India I saw a sign on a railway compartment: "For Dheds [outcast] Only." Now the change: until recently an outcaste has been the Minister for Railways! And said a Brahman colleague, "He is an exellent Minister." The revolution was bound to come—bound to come in a violent or nonviolent form. Fortunately, in the southern United States it is taking a nonviolent form, thanks in large measure to Dr. Martin Luther King. I was deeply grateful when he said to me in an interview with him, "I got my first inkling of the possibility of nonviolent non-cooperation from your book on *Mahatma Gandhi—an Interpretation.* And I determined to apply the method to the doing away with segregation in our land." Was I grateful, for I had thought that the book had not accomplished much! And here it was helping to accomplish a nonviolent revolution!

The outcastes of Kerala were denied the right of certain roads. Some outcaste Christians took a procession on that road. They met a Brahman. He could not go back and there was water on each side of the road. So the only thing he could do was to get out in the water up to his neck while the outcastes had the road! The dispossessed are on the march—the social revolution is on. And it can't be stopped for it has behind it the ground swell of a world revolution. A Negro minister put it this way, "The bell is tolling and the tide is rolling in, and you can no more stop it than you can turn back the tides of Hampton Roads with your two hands." And no right thinking man wants to stop it. For all of us are bound in every man's bondage; we are free only in every man's freedom.

O Lord Christ, we thank Thee that as the Son of man Thou art behind the rise of the sons of man. Thy Spirit is stirring the spirits of men to throw off old bondages and old yokes. We watch with bated breath this rise of man. May it come out at Thy feet. Amen.

AFFIRMATION FOR THE DAY: *Since I stand with the Son of man I will stand with the sons of men in their upward rise.*

THE WORD OF DEMOCRACY BECOMES FLESH IN LINCOLN

We are looking at the Word become power when the Word becomes flesh. The word of democracy was a poor ghost until it became flesh in Lincoln. It existed in the early documents of our fathers, beautifully stated, but it lacked dynamic—lacked it till Lincoln came.

Then the word of democracy became flesh in a person. It looked out of his compassionate eyes, it touched us with his great rugged redemptive hands, and then it shook the world like a passion. We saw democracy take flesh. More books have been written about Lincoln than any ten Americans—over 8,000. And over 100,000 pamphlets and articles have been written about him. Why? Because we feel that in Lincoln we *see* democracy; in others we *hear* it.

And we see it never so clearly as when Lincoln as the victor went into Richmond to take over the seat of the Confederacy. He went into the room where Jefferson Davis had sat at his desk. There alone he stayed so long that when those waiting were wondering what was detaining him and having opened the door a bit they found him seated at the desk with his hands up to his head weeping—weeping for the fallen sons of North and South. There was Democracy personified, bowed in grief. A grateful nation cannot forget that sight.

Paul writes an unforgettable sentence: "That now as always the greatness of Christ will shine out clearly in my person" (Phil. 1:20 NEB). When we think of Paul, the greatness of Christ shines clearly in his person. When we think of Lincoln, the greatness of Democracy shines clearly in his person. One of the greatest eye doctors of India performed over 100,000 operations on the eye. When I asked him how he began it all he said, "As a young doctor I couldn't get any patients. So I waited in my office for a blind beggar to go by, and I would rush out and pull him into my office and operate on him before he had time to protest. I was mad after eyes." The greatness of Devotion shines clearly in his person.

O Jesus my Lord, the greatness of the Father shines clearly in Thy person. When we see Thee we see the Father. And what a Father we see! We cannot love Thee without loving Him. We love Thee both and find Thee One. We are grateful. Amen.

AFFIRMATION FOR THE DAY: *The Word of Victory shall become flesh in me today and look out of compassionate eyes.*

"THAT IS WHAT I WANT"

Only as the Word becomes flesh does the Word become power. Admiral Sato was the commander of the Japanese submarine fleet at Pearl Harbor. I asked him how many submarines he had, and he replied, "Nineteen and a few suicide, pick-a-back type." When I asked him how many of these submarines got into Pearl Harbor, he replied, "Possibly one of the suicide type." (Incidentally, that disposes of the controversy about whether President Roosevelt ordered the submarine net to be lifted before the mouth of Pearl Harbor to allow the Japanese submarine fleet to come in, in order to get America into the war in the Atlantic by the back door. If the net had been lifted the whole of the Japanese submarine fleet would have gone in instead of possibly a suicide type.)

Admiral Sato really believed the emperor was divine and carefully indoctrinated his naval officers in the Naval Academy. When the war came to an end, his world fell to pieces—his admiral's position gone, his income cut off so that he had to work on a farm for his livelihood, and then the emperor announced that he was not divine—his religion was gone. I asked him what happened to his thinking when the emperor announced that he was not divine. "My world turned upside down," he replied. He became bad-tempered, lashing out at everybody and everything. He contemplated suicide. A member of a church asked him to come to the church and get a faith. But it was the Word of faith become word, so he replied, "Oh, I have no time for that." But one day in a prayer meeting in a home he saw something he had never seen before—saw it in the faces of women who had suffered, had lost their husbands in the war, and yet were poised and radiant. "That is what I want," he said to himself as the tears rained down his cheeks. It was the Word become flesh. He was baptized on Easter day. When I asked him if the vacuum within had been filled he smiled and put up his three fingers (Jesus is Lord!). He heard preaching, received an invitation to accept a faith, but only when the Word of Faith became flesh in simple women did it become power.

O Divine Redeemer, we thank Thee for those who so quietly and so unobtrusively show us the Word of Victory become flesh in their own persons. Help me this day to show that Word become flesh in me. In Thy Name. Amen.

AFFIRMATION FOR THE DAY: *If Christ is lifted up in me He will draw men to Himself.*

"I WHO BEGAN AS A MIRACLE HAVE LOST FAITH IN MIRACLES"

This story illustrates the Word of flesh become power. Bishop Chandu Ray, Anglican bishop in Pakistan, was a Hindu teacher in Bishop Cotton School, Simla, when Rev. George Sinker, later a bishop, was principal. Sinker's eyes became dangerously bad and an operation was to be performed the next day. Sinker said to Chandu Ray, "If I lose my eyesight, will you promise to read the Bible to me every day?" He said he would. "Then begin now," said Sinker. He read, "Whatever you ask in my name I will do it." Chandu Ray said, "If your Christ is real why can't we ask Him to heal you? And if He is real, I will follow Him." They prayed and wept all night.

The next morning the British doctor examined him. He was puzzled and sent for one instrument and then another. The doctor said, "I cannot understand this. What happened last night. Did you weep?" He was told that they did. "Well, the pressure is gone, and I've decided not to operate." The eyes got well. Chandu Ray said, "He saw, and I saw too! I was converted through it." He went to a theological college in Calcutta, but his faith was nearly wrecked. He came back and began preaching question marks. A New Zealand missionary said to him, "Chandu Ray, what is the matter? You have lost something." It made him angry. Then he broke down and told her all, "I, who began as a miracle, have lost faith in miracles." She gave him a book, *The Christ of the Scriptures.* He found Him again and later became a bishop. One day he felt impelled to go to a certain man to get him to translate the Bible into Gurmukhi. But the man was dirty, unkempt, and a drug addict. But the Voice persisted: "Go to him." He did three times. The man said, "Why do you come? You don't love me." He broke down and told what was in his heart. "But how can I ask you if you're a drug addict?" The man said, "Come back tomorrow. You pray and I'll pray." The man was changed. He never touched drugs again. And he did a magnificent job of translation, and the two Sikhs who helped him translate were converted.

O Father, as Thy servant Chandu Ray saw a miracle before his eyes and became a miracle, help me, who has seen the miracle of Jesus and lesser miracles, to become a miracle. May my life today be a miracle of grace. Amen.

AFFIRMATION FOR THE DAY: *I will not believe in miracles; I'll be one.*

"YOU DIDN'T GET THAT OUT OF A BOOK"

We are considering the Word become flesh as the Word become power. My granddaughter of sixteen surprised us with this: "This professor talked about a philosophy of life and he had none." At sixteen she saw through it at once! Another girl said of a professor, "They give us bigger words for what we already know." She too saw it was the Word become word—bigger words, but the same words still.

On the other hand they see the reality too. A candy manufacturer, outstanding and influential and generous, came to the conclusion that his spiritual life was shallow and ineffective because he was giving his money to God but not himself. He made his surrender to Christ and became a new man. He called his men together and told them what had happened to him. He said to them, "When you become bitter in soul don't pour it into the candy—it won't taste good. Come and pour it into my ears, and I'll see what I can do to help you. Moreover, I'm setting up a prayer chapel in the factory, and if you get down and discouraged and upset, go into the chapel and pray—on company time." When he taught his Sunday-school class the next Sunday, one of his class, a young married woman, came up and said: "Well, Mr. Brock, you didn't get that out of a book." She saw the difference, felt the difference, and there was a difference—the Word had become flesh. That which was from the heart reached the heart.

In Ceylon there was a big political gathering. When two politicians came in, each was greeted with applause. But when a Christian lawyer came in, a man noted for his integrity and service, the crowd arose, stood silently with folded hands—an act of reverence. Their respect was too great for applause.

Preaching is for the few. Witnessing is open to all. And you don't have to be a saint to do it—just a sincere, imperfect follower of a very Perfect Lord.

Dear Lord and Father, we thank Thee that we have the privilege of being Thy witness. We don't need to know much in order to do this—nothing except to know what happened to us. So we shall be Thy joyful witness. Amen.

AFFIRMATION FOR THE DAY: *Anything that meets my need as a man will probably meet the needs of other men.*

"HE'S OFFERING ME SECURITY"

We ended yesterday with the emphasis that personal witness is personal power. A very sensitive woman was listening to a speaker and she said to herself, "Listen ears, this is not preaching, this is revelation." When such a speaker is speaking you hear more than you hear and see more than you see. The life behind the words witnesses.

We had in our Ashrams this summer in America Sister Lila, a Greek Orthodox nun of the Bethany Convent in Jerusalem. I first met her in India. She is an expert masseuse. And as she gave me a massage I asked her, "What is the meaning of life?" And without a moment's hesitation she replied, "The meaning of life is to love." And she literally makes that the meaning for her—she lives by and for love. She loves everybody, so all doors are open to her. Hindus dying by the Ganges would ask to hold her hand as they slipped into the unknown. I was so impressed by her amazing capacity to love everybody that I wrote her a letter suggesting that I allow me to provide her bare travel expenses and food, and then she could be free to serve everybody—Hindus, Mohammedans, and Christians—with her message, for she travels about without money, trusting God implicitly. Someone told me of her reaction when she got the letter, "Why it is a temptation of the devil. He is offering me security and I don't want security—I want adventure in the will of God." She let us have a glimpse of a New Testament Christian. What she said was illuminating, but what she did not say was more illuminating—it was what she was—the Word made flesh.

O Jesus, we thank Thee for Heaven-sent souls like Sister Lila, the breath of another world upon our spirits. In them we see revelation. We thank Thee. Amen.

AFFIRMATION FOR THE DAY: *In some small way may the words said of an Abbe, as he was about to speak to a mob in the French Revolution, be true of me: "Forty years of pure living are about to address you."*

THE MARKS OF A CHRISTIAN CHURCH

We have many modern discussions on the nature of the church. But they are for the most part discussions, not demonstrations. They show a high blood pressure of creeds and an anemia of deeds. The New Testament is different—it does not discuss the theoretical nature of the Church—it gives us a demonstration of the Church. We see it at Antioch. "And in Antioch the disciples were for the first time called Christians" (Acts 11:26).

In those days they gave names according to characteristics. Simon was surnamed Peter, a rock; Joseph was called Barnabas, Son of consolation. So at Antioch a name was given which fitted the group—the characteristics of Christ were in this group, so they were called the Christ-ians. The group formed a Christian church—the words "Christian Church" become flesh. We must examine its marks.

First, *it was essentially a lay church*. It was founded by laymen and laymen constituted and carried on the church. That made it true to the essential nature of Christianity as a lay movement. "Now those who were scattered because of the persecution that arose over Stephen traveled as far as Phoenicia and Cyprus and Antioch, speaking the word to none except Jews. But there were some of them, men of Cyprus and Cyrene, who on coming to Antioch spoke to the Greeks also, preaching of the Lord Jesus. And the hand of the Lord was with them, and a great number that believed turned to the Lord" (Acts 11:19-21). This church was founded by a lay group, scattered under the persecution which arose over Stephen, a layman. That fixed the New Testament Church as a lay church. Jesus and the disciples were laymen, no hands having been laid on them in ordination, and the Seven, the lay group, became the center of spiritual contagion. Paul, a layman, became the spearhead of this lay movement. The Christian movement continued a lay movement until the third century when it was changed into a clerical movement and the laymen pushed to the margin.

O Father God, Thy church is for Thy children, for all Thy children. Save us from dividing Thy family into clerical and lay. For we are all clerical and all lay. We are persons for whom Christ died. And we are one family, hence equal. Amen.

AFFIRMATION FOR THE DAY: *If the Christian movement is a lay movement then I will be at home there.*

NEXT GREAT SPIRITUAL AWAKENING
WILL COME THROUGH THE LAITY

We are examining the Christian Church as seen in the New Testament. It was a lay church. The word *laos* in Greek, from which the word "laity" comes, means literally, "the chosen people of God"—the laity were "the chosen people of God," not only by language derivination but by divine appointment and intention. And this conception and practice held there till the council of Nicea when the Church authorities made it into a church of bishops and clergy, and laymen were relegated to the margin; being a layman was a concession to human frailty, tolerated as second-class. This was perhaps the greatest tragedy that ever struck the church. Revival will only come when the New Testament emphasis is rediscovered. The next great spiritual awakening will come through the laity. The ministers will be the guides and spiritualizers of an essentially lay movement.

Second, *the New Testament church had the marks of the cross upon it.* It was established by a lay group which had suffered for its faith—"Those who were scattered because of the persecution that arose over Stephen." Their faith had cost them something, so it was worth something. It was precious as gold tried in the fire. If the lay group is to be the center again of the Christian movement it will again cost them something to be Christian. Then and then only it will be worth something.

Third, *the Church at Antioch was founded by men who made it interracial.* The Jewish laymen from Jerusalem preached only to the Jews, but laymen from Cyrene and Cyprus, with larger racial contacts and sympathies, preached the Word among the Greeks. So the church was made up of Jews and Greeks. And Negroes. "Now in the church at Antioch there were prophets and teachers, Barnabas, Symeon who was called Niger"— literally "the black," the word from which we get the word "Negro." Symeon was not on the margin, tolerated—he was a "prophet" or "teacher," and laid his hands on Barnabas and Paul. So Barnabas and Paul were commissioned or ordained by a Negro to preach the Gospel to white Europe (Acts 13:1).

O Father, help me to be a good member of a fellowship which knows no boundaries of race and class. Help me to see beyond the extraneous to the real persons. And help me to treat people as though they were what we expect them to be. Amen.

AFFIRMATION FOR THE DAY: *I belong to a Kingdom that knows no frontiers of race and class. I will demonstrate that today.*

THE MARKS OF BARNABAS AND PAUL WERE UPON THIS NEW TESTAMENT CHURCH

We are examining the Church at Antioch as the Word of the Christian church become flesh in a group.

Fourth, *this New Testament Church had the marks of Barnabas upon it.* Those in charge at Jerusalem were wise in sending a layman like Barnabas. Had one of the apostles been sent it would have interrupted the lay character of the Antioch Church. This choice fitted in. For Barnabas was one of the most beautiful characters in the New Testament. He was a man, a Levite, from Cyprus, who sold a field and laid the proceeds at the apostles' feet. His name had been "Joseph" which literally means "one more." He probably belonged to a large family, and when they came to him they ran out of names and simply named him "one more," that is, Joseph. But when he surrendered his all he came not under the law of addition, but of multiplication. They said, in effect, "He is not just one more. He is a multiplication table—he is contagious so we will name him Barnabas, Son of encouragement" (Acts 4:36, 37).

He encouraged everybody. He took Paul when the authorities at Jerusalem were afraid of him and presented him as real. And he took John Mark when Paul refused to take him. He was big-souled. "When he came and saw the grace of God, he was glad"—he could rejoice in the work of others. Smaller men would have picked flaws to make a place for themselves. Not he. No wonder they could say of him: "For he was a good man, full of the Holy Spirit and of faith" (Acts 11:23, 24). The spirit of Barnabas went into the making of this New Testament Church.

Fifth, *the spirit of Paul went into the church and the spirit of this church went into Paul.* When Barnabas saw this type of Christianity he said to himself, "This is the kind of Christianity that young man Saul needs. I must expose him to it." So he went off to Tarsus, sought out Saul, and brought him to Antioch. One of the best things Barnabas ever did. The Church and Paul cross-fertilized each other and both were enriched.

O Father, help me to give and get from the fellowship this day. Give me the teachable heart, ready to learn from anybody. And ready to give of what Thou hast given me. May "take and give" be my rhythmical heartbeats this day. Amen.

AFFIRMATION FOR THE DAY: *Taking with both hands and giving with both hands—my aim and practice.*

A CHURCH THAT CARED

Yesterday we said that the spirit of Paul went into this church at Antioch and the spirit of this Church went into Paul. It was after his contact with Antioch that Saul was changed into Paul. They must have felt that a change in Paul necessitated a change in name—he was enlarged and universalized after his contact with Antioch, no longer the Jew Saul, he was the Roman Paul.

Sixth, *the Church at Antioch was a church that cared.* Van Hugel has defined a Christian as "one who cares." Well, the Antioch church was Christian, for it cared—cared that the believers in Judea were in need of economic help. "And the disciples determined, every one according to his ability, to send relief to the brethren who lived in Judea" (Acts 11:29). That caring was a pattern for the church of the ages: "determined, every one according to his ability, to send relief." Note that phrase: "everyone according to his ability"—suppose that were the standard and determination—note the word "determined"—of every church in Christendom! What couldn't be done! They did it according to that pattern!

Seventh, *their spirituality functioned in material terms and also in social terms.* In the church at Antioch there was Symeon, a Negro, and also "Manean, a member of the court of Herod the tetrarch." Not only were racial distinctions transcended but social distinctions. Manean was from high society, and the Negro was probably from a much lower society. But here race and class distinctions were canceled—a man was a man for whom Christ died.

The social prejudices die hard. A man went to his pastor and said, "If you lay off your emphasis on race justice, here is a check with five numbers." The pastor left the man with his check and kept his soul. He was a Christian; he could do no other. For the Christian faith is class—and race—blind.

O Father God, save us from building a house of God with Thee left out. For where Thy children are excluded Thou art excluded. To have a house of God without Thee is to have a body without a soul—a corpse. Save us from choosing a corpse. In Jesus' Name. Amen.

AFFIRMATION FOR THE DAY: *I belong to a Kingdom that knows no limits of race and class and color—a Kingdom Unlimited.*

THE CONSERVATIVE AND THE RADICAL

We come now to the next mark of the Christian church as seen in Antioch. Eighth, *the church at Antioch held within itself the conservative and the radical.* The account says: "Now in the church at Antioch there were prophets and teachers" (Acts 13:1). The "teachers" are usually the conservative element in society, passing on the lessons and values of the past to the next generation. The "prophets" are usually the radicals, wanting to apply those lessons and values to wider and wider areas of life. There is usually a tension in every group and society between these two—the conservatives pulling back and the radicals pulling ahead.

But these two are necessary for any progressive society—we need to conserve values, and we need to apply values to larger and larger areas of life. If the Negro is treated as a person and not as a Negro, we will find in the South white radicals and Negro radicals on one side in politics, and conservative whites and conservative Negroes on the other. That is a good division. Jesus said, "Every scribe who has been trained for the kingdom of heaven is like a householder who brings out of his treasure what is new and what is old" (Matt. 13:51). Note: "what is new"—the radical, and "what is old"—the conservative. So the kingdom of heaven holds together the radical and the conservative, the new and the old. But note the "new" is first. For the Christian faith is "the Great Change"—it is pressing on the "is" in behalf of the "ought to be." So it is primarily radical, secondarily conservative. But both are needed in society, and the Church must hold them together in a living blend. To try to make a church out of one or the other is to bring spiritual disaster.

Jesus was a living blend of conservative and radical. He said: "Think not that I am come to abolish the law and the prophets; I have come not to abolish them but to fulfill them" (Matt. 5:17). And then He presented the kingdom of God which demanded total change. He was conservative and radical. The Church must be the same.

O Jesus, save us from trying to make Thee only conservative or only radical. For that brings us the limited Christ. We want Thee for what Thou art. Gather us into Thy greatness and help us to be great with Thee. Amen.

AFFIRMATION FOR THE DAY: *I shall be like the man who looks at the mirror on the side of the car and sees the road behind while going ahead.*

COLLECTIVE GUIDANCE

We continue our study of the word of the Church become flesh in Antioch.

Ninth, *the Church was sufficiently united so the group as a group could get collective guidance.* "While they were worshiping the Lord and fasting, the Holy Spirit said, 'Set apart for me Barnabas and Saul for the work to which I have called them.' " (Acts 13:2). Here was a group so attuned to God and so attuned to each other that the Holy Spirit could give them a united guidance. We would have thrown it open to debate, then have taken a vote, and the majority would have ruled. This would have left a disgruntled minority. But their method of guidance was different, they desired to come a common mind—and did—under the guidance of the Holy Spirit. "It seemed good to the Holy Spirit and to us"—that was the classic phrase that characterized the early Church.

And note again, "The Holy Spirit said, 'Set apart for me.' " And again, "So, being sent out by the Holy Spirit . . . " (Acts 13:4). The church, unlike the modern church, did not insist on their label being put on the sending. They did not say, "Missionaries, sent out by the Antioch Church, through the Holy Spirit." We would have had our denominational labels, prominently displayed. "There is no limit to the good you can do provided you do not seek credit for it." That Church asked for no credit and forgot themselves into immortality. We cannot forget those who forgot themselves.

And it did something for Paul and Barnabas to be sent out by the Holy Spirit and not by a church alone. Success and failure were irrelevant—to be true to the call of the Holy Spirit was the only thing that mattered.

So power not their own was working creatively through the Church. It was a contagious center of the new life. The Word became flesh and the flesh became Word.

O Holy Spirit, make me the center of contagion. I offer my powers to be made creative with Thy touch. Thou Spirit of Creation create through me. Create hope, love, joy, and new life in others through me. I can cooperate in creation. Amen.

AFFIRMATION FOR THE DAY: *The Creative God makes me creative.*

HELD TOGETHER IN SPITE OF DIFFERENCE

We note the next mark of the Christian church. Tenth, *this church held together good men who honestly differed—held them in spite of difference.* Paul and Barnabas had a contention—a contention over taking John Mark on another journey when he deserted them on the first journey. Barnabas' viewpoint: "But, Paul, you don't break a man when he makes one break. Our movement is a redemptive movement—we believe in the Gospel of Another Chance." Paul's viewpoint: "But, Barnabas, we must keep our movement clean. We must hold to the Gospel of the Pure Church." Here were two issues out of which two denominations could easily have grown: One, around the issue of the Gospel as Redemption; the other, around the issue of the Gospel as Purity. But no two denominations resulted. Why?

The account says: "And there arose a sharp contention, so that they separated from each other; Barnabas took Mark with him and sailed away to Cyprus, but Paul chose Silas and departed, being commended by the brethren to the grace of the Lord" (Acts 15:39, 40). That "being commended by the brethren by the grace of the Lord," is a part of one sentence and could refer to both Barnabas and Mark and Paul and Silas. In other words they held together brethren in difference. They commended both to the grace of the Lord—and they both needed it!

And this bigheartedness in holding together brethren in difference paid off. John Mark was redeemd, became "profitable" to Paul "for the ministry," and wrote a Gospel. So this Church in commending both groups to the grace of God was redemptive.

These ten marks of a Christian Church showed that the church at Antioch was the Word become flesh in a group. No wonder they were first called "Christians" at Antioch. This group was an organism of the Holy Spirit. Without these ten marks the church is an organization of man—the Word become word. Hence powerless.

O Holy Spirit, we pray Thee to make us into the image of the group at Antioch—an organism of the Holy Spirit. And may the Holy Spirit make us into the image of Christ so we can be truly called Christ-ian. In His name. Amen.

AFFIRMATION FOR THE DAY: *We "are organs one of another," therefore can be "an organism of the Spirit."*

THE WORD BECOMING FLESH
IN GROUP MOVEMENTS

We have looked at the Word of the church become flesh in a group—the group at Antioch. We now leap from the ancient world to this modern world and look at another attempt to make the Word of the Kingdom become flesh in a group.

There has been a great growth of group movements in modern days. They are attempts to put back into the church the koinonia, the fellowship of the Acts. I used to think that the church was born out of pentecost, but the church is not named until the eighth chapter of Acts. It was the koinonia which was born out of the pentecost, for the koinonia is mentioned in the same chapter with the coming of the Spirit: "And they devoted themselves to the apostles' teaching and fellowship [koinonia], to the breaking of bread and the prayers" (Acts 2:42). This koinonia was a close-knit fellowship across all racial and class boundaries, transcending age and sex. It was a fellowship of the Spirit. The group became an organism of the Spirit. This Group became the soul out of which the body of the Church grew; the organism out of which the organization grew. Where you have the koinonia you have the Church, but where you do not have the koinonia there you do not have the Church—you have an organization without the organism.

These modern Group movements are attempts to put back the koinonia into the Church. The Church should be that koinonia itself, but it is often, more often than not, an impersonal collection of believers who meet once a week to worship together—hear a sermon. It is not a close-knit fellowship. One of these attempts to produce the koinonia is the Christian Ashram. It came out of India, the word "Ashram" being from the Sanscrit, A = from, and *shram* = work, a retreat from work. A retreat, a forest school, under a Guru, or Teacher. We have taken the form and have put a Christian content into it making a Christian Ashram.

O Lord Jesus, we thank Thee, for the stirrings of the Spirit which are driving men to seek for a fellowship of the Spirit, a fellowship where we find Thee and our brothers. And where love reigns. Make us worthy of that koinonia. Amen.

AFFIRMATION FOR THE DAY: *"A fellowship of all who love in the service of all who suffer."*

"JESUS CHRIST IS THE GURU OF THIS ASHRAM"

The Christian faith is a universal faith and as an expression of that universality it picks out local forms and uses them. Coming in contact with Greek thought it picked out the conception of the Word—a conception not native to Hebrew thought, and put a Christian content into it: "In the beginning was the Word." Coming in contact with Indian thought, it saw in the Ashram a form it could use. This did not mean that the Christian Ashram would be an amalgam of Christianity and Hinduism. Eclecticisms pick and choose, syncretisms combine, but only life assimilates. Christianity repudiates eclecticisms and syncretisms, but it is life, so it assimilates. But in assimilating it changes. A plant reaches into the soil and picks out elements akin to its nature and takes them up into the life of the plant, but in taking up it changes these elements into the likeness of its own nature, according to the laws of its own being.

So we took up the framework of an Ashram and put a Christian content into it. The Hindu Ashram is organized around a Guru, or Preceptor—we too would have a Guru, but not a human Guru, only divine shoulders can bear that responsibility— "Jesus Christ is the Guru of this Ashram" is a motto on the walls of the Sat Tal Ashram, with us the original Christian Ashram. Around Him the Ashram would revolve. That was important, for as we have all denominations in the Ashram fellowship we could have a center of unity: everyone who belongs to Christ belongs to everyone who belongs to Christ. If we say, "What do you believe?" we go apart. But if we say, "Whom do you trust?" we come together—one Name upon our lips, one loyalty in our hearts. Our non-Christian friends too can come, often saying, "We love your Christ, but not your Christianity." If the Center of our faith is Christ, the center of that Center is "the Word become flesh." That determines the center of our emphasis: this Group must be the Word of the Kingdom become flesh.

O Lord and Savior, Thou art the center of our loyalty and our love. Help us to make Thee the center of our manifestation of Thee. May we be the Word made flesh. Let men see in us the Kingdom—the Kingdom in shoes. Amen.

AFFIRMATION FOR THE DAY: *"A conspiracy of love to keep each other at our best."*

NOT FIND AN ANSWER BUT BE THE ANSWER

In a conference the participants confer together to get verbal answers to verbal questions—it is the Word become word. Resolutions are drawn up telling what is wrong with men and things, and they go away complacent but not converted. In a retreat someone speaks and in the light of what is said one cultivates his spiritual life, but there is no attempt on the part of the group to be the Word of the Kingdom become flesh in the group. So the Christian Ashram is not a conference or a retreat—it is an attempt not to find an answer, but to be the answer—the Word of the Kingdom become flesh, a Kingdom in miniature. Imperfectly, of course, for it is made up of very imperfect people, but in some real way the New Order realized. Universalize this and you have the answer.

But if this is done, we have to get down barriers. The kingdom of God, which is God's redemptive invasion of us, would invade us, but we put up barriers. So we get down barriers. First, the barriers of race and class. We believe the Kingdom is blind to class and race—it sees a person as a person for whom Christ died. So a motto on our Sat Tal Ashram walls says, "Leave behind all race and class distinctions ye that enter here." Second, we get down barriers between those who have titles and those who do not have titles—titles divide. So we lay aside all titles—there are no more bishops, doctors, reverends, judges, just "Brother Stanley" and "Sister Lila." This has a psychological leveling effect. It is not easy to be high and mighty when you are called by your first name. And the term "Brother" and "Sister" denote that we are "a Family of God." As a Hindu member of the Ashram said, "Since there are both sexes here this term Brother and Sister has an antiseptic influence upon our relationships." One of the mottoes on the wall says, "This is a place of freedom through discipline." The sexes have found their freedom through their discipline. We have never had any problems in this regard.

O Jesus, Lord and Savior, help me this day to find my freedom through my inner disciplines. I shall love Thee supremely and love others subordinately. All my loves shall obey and fit into my love to Thee. In Thy Name. Amen.

AFFIRMATION FOR THE DAY: *May all my outer restraints move within and become inner restraints.*

THE REAL BARRIERS ARE WITHIN

We are looking at the barriers we put down in the Christian Ashram.
Third, we got down the barriers between those who work with their hands,
and those who do not. Those who do not work with their hands are
supposed to be high caste and those who do are supposed to be low caste. So
we have a work period each day when everybody works with his or her
hands. We appoint a head of this, whom we lovingly call "Pharaoh," who
puts the children of Israel to their tasks. "Work is love made manifest," so
we manifest our love through work.

Fourth, the barrier between youth and older age. In a youth gathering
they think youth, and in an older age gathering they think older age. But
each needs the cross-fertilization of the other. A little boy of nine stood up
in the Overflowing Heart in the Ashram and said, "I didn't think Brother
Stanley could convert me. I thought it would be over my head. But it
wasn't. When he asked for those who would offer themselves for the
Christian ministry, I stood up. For missionary work abroad, I stood up.
For full-time service as laymen, I stood up. I was ready for anything. This
is wonderful!" Fifth, the barriers between denominations. We mention
the groups which have nurtured us when we are introduced, and then we
go beyond them to the feet of Christ. Around Him we are one. Sixth, the
barriers between teachers and taught. In the early morning devotional
period we spend it half in silence with our Bibles and devotional books and
half in sharing what we have found. So that everyone becomes teacher and
everyone taught. We try to make everyone creative!

But the biggest barriers are within. Seventh, we get down inner
barriers. The first day we have "The Morning of the Open Heart." We ask,
Why have you come? What do you want? What do you need? The last is
the most important. So we ask the group to tell their needs. But we hasten
to add that they are not pressed to tell their needs, and that they won't be
out of the fellowship if they don't tell them, but they will be poorer and we
will be poorer if they don't.

**O Savior Divine, we stand before Thee and our needs stand out
like a sore thumb. For Thou dost silently judge us and yet believe in
us at the same time. Thou dost send us to our knees and raise us to
the highest heavens. We thank thee. Amen.**

AFFIRMATION FOR THE DAY: *My Father knows me completely and yet loves me
    completely.*

GOD HAS A PRIVATE OFFICE

We remind the group that there are some things they do not need to share with the group, that God has a private office where He deals with matters that concern others. They can be talked over in the presence of God and perhaps another person. I wouldn't have believed that a group of from fifty to four hundred would tell their needs straight off, but they do. We tell them that there is not a group of the attained, an inner circle, working on the unattained. That would set up a strain within the group, a tension. No, we begin in a fellowship of need. We remind them that if they act as though they have no needs then we have their number—they have the greatest need of all—they have the need to see their need and to tell those needs. For to get one's needs up is half way to the solution.

I had an Ashram among the lay leaders of The Methodist Church. The general secretary of this movement said, "Brother Stanley, these lay leaders may close up on you and refuse to tell their needs. They are the attained. They tell others what to do. So don't be surprised if they close up." "All right, Brother Bob," I said, "this is what we are going to do: I'm telling my needs first and you are telling your needs second, and then we will see what happens." We did and every last man told his needs—glad to. They will do it throughout the world—Japanese and Koreans, who are very buttoned up—"You won't know whether I'm sad or glad—I'm a Japanese, a Korean"—they will all do it without urging, glad to get bottled up things up and out. We take from two to five hours in the "Morning of the Open Heart," and in a few hours we know each other better than if we had been together for months and years without this catharsis. And the moment we do it we are on the Way.

A comment, "Good gracious, have you got all the disrupted people in the country together here in this Open Heart?" "No," I replied, "you have a cross section of the church life, turned honest. They have been putting on a front, now they are simple and honest—and on the way to release and reality."

O Savior, we thank Thee that Thou dost want to save us from hidden, festering sins as well as open sins. Thou dost want to save us from sin. And we want to be saved from it. For sin is our only enemy. Save us from that and we are saved! Amen.

AFFIRMATION FOR THE DAY: *"Thou shalt call His name Jesus for He shall save His people from their sins"*—my first sermon in India.

"THE OVERFLOWING HEART"—THE CLIMAX

After the Open Heart we go through the week—the Ashram usually lasts for a week in the West, a month at Sat Tal in India—with a regular daily program: 6:00, rising bell; 6:40, corporate devotions; 7:30, breakfast; 8:30, the Bible Hour; 9:30, the Church at Work Hour; 10:30, The Work Hour; 11:30, Brother Stanley's Hour; 12:30, lunch; 1:15, Family Hour; 1:40, recreation; 3:30, Special Interest Seminar, 4:30, Hour of Witness; 6:00, supper; 7:00, prayer groups; 8:00, Brother Stanley's Evangelistic Hour; 10:00, silence.

We have silence from 10:00 P.M. till the middle of the Devotional Hour at 7:00 A.M. In the Sat Tal Ashram we have Thursday as our day of silence. The Family Hour is the Hour in which we bring up anything for constructive criticism or change. If it is worthy of change, we change. But if they don't bring it up at the Family Hour, they must not bring it up any other place. There must be no secret criticism. The fellowship must be relaxed, knowing that if there is no open criticism there is no inner.

We have a Prayer Vigil running through five days throughout the twenty-four hours in shifts of an hour. There is a chart with spaces of an hour in which the individual signs up. Also, a Prayer Request Book in which individuals can write their requests for prayer. So the participants take that Request Book and spend their hour in praying for these requests. Others can join this hour, but one is responsible. The spiritual temperature goes up when the Prayer Vigil begins. The general public is invited to the evening evangelistic service. We have a communion service and a silent meal the last morning.

The Morning of the Overflowing Heart, following the Communion, is the climax. Here the cream arises to the surface. We see what the Holy Spirit has done. We take from two to five hours to tell what has happened to us. The results are amazing. From ninety-five to ninety-eight percent will be cleaned up and cleared out and transformed.

O God our Father, we thank Thee that there is a possibility of change. We are made for change. And we can be changed radically and permanently when we submit to and respond to Thy redemption. This is our open door. Amen.

AFFIRMATION FOR THE DAY: *"Behold I stand at the door and knock"—my opening of the door is my Open Door—to His Everything.*

HEALING A PART, BUT NOT THE CENTRAL PART

In the Morning of the Overflowing Heart we do not get them to tell what has happened to them to get certificates for the Ashram, nor to praise the speakers, but to be like the leper who turned back to lay his tribute of gratitude at the feet of Jesus. To tell it fixes it—the expression deepens the impression.

It is usually said that you cannot have a fellowship in a group larger than thirty. We find it possible to weld a group into a living fellowship all the way from thirty to four hundred. It is the "Open Heart" and the "Overflowing Heart" that do it. With those two things out it is a discussion group. Those two things make it a quest. We begin with ourselves and working out to the world and its problems. The Ashram is deeply Christ-centric and church-centric.

One service we make a Healing Service. We find that many more are healed by the indirect approach, that is, to get people cleared up spiritually first and then a large percentage of diseases drop off, for they are rooted in the mental, emotional, and the spiritual.

We have emphasized "The Little Ashram" where we turn the redemption power of the Ashram movement into the local church to make better pastors, officials, and members. We telescope the whole of the Ashram program into one day, beginning with the Open Heart and ending with the Overflowing Heart. It works amazingly. The "Little Ashrams" are springing up in many places. The United Christian Ashram movement which began in 1930 at Sat Tal, India, when three of us met—an Indian minister, a retired English missionary, and myself—three nations—has now spread to twenty-one countries, eighteen Ashrams in the United States, with about sixty in all. It is now a world movement with headquarters at United Christian Ashrams, Damascus, Maryland 20750, and has a magazine, *Transformation.* This expresses its outlook and purpose. We do not say the Ashram is the only way, nor the best way—it is a way to the Way. It has been called "a healing of love to mind, body, and spirit." It is an attempt to make the Word of the Kingdom become flesh in a group.

Dear Lord and Father, we thank Thee for these cells of the New Order. Make us humble enough to be used of Thee individually and corporately. Make us sensitive enough to be willing to be led of Thee into deeper and deeper explorations of Thee. Amen.

AFFIRMATION FOR THE DAY: *Our morning greeting: "The Lord is risen"
. . . "The Lord is risen indeed." We too can rise!*

"WHAT A TRAGEDY WHEN CHRISTIANITY BROKE WITH CHRIST"

A Hindu said at the close of one of my meetings, "As the speaker has gone on, two thoughts have been going through my mind. One was, what a tragedy it was when Christianity broke with Christ. And the other was, what a world awakening would come if Christianity and Christ should come together again." Is the Hindu right? Has there been a break between Christianity and Christ?

Many would answer, "Yes," and point to this, that, and the other as the points of break. Some would say that the point of break is at the place of the Bible, so we have the Bible Presbyterian Church and the Bible Church Missionary Society as attempts to mend that break. Others would say it is at the point of the church, so we have church-centric movements and emphasis. Others would say it is at the point of the person of Christ. "We don't mention Jesus Christ in our denomination any longer," said a Christian in Holland, "for we feel He belongs to the past, outgrown." Others would point to evangelism as the point of break. "Conversion," they say, "has been replaced by religious education." Still others would point to the ministry as the point of break. "Your ministry isn't valid unless you are in line with apostolic succession."

Each of these might feel that they have found the point of departure with Christ. But I am persuaded that the real point of departure is at the point of turning the Christian faith into the Word become word instead of the Word become flesh. That is the real point of departure with real results in the consequent effectiveness of the Christian faith in the world. The Christian faith is organized for the most part around the conception of the Word become word. Its "services" are verbal services, ritual; its preaching is not practicing but proclaiming; its religious education is learning about, instead of living out.

O Jesus Lord, we come back to Thee to learn again Thy Way. For Thy Way is a Way—a Way to walk upon. May all my words become flesh in Thee today. And may the Kingdom be seen in me today. Amen.

AFFIRMATION FOR THE DAY: *Show me where I have broken with Thee and I'll mend it immediately.*

"MY DEEDS . . . ARE MY CREDENTIALS"

We said yesterday that the real break of Christianity with Christ was that Christianity has been, and is, organized around the Word become word, verbalism, while Christ is the Word become flesh, vitalism. The creeds are verbal, and if you can repeat them you are correct. But the fact is that the only creed you believe in is the one you believe in enough to practice. Your creed is what you act upon daily.

The Communists believe that this unity of creed and practice is something which they invented. But the New Testament is filled from start to finish with this—it is its theme. In a hotel in Moscow I asked a waiter why the dining room was so empty. He replied, "These officials eat in their rooms so they can have their vodka and their women without anyone seeing them." Only Jesus could say, "Nothing have I done in secret." His life was an open book. From the simple deeds He did day by day men saw universal meanings. His attitudes and words and deeds suddenly became to men luminous with meaning—universal meaning. We know nothing about the universal except as we see it in the particular. We see the character of the universal God in the character of this particular—Jesus. Jesus could say, "My deeds done in my Father's name are my credentials" (John 10:26 NEB). "My deeds . . . are my credentials"—the Word become flesh.

A professor wrote in the Bibles of the students graduating from a theological seminary: "And the Word became flesh." It was a flourish at the end of a course in which for four years the Word had become word. It was a flourish but not the working force. It was a postscript and not the body and soul of the course.

When someone asked Mahatma Gandhi for a message to Gandhigram he replied: "My life is my message." But he finally gave in and gave a message, "Success attends where truth prevails." The message and the man were one.

O Jesus in Thee, the Message and the Man were one, speaking the same thing, for they were the same. Truth prevailed in Thee for Thou wert so truthful that Thou wert Truth. Teach me Thy secret—Thy secret of the Word and the flesh—one. Amen.

AFFIRMATION FOR THE DAY: *"My life is my message"—if so what does it say?*

GAINED A PRECARIOUS LIVING BY WASHING
ONE ANOTHER'S CLOTHES

"What is there in this man's words? He gives orders to the unclean spirits with authority and power, and out they go" (Luke 4:36 NEB). What is there in this man's words? This: This Man's words were the Word become flesh. And therefore it was with authority and power. With us it is different; we quote authorities and become powwow.

Theological discussions are largely raising and refuting other theologians' ideas—reminding us of the people in the South Sea Islands who gained a precarious living by washing one another's clothes. It is all about as effective as the top tile of a roof in Japan which is usually some symbol of water so that the roof will not take fire—the word of protection become symbol, a word. A fire hose would be the word of protection become flesh.

The break of Christianity with Christ, turning Him into the Word, become word, was the most disastrous break possible. For it gave up the one thing in Christianity that makes it unique—the Word become flesh. All the other faiths have the Word become word, but only the Christian faith has the Word become flesh.

The Bhagavad-Gita, the most popular Hindu book, has in it many parallel ideas with Christianity. Difference? It is the Word become word. It is a philosophical treatise with no historical reality. The historical Krishna was not worth looking at and the philosophical Krishna never existed. It is a philosophy with no facts—the Word become philosophy. No wonder salvation is said to be found by touching the feet of a Guru or Teacher. In one place in Bhutan the sight of the temple brings salvation. Or salvation comes through bathing in sacred rivers or sacred tanks, which brings forth from Tagore the comment that "washing away sins which are moral by water which is material is materialism." Where there is no historical reality in the Guru—the Word become word, then there is no historical reality in the salvation—it is verbal and word juggling. No reality in the faith nor in the faithful.

O Jesus Lord and Savior, save me from make-believe. Thou who are Reality make me real. May my words be indistinguishable from my deeds and may my deeds be indistinguishable from my words. In Thy blessed name. Amen.

AFFIRMATION FOR THE DAY: *John the Baptist tried to make men better; Jesus made men different.*

JESUS NEVER USED THE WORD RELIGION

We said yesterday that the making of Christianity into a system of theology instead of the Word become flesh was the most disastrous break with Christ. It led to a study of comparative religions, matching ideas with ideas. And the one that had a superiority of ideas was superior. But that was the Word become word. And those trained under the comparative religious regime have little or no message—they proclaim a few superior ideas and that is their message—and it is no message.

Jesus never used the word "religion." He never conceived of His coming to start another religion alongside other religions, a little superior, more moral. No, He came to set His Gospel over against human need, whether that need be in this religion, that religion, no religion. And He was the Gospel, the Word become flesh. That means a head-on confronting of human need by Jesus Christ, the Word become flesh. There and there alone lies the uniqueness of our Gospel. It is not a word uniqueness, but life uniqueness. To abandon the vital in favor of the verbal was the greatest and most disastrous break of Christianity with Christ.

And the converse would be true. As the Hindu said, "What a world awakening would come if Christianity and Christ should come together again." He was profoundly right. And the coming together must not be here and there, a patched up reconciliation. It must be a complete reversal, a repentance—a repentance from the Word made word to the Word made flesh.

I was talking to the president of India, Dr. Radhakrishnan, and I told him of the four things Mahatma Gandhi had suggested to us as Christians, and I asked him what he would suggest forty years later. He replied, "The same thing—practice your faith." A Russian bishop went to see Stalin to ask him to become a Christian and Stalin replied, "I will, if you can show me one."

O Lord and Teacher, teach me for Thou art Lord. Thou dost possess me so now teach me. I am teachable. I am ready to put into operation whatever Thou dost teach me. I will learn by doing. I am in a state of Yesness to Thee. Amen.

AFFIRMATION FOR THE DAY: *I stand at attention, like Ananias, and say, "Here am I, Lord"* (Acts 9:10).

"CONVERSION? I HAVEN'T THE SLIGHTEST IDEA WHAT IT MEANS"

This abandonment of the Word became flesh in favor of the Word become word and its results are seen in this: A professor of religious education in a Methodist theological college said to a friend of mine, "What do you mean by conversion? I haven't the slightest idea of what it means." He was brought up in a theological climate where Christianity was a system of thought to be learned. The knowing would heal you of your moral and spiritual ailments. It is salvation by knowledge—a lineal descendant of Gnosticism, the Knowers. If you know about it that saves you. That is proving its sterility in the realm of religion and in the realm of psychology and psychiatry.

In the realm of religion it is producing uncertain believers. "Here you found Him?" "I hope so." "Do you know Him?" "Maybe." "Have you assurance?" "No, I'm afraid not." This making Jesus Teacher and Lord is putting the Methodist and other churches back in the days of Wesley before his conversion. There Wesley was depending on knowledge and discipline. It left him empty. But when he passed from knowledge and discipline to surrender and faith and acceptance—made Jesus Lord, then He became Teacher—and how! Wesley's whole being became illuminated—mind, body, spirit. He was converted from Teacher and Lord to Lord and Teacher. And the conversion was profound. And he had a message—a message that set the world on fire. Religious education, as in the person of this professor, knows little or nothing of conversion. For it doesn't believe in it, nor depend on it—it depends on information, not transformation. So it produces moonlight, not sunlight—information about secondhand moonlight, not sunlight firsthand: "This is eternal life that they might know Thee"—not know about Thee, but "know Thee" as Lord and hence Teacher. Hence religious education doesn't produce men of passion, men with a message.

O Jesus, Lord and Teacher, help me to be Thine, and then I shall open my ears to all that is Thine. I shall be on fire to know about Thee since I know Thee—know Thee as my Lord and Teacher. Teach me, teach me, for Thou hast me—wholly. Amen.

AFFIRMATION FOR THE DAY: *The Christian answer is the Christian as the answer.*

CHURCHES FILLED WITH UNCERTAIN BELIEVERS

We said yesterday that the reversal from Teacher and Lord to Lord and Teacher would result in nothing less than a world-shaking upheaval in religion. It would turn our religious world upside down—and rightly, for it is wrong side up. It has broken with Christ and has made Christianity into the Word become word, instead of the Word become flesh. You are a Christian if you can repeat the catechisms, say the creeds, and promise to be loyal to the Church. That has filled the churches with uncertain believers living on question marks, and spiritually noncontagious. And it is filling the pulpits with men who are strong on assertions and weak on assurance. It is proving sterile in religion.

And in psychiatry. Psychiatry has had as its working basis—insight. Give a patient "insight" and it will automatically cure him. That has about run its course—it is proving to be near bankruptcy. Our mental institutions are filled with people who have have "insight" into what is the matter with them, and yet they remain in the institutions uncured, year after year. Why? Because "insight," knowledge about themselves, won't cure them. Can't. For the disease is not lack of insight, it is something else. It is the lack of giving love and receiving love. Until the patient is willing to give and receive love no amount of insight will cure him. Someone asked the head of a mental institution why they didn't have more guards in the institution—weren't they afraid of an uprising? "No," replied the other, "there is no danger of an uprising for the insane never organize." Why? Each is wrapped up in himself, cares little or nothing about others. If he began to care about others, that moment he would be on the road to health. It is self-centered preoccupation that is the disease. No amount of "insight" will cure that unless the insight is accompanied by a self-surrender to God and an outgoingness to man.

O Jesus our Savior, save us from turning from the Savior to cisterns that can hold no water. We want the Living Springs. Thou art that Spring fresh from the heart of the Eternal. Evermore give us this Water. Amen.

AFFIRMATION FOR THE DAY: *Nothing automatically cures me without my response and obedience.*

"THIS DREAM HAS DREAMT ITSELF OUT"

We saw yesterday when psychiatry turns from insight, from self-knowledge, to self-commitment—the receiving and giving of love, cure sets in at once. Victor Frankl has put it this way: "The dream of half a century has centered around mechanisms to explain and techniques to heal neurotic diseases. I believe that this dream has been dreamt out."

In both psychiatry and religion the dream of half a century that knowledge was the key to mental and moral cure has dreamt itself out. In both realms it has proved itself sterile. In both realms a new beginning can be made by self-commitment. In the realm of religion self-commitment to Jesus Christ; in the realm of psychology self-commitment to the receiving and giving of love—have opened the gates, to change and recovery, conversion.

In my Listening Post which I have in the early morning the Lord said to me, "You belong to me wholly, so there is nothing to fear from things, persons or events." Wonderful release. The first and most basic need is "to belong." That fits in with the statement of Jesus: "If I your Lord and Teacher"—first Lord, secondarily Teacher. This also fits in with "called to belong to Jesus Christ" (Rom. 1:6). The end of our calling is not to know good, do good, or be good—the end of our calling is "to belong." The knowing, doing, and being good come out of our belonging to Jesus Christ.

Here were two sisters—beautiful, educated, talented. They had everything—and nothing. They were frustrated because their life purposes had not been fulfilled. One said, "I've been a lousy Christian." The other said, "All my life I've been committed to nothing—to nothing except the rat race in which I live." Both of them in prayer surrendered themselves to Jesus Christ. If they belong to Christ then life will belong to them.

O Jesus Lord and Teacher, when we experience and express Thee this is not foolishness. It is sense—the only Sense. It is Wisdom—the only Wisdom. When I know Thee I know. When Thou art Lord, thou art Teacher—and what teaching! Amen.

AFFIRMATION FOR THE DAY: *I will be a Christian realist knowing that in Christ I'm dealing with Reality.*

"DWELL WITHIN THE REVELATION
I HAVE BROUGHT"

This verse is of the greatest importance in our study of the Word become flesh: "If you dwell within the revelation I have brought, you are indeed my disciples; you shall know the truth, and the truth will set you free" (John 8:31, 32 NEB). What was the "revelation" He had "brought"? Was it like the "revelation" the Hindu Vedas brought? They say that Sanscrit is an eternal language and the Vedas written in that eternal language are eternal. But the revelation was in a language—a verbal revelation. The Koran was dictated by God in a heavenly language, Arabic, but it was dictated—a verbal revelation. The Sikhs treat their sacred book, the Granth Sahib, as if it were a person; they keep it under mosquito nets, fan it, and put it to sleep. It is a book—a verbal revelation. The Old Testament centered around the Law: "We have a Law," said the Jews to Pilate. It too was verbal revelation. All the philosophies and moralisms are verbal revelation. They are, one and all, the Word become word.

What was the difference in "the revelation I have brought"? Note, "I have brought"—it was not "the revelation I have uttered"—it was "brought"—brought in His own Person—the Word become flesh. That sets this "revelation" apart, unique. You can't study it alongside these other "revelations," so called, for they are not in the same category. One is taught, and the other is brought. And the words He uttered were a part of the bringing, for His words were the revelation of His own self, every word operative within Himself. So His words were deeds, and His deeds were words.

Now note: "If you dwell within the revelation I have brought"—if you "dwell within," not dabble in or delve in, but "dwell" in—make it your home, your life commitment, your very life, then with that standpoint and viewpoint you are His "disciples and you shall know the truth and the truth will set you free." Now you know the truth because you belong to the Truth.

O Jesus, Thou art the Way, the Truth, and the Life. And when I take Thee as the Way—the way to live, the way to be, then I find Thee as the Truth. Thou dost not bring me truths—Thou art the Truth. This makes me free. Amen.

AFFIRMATION FOR THE DAY: *I shall not be a visitor—I shall dwell within the Revelation Jesus has brought.*

DOES THE TRUTH ALWAYS MAKE MEN FREE?

We saw yesterday the wonderful clarity of this verse: "If you dwell within the revelation I have brought, you are indeed my disciples; you will know the truth, and the truth will set you free" (John 8:31, 32 NEB). The "revelation" He "brought" is the Word made flesh. Then if I "dwell within" that "revelation" then that Word must become flesh in me. I do not verbally accept His teaching—a creed to be believed—I vitally accept Him as my Savior and my Lord, the Life of my life, the Being of my being, my very all. This means not mind-surrender—the acceptance of Truth, but self-surrender, the acceptance of the Truth by life identification with that Truth. Then, and not till then, are you "my disciples." Then "you are indeed my disciples"—note the "indeed"; otherwise you are His disciples in intellect, in outer allegiance, but not "indeed."

Now note the last portion: "You will know the truth and the truth will set you free." We take this sentence, detach it from "the revelation I have brought," and make it stand as the charter of intellectual freedom. It is over the gates of Johns Hopkins University. But it is completely detached from "the Word become flesh"—"the revelation I have brought." And detached from the Truth incarnate, it does not necessarily make men free. Free intellectualism is free to get tangled in its own verbalisms, free to be mixed-up and muddled with no key to this business of living. For instance, a medical doctor said, "I've never seen a Freudian psychiatrist who wasn't a problem dealing with problems."

A Ph.D. said in disdain, "Do you mean to say that I, a Ph.D., will have to bend the knee and say I'm a sinner?" He didn't have to, but if he didn't he was left high and dry and empty! Another Ph.D. came to me and said without preliminaries, "I want to be saved." Refreshing. In five minutes he was up from his knees, humble and happy—and full.

O Lord Christ, when we are detached from Thee, the Vine, we become dead branches, trying to live apart from Life, Forgive us this folly. For when this happens our wisdom is foolishness. We know and we don't know. Help us to know Thee. Amen.

AFFIRMATION FOR THE DAY: *All my truths must be related to the Truth or they cease to be truths.*

TRUTHS NOT ANCHORED TO THE TRUTH
ARE NOT REDEMPTIVE

We must spend one more day on: "If you dwell within the revelation I have brought, you are indeed my disciples; you shall know the truth, and the truth will set you free" (John 8:31, 32 NEB). We must add a verse which really belongs to this. "If then the Son sets you free, you will indeed be free" (vs. 36). Here the truth which sets men free is synonymous with the Son who sets men free. The abstract truth does not necessarily set men free—it's the incarnate Truth that sets men free. This is important.

Education, psychiatry, religious education, and non-directive counseling have for the most part gone on the assumption that it is the truth, the insight, that sets people free. That assumption is now proving sterile. For truth that is not anchored to the Truth, the Incarnate truth is truth that is non-redemptive, for it has no ultimate meaning or purpose, no goal, no cohesion running through it. Unless that truth leads to the Truth, the Son who makes you free, it is not transforming. It is informing, but not transforming. For to be introduced to the Son, the Truth, means surrender, allegiance, obedience, life-committal—that is transforming, it sets men free. It issues in conversion—Christian conversion, regeneration. Those other procedures—education, psychiatry, religious education, non-directive counseling—may produce marginal change, reformation, but not regeneration. Regeneration takes places when the self surrenders itself as the center to Christ, the Truth, the Son, as the center. Then the Son makes you free. Neither abstract truth, nor concrete truth about yourself, sets you free. You are free when the self surrenders itself to the Son—then He makes you free.

The four procedures mentioned above are the Word become word, and produce in their own image—the word become word. But the Son, who is the Word become flesh, produces in His image—those who surrender to Him do become the Word become flesh. They find and are free.

O Jesus, Thou Son of the Living God, when we come to Thee we are set free. We are set free from the past, the present, and the future—we are set free. We walk the earth free—free because bound to Thee. And this is "indeed" freedom. Amen.

AFFIRMATION FOR THE DAY: *In Thee I am free to be the best that I can be.*

SELF-CENTERED AND SELF-CONTAINED TRUTHS
TURN OUT TO BE LESS THAN TRUTH

From what I said yesterday it would seem that I am prejudiced against modern education, psychiatry, religious education, and counseling. I am in favor of all four and am carrying on all four directly or indirectly. What I am opposed to is these directives becoming self-contained, self-sufficient, unrelated to anything beyond themselves, making truths the end, unrelated to the Truth, the Incarnate Truth. The consequence is that since they have no starting point they have no goal. They turn around on themselves. They know more and more about less and less.

Let them put one point of the compass on Jesus Christ, the Truth, and then let the other point sweep as far into truths as it will—then these would be coherent truths, related to Truth. With a Starting Point they would have a Goal. In Him all things would cohere. Out of Him all things are incoherent. The universe is a multiverse, nothing to hold it together.

Take nondirective counseling—taken over by Christians from secular psychology—what relation has it to "the revelation" Jesus has "brought"? Suppose Jesus had gathered people about Him on the Mount and had said, "Now, boys, talk about yourselves, talk freely, and I'll throw in a question now and again." Instead of the Sermon on the Mount with its "I say unto you," we would have had a lot of confused question marks. A mess, not a message. Question marks, but not exclamation points. And the people would at the end say, not that "He speaks with authority," but, "We are not sure of His position, not sure of ourselves, not sure of anything. We just are not sure." This kind of approach would not produce people who "were astonished at His teaching," but people who are astonished at nothing and agnostic about everything. There is nothing to be astonished about—there is only good news, but no Good News. And no conversions, for there is nothing to be converted to. It is all "flesh."

O Jesus Lord and Redeemer, Thou dost not leave us with "flesh," for Thou art the Word become flesh. Amid the flesh there is this blessed, blessed light of the Word. In its light we see life, and what a life, and what possibility opens. We thank Thee. Amen.

AFFIRMATION FOR THE DAY: *Truth that doesn't lead me to His feet is truth astray, light turned to darkness.*

A FOURFOLD EXPRESSION

The Christian Gospel commands you. But what it commands is what our human nature demands—demands for its fulfillment. This verse shows this vividly: "The aim and object of this command is the love which springs from a clean heart, from a good conscience, and from faith that is genuine. Through falling short of these, some people have gone astray into a wilderness of words" (I Tim. 1:5, 6 NEB). Now note how the total person is fulfilled: Love springs from a clean heart (the affectional nature), from a good conscience (the volitional nature), and from a faith that is genuine (the intellectual nature). The whole person made up of feeling, will, and intelligence is expressed in love. And if it were then it would be perfectly fulfilled. And psychology would agree. For life would agree. Nothing could be more healthy than a personality expressing itself by a clean heart, a good conscience, and a genuine faith—expressing itself in love.

Expressing itself in love would mean that the person is outgoing. The tyranny of self-preoccupation is broken. The person who is outgoing in love is a healthy person and especially healthy if it includes emotions, will, and intellect. To be loving in emotions only may produce the sentimentalist in religon. To be loving in will alone may produce the man of morality in religion, but not very tender and sensitive. To be loving in mind alone may produce the intellectualist in religion. But loving in the total person—emotion, will, mind—makes the most well-rounded, symmetrical person imaginable.

But when this kind of Christian expression is bypassed, or as the verse puts it—"Through falling short of these, some people have gone astray into a wilderness of words"—then it is the Word become word. This passage when acted upon is the Word become flesh, but to fall short of it, or depart from it means "a wilderness of words"—the Word become words.

O Lord Christ, Thy commands set us free. Our humanisms apart from Thee send us into a wilderness of words. Save us from the wilderness of words which try to cover up our barrenness. Thou art the Son who sets us free—free indeed. Amen.

AFFIRMATION FOR THE DAY: *Not a wilderness of words for me, but the Way!*

"HE WILL GUIDE YOU INTO ALL THE TRUTH"

To leave the Word become flesh means to run off "into a wilderness of words" to cover up the falsity. For when you leave the Word you turn to words—a wilderness of words.

How refreshing this is: "When the Spirit of truth comes, he will guide you into all the truth. . . . He will glorify me, for he will take what is mine and declare it to you" (John 16:13, 14). Here "the Counselor," "the Spirit of truth," not only reveals truths to you—"He will guide you into all truth"—guide you into possession of the Truth. He guides you into the word becoming flesh in you. How different this is from the goal of "insight"—the word become word. This is not mere insight; it is the possession of Truth and possession by Truth—it is "into" and not around the edges of.

And the Truth into which the Holy Spirit guides us is the Incarnate Truth: "He will take what is mine and declare it unto you." He unfolds what is infolded in Jesus. This provides for a continuing revelation. The revelation is fixed in Jesus, but it is dynamic and unfolding by the Counselor, the Spirit of Truth, unfolding that fixed Revelation. It is therefore never outgrown. The more you see in it the more you see there is to be seen. It is fixed Goal, but is a flying Goal. You never catch up to it. And yet every moment you are caught by it.

This is why there is a freshness about Jesus which never dims. I go to my Bible every morning with a pen in hand expecting some fresh insight to come—an insight which I can note on a margin. And it seldom or never fails to come. You are striking deeper and deeper layers of truth all the time. This is a Divine Book for it reveals the Divine Person. Out of the words arises the Word. This Book creates expectancy. I am satisfied and yet on the stretch. And I know there is no end to This. This is It and forever!

O Blessed Spirit of Truth, hold Thy torch before His face that I may see Him more clearly. Then inspire me to love Him more dearly and follow Him more nearly. For I am mad after Him. Make me more mad. Amen.

AFFIRMATION FOR THE DAY: *I am under an unfolding Revelation and an unfolding Redemption.*

"HE WOULD GO ON GIVING HIS MESSAGE"

I mentioned the Chinese cook who brought in a cake to celebrate my twenty-fifth anniversary as a missionary with the quotation from the classics on it: "Through the ages one word," meaning through the ages I had one Word, one message—Jesus. The cook was profoundly right. But if your message is a philosophy, a moralism, you cannot have "one word," you have to have many words and different words or else your messages become stale. Hence the search, the frantic search for something new. And this search ends in frustration for every emphasis exhausts itself sooner or later—every emphasis except one—Jesus.

Someone spoke in the presence of an Indian governor about an honor that might be conferred on "Brother Stanley." The governor replied, "It would be nice, of course, but if it didn't come it would make no difference—he would go on giving his message." Quite true. I'm not "an angry man," as some writers style themselves. But I am "an excited man," an excitement that issues in calmness, an excitement that becomes tranquility, an excitement that sets me on fire, but, like Moses' burning bush, I'm never consumed. I've never taken a headache tablet, nor a tranquilizer. I said to a government official, an income tax officer, "What is your biggest headache?" He replied, "I have no headaches, I belong to Jesus." A pastor told this story, "When I came to the Camp Sierra Ashram I had sinus so bad I had to have six handkerchiefs a day. But when I surrendered to Jesus Christ my sinus trouble was gone. Now I have one handkerchief a day—to wipe perspiration here in Honolulu." An income tax man, efficient, but with no headaches; a pastor in Honolulu with only one handkerchief. Small things? Yes, but exciting, for Jesus Christ is performing miracles, big and little, all up and down the line, for big people, little people, for all people. No wonder through the ages I have one word, and I hope my last gasp will be, "I commend my Savior to you."

O Jesus, my Lord, I can sing of nothing but of Thee. And when I sing of Thee the music of the spheres joins my song and sings with me. For in Thee I've caught the joy of Life, the power to live and the Eternal in the now. Amen.

AFFIRMATION FOR THE DAY: *I shall speak many words, but underlying them will be "one Word."*

"THE OFFENSE OF PARTICULARITY"

A doubt begins in some minds. It is this: Can the Universal God be revealed in a particular happening, in a particular period of history, in a particular country, in a particular Man? Can you pack the Universal in the Particular? Does not the Universal need the Infinite Mold? Does not philosophy then with its universal concepts become a better medium to express the Universal than the Word became flesh? This question expresses what Dr. J. S. Whale calls the "Offense of Particularity." But it is through the knothole of the fence of particularity that we see the vast vistas, the universal. You can only see the Universal in the particular.

You cannot tell whether a thing is true by considering it abstractly. You can only tell whether a thing is true when you see it operative. Put it under life and see what life does to it, and then you can tell whether it is true or false. Jesus gave that test: "By their fruits shall ye know them"—the outcome is the criterion. "So live," said Kent, "that every act of yours could be a universal norm." Jesus did that—He so lived that every act and attitude of His could be, and is, a universal norm. The highest adjective descriptive of character, in any language, is the adjective Christlike. We can apply it to God or man and nothing higher could be said of either. This universal had to be seen in the particular—in Jesus. He is the Universal Concrete.

When India wanted to pay her highest compliment to her highest son, Mahatma Gandhi, they called him "the Christlike man." Why not the Buddha-like, the Krishna-like, the Mohammed-like man? Because in them the particular-in-particular was seen. In Jesus the Universal-in-Particular was seen. The Word became flesh and then the flesh became word—and what it said was: "Universal." The Everywhere came into the Here, and the Here was Everywhere!

O Jesus, Thou art the Universal become the Here. And through Thee I see the Universal. And what I see sets my heart afire to see more. To whom else shall we go for Thou hast the words of eternal life? Eternal Life speaks in Thy life and we ask no more. Amen.

AFFIRMATION FOR THE DAY: *If I attend to the Particular the Universal will take care of itself.*

"THAT GAS LANTERN IS TEACHING ME
MUCH ABOUT YOUR JESUS"

The Universal cannot be seen in a Universal concept. The Universal can only be seen in the Universal-in-Particular. In one of our Ashrams in Japan a Japanese professor specializing in Buddhism was lecturing to our Ashram group on how to make Christianity really Japanese. He said, "Teach pure Christianity and it will be universal and will fulfill Japanese culture." He was right. You do not have to water down the Christian faith to make it fit into other faiths and other cultures to make it more universalized. You do not universalize it by that process; you make it fit into the non-universal and thus it becomes non-universal in the process.

A Hindu said to a Christian speaker, "You talk about Christ. We can talk about God, but you must talk about Christ." You really need to talk about Jesus before you can talk about God, but the Hindu was right. He saw in Jesus Christ something universal. For the real Christian is the most universalized person on this planet. He works by love and love in the universal language.

Some Christian boys were going out to the villages by night to inoculate chickens against chicken diseases. They had to go at night, for the chickens were feeding in the fields by day. A Mohammedan watched these boys doing this inoculation without compensation and said to the missionary, "That gas lantern is telling me much about your Jesus." He saw through that lantern into the Christian faith and saw it was "the light of the world." Through this particular he saw Jesus who is the Universal-in-particular. If you chemically analyze a sunbeam you can find out the universal sun. In a single act of love you find out the nature of the Christian faith. "The publicans and sinners drew near to hear him"—here was Holiness that instead of repelling was compelling. Here was the Universal-in-the-particular.

O Jesus, in Thee we see in understandable form the Eternal God. Thou art God simplified, approachable, lovable. We would never have known that God is love, unless we had seen it in Thee. Thou art the Speech of Eternity translated into the language of time. Amen.

AFFIRMATION FOR THE DAY: *May my "gas lamp" of lowly deeds and attitudes tell others much about our Jesus.*

"WHEN I SAW THOSE PLAGUE-STAINED HANDS I SAW THE MEANING OF THE CHRISTIAN FAITH"

We are looking at seeing the universal-in-the-particular. Before independence I was speaking in an Indian State, and the Hindu Prime Minister was the chairman. He said in his remarks,

"I could not help but contrast this meeting tonight with the meetings I attended as a boy. There we used to heckle the missionaries and throw rotten fruit at them. But here this great audience sits in pin-drop silence listening to the Christian message. What has made the difference? Perhaps this: Nearby is the great Miraj mission hospital where Indian and foreign doctors tend to poor and rich, night and day. Nearby is a leper colony where they work on the sores of lepers and heal them. Then a little further is an outcaste village where these outcastes are washed body, mind, and spirit and given back to India as honored and respected citizens. I had to go to inspect a plague-stricken town, which had no inhabitants; all had fled to the fields. Going through the deserted town I saw a lady missionary coming out of a house with her hands extended. She came up to me and said, 'I'm sorry I can't shake hands with you, for my hands are plague-stained.' When I saw those plague-stained hands, I saw the meaning of the Christian faith."

Through the particular—the plague-stained hands—he saw the Universal. It is the only possible way it can be seen. To talk about the Universal in universal language is to end in meaningless words. You see the universal-in-the-particular or you don't see it.

During the days when India was struggling for her independence I was on the train, and the toilet in the bathroom was filthy. So when the train stopped at a station, I got out, borrowed a sweeper's broom, came back and cleaned it. Some Brahmans in the train asked me in astonishment, "Who are you?" When I told them I had stayed with Mahatma Gandhi in his Ashram, they said, "Now we understand." Through that little incident they saw the universal. They wanted to see more.

O Lord and Savior, we see in Thy lowly acts the highest meanings of life. We study one of Thy words and find a universe. We listen to a sentence and we hear the whole meaning of existence. When we see Thee—we see! Amen.

AFFIRMATION FOR THE DAY: *My smallest act can reveal the greatest meanings.*

"O GOD, MAKE ME LIKE CHRIST"

We are considering the fact that we can only see the universal through the particular. When Dr. Kagawa, the Japanese saint, read the story of the crucifixion for the first time he was overwhelmed with emotion. "Is it true that cruel men persecuted and whipped and spat upon this Man Jesus?" he asked. "Yes, it is true," he was told. "And is it true that Jesus when dying on the cross forgave them?" "Yes, it is true." Then Kagawa burst into prayer: "O God, make me like Christ." And that became his life prayer. He saw the Universal through that particular. When he was in America someone heard him speak and as he walked home with a friend he remarked, "Well, he didn't say much, did he?" For Kagawa was a poor public speaker. "No, he didn't say much," said the friend, "but if you are hanging on the cross you don't have to say much."

I quoted that to our Sat Tal Ashram group and the Hindu secretary of Mr. Venugopal, the Financial Secretary of the Railway Board who has all the finances of the railways in his hands, and who is perhaps the outstanding Christian of India, thoughtfully said, "Mr. Venugopal doesn't have to say much, for he too is hanging on the cross." He is the Word of self-sacrifice become flesh.

A Hindu said this about a missionary doctor: "Dr. Hicks is a saint; no, he is a god." Some of his employees had stolen powdered milk. They were brought before the court. The judge said they were guilty and must be fined. "No," said Dr. Hicks, "I am guilty. They are under me. It was my fault. I will pay the fine." "Nobody but a god could do that," said the Hindu. The Hindu saw the universal in the particular. When the Universal Word becomes the particular flesh it burns our souls as when a burning glass gathers the scattered rays and focuses them on a single point.

O Lord God, men see Thee more at the cross than through volumes of the philosophies. They bring us words. But the cross brings us the Word of Love become flesh. We see and our knees bend and our hearts melt. We thank Thee. Amen.

AFFIRMATION FOR THE DAY: *A God on a cross—what a lowly thing! And what a High God!*

"LORD, DO NOT HOLD THIS SIN AGAINST THEM"

Stephen was not supposed to be a speaker—he was supposed to serve tables, but he made the longest speech made in the New Testament. But we do not remember the long speech, we remember a single sentence. Amid a shower of stones "he knelt down and cried with a loud voice, 'Lord, do not hold this sin against them' " (Acts 7:59). That "loud voice" drowned out his own speech and shook the ages. The word of forgiveness became flesh. And even this "loud voice" was not as loud as this account: "And gazing at him, all who sat in the council saw that his face was like the face of an angel" (Acts 6:15). When they were lying about him, the lies falling upon him burst into light—the lies became light. This was the word of victory become flesh.

An equally great revelation of the Universal in the particular was seen in the story of Ananias going into the room where the blind Saul was staying in Damascus. Ananias had hesitated to obey the command of Jesus to go to Saul, "How can I? He has come down here to murder us as he did the saints at Jerusalem." He trembled, but he trembled bravely and went and said two words, but those two words opened the gate of life to the greatest Christian of the centuries. He went in to him, laid his hands on him, and said, "Brother Saul," and when he said that, Saul's frame must have shaken with sobs: "My God, they're calling me 'brother,' I who have come down here to murder them." Through this human forgiveness Saul saw the divine forgiveness in Jesus Christ—saw into the heart of redemption and was converted. I say "converted," for Saul was stunned and blinded on the Damascus Road, but not converted. He was only converted when he saw through the two words, "Brother Saul," the meaning of redemption. He saw the universal through the particular. He saw the universal not through a discourse but through a deed. The Word had become flesh in Ananias.

O Lord and Savior, help me this day to open the gates of life to someone by some deed, some word, some attitude. I may do it as hesitatingly and tremblingly as Ananias did, but help me to do it as sincerely and lovingly. Amen.

AFFIRMATION FOR THE DAY: *When I can't do anything else I can always love.*

"NOW I SEE THE MEANING OF CHRISTIANITY"

We are meditating this week on the Universal in the particular. Two men spoke at Gettysburg—one a man of very eloquent words, Everett Edward Hale, and Abraham Lincoln, a man who that day used few words. No one can remember any of the words of Hale, but we cannot forget the words of Lincoln. Hale was the word of democracy and freedom become word, but Lincoln was the Word of democracy and freedom become flesh. We heard it in Hale and saw it in Lincoln. One dies and the other lives. Hale put the universal in universal words, and Lincoln put the universal in the particular—in himself. So his particular words became universal words.

In an orphanage Mrs. Murphy was the loving mother of them all. One little boy said the Twenty-third Psalm, not the way it was written: "Surely goodness and mercy shall follow me all the days of my life," but this way: "Surely good Mrs. Murphy shall follow me all the days of my life." To him goodness and mercy had become flesh.

If a man, really in love with his wife and away from home, were offered a book on "Love," instead of going home, would he not reply: "I want my wife"? The picture of the dog listening to "his master's voice" is good advertisement, but no dog will be content with the canned voice of his master—he wants his master. The word of his master become word is not a substitute for the word of his master become flesh.

At the close of the war some young American boys and girls went to Germany to work on the ruined cities to restore them. At first the German workmen viewed with sullen suspicion this approach to bridge the chasm of hate. It couldn't be real. But when they saw these young people dead tired at night they melted. A German workman gave them a piece of his precious cake and said, "Now I see the meaning of Christianity." That piece of cake was a sacrament of the Word become flesh—the Universal in the Particular.

O Lord God, help me this day to make every act of mine a sacrament—a sacrament of the Word become flesh. Help me to show in every situation the reconciliation I have received from Thee. May every little thing be big and with meaning. Amen.

AFFIRMATION FOR THE DAY: *A cup of cold water given in His name can be a revelation of God.*

A BOOTBLACK: "I LOVE TO WORK FOR JESUS—
I DO IT FOR HIM"

We come to our closing day this week on seeing the Universal in the particular. Jesus was the Universal Particular, the Absolute Concrete. And we see this Universal Absolute through the Particular.

For instance, we talk in high-sounding language about bridging the chasms of hate between nations and making a brotherhood, but this illustration lingers in my mind after the brotherhood phrases die out. In 1949 on my first of six visits to Hiroshima, Japan, where the first atomic bomb fell, I stayed in a quonsett hut as the guest of two women. One, an American woman who had lost her husband in Okinawa, of course, by Japanese bullets. The other was a Japanese woman who had lost her doctor husband and her whole family when the atomic bomb fell on Hiroshima, dropped by Americans. These two Christain women lived together as sisters in a deep fellowship. They were the word of healing fellowship made flesh. And it was an unforgettable experience to be in that home.

A Hindu doctor was opposed to Christianity. He went to London and there having a shoeshine, he noted that the boy did it so neatly and cheerfully and sang while he did it. The Hindu asked him why? And the boy replied, "I am a Christian. I love to work for Jesus—I do it for Him." All the prejudice against Christianity faded out of the doctor's heart. He saw it in the bright face of the bootblack—the Word had become flesh.

One of my most luminous moments in India was this one: [I previously mentioned the fact that we give the few servants at the Ashram a holiday once a week and we volunteer to take their jobs, including the sweeper's job, cleaning the latrines by hand.] When we began it, of course, as the head of the Ashram I would be expected to volunteer and did. When the sweeper came back at eventide he stood before my window with folded hands and his face wreathed in smiles but without a word. I saw the whole social revolution in that man's face. He said nothing—and everything!

O Lord Jesus, give me the passion of that bootblack who used his little and made it into the much. I have much more than he had, but am I using my much the way he used his little? Forgive me for my comparative lukewarmness. Amen.

AFFIRMATION FOR THE DAY: *Whether I have little or much is not the chief concern, but who has my little or my much.*

"WHAT IS THIS? VIEWING CHERRY BLOSSOMS WEARING A LONG SWORD!"

We have been looking at the Universal being seen through the particular. We must now look at the Universal not being seen because there was no particular. We would call this the paralysis through the absence of the particular. Where there is no particular the Universal fades out.

Of a pastor it was said, "He preaches like an angel to get people converted, but he wouldn't go across the street to bring a person to Christ." His preaching proclaimed the Universal, but there was no particular, hence no Universal. The Word was the word become word and hence dead.

A Hindu was presiding over a Christian lecture. The lecturer said: "Before we go on let us settle certain things: First, there is one God." They agreed. "Second, that one God is personal." The Hindu chairman interjected: "If you agree to that you might as well go off and be baptized and come back." He saw that if God is personal He would do as the Christians say: "Become Incarnate." The Universal would become particular.

The Japanese newspapers carried this: "What is this? Viewing cherry blossoms wearing a long sword!" The viewing of cherry blossoms meant communing with beauty and the long sword meant fight. The universal had a contradictory particular, hence the universal was negatived.

A man in the steel helmet of the Crusaders and the armor of a knight peddled lead pencils in an Italian street for forty years. With all that symbolism of bravery and crusaders' zeal peddling lead pencils! Many preachers clad in gorgeous robes are peddling lead pencils—bits of poetry and clever quips.

The Turks with their leisurely ways were impressed with the American slogan, "Do it now." So they decided to adopt it and thus they put it out: "Do it now, if you have the time." The "Do it now" was the universal but "if you have the time" canceled it out. The universal had no particular.

O Jesus Lord, save us from canceling qualifications. May we give and give with no strings attached. Help me to give as Thou dost give with nothing held back. For to qualify is to cancel. I would give with both hands. Amen.

AFFIRMATION FOR THE DAY: *"If you wish to go the whole way, go, sell your possessions . . . and come follow me" (Matt. 19:2 NEB).*

"DRUNK WITH THE WINE OF HIS OWN WORDINESS"

We continue to look at the cancelation of the universal by failure in the particular. An Indian friend described the attitude of a man "drunk with the wine of his own wordiness" who "described the Universal God in glowing terms in a public meeting and then would probably go home and worship a three-legged cow if he met one." He canceled out his verbal universal by his particular. The universal had no particular and therefore was no universal.

In Japan we presented the plan of Federal Union of the churches around Christ as the center. A leading layman got up and said, "All the chuches in this city have already come together in a union. We united around a common graveyard." The union was around the dead! The universal—the union—had no particular except the graveyard—hardly a basis of union!

People have become tired of words—they have become slick like much-used coin, so in many places instead of words they have turned to pantomime, acting out the words. But this is acting out the words, instead of acting. It is the Word become shadow instead of the Word become flesh. It is this side of reality.

The whole trend of TV addiction is a symptom of escapism—action by proxy instead of action by person. We let someone else do the acting for us—on a screen. Those who give themselves to this deteriorate. For it is the Word become picture instead of the Word become flesh. A nation of TV viewers is no substitute for life-doers. It becomes a nation of secondhanders, incapable of coming firsthand with life. At the close of the average movie you are not supposed to do anything—you are supposed to feel. But impression minus expression equals depression. So it ultimately ends in depression.

O Lord and Savior, save us from the make-believe, the halfway, the substitute. We would be firsthanders. Take from us the willingness to be persons just-this-side-of-reality. We want to see Thee and embody Thee. Fully and wholly. Amen.

AFFIRMATION FOR THE DAY: *Halfwayism in dedication is whole-wayism in decay.*

AFRAID OF FALLOUT
AND PRODUCING IT ALL THE TIME

We spend one more day on substitutions for the Word become flesh. I listened to an American doctor, sent to Hiroshima, Japan, to study the effects of radiation and fallout from the atomic bomb. All the time he was describing the devastating effects of atomic fallout he smoked cigarette after cigarette, apparently unconscious that the fallout in his lungs from the cigarette smoking was causing greater devastation than the fallout from the atomic bomb. It was killing more people, silently and persistently, than the bomb has ever killed and may ever kill. A cartoon in an Indian paper showed a man smoking and saying, "All this talk about lung cancer from cigarette smoking? I have made a vow to myself never to read this kind of thing again." That vow did away with the danger, of course! It was the word of escape became vow instead of flesh. We see the spectacle of people in the West building costly bomb shelters when day by day, hour by hour a deadly fallout is taking place in their lungs.

Nearly all our major and minor upsets come from this refusal to stand responsibilty. People try to escape responsibility by retreating into illness, into illusions—an escapism. A patient in a mental institution had a passion to take pictures with as small an exposure as possible. He succeeded, so he thought, when the picture was large and the exposure small. He gave away his life strategy. He was trying to withdraw from life, exposing himself to life as little as possible so life would not hurt him. He was trying to escape life—responsibility. And landing in mental and emotional upset. He was willing for the word of life contact to become word—small exposure—but not willing for it to become flesh—life participation.

Nearly all our major and minor upsets come from this refusal to stand up to life and accept responsibility. We hear sermons, read books, listen to exhortations, but these impressions never become flesh. This is the prime cause of our sense of frustration.

O God, our Father, we pray Thee to save us from dodging out of responsibility into unreality, into half-acceptances and half-obediences. Help us to be all-outers. For we cannot be too all-out if we obey Thy Son. For we are in Reality all the way, when we are in Him. Amen.

AFFIRMATION FOR THE DAY: *No straining at gnats and no swallowing of camels for me today.*

"IN ALL THESE THINGS
WE ARE MORE THAN CONQUERORS"

We are now ready to listen to a very important verse from Paul: "I appeal to you therefore, brethren, by the mercies of God, to present your bodies as a living sacrifice, holy and acceptable to God, which is your spiritual worship. Do not be conformed to this world but be transformed by the renewal of your mind, that you may prove what is the will of God, what is good and acceptable and perfect" (Rom. 12:1, 2).

After wandering around in the Old Testament in the ninth, tenth, and eleventh chapters of Romans and getting mixed up with an impossible view of predestination, Paul returns to his Christianity when he left off his excursion which began at the end of the glorious eighth chapter. In that eighth chapter he said something important when he said this: "No, in all these things we are more than conquerors through him who loved us" (Rom. 8:37). Here he set the Christian victory "in"—"in all these things . . . conquerors." This makes the Christian victory different. In Buddhism it is: "apart from all these things"; in Hinduism: "above all, these things"; in Communism: "as a part of all these things"; modern secularism: "through all these things." The Christian gains his victory not "apart from," nor "above," nor "a part of," nor "through," but "in." The victory is found not by escape from, nor by escape into—but "in." The Christian gains the victory "in"—the Word has become flesh, but he never becomes "these things." He is in the midst of, but not of. He participates but always inwardly he is different. He lives in two worlds at once—the kingdom of God and the kingdoms of this world. He lives his life in the flesh but the flesh is in control of the Kingdom. He seeks that "first," last, and always. Therefore he walks by the Spirit and not by the flesh. And the flesh becomes the instrument of the outer manifestation of the Spirit. The human Spirit and flesh are under one control and the victory is worked out "in." No dodging, no escapism—it's all "in."

O Jesus Lord, we thank Thee that Thy victory was "in," even when that "in" meant a cross. Teach me to accept the "in" as the sphere of my victory too. For I want no paradise if it turns out to be a fool's paradise. I want the paradise of Thy reality. Amen.

AFFIRMATION FOR THE DAY: *Let all my victories be "in"—no escapism, no drugs, mental or physical.*

NOT GHOSTS BUT EMBODIED BEINGS

We turn now again to Paul's exhortation: "I beseech you therefore, brethren, by the mercies of God, that ye present your bodies a living sacrifice" (Romans 12:1 KJV). This "therefore" picks up the thread of the discourse broken by the interlude of the three intervening chapters and emhasizes the "in." If the victory is to be "in," then you "must present your bodies." The word of victory must be wrought out in physical relations or not at all. We are not ghosts, we are embodied beings and the victory must be wrought out as embodied beings.

But why "by the mercies of God?" Does it mean that it is a merciful thing for God to invite us to present our bodies a living sacrifice? Yes, for if you do not present your bodies as a living sacrifice you will be in for trouble, deep trouble with your bodies. For the body that isn't offered to God is offered to Trouble and Sorrow, both with capitals. For the body that doesn't fulfill the purpose of God will be a body that is full of conflicts and self-created diseases. Why is there more aspirin sold in the United States than in all of the rest of the world? It is because we need these painkillers to rectify homegrown pains. Dr. Sadler, the great psychiatrist, said that "if we lived in a truly Christian way half the diseases would drop off tomorrow morning and we would stand up a new healthy human race."

So it is not sacrifice if you offer your body back to the Creator for Him to teach us how to live with it. The sacrifice is the other way round. For if you don't offer your body to God, you have to offer your body to doctors, to pharmacists, to hospitals—you offer your body to the altar of Trouble. So it's by "the mercies of God" that you are asked to offer.

O God, our Father, our bodies made by Thee, and for Thee, live in Thee. Outside of Thee they fulfill the description—"this body of death." So we come with our bodies to learn how to live and to live abundantly. Amen.

AFFIRMATION FOR THE DAY: *My flesh and my spirit in partnership with thee will be partners in Thy Cause.*

SPIRITUALIZATION—FIRST REFUGE OF THE
SKEPTICAL MIND

We saw yesterday that it was a merciful thing for God to ask us to offer our bodies as a "living sacrifice." The emphasis is on "living." The body that belongs to Jesus Christ is a "living" body. It can throw off disease germs, it can absorb hard knocks, it has a built-in repair shop, balancing the accounts by throwing off fatigue toxins each night; it is dedicated to health, not disease, so it breathes health, exudes health—it is health. If I am His, I am a "living sacrifice." If I am not His, I am a dying sacrifice.

No wonder then Paul said, "Present your bodies as a living sacrifice." This fulfills this voice: "Lo, I come to do Thy will . . . a body Thou hast prepared me"—the will of God was to be done in and through the body.

But we often do what the New English Bible does when it says, "I implore you by God's mercy to offer your very selves to him a living sacrifice." It substitutes "your very selves" for "your bodies." In other words they spiritualize it. Now spiritualization is the first refuge of the skeptical mind. When we don't know what to do with a thing we spiritualize it. That takes it out of the concrete and puts it into the abstract. For instance, when Jesus said that the first item in His Good News was "the gospel to the poor," we make this the spiritually poor, for that takes it out of concrete relations and puts it into the Word made word. Renders it innocuous.

Paul says the presenting of the body is your "spiritual worship." The spiritual is only spiritual when it is presented in incarnate terms. When you lift it out of material relations you make it the Word become word so that the spiritual has lost its spirituality and become verbal. So Christianity which is not the Word become flesh is less than Christianity.

O Lord Jesus, when we fellowship with Thee totally we fellowship with Thee. If not totally then with an abstraction, a fiction. Save me from denaturing Thee and help me to take Thee as Thou art that Thou mayst take me as I am. In Thy Name. Amen.

AFFIRMATION FOR THE DAY: *"I am in Nero's prison, but I'm not Nero's prisoner"—I'm bound to the earth but not earthbound.*

THE BODY IS HOLY IF WHOLLY HIS

Paul goes on in his passage and says that this presenting of the body is not only "spiritual worship," but it is "holy and acceptable." This word "holy" strikes at the whole Greek idea that the body is "impure," only the spirit is "pure." This says the body offered to God is "holy." For what the holy God has is "holy." There is no such thing as a "holy place," or a "holy shrine," things in themselves are not holy. It is whether God's holy possession and purpose run through it. If a selfish, secular purpose runs through it, it is unholy, whatever its label.

This offering of the body is "acceptable to God." Does that mean that if the body is not included, if it is only "spiritual," it is not "acceptable"? It would seem so. Then if the Word doesn't become flesh it is an unacceptable word to God. That would cancel out a lot of our so-called "services" as unacceptable, for there is no intention or attempt to make the Word preached to become flesh in the individual or the group.

An Indian friend quoted the verse, "God has made of one blood all nations," and an American arose and said, "I believe in the whole Bible except that verse." In many churches if a Negro were brought into a World Brotherhood Service it would break up the service. The Word become word.

"That you may prove what is the will of God, what is good and acceptable and perfect." This gives the only way to prove what is the will of God—put it under life, the total life, physical, spiritual, mental, and then you can find out the will of God for it will prove itself to you. When you present the total person to God then God can prove Himself totally to you. But if you present a portion of yourself—the spiritual—the verification will be as hazy as the presentation.

When there is a total presentation then you will find that the will of God is "good," so "good" that it is "acceptable," and so acceptable that it is "perfect." For the will of God totally fits the total person when it is totally presented. You "prove" that, not by logic, but by life. The Word becomes flesh.

O Blessed Father, we thank Thee for Thy blessed will. Thy will is our highest interest always and everywhere. When we find Thy will we find our own—our own deepest will. May Thy will be "acceptable" to me in everything. Amen.

AFFIRMATION FOR THE DAY: *God's will is first "good," then "acceptable," then "perfect." My will starts out "perfect," then "unacceptable," and then "not good."*

"WE DO NOT WORK TO THE VICTORY BUT FROM THE VICTORY"

We are now in a position to emphasize the fact that the Christian faith is not a verbal faith to be believed, but it is an offer to be accepted. If it were a philosophy you would verbally accept it and act on it as far as you are able. "As far as you are able" is important, for it would depend on you and your resources—a human whipping up of the will. But the Christian Gospel is quite different—it doesn't depend on what you do, but on your acceptance of what God has done. This doesn't mean that you don't do anything, a sort of quietism. You do everything, but only after you have accepted what God has done. You love because He first loved you; you do because of what He has done; you give because of His giving.

A theological professor in England asked his students whether the Gospel they preached was a demand or an offer. With one accord they replied that it was a demand. "Think again," said the professor. "Well, it is a demand and an offer," they replied. "Think again," said the professor. And they finally came to the conclusion that if it is the Christian Gospel it is an offer. Since the center of the Gospel is the Word become flesh it is an offer within life to life. He makes available what he has wrought—not merely what He has taught, but what he has wrought. He offers His wrought-out Victory as our very own. We plug in at His highest point.

So all His promises are performances become available to the receptive. We do not have to take His verbal promises and make them real. We take His vital performances and accept them as our own and live by them. As Mary Webster says, "We do not work to the victory, but from the Victory." We begin with His victory and by receptivity make it our own. So it doesn't depend on our reserves, but on His Resources. "Not my responsibility, but my response to His ability." Not my mental approval, but my appropriation.

O Jesus, Lord and Savior, I see the point of my failure. I screw myself up mentally to believe when I should be letting go and trusting and appropriating. I try to make Thee willing, but Thou art waiting for my willingness. Amen.

AFFIRMATION FOR THE DAY: *Since God is in a state of Yesness to me, I shall be in a state of Yesness to Him.*

THE GOSPEL IS DIFFERENT:
IT IS GOD TAKING THE INITIATIVE

We are meditating upon the fact that the Gospel is different—it is God taking the initiative. He offered Himself up for us all and now He offers His all to us—for the taking. "For the taking"—provided *we* take it—the whole person. You cannot take it with your hand and leave your heart, your very life out. The whole person must take. Like produces like. His was a whole offering and it produces a whole taking in us.

But what do we do? We conceive of His promises as beautiful promises—to be framed and put on a wall. A man was given a check and he was so grateful, for he was very poor, that he framed it and put it on a wall. Framed it instead of cashing it! Another man was so grateful for a check that he set it to music and sang it. That is what we do with the promises of the Bible—we set them to music and sing them instead of cashing them and living by them. We make the Word become flesh into the Word become rhythm—rhythm instead of realization.

A man said to me, "My whole family swims, but I don't." I asked him why, for he looked robust. "Well," he replied, "I am afraid of water, so I fight it. I don't trust myself to it." That was the point of failure. He didn't trust, therefore, he didn't entrust. We have to trust and entrust.

A little red hen sat on a barrel of wheat and starved to death. All she would have had to do would have been to turn and eat and live!

A Hindu woman lost her husband by an accident. She said to a Christian friend, "If he had only come home alive I would have fought with the gods for his life." Some Christians "wrestle" with God, some bargain with God, but some know that we do not have to overcome God's reluctance—we have to lay hold on His highest willingness. The Word has already become flesh. It becomes flesh in us when we take it.

Blessed Lord, this must be Thy greatest hurt—the hurt that we do not take. Thou hast given Thy all and we take little driblets. Thou art giving with both hands and we take with two fingers. Help me to take with both hands, with open heart. Amen.

AFFIRMATION FOR THE DAY: *God's two steps toward me will be met by my two steps toward Him.*

"IT'S POURING DOWN—IT'S POURING DOWN— TAKE IT"

We are studying the Christian faith as realized potentiality, as Everywhere brought into the Now, as Everything brought into the Here.

A girl was an ugly personality, no friends. But Estelle Carver got her to write out this verse and place it in the corner of her mirror: "I, Janet, chosen of God, holy and beloved" (a paraphrase of Col. 3:12). She read it day by day, made it her own, and became exactly what she read. In six months she was transformed. It could have been done in six minutes.

In a Greek convent in Jerusalem two pictures linger in my mind. Sister Lila lives there and is a saint. She lives in a state of vibrant joy and vitality. She said to me, "What can I do for you? What can I bring you?" I replied, "I want nothing except more grace." "Well," she said, "take it. It's pouring down, it's pouring down—take it." And when she said it you knew she was doing that very thing—she was taking it.

On the other hand, in the same convent I saw a lovely painting of a woman who had spent twenty years in the desert atoning for her sin of adultery. Haggard and worn from her twenty years of austerity and fasting she was at last being given the holy communion by a priest in the desert. She had atoned for her sins. This is not the Word become flesh—it is the flesh trying to become word—the flesh atoning for its own sins. It is the Hindu conception, but not the Christian.

And yet one seems cheap and the other expensive. But the reverse is true. Sister Lila takes grace as it pours down and she pours out her life as an offering of gratitude for grace. The desert penitent had no message to give—all she could do would be to warn others of how expensive sin is. But no message of the wonder of grace. It was an egocentric attempt at salvation. Hence no song to sing. But Sister Lila's life itself was a song—a lyrical song of the wonder of redeeming grace.

O Lord God and Savior, save me from thinking I can save myself by my goodness or by my efforts. For my goodness is not goodness when it is a substitute for Thy grace. Give me the grace to take Thy grace and then I'll have Thy goodness. Amen.

AFFIRMATION FOR THE DAY: *An organism can expend as much energy as it takes in and no more.*

LIVING IN A STATE OF YESNESS TO GOD

We are considering the fact that the Christian faith is not a creed to be believed, but an offer to be accepted. This is important. On my way out to India fifty-four years ago a chaplain on board ship spoke of the beauty of the Prayer Book prayers and then added, "But you don't believe God answers prayer, do you?" Prayers beautiful, but the Word become word, not the Word become flesh.

On the other hand, Sister Lila lives in a state of Yesness to God—and to life! She says, "Don't ask me to do a thing unless you really want me to do it for I may say yes." So you're careful what you ask her to do. To live in a state of Yesness to God fits in with the revelation in Christ, for He is the Yes. "For all the promises of God find their Yes in him" (II Cor. 1:20). Or as Moffatt puts it: "The divine 'yes' has at last sounded in him." So when Sister Lila lives in a state of Yesness, she is but echoing the Divine Yes in Jesus Christ. He has Yessed every promise of God and therefore it all awaits the human Yes. To live in a state of Yesness is to live in a state of receptivity, drawing on Him every moment for everything.

At a church supper grace had been said and there was an awkward pause; no one wanted to be the first to begin, but the silence was broken by an impatient boy, "What are they waiting for?" And that is what we can say to ourselves and to the Christian world, "What are we waiting for?" The Yes has been sounded in Him. The Japanese have the custom of having grace, and then begin eating only when someone, or a number in unison call out: "I will take." That "I will take" makes the word of food become flesh.

A judge said to me, "The wires are all connected and everything is ready, but I'm afraid to press the button." Afraid of light coming into his darkness, afraid of fullness coming into his emptiness—afraid to say Yes to His Yes.

O Divine Yes, Thou hast thrown open the Resources of Divine Grace, and we stand fearful of taking those Resources. We plead our unworthiness when Thy worthiness is the very thing open to us. Forgive us our stupidity. Amen.

AFFIRMATION FOR THE DAY: *Anyone can take. So whatever my limitations I'll not be short on taking.*

"I REFUSE TO ACCEPT MY LIMITATIONS"

Everything in Jesus is present tense. Heaven? You can have it now—in Him. Apocalyptic? You can live in "realized apocalyptic." "When they have experienced the goodness of God's word and the spiritual energies of the age to come" (Heb. 6:5 NEB). "Experienced . . . the spiritual energies of the age to come." You can live tomorrow today! Last night a polio cripple, unable to walk, told me that her priest had said, "Yes, my child, you will enjoy happiness in heaven." But she saw the possibility of living in heaven now through surrender to Jesus, took heaven as her portion now, and is radiantly happy and useful in teaching seventy children. She went past the priestly "No, not now," and took the immediate "Yes" of Jesus and is a center of spiritual contagion.

A minister radiantly happy and useful at eighty-three said, "This is my life philosophy: In view of the resources of God I refuse to accept my limitations."

A critic said to Sister Mary, "I don't believe in your way of life," and she quietly replied, "Well, the difference between you and me is that you are digging for oil and I'm pumping it." She had learned to take, and it made the difference between the frustrated critic and the fruitful Christian.

When Jesus breathed on His disciples He said, "Receive ye the Holy Spirit"; it could be translated, "Take ye the Holy Spirit"—it is active. Everything in Jesus is open and everything is present. Jesus brought God into the Now.

A couple who had turned their backs on Jesus and were trying to climb the ladder to God by their renunciations said rather wistfully, "We have a long way to go." In Jesus it's never "a long way to go"—it's all in the here and now. A student in Japan said, "Stanley Jones tonight gave instances of people finding God now. I don't think that can happen." The next morning he appeared at the door: "Sir, it has happened—to me."

O Jesus, we do not have to climb up to heaven to bring Thee down, for Thou art here. If I'm in a hole Thou art in the hole with me—to release me. All I need to do is to stop turning my back on Thee. Thou art here. Amen.

AFFIRMATION FOR THE DAY: *In view of the Here-ness of Jesus I am not alone and I am not without adequate Resources.*

HOLDING TO CRUSTS

We are looking at the fact that the Christian faith, interpreted as the Word become flesh, is God's eternal Yes to us. And our response should be an attitude of Yesness—a Yes to His Yes. A cowboy was converted late in life and brought over into his Christian life his cowboy language and attitudes. He was asked by a pastor with whom he was taking breakfast to say grace. He prayed, "Lord, I ain't askin you for nothin, but I'm a-thankin You for everything." He had passed the stage of asking to the stage of receiving, continuously receiving and continuously thanking, a state of Yesness. His attitude was not achieving but receiving. The achieving came out of the receiving and not the other way round.

A man was arrested in Ceylon and brought before a court for digging up a grave and removing a skeleton. Asked why he did it he replied, "I wanted it for meditation." He wanted to meditate upon a skeleton! But before we smile at the man in Ceylon let us ask ourselves how many Christians meditate upon dead Bibles, dead doctrines, dead rituals. They don't expect to receive anything from a living Christ. Inwardly dead with an open Bible in their hands. They don't take it—they take it in their hands, sleep with it under their pillows—anything except taking it as their very own.

Or they cling to some outworn doctrine instead of receiving the living Christ. A child was taken from a war area where he had been going into garbage cans in search of scraps of food. He was taken to a home, washed, but his hand was clenched; they had to pry it open and found a crust of bread—this clenched crust with abundance of food next door. We hold on to our moldy doctrines, clenching desperately, when if we would open our hands and heart we could have the Living Bread.

O Living Bread, help me to throw away my moldy crusts and to eat forever of Thee. For without feeding upon Thee we are lean and empty. Feeding on Thee we are satisfied to our depths. Evermore give us this Bread. In Thy name. Amen.

AFFIRMATION FOR THE DAY: *My good is often the enemy of His best, my crusts keep me from His loaf.*

"HAS ANYONE TOLD YOU TODAY?"

We are looking at the Word become flesh as availability—now and anywhere for anybody. A young Dutchman became enamored of Eastern mysticism. He sat for fifteen days on a peak of the lower Himalayas gazing at the higher peaks and the eternal snows upon them. The fifteen days he fasted and meditated upon their eternal whiteness hoping that some of that purity would come within him. Nothing happened. Nature mocked him. His Bible was unopened beside him. He opened his Bible and the living Christ walked straight into his heart. The nature worshipers are always secondhand, this side of Reality.

A woman secretary was the point of tension in the office. Her boss said to her one day as she entered, "Has any one told you today?" "Told me what?" she replied. "That God loves you." She broke down and wept, accepted the love of God in Christ, and is now the spark of life in that office.

A mathematician in an atomic center said to me with a tense eagerness, "All the kindling wood is laid, ready for the fire to burst forth." When I saw him again he was on fire. He had applied the match of receptivity!

To be empty in the face of this Fullness is tragedy—and stupidity! A man who had never traveled went across the Atlantic and provided for his food—bananas and peanuts. He got tired of this diet and went to the steward to see if he could buy a good meal. Found to his amazement that all his meals had been paid for—in the ticket! He was like many—spiritually starved when all they need is paid for in Christ!

It's all open—to the receptive. Two high school boys went to the altar and gave witness that they were saved. An old man got up, "Something is wrong here. I went to the altar eleven times before I was saved, and these boys got it in three minutes." An old lady replied, "But they were not so stubborn." "Blessed are the meek for they shall inherit the earth"—and salvation!

O Jesus, Thou art the Eternal Openness. So I take Thy forgiveness for my sin; Thy fullness for my emptiness; Thy victory for my defeat; Thy healing for my sickness; Thy strength for my weakness; Thy all for my nothingness. Amen.

AFFIRMATION FOR THE DAY: *I am what my receptivity is, no more, no less.*

CAN THE FLESH BE REDEEMED?

We have been looking at the healing of the soul by surrender and appropriation and obedience. What about the body? If the "flesh" is an instrument of this redemption does it partake of that redemption?

Plato said, "If the head and the body are to be well you must begin by curing the soul." We have emphasized the curing of the soul. But the healing must be passed on to the body if it is to be the Word become flesh.

Physical healing is not the central emphasis of the Gospel. If you make healing central that leaves you at the center—God serves you, keeps you well. And anything that leaves you central is off-center. God is the center, and reconciliation to Him is the central emphasis of the Gospel. But reconciled to Him you are reconciled with yourself, with your body, with your brother, with nature, with life. This reconciliation brings health.

I have often imagined a convention of bodies talking about the people who inhabit them. A body stands up and says, "Oh my, the man who inhabits me doesn't know how to live. He is full of fears, resentments, self-centeredness and guilts. He ties me in knots, and then doses me with all sort of medicines which have no relationship with what is wrong with me. There is nothing wrong with me. He upsets my functioning. I wish he knew how to live." Another body stands up and says, "It's wonderful to live with the man I live with. He is rhythmical, harmonious, and adjusted. We get along famously together, and I do prodigious things for him. It's a joy to do it." Suppose your body would stand up, would you enjoy it? At least seventy-five percent of all diseases are homegrown ills, the doctors tell us. And the patients will never be well unless they change their attitudes toward life. The life climate is wrong for health.

O Jesus, I would let Thy health and healing into every pore of my being, so that I may live by Thy health. For my body is made by Thee, for Thee, and when I live in Thee I live in my homeland. I thank Thee. Amen.

AFFIRMATION FOR THE DAY: *My body, included in redemption, will realize its inclusion to the full.*

SIXTY TO EIGHTY PERCENT OF PATIENTS HAVE PSYCHOSOMATIC COMPLAINTS

We mentioned yesterday the effects of mind and emotion on the body. Dr. Blaine E. McLaughlin, director of psychiatry at Women's Medical College, Philadelphia, says that sixty to eighty-five percent of all patients in doctors' offices have psychosomatic complaints. He says that ninety-nine percent of all headaches, seventy-five percent of all gastric upsets, seventy-five percent of all skin diseases, and eighty-five percent of all asthma are psychosomatic in nature.

A doctor in our Hiroshima, Japan, Ashram said, "I was taught in the medical college that all diseases were rooted in the body, but my practice has made me see differently. A farmer was a drunkard and felt guilty over it. Then his son in Tokyo began to behave badly, and he felt guilty over this too. His heart began to act badly. But he has a perfectly good heart structurally." A heart specialist in Fredericksburg, Virginia, said to me, "eighty-five percent of people with heart conditions have nothing structurally wrong with them—the disturbance is functional. Fear is the great trouble. I have to spend most of my time telling people they have nothing structurally wrong with them."

A minister told me he lost his personal experience of God in the Seminary. "I went to Mayo Clinic. They could find nothing wrong with me physically. The psychiatrist to whom I went had more problems than I had. He sucked on candy all the time. He said, 'If you want to do it, why don't you do it.' I found myself reading your book on conversion while riding on a bus. There it happened—on the bus! I was converted! I have had a wonderful year—no problems."

A doctor who attended to the medical needs of a General Motors plant in a certain city said, "Seventy-five percent of the executives of this plant have gastric ulcers due to the pressure upon them to succeed or be replaced. I have had no training to deal with these mental and spiritual needs, so I am helpless."

O Jesus Lord and Savior, Thou art not helpless. Thou dost lose no cases surrendered into Thy hands and wholly obedient to Thee. Help me to be one of those—surrendered and obedient. For Thy will is health and healing. I would live in it. Amen.

AFFIRMATION FOR THE DAY: *My resolution: No homegrown ills.*

"IT'S THE SURLY BIRD WHO GETS THE GERM"

We mentioned yesterday that some doctors do not know how to deal with spiritual problems. Some do. A surgeon said to a public audience, "If you don't come to God and surrender to Him you will have to come to me and surrender to surgery. Seventy-five percent of surgical cases begin in functional disturbances and pass into structural disease. Then I get them."

A doctor examining a patient said to himself, "Something is eating this man," and found he had had an affair with another man's wife. It was discovered the night before, hence the colitis. The man confessed it, asked forgiveness and got it, and is well.

But some doctors are problems to themselves. A friend of mine went to see a doctor who was having an affair with another woman and getting a divorce from his wife. She found the doctor walking the floor with a glass of whiskey in one hand and tranquilizers in the other. That picture of an able man, breaking himself upon the laws of God and trying to hold himself together with liquor and tranquilizers—it is the essence of pathos and folly.

A prominent man and his wife led opposition to a pastor because he was treading on their toes. They drew up a bill of complaints to be presented to the Official Board. The wife broke out in hives as the day approached, and he lost his voice, couldn't speak. "There is nothing covered that will not be revealed"—sometimes in hives and lost voices!

A businessman in the Oslo Ashram had a nervous breakdown. Someone had been put in over him. He was resentful and bitter. He surrendered himself and his resentments to God and the next morning he said, "It's all gone—I'm well." And he was. Dr. Karl Menninger says, "Guilt changes the physical structure of the body and makes the person more susceptible to disease." "It's the surly bird who gets the germ."

Dear Father, Thou hast written Thy laws within us. Help us to obey those laws and thus obey the purpose for which we were made. Amen.

AFFIRMATION FOR THE DAY: *Health is my heritage—I shall take it and make it a gift and an achievement.*

ALL MENTAL ILLNESSES ARE
A RETREAT OUT OF LIFE

If one wants to be well, for a purpose, it helps tremendously in being well. When Jesus asked the man at the pool, "Wouldst thou be made whole?" it was important. Some people want to be well but not whole—whole as a person. They want to be well of the disease, but not whole in the total person—body, mind, and spirit. Unless you will total health you have no right to ask to be well. For being well may mean going back to the old selfish ways of life.

A woman was operated on for a heart condition. When she was told the operation was successful she was furious. It meant that now she would not be the center of attention as an invalid. She would have to take responsibility and get attention by what she produced instead of by what she suffered, so she was frightened and angry. A man who was going blind was operated on and his eyesight restored. He said, "I had been living back in the shadows, protected from life and its responsibilities. Now I felt my defenses were all down. I was right out there in the center of things. I was afraid for I felt naked. I did not want to assume the responsibility of facing life."

All mental illnesses are a retreat out of life—a retreat into the unreality of concepts and phrases and illusions. It is the word become word. All healing is the positive assuming of responsibility. Sten Nilsson, a missionary to India, was given up to die when he was a boy. The doctor said to the mother, "You need not send for me to make out the death certificate, I'll write it now." He did. But Sten, when he heard it, said, "I do not intend to die. I intend to be a missionary." The next day he got up, was well, and has been well ever since, the picture of health. The champion weight lifter of Canada met with an accident and couldn't be an athlete any longer; he was frustrated, argued with God and himself. He surrendered to God and is now a well man!

O Jesus Lord and Healer, help me to face up to everything with Thee. For in Thee there is health and wholeness. Help me to take nothing lying down, all standing up. For in Thee is everything I need—and more. I thank Thee, thank Thee. Amen.

AFFIRMATION FOR THE DAY: *I am as well as I want to be, if my "want to be" includes cooperation with God.*

A PRESCRIPTION FOR HEALTH:
THE NINE BEATITUDES

We are emphasizing the will to be well. Tommy Kano was an asthmatic boy and became the champion weight lifter of the world. Secret? He asks himself the question before he lifts: "Do I want to lift this?" When he says he does, he does lift it!

But the will to health must not be the willing of the will only—it must be the willing of the total person. There are two extremes in regard to finding of health—one to depend on science alone; the other to depend on miracle alone. Both of these bring disappointment. There is a third way: the way that obeys the laws of health on the one hand and depends on the resources of God on the other. These are the alternate beats of the healthy Christian heart.

A psychologist went throughout the world looking for the positive qualities that make for health. He came back and found them in the New Testament. More specifically Dr. Frank Sladen, of the Ford Hospital, Detroit, found these positive qualities in the Beatitudes. "Sister Mary" reminds us that the Beatitudes are Be-atitudes not do-atitudes. The doing comes out of the being.

We will take these nine beatitudes as the Christian prescription for health. First, *Blessed are the poor in Spirit, for theirs is the Kingdom of heaven.* The word for "poor" is *anav,* literally, a chosen poverty, so chosenly poor, that they are poor enough to receive. It could be translated then: "the receptive in spirit." This means that you are willing to change, willing to break up old thought patterns, old habits, old ways. And be willing to take new thought patterns, new habits, new ways. This means surrender. And complete surrender. No yes and no—it must be yes to change. You must empty your hands of old ways and be ready to have them filled with new ways—God's ways.

O Lord Jesus, we come again as little children—open and receptive. Our hearts and our hands are empty and open to receive Thy health, Thy healing, Thy self. We do not do this tomorrow—we do it now. For we want Thy healing now. Amen.

AFFIRMATION FOR THE DAY: *I will take this first prescription: I will be humble enough to acknowledge my need and receive.*

ALWAYS RIGHT, HENCE ALWAYS WRONG

We are looking at the Beatitudes as giving the mental and emotional and spiritual positive attitudes which produce health. Second, *Blessed are those who mourn, for they shall be comforted.* "Sister Mary," a radiant soul, said to me, "There is one verse I don't know how to practice: 'Blessed are those who mourn.' I don't know how to mourn. I am so happy I don't know how to mourn." Nor could I tell her, for I too was too happy to mourn. But I could tell her that the meaning was probably the ability to say, "I am sorry. I made a mistake." This is the greatest catharsis I know. But some people have not learned that secret—they are always right, hence always wrong. Confession leads to correction and correction leads to conversion. Without confession there is no conversion. One of the finest Christians I know had the vice-presidency of a company at a $20,000 salary. He resigned. The president said to him, "You are young and inexperienced. You do not understand the intricacies of business." The young executive quietly said, "I know the difference between right and wrong," and went out. It's a healthy attitude and brings health.

Third, *Blessed are the meek for they shall inherit the earth.* The meek have been looked on as the weak. Nothing could be further from the truth. The meek are so sure of their resources and of their goals that they can afford to be meek. Others have to be proud because they are so unsure of themselves and their goals. The meek could be called the assured, for they are meek enough to take the resources of God.

Fourth, *Blessed are those who hunger and thirst for righteousness, for they shall be satisfied.* This beatitude is the turning point from the receptive attitude in the first three to the outgoing aggressive attitude in the next three. For receptivity means response—response to God's ability. The hunger and thirst mean that in appropriating the righteousness and assimilating it you become righteous, and righteousness means right action. You are righteous and you do righteousness. In the being and doing you are "satisfied."

O Jesus Lord and Savior, make my hunger and thirst for righteousness as pressing as my hunger and thirst for food. And help me to be as receptive to righteousness as I am receptive of food. I don't want to be satisfied physically and starved spiritually. Amen.

AFFIRMATION FOR THE DAY: *To say "I am sorry" is a catharsis.*

INWARD CONFLICT CHIEF CAUSE OF ILLNESS

We continue the positive attitudes making for health. Fifth, *Blessed are the merciful, for they shall obtain mercy.* At the heart of mercy is forgiveness. We forgive everybody for everything. And we ask forgiveness. A misson college in India was on strike for twenty-one days and the college closed. An official in the college said a rude thing to a student. The student union, which the student represented, demanded that he apologize not only to the one student but to the whole student union. Over that the college was tied up for twenty-one days. Ask for forgiveness and give forgiveness to everybody or you're tied up physically.

Sixth, *Blessed are the pure in heart, for they shall see God.* The pure in heart are the undivided in heart—the single-hearted. Inward division causes more unhealth and unhappiness than anything else. I asked a young woman missionary about to be sent home from the Congo what she thought was the matter, and she replied, "I'm sitting on a lid." "What is under the lid?" I asked. "Two people—one who doesn't want to be a missionary, and the other a person who is afraid if she isn't a missionary she will be lost." I replied, "You don't want to be either of those—surrender of the divided self will solve it."

Seventh, *Blessed are the peacemakers, for they shall be called sons of God.* A little girl came down one morning and said to her mother, "What a beautiful day." And the surprised mother said, "But how can you call this weather beautiful?" "But, mother," the girl replied, "a beautiful day has nothing to do with the weather." She reconciled her mother to the weather and had a more beautiful day for herself. The peacemakers make a new world around them and within them.

Eighth, *Blessed are those who are persecuted for righteousness' sake, for theirs is the kingdom of heaven.* You cannot be healthy unless you stand for something—even at cost.

Ninth, *Blessed are you when men revile you . . . rejoice and be glad.* Nothing makes a person healthier than joy in spite of. Joy on account of is neutral, but joy in spite of is positive, hence health-giving.

O Jesus, Thou didst rejoice in spite of. Give me that positive joy that can laugh at the "is," for it is living in the "ought-to-be." Make me incorrigibly happy, and then I shall be incorrigibly healthy. Joy makes me glow with health. Amen.

AFFIRMATION FOR THE DAY: *I will rejoice when there isn't anything to rejoice about except my rejoicing.*

"IT IS INHERENT FOR THE CHRISTIAN TO PROPAGATE HIS FAITH"

We now come to the consideration of the Word become flesh and evangelism. An interesting incident took place when India's new constitution was being passed in the National Legislature. In the portion where it says that each individual has "the right to profess, practice, and propagate his faith," that word "propagate" was a question mark to many. In the midst of it a Hindu said this, "To the Christian it is inherent to propagate his faith. If he is faithful to his faith he must propagate his faith. So if you do not allow him to propagate his faith you do not allow him to profess and practice his faith." That argument swung the situation and it was adopted. The Hindu saw clearly that to propagate his faith is inherent in being a Christian. Then why don't all Christians do it? I can only testify.

I underwent a half-conversion and joined the church. A revival came on. I was urged to win someone. I tried but was rebuffed by my own lack of having anything to give. It was my first and my last attempt to win someone, until I had found something for myself. What I said was the Word become word. Then came the real thing—I found a conversion for myself, the real thing. The word of conversion became flesh. Then conversions began to happen right and left. My first convert was my grandmother at eighty-two years of age. It was the day after Christmas, and she said that she would possibly not be here by another Christmas. So I asked, "But you're ready to go, aren't you?" The tears began to flow down her cheeks and she said, "No, I'm not." We knelt and in the midst of our praying she entered. Again, my mother came to the altar of prayer. When I knelt beside her I asked, "What do you want?" And she replied: "I don't know, but I want what you have found." The whole family came in. When I tried to win others with the word of conversion become word it was a failure. When the Word became flesh it was a success.

O Jesus, my Redeemer, I can only give as I take from Thee. May my words be a revelation of a fact—the fact of conversion in me. That which is to reach the heart must come from the heart, so let my words about conversion come from conversion. Amen.

AFFIRMATION FOR THE DAY: *Nothing is mine unless I share it.*

NOT GOD'S LAWYER BUT HIS WITNESS

This necessity of the Word becoming flesh in winning others to Christ was burned into my very soul by an unforgettable experience in the very beginning of my ministry. I had begun to study law, but the law dropped away and the ministry gripped me. I told my pastor. He was very happy and said he wanted me to preach my first sermon three weeks hence. I was scared but I had three weeks in which to prepare. My idea was that I was to be God's lawyer and argue His case for Him. A big crowd was there—all my relatives came and the Jones family is large! And they were anxious to see the young man do well.

I began on a high key—too high. I used a word I had never used before—and I've never used since—"indifferentism." When I used that word, a girl attending college put down her head and smiled. It so unnerved me that when I came back to the thread of my discourse it was gone. My mind was a perfect blank. I clutched wildly for something to say but nothing came. Finally I blurted out, "I'm sorry, but I've forgotten my sermon." Six sentences and I tripped over that word "indifferentism." This was the beginning of my ministry—a dead failure. I started down the pulpit steps to go to my seat when God said to me, "Haven't I done anything for you?" "Why, yes," I replied, "everything." "Couldn't you tell that?" "Well, I might." So instead of going to my seat I came around in front and said, "Friends, I see I can't preach. But you know my life is different in this community. And though I can't preach I'm going to witness for Him the balance of my days." I said some more things like that. At the close a young man came up and said, "Stanley, I want to find what you have." I have often wondered what he saw that he wanted amid the wreckage of things that night. But he knelt with me and was converted. He became a minister, and his daughter became a missionary to Africa. As a lawyer I was a failure; as a witness I was a success. I had found through a hard experience the keynote of my ministry—I was to be a witness—the word of redemption become flesh.

O Lord Jesus, help me to be Thy witness. I cannot argue people into the Kingdom, but maybe I can show them the Kingdom at work in an unworthy life. I can show Thee as a Savior because Thou art saving me. Amen.

AFFIRMATION FOR THE DAY: *Not to witness for Christ is to witness against Him: "He does nothing for me."*

"SUFFERING FROM A HALLUCINATION?"

I recounted yesterday how God burned into my inmost soul the deepest lesson of my life: I was to be His witness—the word of experience become flesh. In my first book, *The Christ of the Indian Road,* I said, "Just as family training cannot rise above family character, so Christian preaching cannot rise above the Christian preacher." I determined I would be a witness. So I have witnessed before high and low, kings and peasants, what Christ has done for a bankrupt life.

I was asked to speak before the psychologists of Columbia University. And they assigned me my subject: "Your personal religious experience." Of all the places where I did not want to bare my soul it was before those mechanistic psychologists of Columbia, for I knew what they would do. They would put me on the operating table and practice mental vivisection. And when they got through I would be a museum specimen, ticketed and labeled. But I was not on trial, the reality of the thing I held was on trial, so I would let them break it if it could be broken. The hall was filled, and for an hour I told them what Christ had done for a bankrupt life. They began to ask questions at the close. One man asked, "Isn't it possible that you are suffering from a hallucination?" "Yes," I replied, "it is possible. But if it is a hallucination then it is in spite of the attitude I've taken, for I've put my faith out before the non-Christian world, and I've said, 'Brothers, break it if it can be broken. If it can be broken it must be broken. I don't want to live in a paradise if it turns out to be a fool's paradise.' So they have smitten on it for a quarter of a century but the more it is smitten upon the more it shines. Besides if it is a hallucination it has given me exactly what I've needed so that it has done me more good than my former sanity." They broke out in applause. The questioner, surprised, said: "It looks as though I'm in a minority here tonight." He was, for some psychologists do survive being psychologists and do remain persons.

O Christ of the Emmaus Road and of Every Road, our hearts burn within us as we talk to Thee and companion with Thee by the way. Thou art Reality and to experience Thee is to experience self-verifying Reality. My heart burns now. Amen.

AFFIRMATION FOR THE DAY: *What my eyes have seen and my heart has known, shall my tongue refuse to tell?*

LAY WITNESSING THE CENTER OF OUR FAITH

If the very nature of the Christian faith is the Word become flesh then the very nature of the expression of that faith is witnessing—the Word become flesh. But almost the whole of the Christian expression is on preaching—the Word become word. This points to the fact that in a major change, the emphasis must be on the part the laity plays in the Christian movement. Lay witnessing must be the major emphasis. For ministers, priests, missionaries, and evangelists like myself will never win this world for Christ. And if we could it would not be good, for the lay people of the churches would be denied the growth and development which comes from sharing their faith and winning others.

The fact is that the Christian faith is a lay movement. Jesus was a layman. The religious system of the day gave Him no license or credentials. His call was from God and not from man. He was not ordained in the ordinary sense of laying on of hands. When the religious leaders asked Jesus for his credentials He pointed to the changed people around Him—credentials in flesh and blood. Nor were His disciples ordained by the laying on of hands. They were ordained: "Ye have not chosen me, but I have chosen you, and ordained you" (John 15:16 KJV). The Divine choice was the ordination. So if there is an "apostolic succession" by the laying on of hands the apostles were not in it. But the apostles began to be possessive of the movement, began to argue who was first in the movement, forbade others from casting out devils because "they followed not us," wanted to call down fire on those who would not receive them. Instead of the movement possessing them they began to possess the movement. So Jesus had to reemphasize the lay emphasis in the movement by appointing the seventy laymen to whom He gave the same commission He gave the Twelve. He was immediately behind them, to reject them was to reject Him, to receive them was to receive Him.

O Jesus, Savior and Leader, lead us back to Thy original purposes, back to Thy mind. For if we are outside Thy mind we are outside Thy power. And without Thy power we are fruitless. And we would be fruitful. Amen.

AFFIRMATION FOR THE DAY: *When I am witnessing I am not witnessing to myself, a ransomed sinner; I'm witnessing to a ransoming Savior.*

SEPARATING WHAT GOD HAD JOINED

We are looking at lay witnessing as the basis of our faith and the basis of the future of our faith—if it is to have a future. For the Word become word has run its course. The Word become flesh must now take over.

At Pentecost the Holy Spirit was not given to the Twelve but to the hundred and twenty. Man as man was equal before God. So the Holy Spirit was not given to a priest, a prophet, or a pope, but to a person. The cipher added to the twelve made a new world. And the women too received the Holy Spirit on the same basis as men, and this included Mary the mother of Jesus. The last thing we see of the Virgin Mary was that she was praying for the Holy Spirit on the same basis as the rest of us. To try to save the situation some Roman Catholic friends say that because she was there and prayed, the Holy Spirit was given in answer to her prayers! Which of course is an unwarranted assumption, just as the other "assumption" is an assumption!

When a dispute arose over the distribution of food in Acts 6, the apostles did something that has always been looked on as wisdom, but is now seen as disaster. They said, "We will devote ourselves to prayer and to the ministry of the word," and appointed the Seven to look after the material side of the movement. This separated the spiritual from the material—left the spiritual unrelated and the material unredeemed. They put asunder what God had joined in the Incarnation when the Word became flesh. What happened? A strange and significant thing: the Seven became the center of spiritual power. It was Stephen, one of the Seven, who precipitated the revival in Jerusalem and brought on his own martyrdom. It was Philip who first preached the Gospel outside Judea and had a revival in Samaria. The apostles sent down Peter and John to regularize what they couldn't produce.

O Father, Thou hast hid these things from the wise and prudent and revealed them unto babes. Thou hast ordained that the spiritual must function in and through the material or not function. Teach me this day to let all life be the Word become flesh. Amen.

AFFIRMATION FOR THE DAY: *Witnessing is for the sincere, not for the perfect.*

A TONGUE-TIED COLONEL
FREED THROUGH WITNESSING

Without this lay witness the life of the layman is routine and non-creative. Taking up collections, ushering, and sitting on committees is hardly worthy of a vital layman.

> When Wellington beat Bonaparte
> . As any child can tell,
> The House of Peers throughout the war,
> Did nothing in particular and did it very well.

Lay witnessing does something to the witnesser. This is a conversion that converts the converter. A couple in India were about to break up the home. They both surrendered to Christ and won sixty people to the new life; they started a congregation which has become a church in the suburbs of Bangalore.

In America an army colonel who had home troubles tried to commit suicide. He was converted and joined a lay evangelistic team going out two by two. The layman in charge said this colonel was the most tied-up person he had ever seen. Didn't say a word on the first three visits. The layman said to him, "The next one is yours. You are to lead off." The colonel replied, "I will on one condition: if I fumble the ball you will pick it up." The layman agreed. But there was no fumbling as they called on a judge and his wife. The layman said, "I never saw such a change when the man began. He literally poured out his soul to this judge and his wife. He seemed inspired." He won the judge and his wife to Christ and the church. Then that same night he went to the leading oil man and won him to Christ—three in one night. Now he was free and on his own, transformed in helping to transform others.

Here is a simple woman of seventy in the Philippines who goes from barrio to barrio and talks to people about her Savior, night and day. Congregations have sprung up in every town as a result of that woman's witness. Her witness is more powerful than preaching!

O Divine Spirit, set my heart aflame with the love of Christ. For if I am not aflame with His love I shall be aflame with the love of myself. Save me from myself that I may save others. For in saving others I shall save myself. Amen.

AFFIRMATION FOR THE DAY: *I am as strong as His strength, good as His goodness, free as His freedom.*

"LET HIM WHO HEARS SAY 'COME' "

In the final chapter of revelation is this verse: "The Spirit and the Bride say, 'Come.' And let him who hears say, 'Come' " (Rev. 22:17). The Spirit is saying within every man, "Come." For Christ is what the human heart is made for. So our longings are longings for Him, often wrongly interpreted. But the Spirit is saying "Come." And the Bride, the church, is saying "Come." Often the church instead of saying, "Come to Christ," says, "Come to me." Then we have Churchianity instead of Christianity. But it is not enough to have this collective call—it must be individual. The general word of call is often the Word become word, in the individual it must be the Word become flesh. He who hears must say "Come."

A layman heard his pastor preach on this text. It awakened him. "All my life I've been hearing, but I've never said to anyone 'Come.' Time for me to begin." He did begin and never stopped, and was transformed by it.

Gaston Morris is a cripple who goes about on crutches because of arthritis. In one year he won two hundred sixty people and the next year one hundred fifty. He did this while carrying on his real estate business.

Recently I was in Taiwan and saw a cave with a chapel beside it put up in memory of a tattooed old grandmother, who used to sit in that cave all night and teach the headhunters the Gospel. When the missionaries came back after the war was over they found ten thousand of these headhunters had become Christians. No missionary or pastor—just a dedicated old lady in whom the Word had become flesh.

The young people of a church in Phoenix, Arizona, go out on Sunday afternoons. Fifty-five young people called on one hundred ten other young people and won fifty-five, every other person! They have little gold "wish bones" which they wear on their lapels. When someone asks them what it means they reply, "My dearest wish is that you become a Christian." The wish had become flesh.

Dear Lord and Father, may all my wishes become wills. May I not only wish people to come to Thee, but may I will it. May all my impulses become pulses. May I hear and say, "Come." May my words be words of invitation. Amen.

AFFIRMATION FOR THE DAY: *Definition of evangelism: "One beggar telling another beggar where to find bread."*

THE MOTIVE AND INCENTIVE FOR MISSIONS?

But someone asks, "What is the incentive and motive of evangelism and missions?" Why should we do it? Why should millions of men and more millions of money be marshaled for the work of Christian missions throughout the world? Is it a species of religious imperialism—a kind of paternalism toward the "lesser breeds without the law"?

The reply of some would be the words of a famous man who asked that question: "Look to your marching orders. Did Jesus not say, 'Go therefore and make disciples of all nations'? That settles it." But while the command is weighty, it doesn't settle it. For suppose this command were something read back into the account by the early Christians and did not originate with Jesus, as some would say. Then your whole enterprise resting on a single passage collapses. It is precarious to have it rest on a single passage. Besides, if it is a command only, then it is the Word become word.

The reply of others would be, "People need it. The incentive rests on the need of the world." It is true that people need it. But if your incentive is the need of people—a humanitarian motive, then the motive will wear thin. Those who come to the mission lands through humanitarian motives usually exhaust their humanitarianism and go home. They peter out.

Neither command nor concern are sufficient motives. Then what is the sufficient motive? The biographer of Lord Grey recorded that Grey once said: "The case against God is mountainous and watertight, unless we can believe in the Incarnation where God comes into this world to sacrifice Himself for it." He is right. And the case against missions is the same unless you can believe in the Incarnation. If the Incarnation is a fact, then the case for missions is "mountainous and watertight." Missions then become inevitable and compelling.

O blessed Father, we are on solid ground if Thou hast come to our earth to redeem it at deep cost to Thyself. In that case we have no alternative but to tell the goodness to everybody everywhere. We cannot but speak it. Amen.

AFFIRMATION FOR THE DAY: *If He came, I must go!*

WE DO WHAT HE DID

We ended yesterday with the conclusion that neither command nor concern are sufficient motives for missions or evangelism. But if the Incarnation is a fact; if God has redemptively invaded us; if He has gone to the very bottom of our need, tasting sin and death for us to lift us to a free, full life in communion with Himself, then that changes the picture. This means that our motive is in God—we do what He did. The cross means God tasting the bitterness of sin and death—tasting what we taste. He "drank our poison that we might ambrosia taste." If that be true then not to tell it and share it would be the highest sin of ingratitude.

So last command or no last command, marching orders or no marching orders, we must be missionaries of the Good News. The last command and the marching orders are inherent in what God has done in Christ. Wipe out the last command and we would still go—driven from within. An African woman was converted in a mission hospital and in walking back the seventy-five miles to her home she stopped in seven villages, about ten miles apart, witnessed to what Christ had done for her and established seven congregations on her way back. She had never heard of the last command, but she heard from within the imperious drive of gratitude to tell what God had done for her in Christ. A Chinese pastor was not allowed to preach the gospel to the Chinese indentured coolies working in the mines. So he sold himself as an indentured coolie, practically a slave, and worked in the mine so he could preach to them and witness to them as he worked. No last command would make him do that. But God's doing would make him do it. So our motive for missions is as broad-based as God. If we hold our peace the stones would cry out, the hard bare facts would proclaim the Good News.

O Blessed God, forgive us our guilty silence when we refuse to share what Thou hast done for us. That guilty silence brands us as traitors, makes every one of us a denying Peter and a betraying Judas rolled into one. In Jesus' name forgive us. Amen.

AFFIRMATION FOR THE DAY: *If we are not evangelistic we will soon cease to be evangelical. If something doesn't happen through us, something will happen to us.*

JOHN 3:16 AND I JOHN 3:16

Note the last command, "Go you into all the world." It is the greatest missionary verse. But great as it is, listen to this one: "For God so loved the world that he gave his only begotten Son, that whosoever believeth in him should not perish, but have everlasting life" (John 3:16 KJV). That verse is "our marching orders." If God did that we must do this. But we take this John 3:16 and forget this I John 3:16: "By this we know love, that he laid down his life for us; and we ought to lay down our lives for the brethren." But why do we remember the first and forget the second? The answer is simple: In the first we see what God did for us, and in the second we see what we ought to do for others—lay down our lives. We have no right to the first to make it our own unless we take the second to make that our own. The second is the first become flesh in us.

In the early church there were two breakings of bread—one, the bread of the communion, and the other, the bread of the love feast. The first symbolized our sharing His broken body, the second symbolized the sharing of our bread with our brothers—communion with God and communion with man. The last dropped out of church practice, the first remained. It was easier to accept what He did than to accept what we must do. This is a symptom of the whole tendency to make the Word become word instead of the Word become flesh.

That shift from the Word become flesh to the Word become word is the most disastrous and fatal shift within the Christian faith. Beside that shift all shifts are marginal—this is central. For if the Word doesn't become flesh it doesn't become anything. It is a word.

Note this I John 3:16: "By this we know love, that he laid down his life for us." "By this we know love"—how? By description, by philosophizing, by moralizing? No: "that he laid down his life for us." The Word of love became flesh. Only then could we know what love is. It is the Way: The only Way!

Blessed Savior, how could we know love except we had seen it in Thee, had seen it in Thy laying down Thy life for us? Only there at the cross do we know it. And what we see sets our hearts aflame to tell it to everybody, everywhere. Amen.

AFFIRMATION FOR THE DAY: *"He gives seed to the sower" and only to the sower. If I do not sow I'll have nothing to sow.*

"I KNOW THAT MY REDEEMER LIVETH"

We are looking at the motive for missions and evangelism. The only adequate motive is based on what God has done. He went on a mission—He was the first missionary; He came to us to redeem us. Then when we do the same, we are in line with what God has done and is doing. He is still coming—He is still a missionary and an evangelist. He only asks us to do what He has done and is still doing. When God stops His missionary activities so will I. Until then I keep on, not specially elated by success nor depressed by failure—they are irrelevant. To be true to what I see God doing in Jesus Christ is the only relevancy.

On my return after my first furlough, I said in England, "The romance of missions for me is gone. I know what I am going back to. Tell me I will never have any success, that it will all end in failure, I would go on. To be true to the highest I have seen in Christ is the only thing that matters now. I am a missionary, regardless of success or failure." At this writing I have been a missionary fifty-five years. Give me back my choices to make over again, and I would make them as I have made them. With this proviso—that where I have been untrue I would be true.

A few days ago I stood in Tellapale, Ceylon, where one of the original five who constituted "The Haystack Group," which took refuge in a storm under a haystack in Massachusetts, prayed that "a way might be opened to carry the Gospel to the regions beyond." Out of that haystack prayer meeting, modern missions were born, far as America was concerned. One of those young men, Richards, came to Tellapale and lived for six years and was buried there. For six years he was frustrated by ill health, and one by one he had to give up his ambitions to be an effective missionary. But his last words were, "I know that my Redeemer liveth." That revealed his undeterred motive—"my Redeemer." Jesus had redeemed him and the missionary enterprise for him.

O Lord Jesus, Thou dost redeem everything Thou dost touch and Thou dost touch everything. We thank Thee that thou dost redeem Missions for us. For looking into Thy Face we cannot but speak of what we see. And how we love telling! Amen.

AFFIRMATION FOR THE DAY: *"Out of the abundance of the heart the mouth speaketh,"* so if my mouth doesn't speak, it speaks of emptiness within.

"BUT I DECIDED TO STAY"

We continue to look at the motive for missions and evangelism. The last incident we gave yesterday might have given the impression that Christian missions is a grim-faced business. It isn't. It's joy—in spite of, if not on account of. Alongside this grave of Richards was the grave of Dr. Poor—he lived longer, joyously. He was stricken with cholera and said to Dr. Green, another missionary, who attended him, "I don't think there is much hope for my recovery. I am a Poor patient and you a Green doctor." Joked on his deathbed!

When Bishop Warne visited me in a Lucknow, India, hospital when I was struggling with tetanus, he leaned over to get my last words. They were: "Bishop, please don't take away my work from me. I'll be well and able to take care of it." Hope when there was no hope!

Today I talked with a young woman missionary treasurer of the women's society of The Methodist Church in India, and she told me that she was ordered home by a Hindu doctor, for she had filariasis, elephantiasis. She decided she would not go and would be well. Two years later when she presented herself to the same doctor, he was amazed and said, "But I sent you home." And she quietly said, "But I decided to stay." "Well, then I'll do all I can to help you stay," he thoughtfully replied. She is well and will take over the Lee Memorial Mission which is itself based on the heroism of the Lees who lost their six children when the whole family was buried in a landslide in Darjeeling. They decided that since their lesser home was broken up they would set up a bigger one. For over sixty years there have been about three hundred children, waifs gathered from the streets of Calcutta, in that home. Nothing, absolutely nothing could have given them the motive and power to turn that tragedy into triumph, except the fact of what God had done in Christ.

O God, our Heavenly Father, what Thou hast done holds us to what we should do. This is the only thing that suffices us. We can follow the God who shows us the way and doesn't merely point the way. We are thankful. Amen.

AFFIRMATION FOR THE DAY: *If I do not witness, I will soon have nothing to witness to.*

THE WORLD IS A MISSION FIELD AND GOD
THE FIRST MISSIONARY

Both the motives of the last command and the needs of men are inadequate. The last command would suffer from what we are pointing out in this book—it would be the Word become word. And the motive of the needs of men would suffer from the same disability—God would point out the needs of men to us but would do nothing to meet those needs Himself. He would have to come to get us to go.

I have shared with you my first sermon and its failure, enough to dampen my zeal for the ministry. My first missionary adventure was also enough to dampen my zeal for missions. It was a home mission adventure in the mountains of Kentucky. Jim Ballinger, a singer, and I started to walk from Junction City two miles to where we were to stay for the night. It was cold and raining hard, and I was carrying two suitcases, one filled with books. As we walked along the railway tracks, to encourage my companion I called out, "Jim, I believe the stars are coming out." Just as I said it I went over the side of a steep fill. I saw stars all right! On my way down the muddy embankment I lost my two suitcases. So I had to feel over that embankment in the dark to find them. When we got near the house a gust of wind blew off my felt hat. Impossible to find it—never did, for snow covered everything the next morning. When we got to the yard a creek had arisen, so I had to take a leap toward the other bank weighted down by two suitcases. I hit somewhere near the middle! At midnight we arrived, and our host was not expecting us! When we arrived in the mountains the next day I was invited to a one-room cabin where I was to stay—and there was one bed. My host said at bedtime, "You take the far side." Then he got in and then his wife. In the morning we reversed the process! Real hospitality! I preached in a schoolhouse, and when I preached on "Thou shalt not kill" my hearers turned pale. This experience dampen my zeal? No, whetted my appetite for more.

Dear Father, we see through Jesus what ought to be—and is! And the "is" is more wonderful than the "ought-to-be" for it "is"! We see it and love it and bow in deepest gratitude. Oh, the wonder of it all! The wonder of it all! Amen.

AFFIRMATION FOR THE DAY: *His hand is on my shoulder, His love in my heart, His words upon my lips.*

"I WOULDN'T DO THAT FOR A MILLION"

A Christian and a non-Christian were discussing the possibility of putting a non-Christian on the Board of Management of a student center in England. The non-Christian said, "You began this Center didn't you? We had better leave it as it is. Whatever you Christians begin, you carry on. We take things up and drop them. You have a strange persistence." Why? Because God in Christ had a strange persistence. "He set his face to go to Jerusalem"—and went.

Yesterday I talked with a couple with Unitarian leanings—cultured, earnest, and lovable—but they were leaving India after a year. Their altruism faded under the hard realities. No cross that turned defeat into victory sustained them. God taught us, but didn't come Himself. The motive failed.

Mary Reed's name is a name to remember with reverence. She lived among the lepers in the Himalayas, herself having been cured of leprosy, but she never returned to her American homeland. In her old age her faithless servant robbed her of everything, even transferred her to a poor bed in order to get possession of the better bed. I met a British lady doctor missionary on her way to take over Mary Reed's work. Did she know of this faithlessness and ingratitude? Yes. But she was going "for Jesus' sake"—and going gladly!

When someone asked Bishop Bashford why he buried himself in China he replied, "Because I believe in a resurrection." But he could not have believed in his own resurrection if he had not believed in His Resurrection.

A nurse was washing the sores of lepers in a mission field. A visitor from the West was watching her. He said to her. "I wouldn't do that for a million." The nurse replied, "Neither would I." But she would do it "for Jesus' sake."

Neither command, nor need, nor money, nor anything is a motive for missions. What God has done, we must do. Jesus is our message and our motive.

Dear Lord and Father, as Thou hast come, so we must go. We look into Thy face in Jesus and then we look into the face of our brother's need. Then we spend the balance of our days to try to bring them together. This suffices us. Amen.

AFFIRMATION FOR THE DAY: *Jesus Himself is my motive and my message—what better, what higher, what more?*

THE INCARNATION AND THE KINGDOM

We come now to one of the most important aspects of the application of the Word become flesh—its application to the Kingdom of God. For if this Incarnation is God's Incarnation then it must have total meaning for the total life. The Christian conception of the Incarnation is unique in that the incarnation is not only to be in a person, but in an order, the kingdom of God. Jesus made Himself and the Kingdom of God synonymous. He used interchangeably "for my sake" and "the Kingdom's sake." He was the Kingdom. One's relationship to Him determined one's relationship to the Kingdom. Not only was absolute love embodied in Him, but absolute authority. God was not only redeeming in Jesus, He was ruling in Jesus. The Incarnation is redemptive rule. The Kingdom came with Jesus. The Kingdom is Jesus, and Jesus is the Kingdom. The Kingdom is the Christlike spirit universalized. So the Incarnation is not only in a personal body, but also in a cosmic body. To have relations with Him is to have relationship with an Order. Religion is at once individual and social.

So when people talk about an individual gospel or a social gospel they are dividing what God has joined in the Incarnation. God is not a half-God ruling over a half-realm. He is God and the sum total of Reality in His realm. An individual gospel without a social gospel is a soul without a body, and a social gospel without an individual gospel is a body without a soul—one is a ghost and the other is a corpse. Together they make a living person. So when the Incarnation includes the Person and the Order then it meets a total need. They are one. So a personal Incarnation without a corporate Incarnation would be a half-redemption. Jesus incarnating the Kingdom is a whole redemption.

O Blessed Lord and Savior, we thank Thee for Thy all-embracingness. Thou wast located in a body and yet the cosmic was Thy body too. When we find Thee we find Everything, including ourselves. We thank Thee. Amen.

AFFIRMATION FOR THE DAY: *I am made to be ruled; therefore, I welcome the rule of God—the Kingdom of God.*

"WE WANTED SOMETHING THAT WOULD BRING LIFE INTO TOTAL MEANING"

An English bishop said, "Stanley Jones seems to be obsessed with the kingdom of God." My reply was, "Would God that I were. It would be a magnificent obsession." For Jesus was obsessed with it. He used the phrase or its equivalent one hundred times. And, depend upon it, anything He used that often is important, the ages being witness, for He was never misled by a subordinate issue, never got on the marginal, the unworthwhile. And He made the Kingdom central. Why?

I was speaking on the Kingdom in Germany after the war, and on the front seats sat a number of prominent German religious leaders, among them Dr. Neimuller. They kept pounding the benches as I spoke. I asked them at the close, Why? They replied, "You are the first one who seemed to understand why we turned to Nazism. We wanted something to bring life into total meaning and guide it to total ends. Life for us was compartmentalized, at loose ends; we wanted something to command and guide us totally. We chose the wrong totalitarianism, Nazism; what we really were after was the Kingdom of God."

It has taken humanity two thousand years of trial and error to come to the place where we could really understand the meaning and necessity of the Kingdom of God. The rise of modern totalitarianism—Fascism, Nazism, Communism—is the outcropping of a felt necessity for something to bring life into total coherence, total meaning, total goal. These man-created totalitarianisms are wrong, disastrously wrong, but down underneath what they wanted, if they only knew it, was the Kingdom of God. They will break down, as all half-answers do, and leave a vacuum, and it is then that man will finally be predisposed to listen to and receive the Kingdom of God. That time is now ripe. For mankind now has been driven with its back to the wall—it is now God's totalitarianism, the Kingdom of God, or total destruction.

Dear Heavenly Father, Thy love is forcing us to an awful choice—the choice between Thy way and our way. Thy way means total redemption and freedom, our way means total ruin. Never in the long history of choices have we had such a choice. Save us. Amen.

AFFIRMATION FOR THE DAY: *The Kingdom is God's total answer to man's total need.*

"EVERYTHING ELSE HAS FAILED US
SO WE ARE TRYING THIS"

Mahatma Gandhi, seeing the necessity of presenting to India some total conception, some program of total reconstruction, put forth *rama rajya*—the kingdom of Rama, the kingdom of a mythological figure. But it was so faint and colorless and contentless that it has faded out of the minds of India as an issue. I sat with a group of officers in the Pentagon at lunch. I asked them whether the religious spirit was growing in the armed forces, lessening, or as it was? A colonel replied, "Among the thoughtful it is growing." I asked him, Why? He replied, "Well, we've tried everything else, and it has all let us down, so we are now trying this." Everything, literally everything has failed man and now man is ripe, dead ripe, for God's answer, the Kingdom of God. Joseph said to Pharoah, "It is God's answer that will answer to the Pharaoh." Now we can say, "It is God's answer which will answer to a dissilusioned and floundering humanity and that answer is the Kingdom."

What did Jesus mean by the Kingdom of God? He said, "When you pray say, 'Our Father . . . Thy kingdom come, Thy will be done, on earth as it is in heaven.' " The second phrase explains the first—the coming of the Kingdom was the doing of the will of God on earth as it is done in heaven. How is the will of God done in heaven? In the individual will? Yes. In the collective will? Yes. In the total social arrangements of heaven? Yes. It is a completely totalitarian order demanding a total obedience in the total life. Then may Thy Kingdom come on earth as it is in heaven. It is the coming of a completely totalitarian order demanding a total obedience in the total life. Wouldn't that mean total bondage? Strangely enough, no. For this is a complete totalitarianism, which when you totally obey it you find total freedom. I do not argue, I testify: The more I belong to Christ and His Kingdom the more I belong to myself.

O Father, we thank Thee for this total bondage which becomes total freedom. Thy will is our freedom. Our wills against Thy will is our bondage. This is the best proved fact of history. Save us from further hesitation. Amen.

AFFIRMATION FOR THE DAY: *At last I have found my homeland—the land of my perfect freedom.*

GOD'S TOTALITARIANISM = FREEDOM;
MAN'S TOTALITARIANISM = BONDAGE

We finished yesterday by saying that if we obey totally God's totalitarianism we find total freedom. Bound to Him I walk the earth free; low at His feet I stand straight before everything else. This is an essential difference between God's totalitarianism and man's. If you obey totally man's totalitarianism—Facism, Nazism, Communism—you find total bondage. This is then its final doom, for man is inherently made for freedom and will finally revolt against chains.

But, says someone, this Kingdom of God is hazy. What is the content and what is the program? We have mentioned before the Nazareth Manifesto in another setting. We repeat it in this Kingdom setting. After struggling with temptation for forty days—temptation as to how to bring in the Kingdom—Jesus came to the synagogue at Nazareth and announced His program: "The Spirit of the Lord is upon me"—how would that spirituality function? In mystical states of emotion? No, in a very definite fivefold program: "because he has anointed me to preach good news to the poor"—the economically disinherited; "He has sent me to proclaim release to the captives"—the socially and politically disinherited; "and recovering of sight to the blind"—the physically disinherited; "to set at liberty those who are oppressed" (or as Lamsa's translation puts it: "to strengthen with forgiveness those who are bruised," so the bruises must be moral and spiritual)—the morally and spiritually disinherited; "to proclaim the acceptable year of the Lord," or "the Lord's Year of Jubilee" (if this translation is correct then it referred back to the Jewish Year of Jubilee when every fifty years all land was redistributed, all debts canceled and all slaves freed and the nation begin on a closer appropriation of equality)—a fresh world beginning on the basis of a more equitable distribution of goods and opportunities (Luke 4:18-19). So this new order would touch the economic, the social and political, the physical, the moral and spiritual, and the collective—the whole of life.

Dear Lord and Father, we thank Thee that Thou art out to redeem the whole of life, to make us new totally—individual and collective. We need regenerating—a total regenerating. We ask for it, without it we perish. Amen.

AFFIRMATION FOR THE DAY: *The Kingdom is a total discipline which brings total deliverance.*

THE KINGDOM WAS LEFT OUT OF THE
HISTORIC CREEDS

We saw yesterday that the total life was to be totally redeemed by the coming of the Kingdom. What happened with this breathtaking program and conception? Jesus stayed with the disciples for forty days after the Resurrection and talked about what? "Appearing to them during forty days, and speaking of the Kingdom of God" (Acts 1:3). His last emphasis was on the Kingdom. "Get this straight," He was saying, "for if you get this straight all the ages will go straight with you." Did they? Alas, this conception was too big for their small hearts, for they said to Him, "Lord, will you at this time restore the kingdom to Israel?" (Acts 1:6). They reduced this universal Kingdom to a nationalism—Do we get back our self-government? They didn't reject it—they reduced it. That is what we have been doing ever since.

The church reduced the Kingdom or even eliminated it in the forming of the creeds. In the third century in the making of the creeds, the Apostles' Creed and the Athanasian creeds do not mention the Kingdom. The Nicean Creed mentions it once marginally beyond the borders of this life in heaven: "Thy Kingdom is an everlasting Kingdom." But this was after the "resurrection"—a heavenly Kingdom. So the three great historic creeds mention once, beyond the borders of this life, in heaven, what Jesus mentioned a hundred times. A note, a very important note, had dropped out of the Christian faith. A crippled Christianity went across Europe with a crippled result. The Kingdom of God was pushed into the inner recesses of the heart as mystical experience now and pushed beyond the borders of this life in heaven, as a collective experience. Between this inner mystical experience now and the collective heavenly experience, vast areas were left out unredeemed—the economic, the social, and the political. A vacuum was created in the soul of Christendom. Into that vacuum moved man's totalitarianisms and took over.

O God, forgive us, forgive us, that we have lost the central emphasis of Thy Gospel, the Kingdom. We deserve the fate that has come upon us. Help us to recover by Thy grace Thy Kingdom again. It is our only hope. Save us. Amen.

AFFIRMATION FOR THE DAY: *When I criticize the Creeds for leaving out the Kingdom, I criticize my deeds for doing the same.*

AN ALIEN PHILOSOPHY OF LIFE MOVED IN

We ended yesterday at the place where we lost our totalitarianism, the Kingdom of God and man's totalitarianisms—Fascism, Nazism, Communism—moved in and took over. They said to us, "We will give you your inner mystical states now and your collective experience in heaven, but we will take over the rest—the economic, social, political—and we will run them by our means and direct them to our own ends." We were shocked, and rightly so. For an alien philosophy of life undertook to replace the Christian basis of life. Now we are in a state of confusion and shock. Maybe this is God's shock treatment of us—to shock us out of our unchristian ways back to His way—the Kingdom of God.

But we must remember that we created the vacuum into which the totalitarianisms entered. And we will never get rid of these totalitarianisms by merely fighting them. We must replace them by a higher totalitarianism, for man is made for a total obedience. William Penn said, "If men will not be governed by God, they will be governed by tyrants."

In 1934, I wrote in my book, *Christ's Alternative to Communism:* "This generation, or at most the next, must decide between materialistic, atheistic Communism and the Kingdom of God on earth." Twenty-eight years have gone by since then, and I would still define the issue in the same terms: "Man's totalitarianism or God's." In the meantime, two of those totalitarianisms have gone down in disaster; the third will follow, broken, I believe, by the very moral universe which they say isn't there. Paul speaks in Moffatt's translation of "the dethroned Powers who rule this world" (I Cor. 2:6). These "powers . . . rule," but they are "dethroned." They are against the Kingdom and anything and everything that is against the Kingdom perishes. Nothing can live against Reality and survive. The Kingdom is the Omega and has the last word!

O Lord Jesus, we thank Thee that Thy Kingdom is an everlasting Kingdom and will have the final word. We see everything go down before its final sway and say. We would identify ourselves with the Kingdom's everlastingness. In Thy Name. Amen.

AFFIRMATION FOR THE DAY: *I will be ruled—ruled by myself, by the herd, or by the Kingdom.*

"THE KINGDOM OF HEAVEN HAS BEEN
FORCING ITS WAY FORWARD"

We saw yesterday that the Kingdom of God is God's final order and has the final word. Whoever has the first or the intermediate word the Kingdom has the final word. This passage is luminous: "Ever since the coming of John the Baptist the kingdom of Heaven has been subjected to violence and violent men are seizing it" (Matt. 11:12 NEB, marg.). Note: "The kingdom of Heaven has been forcing its way forward" by its own inherent truth and reality. But men of force try to use force to further it, but violate the inner nature of the Kingdom ends.

When in Russia in 1934 I was shaken to see them building up a civilization without God. I needed reassurance. This verse "spoke to my condition" during my Quiet Time in Moscow: "Therefore let us be grateful for receiving a kingdom that cannot be shaken" (Heb. 12:28 RSV). Was the Kingdom of God the one unshakable Kingdom? Everything within me answered Yes, and continues to answer, Yes, with increasing emphasis. I went to my Bible the next morning, and this verse arose authoritative: "Jesus Christ is the same yesterday and today and for ever" (Heb. 13:9). Is Jesus Christ the unchanging Person, the same yesterday, today, and forever? Everything within me answered, Yes, and does increasingly. I came out of Russia with an unshakable Kingdom and an unchanging Person—the Absolute Order and the Absolute Person. They were two then. Now they have become one—I see that the Absolute Order—the Kingdom of God, is embodied in the Absolute Person—the Son of God. They are one. The Word of Final Authority has become flesh in Jesus Christ. In Him is not only Absolute Goodness, but Absolute Authority. God not only redeems in Jesus—He rules in Jesus. So the Incarnation, seemingly the meekest and weakest, becomes the strongest. The Lamb is slain, but in the final scene, "the Lamb is on the throne." Jesus is Lord!

O Blessed Lamb, slain since the foundation of the world—ever suffering and ever succeeding, ever crucified and ever upon the throne. We thank Thee that Thou, the Meek, the Terrible Meek, shalt inherit the earth. We will rule with Thee. Amen.

AFFIRMATION FOR THE DAY: *I shake but the unshakable Kingdom does not shake—the one solid Reality in a shaken world.*

THE KINGDOM AND THE CHURCH

We must now pass on to the relationship of the Kingdom of God and the church. Only one church makes the Kingdom of God and the church identical, namely, the Roman Catholic Church. Nowhere are the Kingdom and the church identical in the New Testament. Suppose you would say, "Repent for the Church is at hand." People would laugh. But you don't laugh, you feel like bending the knee if you hear, "Repent for the Kingdom of God is at hand." But the actual emphasis today is largely not on the Kingdom, but it is on the church.

Now I believe in the church. The church is the fellowship of the being-redeemed. With all its faults it is the greatest serving institution on earth. It has many critics but no rivals in the work of human redemption. There isn't a spot on earth where they have allowed us to go, where we haven't gone with schools, orphan asylums, leper asylums, hospitals, churches, everything to lift the body, the mind, the soul of the race. No other institution has done anything like it. The church has been the mother of my spirit. At her altars I found Him.

But you are not saved by the church. The church is the subject of redemption, how then can it dispense it? "Christ is the head of the church, his body, and is himself its Savior" (Eph. 5:23). If the church needs saving, how can it give salvation? If the church takes you by the hand and takes you beyond itself to the feet of the Savior, it is wonderful. But if it stops you at itself and makes itself the issue, it is not wonderful—it is idolatry. The Kingdom is the Absolute, the church is the relative. The Kingdom commands, the church obeys. The church loses its life in the life of the Kingdom and finds itself again.

O Lord God, save us from making ourselves, individual or collective, the end. Thou art the end and we bow the knee there, and there alone. Save us from giving ourselves to halfway houses, trying to make them our home. In Jesus' name. Amen.

AFFIRMATION FOR THE DAY: *I do not belong to the church, I belong to the Kingdom—the church belongs to me, my Kingdom heritage.*

WE DO NOT BUILD THE KINGDOM—WE RECEIVE IT

We have seen that while the church contains the best life of the Kingdom, the church is not the Kingdom. You build the church, you do not build the Kingdom—you "receive the Kingdom." It is built—built from the foundation of the world, built into the structure of Reality—it is Reality.

Jesus went about "preaching the gospel of the Kingdom of God." It was the only thing He ever called His Gospel. But suppose we would go out preaching the Gospel of the Church. People would laugh for the Church is us, writ large.

A disciple came to Jesus and said, " 'Master, we saw a man casting out demons in your name, and we forbade him, because he does not follow us.' But Jesus said to him, 'Do not forbid him; for he that is not against you is for you' " (Luke 9:49, 50). Why did Jesus change this statement? In one place He said, "He that is not with me is against me," but here He said, "He that is not against you is for you." Why? Well, in one place following them was the issue—"he follows not us." And Jesus said, "You are not the issue and following you is not the issue, so if they are not against you they are for you. but I am the issue and following me is the issue, so if you are not with me you are against me." So the issue is not whether I belong to this group, that group, or the other group, but whether I belong to Christ. In other words, the Church is not the issue, but Christ is. I am not saved by belonging to the Church, but by belonging to Christ and His Kingdom.

And yet the ecumenical emphasis of modern times would seem to imply that the church is the Redeemer. Or its position is very close to the tendency in the Roman Church of making Christ and Mary co-redeemers. The modern ecumenical emphasis would seem to make Christ and the church co-redeemers. Both are false. There is one and only one Redeemer—Christ Jesus our Lord!

O Lord Jesus, we cannot see the Father except through Thee, the Son. If we look at Thee through the church, our vision is blurred, for the medium is blurred. In Thee there is no blur, for there is no fault. We thank Thee. Amen.

AFFIRMATION FOR THE DAY: *If I am humble enough to receive the Kingdom I shall be strong enough to do the "greater works."*

IN WHAT SENSE IS THE CHURCH
THE BODY OF CHRIST?

We come now in our study of the Word become flesh, the Incarnation, to the question, In what sense is the church the body of Christ? In several places the church is called the body of Christ. "He is the head of the body, the church" (Col. 1:18). "Christ is the head of the church, his body" (Eph. 5:23).

Does this mean that as once Christ took a body and inhabited it, that the church is now His new body and the church is now the new Incarnation? Has the church replaced the now discarded body of Christ and become the new "body of Christ"? There is, of course, a sense that each individual and each group of individuals devoted to Christ incarnate in some way the Incarnation and are an extension of that Incarnation. But only as they reincarnate the spirit of Christ.

But to make this collectivity of organized Christianity, called the church, "the body of Christ" makes me inwardly shudder every time I hear it used. It is close to blasphemy. Is Christ's "body" like this that I see in the organized church? Last week I was in a city where a church building was padlocked and sealed by court decree because two factions within the church were quarreling over which should be in control. Is that church a part of the body of Christ? I see church assemblies in voting for high church offices, such as bishops, play low, party politics exactly as any political convention. Is that a part of "the body of Christ?" A group of bishops meet to discuss plans for union of the churches, and four bishops of a particular group stay away lest their coming would be a recognition of other bishops whose ordination supposedly is not as valid as theirs. Is that a part of "the body of Christ"? I was shown a court of the Inquisition where an Ecclesiastical Judge sat and condemned heretics, and the wooden statue of Christ on the judge's desk nodded its head in approval when the judge pulled the string! Is that a part of "the body of Christ"?

O Jesus Lord, what kind of a body hast Thou? Are the legs upon which Thou art walking this earth of ours suffering from gangrene or moral leprosy? There must be something wrong somewhere. Teach us how to look on Thee and Thy church. Amen.

AFFIRMATION FOR THE DAY: *I am "the body of Christ" if Christ is in my body, and not because I belong to a group of believers.*

"CHRIST'S AFFLICTION FOR THE SAKE OF
HIS BODY, THE CHURCH"

We are asking, Is the church the body of Christ? A woman requested in her will that she be buried not alongside her husband but in a different section, for she did not want to embarrass her husband by being resurrected and leaving him behind, for he was a Methodist and she a member of another group. Is this a part of the body of Christ? A church in Mississippi has this big billboard beside it, "This church is the only Church authorized by God to represent Jesus Christ in the world." Is that a part of the body of Christ? A body of bishops sit solemnly and decide with whom they will have communion, and the basis is not on the basis of a loyalty to Christ but whether the people concerned have had hands laid on them in a certain supposed "succession." Is this a part of the body of Christ? Then the "body of Christ," with all its spots of wholeness, is disease-ridden—ridden with snobberies and pride and self-seeking.

I can see that there is an inner body of dedicated believers, made up of clergy and laity, who by their very inherent spirit and service do constitute "the body of Christ." That "body of Christ," invisible and potent, and scattered through all denominations, perhaps equally scattered, I can accept with gratitude and joy. But that is not what the modern emphasis, expressed in ecumenicity, is talking about when they are talking about "the body of Christ." They are talking about the organized church as such. If that is what they mean, then "the body of Christ" is a fiction at its best, or a "body" spotted with festering sores at its worst.

If we do not accept "the invisible church" as the real body of Christ, then we must accept Paul's description: "Now I rejoice in my sufferings for your sake, and in my flesh I complete what is lacking in Christ's afflictions for the sake of his body, that is, the church" (Col. 1:24). Here Christ is afflicted for the sake of His body, the Church. He is being crucified in His body. The Church is a continuous crucifixion to Jesus.

O Jesus Lord, dost Thou wear a crucified body—crucified by the very Church which constitutes that body? Art Thou still hanging on the cross and wilt Thou continue to hang on Thy cross until we change? Forgive us, save us. Amen.

AFFIRMATION FOR THE DAY: *"The sufferings of Christ for His body"*—*I can accept that, but save me, Lord, from causing that suffering.*

"THE BODY OF CHRIST" IS A CRUCIFIED BODY

We ended yesterday with Paul's conception of Christ continuing to suffer in His body, the Church. "In my flesh I complete what is lacking in Christ's affliction for the sake of his body, that is, the church." Christ is being afflicted in His body, not because of the persecution of the Christians, but because the body itself is afflicted with its own self-inflicted illnesses.

Because the church is what it is, Christ is still being crucified. "The body of Christ" is a body still on the cross put there by His own followers. He was wounded at Calvary by His enemies, now He is being wounded again "in the house of His friends." Paul says, "I enter that suffering with Christ and add my sufferings to His and thus complete in some measure His sufferings."

I can understand that kind of "body of Christ," for I am a part of it. I am a part of it, at times, as a part of the disease. I must give Him pain—a shooting pain when I lapse into un-Christlikeness. But I am also conscious that a good part of the time I'm part of the cure. But if I am, it is all by His Grace. A friend wrote a letter of gratitude to a prominent businessman who is a Christian from Sunday through Saturday and in all his relationships—contagiously so. The businessman replied, "Where you find anything ugly and mean in my character and life, put that down to me. But where there is something fine and noble and worthwhile, put that down to Jesus Christ." I can say "Amen" to that. When will Jesus come down from His cross of continual pain? When we as Christians come together and take Him down. For He is crucified in our divisions; we press the thorns on His brow when we insert our own ambitions into a Kingdom which is based on self-losing. We drive the nails tighter when we lose our tempers and are ugly-spirited and unloving. "He was wounded for our transgressions," also "wounded" by our transgressions.

O Lord Jesus, we see this continuing Incarnation is a continuing Cross. And we begin to see how expensive to Thee this Incarnation was and is. But now it comes as our opportunity—we can be a part of Thy vicarious sufferings and a part of redemption. We thank Thee. Amen.

AFFIRMATION FOR THE DAY: *"I am a part of the disease or a part of the cure."*
    May I be cure-attituded.

"O JESUS, IF IT WEREN'T FOR YOU I'D NOT BE A CHRISTIAN FIVE MINUTES"

But, someone objects, if Christ's body is a crucified body then how can you continue to believe in His power and redemption? Why doesn't he redeem His own body and come down from the cross? It is the same thing that was thrown "in His teeth" when He hung on the cross before: "Let Him come down from the cross and then we will believe in Him." But He was saving others, Himself He could not save. Now again He is saving others, including His own body, the church, hence He cannot save Himself this continuous pain. But this pain is "a pain divine"—it is redemptive.

A very sensitive and dedicated Christian, after a deep disappointment in some of her trusted colleagues, threw herself on her bed and cried, "O Jesus, if it weren't for You I'd not be a Christian five minutes." He held her steady through that letdown. I believe in the church because I believe in Jesus. He is redeeming it—and redeeming it the hard way. And that church will stand before Him without spot or wrinkle.

But to talk about the church now as though it were the body of Christ in that final sense is unrealistic. Today it is the crucified body of Christ—crucified on the cross of its own unfaithfulness. And we must suffer, as Paul did, to help make up a share of Christ's sufferings for this crucified body. We must feel faithless in its faithlessness, feel a sense of shame in its shameless betrayal—be crucified in its self-imposed crucifixion and be humiliated in its pride. Some bishops at the World Council of Churches in Delhi pompously and piously said: "We've been very generous in being willing to give communion to those not of our denomination." "Willing to give"—but to take? No. And yet they talk about "the body of Christ." Nail-pierced body—yes. And such attitudes are a part of the piercing.

Dear Lord and Father, forgive us that in the name of Thy dear Son we crucify Him again. We defend our ecclesiastical snobberies and offend Jesus in the process. Help us to bear in our own bodies His sufferings for us. In His name. Amen.

AFFIRMATION FOR THE DAY: *I love Him who loves me though He knows me.*

ENOUGH REAL CHRISTIANITY TO ABSORB
UNCHRISTIAN CHRISTIANITY

A woman in India, where because of illiteracy, the people must vote by dropping their ballots into the box with the symbol representing the party for which she wanted to vote, put a garland of flowers on one ballot box and then dropped her ballot in another box. The word of loyalty became word—became flowers, but the word became flesh in something else—another ballot box. Another woman stood with folded hands and said her prayers to the ballot box, but dropped in no ballot. She voted with her prayers but not with her person. A caricature on democracy, it is true. But do these illustrations destroy democracy? No, for there is enough solid democracy in the country to absorb these aberrations and go on its way to express the will of the people.

So the illustrations of the Word become word on the part of the church do not cancel the church and destroy it. For there is enough real solid Christianity within the church to absorb these anti-Christian elements and still go on its way. I walked on a cinder, encased in the bottom of my foot, for fifteen years. It pained me again and again, but still I walked—in spite of! There was enough general health to absorb that alien element and go on its way. So the Christian church has the power to absorb the mistakes and sins of its members and go on its way. It is not a divine institution, but it is a divine-human institution and the Redeeming Lord—the Divine part of the church—redeems the human to the degree that it will let Him. He is the Savior of the Body. I believe in the church because I believe in Jesus Christ. He saves my faith in the church because He saves the church. The Christian movement has a principle and power of self-correction at its heart—the person of Jesus Christ. So Christ saves Christianity, for which I am grateful, for I am a part of Christianity.

O Son of God, I thank Thee that I need not be afraid that the light will go out. For Thou art standing in the midst of the candlesticks to relight them when they sputter and die. The bruised reed Thou wilt not break nor quench the smoking flax. I thank Thee. Amen.

AFFIRMATION FOR THE DAY: *If I did not have a Savior I would be lost. But I do have a Savior, for He saves me from myself and from sin.*

DIVINE AND HUMAN SELF-SURRENDER

At the very center of the conception of the Word become flesh is the fact of the divine Self-surrender. The Christian faith demands of us as its deepest demand, self-surrender. And in the Word became flesh shows God doing the same thing—the divine Self-surrender.

This is an essential difference between the Christian faith and other faiths: in the Christian faith the Divine practices everything He asks us to practice, especially, in regard to Self-surrender. A prominent Hindu philosopher said to me, "Self-surrender is everything." But in saying this he departed from his Vedantism, for in it Brahma is impersonal. You cannot surrender to an It.

In the different faiths it is important to see what happens to the self, the ego. This is important for the only thing we own is just ourselves. What happens to the self is all important. The faiths which came out of India are world weary and personality weary. They want us to get rid of both. Buddha sitting under the Bo tree in Gaya came to the conclusion that existence and suffering are one. The only way to get out of suffering is to get out of existence and the only way to get out of existence is to get out of desire, even for life. "Is there any existence in Nirvana?" I asked a Buddhist monk in Ceylon. "How can there be? There is no suffering, hence there can be no existence." Buddha would get rid of the problems of life by getting rid of life; he would get rid of our headaches by getting rid of our heads. The Vedantic Hindu wants to rise above personality into the Impersonal Brahma. Like a raindrop losing iself in the ocean, so the personal will lose itself into the ocean of Impersonal Being. The personality is wiped out. The Bhakti Hindu merges himself in the object of his devotions. I asked a "holy man" what he wanted? Where had he come from? Where was he going? And what was his name? And to every question there was one answer, "Ram Ram"—the name of his god. His personality was lost in Ram Ram.

O Father, teach me Thy purpose concerning my very self. Art Thou striving to cancel it? To reduce it to zero? I must know, for I want to know where I am headed in my goal. I think I see, for I see Jesus. Amen.

AFFIRMATION FOR THE DAY: *What happens to my self is important, for it is the only thing I own.*

THE THREE DICTUMS OF MODERN PSYCHOLOGY

We have seen that the faiths which come out of India are personality weary. Contrary to this attitude, modern psychology emphasizes the opposite: Know yourself, accept yourself, express yourself. Just as I would reject the Indian attitude toward personality, so I would reject the modern attitudes as they stand. First, you cannot know yourself by studying yourself. You must know yourself in relation to something beyond yourself—you must know yourself in relation to God and His plans and purposes for you. Second, you cannot accept yourself when the self is an unacceptable self—full of conflicts, fears, resentments, unresolved problems. Third, you cannot express a self that is full of itself and unresolved problems. Get a dozen people like that in one situation and the situation is set for clash and confusion and strife.

What is wrong with this list of modern psychology? It needs one thing in front of these three: "Surrender yourself." When you surrender yourself, then everything begins to add up to sense. Surrender yourself to God, and then you know yourself in relation to God. You know yourself in regard to an unfolding destiny as a child of God. You now see you are to be "changed into His likeness." Now you not only know yourself, you can accept yourself. For you now have an acceptable self—a self under redemption. You can love yourself. The Christian faith teaches self love: "Thou shalt love thy neighbor *as thyself.*" Now you love yourself in God—not in yourself which is egoism, but in God which is consecration. You love God supremely and yourselfsubordinately. He accepts you so you accept yourself; He loves you so you can love yourself. So then all self-loathing, self-rejection, self-hate drop away and you stand accepted by God and thereby by yourself.

O Jesus Lord, Thou art teaching me how to live with myself, for I'm learning how to live with Thee. And now since I am able to live with Thee I can live with others and with myself. Blessed adjustment. I am grateful. Amen.

AFFIRMATION FOR THE DAY: *Since in Christ I am acceptable to God, now I'm acceptable to myself.*

"A CORN OF WHEAT AFRAID TO DIE"

There is only one Sin—the Sin of making yourself God—the rest are sins. There is only one Loneliness—the Loneliness of being alone with an unsurrendered self. Geoffery Bull in his book, *When Iron Gates Yield,* says in his narrative of his experience in the lonely life of Tibet: "He had appointed me to stand in solitude upon the threshold of crisis, yet the only loneliness I had need to fear was that of a corn of wheat afraid to die."

"A corn of wheat afraid to die"—that is the deepest loneliness. A minister was prominent and useful. He sat with a prominent layman and talked about becoming a bishop. He was divided. He wanted to be "a big shot," and he wanted to be useful. This conflict divided and disrupted him. His wife left him. He "located" voluntarily, and now he lives in the big house alone—terribly alone. He was "a corn of wheat afraid to die."

When the grain of wheat decides to die it begins to truly live. Mrs. Nobu Jo as a young woman went out to the hills surrounding Kobe and spent three days and nights in prayer trying to find God's will for her life. At the close of the three days and nights of vigil she came down with inner clarity—she belonged to the discouraged and beaten people who were committing suicide at a certain place in the bend of railway track where people threw themselves over the cliff. She put up a sign: "Don't. See Mrs. Nobu Jo first. God is love," giving her address. When I asked her how many people she had actually saved from suicide she replied, "We have a record of 5,000. And a further record of 65,000 who might have committed suicide if we hadn't helped them." When I asked her when she was ninety-two what was the secret of her life she replied, "Full surrender to God and having him always with me." The grain of wheat fell into the ground and died—and yet how abundantly she lived. The secret: "Self-surrender."

Dear God, I thank Thee that Thou hast shown me the way. We see clearly for Thou hast walked the way before us. So I follow in the steps of the consistent God. And in doing so I catch Thy joy. And what a Joy! Amen.

AFFIRMATION FOR THE DAY: *My only enemy—the unsurrendered self; my only open door—surrender that self.*

345

"NOT A GOD HAS WOUNDS, BUT THOU ALONE"

The God who stooped to serve is the God who is now high over all. The God who gave Himself is the God whose feet we want to kiss. Because He was strong He dared to be weak. Browning puts it this way:

> To herald all that human and Divine
> In the weary, happy face of Him, half-God,
> Half man, which made the God-part, God the more!

And as Edward Shillito puts it in "Jesus of the Scars":

> The other gods were strong; but Thou becomest weak;
> They rode, but Thou didst stagger to a Throne.
> But to our wounds only God's wounds can speak,
> And not a god has wounds, but Thou alone.

No other god can speak to my condition, for no other god was ever in my condition. The God that I see in Jesus was in my condition. He has gone through everything I have to go through. So His wounds answer my wounds. Man, in manufacturing their gods out of their imaginations, had to make their gods strong. If they ever were weak they would betray their earthliness, so they had to be always strong, always victorious.

But only of Jesus could it be said, "Jesus, knowing that the Father had given all things into his hands, and that he had come from God and was going to God, rose from supper, laid aside his garments, and girded himself with a towel. Then he poured water into a basin, and began to wash the disciples' feet, and to wipe them with the towel with which he was girded" (John 13:3-5). The consciousness of His greatness—"knowing that the Father had given all things into his hands"—was the secret of His humility—He washed His disciples' feet. Only the Great can afford to stoop. A famous swami washes his feet in milk, and then passes this milk around to his disciples to drink a pseudo-communion. Jesus washed His disciples' feet. We are at the feet of the Man who washed our feet.

O Lord Christ, Thou art Lord because Thou wast lowly. Thou risest high because Thou didst stoop low. I adore Thee for Thou didst not abhor me. I clasp Thy feet, for Thou hast washed mine. I love Thee, love Thee. Amen.

AFFIRMATION FOR THE DAY: *I am girded with a towel—I ask no higher honor.*

"NOW HAVING DONE THIS
I'M READY FOR ANYTHING"

When you go low you can go high. Here was a woman who was put in the dust from a letter from her husband—"Divorced in Mexico." He married a Japanese girl and had two daughters by her. She loved him still and wrote, "Let us be friends. Write to me." He wrote to her that he was dying of tuberculosis in Okinawa. She wrote to him, "Send your two daughters and let me take care of them." This was done, and she took care of them as if they were her own daughters. Then she wrote to the Japanese mother, "Come and take care of your two daughters in my home." She came. When she met the Japanese mother at the airport she prayed this prayer: "Lord, let me love her as I would love for Carl to come home to me." She really did just that. Telling about it she concluded, "I'm the happiest woman in this block." And she was.

Another—a young married woman was bitter against the church and all religion, for the religion of her parents was forbidding and uninviting, based on fear. She became a semi-invalid, in and out of the hospital. The doctors thought she had a brain tumor, but could actually find nothing. Two church women called on her, did her household work for her, loved her. She was converted. All her ailments dropped away; she had been skin and bones, now she is a robust, radiant person.

An ex-superintendent of police in India was converted, volunteered to do the sweeper's job at our Ashram. "Now that I've done that I'm ready for anything," he said triumphantly. And he was! For from that moment he started to go up. After his resignation as police superintendent at forty-two he went on and got his theological education in England and America and is now one of the secretaries of the National Christian Council of India. Ready to do the little, he was ready for the big.

Blessed Redeemer, Thou hast the marks of Thy descent upon Thee. And those marks are not mere scars—they are sacraments of Thy love. Through them we see deeper into the mystery of Thy love. We thank Thee. Amen.

AFFIRMATION FOR THE DAY: *In my trying to be great I am never so small; in my lowliest task I am never so great.*

LOOKING AT THE SO-CALLED "SPOTS" IN JESUS

This week we will gather up and look at the objections that many of the best brains of India have brought against the idea of Jesus Christ as a single and sole Incarnation for all men of all time. If this be true it cuts across the Hindu idea of the many incarnations and renders them irrelevant. Nine incarnations have come, the Spotless One—Kalki—is to come. We believe that Spotless One has come in Jesus. So from their standpoint they have to find spots in Jesus to prove that He is not the Spotless One.

Frankly, as I begin this, I feel somewhat silly. My attitude has been, and is, this: Don't try to defend Christ—present Him, He Himself is His own defense. It is like organizing a society for the defense of the sun since someone throws mud at it. Let the sun be its own defense by shining. So I simply lift up Jesus and let Him defend Himself. But if I now inwardly consent to do this, it is on the basis that all of these so-called "spots" are beauty spots—the very opposite of what His detractors say. So I shall try to interpret these so-called "spots."

The first is His "virgin birth." I have often said I do not believe in Jesus because of His virgin birth. I believe in the virgin birth because of Jesus. His virgin life makes it possible to believe in His virgin birth. An unconverted Jew asked a converted Jew, "Suppose a son were born among us and it was said that he was born of the Holy Ghost, would you believe it?" The converted Jew quietly replied, "I would if he were such a son." If the person were ordinary then the birth must be presumed to be ordinary. But the life of Jesus was not ordinary. No other person has left such an extraordinary influence upon humanity. So if His life was extraordinary I can accept it when it says His birth was extraordinary. He carries the miracle, for He was a miracle.

O Jesus, I look into Thy face and I know that anything good and right is possible. For Thou art that good and right made flesh. I cannot argue about it. I see it and the seeing is believing. And the believing lifts one. Amen.

AFFIRMATION FOR THE DAY: *The spots in Jesus are "so-called," the spots in me are called spots—and rightly.*

LIKE ME AND UNLIKE ME

We add this further word about the virgin birth. In His life He is like me and unlike me. He is like me in that He faces life as a man, calling on no power for His own moral battle which is not at your disposal or mine. He performed miracles—for others, but not one on Himself. He stands praying as I pray, facing God. He is like me. So like me that I can almost put my hand on His shoulder and say, "Brother Man." But when I'm about to do it I cannot, for He steps over on the side of God, confronting me with an offer that no one dare offer another without blasphemy: "Come unto me, I will give you rest." He is like me and unlike me. If He were only like me He could only be my Example. If only unlike me He could only be my Redeemer. But I need someone like me to show me how to live and then someone to redeem me and dispose me to live. I need an Example and a Redeemer. In Jesus I find both. This likeness and unlikeness is in His life. Will it be in His birth? He is like me in that He was born of a woman, unlike me in that He was born of God. The likeness and the unlikeness in His life and birth do not conflict, they coincide.

The incredible myth that Jesus spent the silent years between twelve and thirty in India can be dismissed as wishful thinking without a historical leg to stand on.

The transfiguration scene is objected to as incredible. But is it incredible? Do we not see that goodness and the luminous face are inseparable? It happens in people now. When they are good their faces shine. Then if we had the Perfectly Good would we not have the Perfectly Luminous? The transfiguration scene is not contrary to that law at work—it is a fulfillment. People saw this in Stephen: "And all who were sitting in the Council fixed their eyes on him, and his face appeared to them like the face of an angel" (Acts 6:15). The transfiguration scene is the highest fulfillment of the law: the good are luminous and the perfectly good are the perfectly luminous.

O Jesus Lord, we see Thy face and we see more than Thy face—we see Thy soul. And Thy face is Thy soul exteriorated. Make me shine with Thy goodness within me. I can shine only as Thy light and life shine in and through me. Amen.

AFFIRMATION FOR THE DAY: *"They looked unto Him and were luminous"*—may that be my experience.

ANGER WITH GRIEF IN IT—A RIGHTEOUS ANGER

We take up more of the objections brought against the spotlessness of Jesus. One is that Jesus got angry. "And he looked around at them with anger" (Mark 3:5). "Anger" is one of the five deadly sins of India: *kama* (illicit desire), *krodh* (anger), *moh* (greed), *lobh* (miserliness), *ahankar* (pride). So if Jesus was angry He was not spotless. But note the next words: "And he looked around at them with anger, grieved at their hardness of heart." His anger was grief at what was happening to a man with a withered arm. The religious leaders preferred that the man remain unhealed rather than a Sabbath rule be broken. So those who object to this anger take their places with these religious leaders who prefer unbroken religious taboos rather than healed people. An anger which is grieved at what is happening to others, and not a person piqued because of what is happening to Him, is a justified anger and a sign of moral beauty instead of a moral blemish.

Along with this objection is a similar one—the "woes" which He pronounced on the Pharisees and religious leaders: "Woe to you, scribes and Pharisees, hypocrites! for you are like white-washed tombs, which outwardly appear beautiful, but within they are full of dead men's bones and all uncleanness" (Matt. 23:27). The real question is, Was this truth? It was harsh, but truth is often harsh. It has to be harsh to be healing. Estelle Carver sat in a train reading her Bible and the woman alongside her said, "Please close that book, it upsets me." On the other hand, I sat in the train reading my Bible and a woman going by said, "You must love its Author." The Bible upset one woman and set up another. The Bible is a revelation that not only reveals God, but reveals you. Jesus cut into the cancer of outwardism in religion, but He did it not to cut but cure, and His words have proved the most curative words ever uttered in human history. Up to the time of Jesus' saying this, Phariseeism was respectable, now to call a man a Pharisee is to condemn him. And rightly.

O Jesus, Thy words are often as sharp as a surgeon's knife—and as healing. Thou dost never cut me just to cut me, but to cure me. Thy strictures are more curing than Thy sweetness. So cut me, Divine Redeemer, for I need it. Amen.

AFFIRMATION FOR THE DAY: *His anger is not poison injected, but a lancing to get the poison out.*

FROM WOES TO WEEPING

A prominent philosopher, who has brought up these "woes" pronounced on the Pharisees in his book as a sign that Jesus was not sinless, stood in Kalighat where priests sacrificed goats to Kali, the bloodthirsty goddess, cutting off their heads with a single blow. He stood watching the bloody spectacle and said, "Why do you take the blood of these goats? Why don't you take my blood?" This innocuous remark did not cause the slightest ripple on the surface of a corrupt custom, unworthy of India. It left things as they were. But Jesus' words cost Him His life and He knew they would. They put Him on a cross. He wept over Jerusalem after uttering these words. "How oft would I have gathered you as a hen gathers her chickens under her wings but you would not." His woes turned to weeping. Therefore His words were redemptive—the most brave and redemptive words ever uttered.

Another objection. He said to the Canaanite woman, "It is not fair to take the children's bread and throw it to the dogs" (Matt. 15:26). This sounds harsh, but look at the setting and the ending. The setting: "His disciples came and begged him, saying, 'Send her away, for she is crying after us.' " Evidently they used the usual word "Gentile dog" in referring to the Canaanite woman. Then Jesus took their word and used it of the woman. He must have done it as a gentle rebuke to them, for it was shocking to hear Him use it. His look at them conveyed His meaning. And His look at the woman conveyed His encouraging love, for she saw hope in His words. That was the setting. Here was the ending: " 'O woman, great is your faith! Be it done for you as you desire.' And her daughter was healed instantly." Could stinging racialism bring that result? That fruit could only come from the root of redemptive love—a love that rebuked His disciples and encouraged the woman.

O Jesus, how could racialism be in Thee, Thou Son of Man? How could it be said, "In Christ there is no Greek nor Jew"? We are in Thee "the desire of the nations," friend of the outcast and the redeemer of thieves. We worship Thee. Amen.

AFFIRMATION FOR THE DAY: *Racialism in the Son of Man? Rather I smite my breast and say, "No, in me!"*

351

DID JESUS USE FORCE ON MEN?

Another objection brought by Hindus is this one: Jesus used force on the people in cleansing the temple, therefore, He indirectly backs war. The account says: "There he found in the temple the dealers in cattle, sheep, and pigeons, and the money-changers seated at their tables. Jesus made a whip of cords and drove them out of the temple, sheep, cattle, and all. He upset the tables of the money-changers, scattering their coins. Then he turned on the dealers in pigeons: 'Take them out,' he said; 'you must not turn my Father's house into a market' " (John 2:14-16 NEB). Note the use of physical force: He used it on the tables, for tables cannot understand moral force. He used the whip cords on the sheep and cattle, for they could not understand moral force. But to the men who could understand moral force He said, "Take them out." On the men He did not use physical force, only moral force; on the tables and cattle He used physical force, for they could not understand moral force. So the record is clear: physical force where moral force cannot be understood, moral force where it can be understood.

Another objection: the withering of the fig tree. There were two references to the fig tree—one a parable in words, where the owner of the garden came seeking fruit, but found none and ordered it to be cut down. The vinedresser interceded and asked for a year's extension (Luke 13:6-9). It was a parable directed against a nation having outer leaves of religion but no fruit. Then to point the parable He gave the same parable in act: He found a fig tree with leaves and no fruit: "May no one ever eat fruit from you again." And the next day they found the tree had withered (Mark 11:12-14, 20, 21). He was on His way to Jerusalem to make His final appeal to a nation drifting to its doom. So the withering of a fig tree was justified in the attempt to save a nation. It was a red flag across the road of a nation in the act of destroying itself. It was redemptive.

Dear Lord, forgive us that we get our values mixed. We are sensitive to a barren fig tree and not sensitive to a whole nation bent on its own destruction. We thank Thee for this redemptive act. Put the red flag across my pathway when I go wrong. Amen.

AFFIRMATION FOR THE DAY: *Jesus withering many barren fruit trees in my life to save me, would be my Redeemer.*

EVERY NEW TRUTH BRINGS DIVISION

We come to another objection: "Do not think I have come to bring peace on earth; I have not come to bring peace, but a sword" (Matt. 10:34). That this is not a literal sword is seen from the parallel passage: "Do you think that I have come to give peace on earth? No, I tell you, but rather division; for henceforth in one house there will be five divided, three against two and two against three" (Luke 12:51, 52). So the sword was not a literal sword but a sword of "division." Whenever a higher truth comes it causes division—people take sides inevitably. When the Truth came, embodied in Jesus, then it was bound to cause "division"—and rightly. It is the price of progress; the presentation of a truth upsets people on one level to set them up on a higher level. It is a redemptive upset.

A similar objection: "And he said to them, 'When I sent you out with no purse or bag or sandals, did you lack anything?' They said, 'Nothing.' He said to them, 'But now, let him who has a purse take it . . . And let him who has no sword sell his mantle and buy one. . . . ' And they said, 'Look, Lord, here are two swords.' And he said to them, 'It is enough.' " Or as Moffatt puts it, "Enough! Enough!" (Luke 22:35-38). If He meant this literally, would "two swords" be "enough"? If He had depended on this armament against a hostile, armed nation they would have torn Him and His followers to pieces. What He meant was that the situation is now changed—when you went out before you went into a friendly environment, but now the situation has changed, you are going into hostility. That He did not mean physical swords is seen in the fact that when Peter struck with the sword, "Jesus said, 'No more of this!' And He touched his ear and healed him" (Luke 22:49-51). So the record is clear: Jesus came to give His life and refused to allow His disciples to take the life of others.

Dear Prince of Peace, to twist Thy sayings and Thy spirit and make Thee into a Man of war is to crucify Thee again. For there could be no deeper crucifixion than to make Thee, the Savior, into the Destroyer. Forgive us. Amen.

AFFIRMATION FOR THE DAY: *May my life be so decisive that I cause division—upsetting the lower to establish the higher.*

WAS HE AFRAID TO DIE?

We come to another supposed "spot"—His apparent fear of death in Gethsemane: "And being in an agony he prayed more earnestly; and his sweat became like great drops of blood falling down upon the ground." And His prayer was: "Father, if thou art willing, remove this cup from me; nevertheless not my will, but thine, be done" (Luke 22:41-44). Was He here afraid of death, cringing before it? If so it reverses all we know about Him. For "He set His face to go to Jerusalem," knowing that if He did that there He would end on a cross. Then what was the hesitation and the agony?

Was it not this: In going to Jerusalem He knew that He would precipitate a crisis and He would make a nation take sides—for or against Him. And He also knew they would take the wrong side and would crucify Him. So the agony was this: He who came to save men from sin was apparently making them commit a deeper sin—the sin of crucifying Him—if He went on with this crisis. Wasn't there some other way? He saw there was no other way than to go on and die for the nation and the world. So He came to His disciples and said, "Arise, let us be going." Going where? Why straight to the cross! The end of Gethsemane is not the bloody sweat and agonizing prayer—the end is the triumphant words: "Arise, let us be going" to meet the whole tragic business. And He did, without a moment's wavering.

We have looked briefly at these so-called "spots" and every one of them, rightly understood, is not a place of shame but of glorying. And when He turns and asks humanity: "Which of you convinces me of sin?" we are silent. When we try to find fault with His character, we go away smiting our own breasts saying: "God, have mercy on me a sinner." He stands the spotless Incarnation. The Very Word made flesh. "Lord, to whom else can we go? Thou hast the words of eternal life." For Thou art Eternal Life become flesh.

Dear Blessed Redeemer, when we begin to criticize Thee the words die on our lips. For our very criticisms of Thee become criticisms of ourselves. If we point one finger at Thee we point three at ourselves. Spotless Savior, we love Thee. Amen.

AFFIRMATION FOR THE DAY: *Would that all my blemishes were like His—my blemishes would be blessedness.*

"THROUGH THE PROPHETS . . . IN THE SON"

We come this week to sum up seven vital things in the Incarnation as found in the first four verses of the Epistle to the Hebrews.

When in former times God spoke to our forefathers, he spoke in fragmentary and varied fashion through the prophets. But in this the final age he has spoken to us in the Son whom he has made heir to the whole universe, and through whom he created all orders of existence: the Son who is the effulgence of God's splendour and the stamp of God's very being, and sustains the universe by his word of power. When he had brought about the purgation of sins, he took his seat at the right hand of Majesty on high (NEB).

In these seven statements about the Incarnation the whole of that Incarnation is comprehended.

First, God spoke "through the prophets" but "in the Son." The vital difference: Since it was "through the prophets" it was the Word become word; but since it was "in the Son" it was "the Word become flesh." That is the chasmic difference between Jesus and all others. They brought words—He was the Word! All others had perforce to point to something outside themselves—to truth, to God, to precepts, to principles, to ideas. He knew no more sacred task than to point to His own Person: "I am the Way, the Truth, and the Life" . . . "Come unto Me." That is an unbridgeable difference.

"A great wind blew through the Scriptures and lo, it stood up a Man," and the words became flesh.

The old, in every race, was "fragmentary and varied." They brought truths—He was the Truth. They were "varied"—often so fragmentary that they were at variance with one another—He was the Truth, the whole Truth, and nothing but the Truth. When you see Him you know that this is not a light, a star—this is daybreak. Darkness and doubt are at an end. That is It!

O Jesus Lord and Savior, when we see Thee—really see Thee, then we are like a blind man now looking at the sun for the first time. He doesn't ask, Is this the Sun? He knows it is the Sun. When we look at Thee in faith and surrender we do not ask, we rejoice. Thou self-verifying Christ! Amen.

AFFIRMATION FOR THE DAY: *When our eyes fall on Christ we know all else is relative—This is Absolute!*

"WHOM HE MADE HEIR OF THE UNIVERSE"

We come to the next step in the description of the Incarnation: Second, "Whom he has made heir to the whole universe." This is amazing: Everything will come out at His feet. Why? Arbitrarily so, because God willed it? No. The reason is this: Everything that does not come out at His feet will destroy itself on the way. He is the heir of all things, for everything that refuses Him will go to pieces by its own inherent conflicts and contradictions. This process of elimination is happening now. There is a silent process of the elimination of the morally and spiritually unfit. If you won't live with Jesus Christ you can't live with yourself, and you can't live with others.

A financier kited checks to the tune of $10,000,000. He never took a vacation in eighteen years. Had to spend two hours a day to see what forged checks were due and what new ones to make out to cover them. He gave himself up and said, "I'm glad it's over. I've been in prison for fifteen years. Now I'm free." He was "free" to go to jail! And every person who lives in sin is jailing himself, and if it goes on long enough he executes himself, rendering himself unfit to survive. God doesn't will this—man wills it.

And this happens automatically whether you bear the name of Christ or not. Live according to Him and you live, live against Him and you perish, whatever your name or sign.

The feet of Jesus is the terminus *ad quid*—the terminal point of this universe. "In the name of Jesus every knee shall bow and every tongue shall confess that Jesus Christ is Lord." The rest have stilled their own tongues in self-destruction. A doctor, belligerent and wanting an argument, went up to a missionary and said defiantly: "I don't believe in God; I don't believe in Christ." The missionary quietly said, "Go to hell then." The doctor never said another word. That's where he was.

Jesus, Thou art heir of all things, for if we don't come out at Thy feet we don't come out. We kill this thing called life. We perish. Save us from this self-destruction. Give us sense. Thou art Sense—all else is nonsense. Amen.

AFFIRMATION FOR THE DAY: *Everything I place in Jesus by surrender is safe and secure. Everything, including myself, outside Him is unsafe and insecure.*

"A NOVEL WAY TO END A STRIKE?"

We come to the third item in the Incarnation. Third, "Through whom He created all orders of existence." This verse is the basis of the preceding verse—Jesus Christ is the heir of all things because all things were made by Him and for Him. If so, then the touch of Christ is upon all creation, and everything is made in its inner structure to work in His way. And when it works in His way it works well, and when it works some other way it works its own destruction.

Here in Delhi where I am writing there was a strike on against a newspaper, lasting a year. It was settled by a Christian labor officer. When it was settled the newspaper came out with this headline: "A Novel Way to Settle a Strike." But it was not "novel." The employers dismissed a man for rudeness and refused to reinstate him. The employees went on strike. The settlement: The offending employee would confess that he had done wrong, and the newspaper would forgive him and reinstate him. That settlement wasn't "novel"—it was sense, inherent sense, because it was Christian. The hate, the bitterness, the stubbornness, the self-assertion—they were "novel" and got them nowhere—deadlocked. With the emphasis on the "dead" and on the "locked"—locked in death. But when you are in Jesus and take His way you are life-loosed. Life is free—free to live.

Sin is "novel," goodness is natural. The truly Christian person is the truly natural person. He is not living against the grain of the universe, but with it. He is not barking his shins on the system of things. He knows his way about in a universe of this kind—he knows how to live. I know exactly how I feel when I sin—I am orphaned, estranged, and everything within me cries, "This is not the way." I also know exactly how I feel when I live the Christian way—I am universalized, at home. Everything within me cries, "This is the way!" His way is my way.

O Jesus, we have been so habituated to the unnaturalness of sin that we think it natural. We are afraid of Thy divine naturalness. Help us to see Thee as the supernaturally natural. And live by Thy joy and our joy will be full. In Thy Name. Amen.

AFFIRMATION FOR THE DAY: *On everything I have and am is this written: "Jesus Christ is the heir of this."*

"THE SON WHO IS THE EFFULGENCE OF GOD'S SPLENDOR"

We come to the next portion of the unfolding of the meaning of the Incarnation. Fourth, "The Son who is the effulgence of God's splendour and the stamp of God's very being."

This is an amazing passage and reverses so much of our Christian and non-Christian thinking about God and Christ. A prominent Hindu said to me a few days ago, "God has nothing to do with the law of karma [cause and effect], it operates without Him, He is apart from it in bliss." God was "in bliss" by being apart from the law of sowing and reaping which is operative among men. He maintains His bliss by being apart. But the Christian believes that God finds His bliss and splendour through and in the tragedy of man. Not by philosophizing about it, but by getting into it redemptively.

And Jesus "is the effulgence of God's splendour." God's glory point is the Incarnation where He took it all on Himself. And the center of that glory point is the cross where He felt the acutest pain of all—the pain of our sin. At the Transfiguration Jesus burst into light when He talked about "his departure which he was to accomplish at Jerusalem." But this was the word of the cross become word. But at the actual cross it was the Word become flesh. It actually happened. Therefore the Cross is "the effulgence of God's splendour." His bitterest shame was turned into His greatest glory. The God of the Scars has become the God of the Stars—all worlds.

Gone is the nonsense of Swinburne's words: "O Pale Galilean, Thou hast turned the world into ashes by the breath of Thy mouth." Instead it could be said: "Thou Blessed Risen Savior, Thou has turned Death into a Door, The Grave into Glory and Thou hast become the very 'effulgence of God's splendour.' " He is the saving and the shining point of God. When we think of God's glory we think of Jesus. This is no cheap, tinseled glory—it is Glory, inherent and earned. The Word of Glory become flesh.

O Jesus, Lord of Glory, Thy glory is an expensive glory—the glory of a cross turned luminous. We are not dazzled but drawn by this Glory. For it is a redemptive Glory. We glory in this Glory. We thank Thee. Amen.

AFFIRMATION FOR THE DAY: *"Let the Beauty of Jesus be seen in me, all His wonderful Love and Purity."*

"THE STAMP OF GOD'S VERY IMAGE"

We consider the other portion of the likeness to God on the part of the Son: "The stamp of God's very being." This statement dots the "i's" and crosses the "t's" of the statement: "He that hath seen me hath seen the Father." This is as far as words reach in describing the Word.

Man in his homesickness for his Heavenly Father has looked at nature to see the image of God. He views sunrises and sunsets and mountains and flowers and wonders if God is like that. But the storm rages, thunder rolls, floods arise, and the earthquakes shake; nature is cruel, and man's faith in God's being, like Nature, is shaken with it all. No, God is not like that! The nature-worshipers are confused—and empty.

Then man looks on the work of his hands—on idols. He goes through austerities to wring out of the idol some favor or attention. For instance, in the hottest period with the thermometer 115 degrees in the shade devotees in India will measure their length on the ground for fifty miles to get to the temple to ring the bell, and thus get the attention of the idol. But the idol sits attentionless.

Then man looks to his books for some word from God. But the letters are letters, not life. He drinks of the words, but knows in his heart of hearts that this is not the Word.

Then he looks on the face of Jesus, and in one look he knows his quest is over. Jesus is "the Stamp of God's very image." The doubt now is not whether Jesus is like God, but rather is God like Jesus? If He is, then He is a good God and trustable. If the best of men should try to think out what kind of God they would like to see in the universe, they could not imagine anything better than that He should be like Jesus.

O Jesus, if I should transfer all thy qualities of character to God, I could not do it without lowering our estimate of God. Lower? I heighten my view of Him. What a blessed Son Thou art to show me such a blessed Father. I Thank Thee. Amen.

AFFIRMATION FOR THE DAY: *When I say God, I think Jesus. And unerringly I am right. When I say God and think something else I am wrong—always.*

"SUSTAINS THE UNIVERSE
BY HIS WORD OF POWER"

We consider today the next breathtaking statement about Jesus: Fifth, "Sustains the universe by his word of power." Did the writer of the Hebrews have his tongue in his cheek when he said this? A lone man out of a Galilean village sustaining the universe by His word of power? Seems preposterous. And yet His followers had seen Jesus sustaining everything around by His word of power.

He sustained the world of health around Him—cured the sick with a word. He cleansed and sustained the inner life of men by casting out devils and did it with a word. He lifted the inner guilt from a diseased soul and body and did it with a word: "Thy sins are forgiven thee." He stilled the tempest of a raging sea, and He did it with a word. He raised the dead: "Lazarus come forth"; "My daughter arise"—and he did it with a word. He cleansed the temple and drove vested interests from their places of power, and He did it with a word: "Take these things hence." He opened the gates of Paradise to a dying thief and did it with a word: "Today thou shalt be with me in Paradise." And more than all He said to His disciples: "Now you are clean through the word which I have spoken to you"—and they were. He had cleansed their ideas of God, of man, of woman, of prayer, of eating clean and unclean foods, of paradise, of love, of worship, of human relationships, of forgiveness, of the meaning of life and death—He cleansed everything, and He did it with a word.

No wonder the writer exclaims He "sustains the universe by his word of power." He did it in the little; now through the little they saw Him doing it in the big—in the microcosm and in the macrocosm. They had to see it in the little before they could see it in the big. The Word had to become flesh before it could become cosmos.

Dear Lord and Teacher, Thou didst show us in the little world around Thee the power of Thy word. We had to see it in the minute before we could see it in the magnificent. We see it now in both places. We thank Thee. Amen.

AFFIRMATION FOR THE DAY: *I can never show my greatness unless I show it in the little.*

JESUS IS SAVIOR, THEREFORE "JESUS IS LORD"

The last two statements about the Son bring us to an amazing climax: Sixth, "when He had brought about the purgation of sins." Before He takes His seat "at the right hand of Majesty on high" the last emphasis as to the purpose of His coming was to bring about "purgation of sins." The central purpose of His coming was not to be an Example, a Teacher, a Healer, a Guide but to be a Savior, a Redeemer. And if He doesn't save us now—doesn't save us now *from sin*—He doesn't save us from anything. He doesn't save us from hell, nor to heaven unless He saves us from sin now.

I see now, what I didn't see then, that it was an accurate leading that led me to preach my first sermon as a missionary when I landed in Lucknow fifty-five years ago on the text: "Thou shalt call His name Jesus: for he shall save his people from their sins" (Matt. 1:21 KJV). Not "in their sins" as neo-orthodoxy would imply, but "from their sins" as the New Testament teaches. And this has been "brought about"—not promised, but accomplished, "it is finished." It now awaits my acceptance. He saves me to the degree I allow Him. And He does it now, not in some future purgatory. The only purgatory known in the New Testament is the blood of Jesus Christ. And here is an essential difference between the purpose of the coming of the Incarnation as described in the Bhagavad-Gita: "to punish the wicked and to establish righteousness." Jesus did not come to punish the wicked but to save the wicked. He is the Divine Redeemer not the Divine Executioner.

Then the writer comes to the climax of climaxes: Seventh, "He took His seat at the right hand of Majesty on high." He is at the place of final authority. He has the last word. He is the Omega. So with the most astonishing accuracy and succinctness the early Christians summed up their faith in these words, "Jesus is Lord."

O Jesus, Thou art Lord, not by appointment but by accomplishment. Thy Word is now the last word because it is the Word become flesh. Thou didst stagger under a cross to Thy Throne. We thank thee. Amen.

AFFIRMATION FOR THE DAY: *Let my affirmation be in the face of everything: "Jesus is Lord."*

THE ROUND TABLE CONFERENCE APPROACH

In our Round Table Conferences we gather about thirty people, the best representatives of the various faiths, and of no faith, and we say to them, "We have had the dogmatic, the controversial, the traditional approaches to religion. Shall we take an approach more akin to the method of science? In the scientific method there are three things: experimentation, verification and sharing of verifications. We have been experimenting with this business of religion, using it as a working hypothesis of life, what have you verified in experience? What has become real to you? Will you share with us your verifications? I suggest that no one argue, no one try to make a case, nor talk abstractly, nor preach at the rest of us, but that you simply share with us what you have found in experience through your faith. If you have no faith, if you are an agnostic or an atheist, tell us how that is working. We will not sum up at the close. We will leave the facts to speak for themselves."

I have listened in for years to what the finest and best of the different faiths have said about what they are finding, and if I didn't know the New Testament says that Jesus is the Way I would know it from my Round Table Conferences. Those in touch with Jesus Christ were finding something that those not in touch with Him were not finding. This is sometimes intepreted in a strange way. As I walked home with a Mohammedan gentleman he said, "We Hindus and Moslems must have been more honest and sincere in that Conference than you Christians. For we all said we had found nothing, but all you Christians said you had found something, so we must have been more sincere and honest."

O Jesus, Lord and Savior, I thank Thee that I can call Thee Savior, for Thou dost save me now—save me from what I don't want to be to what I want to be. Without Thee my life would be a mess. With Thee, everything. Amen.

AFFIRMATION FOR THE DAY: *The test of a Savior is that He saves—the only test.*

I FELT I WAS HOLDING IN MY HAND A KEY

We ended yesterday with the statement of the Moslem brother who said that the Hindus and Moslems must have been more honest and sincere because they said they found nothing and the Christians all said they had found something. My reply was, "That is one interpretation; the other is that Jesus is the Way." As I have sat in these conferences I've felt that I was holding in my hand a key. And that key was Jesus. He unlocked everything. Without Him you have the Word become word—a philosophy about life, with Him you have Life—the Word become flesh. Put the non-Christians on the abstract and they are wonderful, put them on finding in experience and they are flat. That doesn't mean that many Christians are not flat too. But they are Christians not in vital, first-hand contact with Christ. They often have "a high blood pressure of creeds but an anemia of deeds." But when the Christian is real he is finding something Real.

Someone has said that "Christians are very ordinary people making very extraordinary claims." Not about themselves, but about their Redeemer. They know they are very imperfect followers of a very perfect Lord. So they say, "Glance at me, but gaze at Christ. Don't follow me, follow Him. 'We preach not ourselves, but Jesus Christ as Lord.' " A Hindu convert said in his prayer, "Save me from vain and magnificent words and give me simple deeds." A good prayer—and needed. But Jesus Christ is proving Himself a Savior to the degree that men expose themselves to Him in simple surrender and faith and obedience. It works, and it works with a mathematical precision—it works to the degree that we work it. It is verified knowledge—and verified across all races and classes and ages.

O Lord Jesus, I know that Thou art a Savior for Thou dost save me, most of all from myself, my chief enemy. We do not boast when we talk about Thee, we testify. "Out of the abundance of the heart the mouth speaketh." We thank Thee. Amen.

AFFIRMATION FOR THE DAY: *"Jesus Christ the same yesterday, today, and forever"*—the only one about whom that can be said, except God; therefore He must be God.

"THE FUNDAMENTAL TENDENCIES OF THE UNIVERSE ARE IN JESUS CHRIST"

In one of our Round Table Conferences a sociologist said this penetrating and important thing: "I find in my study of sociology that the fundamental tendencies of the universe are in Jesus Christ." Note that he found this "in my study of sociology." In the study of the facts he found he was led to the Fact of Christ. And in Him were "the fundamental tendencies of the universe." In other words he found what someone said: "Jesus is the incarnation of universals."

What are some of these "universals" incarnate in Jesus which are also "fundamental tendencies of the universe"?

One can see them at work. First, "the greatest of all must be the servant of all." We call the head of a state a "Prime Minister," or "First Servant." And if he doesn't prove to be the "First Servant" of the people, but is rather servant of himself, we put him out. Not reelected. The cells that serve the rest are normal cells, the cells that do not serve the rest are cancerous, so they are operated on and eliminated. "The Struggle for the life of Others" is the key to survival, says Prokotkin. These are fundamental tendencies of the universe and they are found supremely in Jesus.

Second, you must "love your neighbor as you love yourself." If you don't love your neighbor as you love yourself you can't get along with your neighbor and you can't get along with yourself. God has us hooked. We reject the commandment, and we reject ourselves and our neighbor in the process. It is a fundamental tendency in the universe that you love your neighbor as yourself. This is supremely illustrated in Jesus Christ. When you think of loving, you think of Jesus almost automatically. That "tendency" has become universally associated with Him.

O Jesus, I cannot think of the good without thinking of Thee for Thou art Goodness. I cannot think of the true without thinking of Thee, the Truth. I cannot think of the beautiful without seeing Thee, the Beautiful. I see everything in Thee. Amen.

AFFIRMATION FOR THE DAY: *Whenever I find an intimation of the noble, the good, the true, I find that intimation is illustrated in Jesus.*

FURTHER UNIVERSAL TENDENCIES

We continue to look at "the fundamental tendencies of the universe" which "are in Jesus Christ."

Third, self-surrender to Something Higher. That is a fundamental tendency of the universe. All life is lifted by surrender to higher life—the mineral to the plant, the plant to the animal, the animal to man, and the man to God. Self-surrender is the key to rise. That universal tendency is in Jesus Christ supremely—He surrendered Himself, gave His life a ransom. When you think of self-surrender you think of the Divine Self-surrender—you think of Jesus.

Fourth, the need to belong. In *Conversion* I said that psychology in outlining the basic needs of human nature says they are three: the need to belong, to have significance, and to have reasonable security (p. 243). The first need is to belong. Where the ant does not belong to the anthill, the bird does not belong to the flock, the animal to the herd, the individual man to the kingdom of God, there is a sense of estrangement, of incompleteness. Bertrand Russell and Dr. Radhakrishnan, the great philosopher, were on a radio together in a debate, one telling why he did not believe in God and the other why he did. At the close Bertrand Russell said to Dr. Radhakrishnan privately, "I feel somewhat incomplete because I've not had the comfort and consolations of religion." In other words he felt a sense of incompleteness because he didn't "belong." Jesus said, "Seek ye first the kingdom of God . . . and all these things shall be added unto you" (Matt. 6:33 KJV). Jesus belonged to His heavenly Father and urged men to have as their supreme loyalty the Kingdom of God. This universal tendency to belong comes to completion in Jesus Himself and in His urging men to belong—belong to the Kingdom.

O Holy Father, we thank Thee that Thou has planted these universal tendencies in the universe as men put strings to lead blind men in a race. So these tendencies lead us Home—to Thee. We thank Thee. Amen.

AFFIRMATION FOR THE DAY: *When I belong to Christ then everything belongs to me—I am mastered, therefore master.*

EXAMPLES OF NOT BEING ALIGNED WITH THE FUNDAMENTAL TENDENCIES OF THE UNIVERSE

We pause for another look at the need to belong. A German war orphan was shown a picture in a G.I.'s wallet—his girl friend. The orphan said rather sadly, "I had a picture in my wallet too. But he is dead. It was Hitler. I loved and obeyed him, but he is gone. Have you a picture to put into my wallet?" His family was gone, his hero was gone, everything was gone, could we offer a picture to put in that orphan's wallet? Yes, Jesus Christ, the express image of his Heavenly Father—the only picture that would meet his total need. For the picture would be a Person—and alive!

A priest of a shrine in which forty-nine generations had served as priests said to a missionary friend of mine, "We're defunct. The shrines are dead forms. My oldest son, who is very brilliant, should succeed me in this priesthood, but I'm breaking a line of forty-nine generations, 1,500 years, and am sending him to a Christian college. The future belongs in that direction. I am sending my second son who is of no account into the priesthood." "The future belongs in that direction," for in that direction "the fundamental tendencies of the universe" have come to embodiment in Jesus.

A kamakazi (suicide) pilot who was converted at midnight said in one of our Ashrams in Japan, "I was ready to die for the Emperor, but now I am even more ready to die for Christ, for I feel a greater loyalty for Him than I did for the Emperor." His insight now showed him that "the fundamental tendencies of the universe" were away from the Emperor and toward Christ.

Disillusionment with the half-gods is making men align themselves more and more with Him in whom the wave of the future is seen. The half-gods will go, and God, the Incarnate, will get men's allegiances.

O Lord Christ, we take our roads with dead ends and frustrated, turn back to Thee who art the Way. We thank Thee that we do not have to follow false trails forever, for Thou, the Way, art open. Amen.

AFFIRMATION FOR THE DAY: *I go singing down the days and years, for I am on the Way.*

FUNDAMENTAL TENDENCIES:
FORGIVENESS AND A SECOND CHANCE

Another fundamental tendency: Fifth, the need to forgive and be forgiven. There is a redemptive strain running through the universe. If a hillside is scarred by torrential rains Nature sets to work to cover the scars with trees and flowers. If a bone is broken Nature makes the broken place far stronger than before. Said a woman to a doctor, "With all these germs I don't see how anybody could be well," and got the reply, "Knowing the body with all its provisions toward warding off disease and to recover when diseased, I don't see why anybody should ever be sick." There is a fundamental tendency in the universe toward forgiveness and recovery, toward redemption. That fundamental tendency came to its highest manifestation in the cross where God identifies Himself with our sin, takes it upon Himself, and offers us forgiveness in a nail-pierced Hand. As he forgives so we are to forgive. "Treat one another as you are treated in Christ."

Sixth, the fundamental tendency toward a new birth, a new beginning. There is a fundamental tendency in the universe to give the second chance, a recovery, a new start. This comes to its supreme manifestation in Jesus—He took the nobodies and turned them into the somebodies, made a new world beginning out of cast-off material, threw open the gates of possibility to the impossible. "Recovery," "Transformation" are the twin words written across the whole of the life and purpose of Jesus. "Now when they saw the boldness of Peter and John, and perceived that they were uneducated, common men, they wondered; and they recognized that they had been with Jesus" (Acts 4:13). The worms had come out of their chrysalis and were soaring to the astonishment of all—and their own!

O Jesus, this is the most precious thing about Thee. Thou dost bring the Gospel of the Second Chance. Thou dost not despair of us so we must despair of no man. Help us to treat people as Thou dost treat us. In Thy name. Amen.

AFFIRMATION FOR THE DAY: *"There is a fountain filled with blood drawn from Immanuel's veins, and sinners plunged beneath that flood lose all their guilty stains."*

RELIANCE ON CHARACTER AND AUTHORITY
FROM WITHIN

We come to the next fundamental tendency of the Universe. Seventh: The tendency to make character the basis of leadership and survival. Among the lower forms of life, the secret of leadership and survival is strength of physical character, among the higher forms mental and moral character. In Jesus this comes to its highest form in moral and spiritual character. Here we see the highest moral and spiritual character ever seen upon our planet. You can transfer every moral and spiritual characteristic of Jesus to God without lowering your estimate of God. Lowering? You heighten your estimate of God when you think of Him in terms of Jesus Christ. You simply know nothing higher to say about God or man than to say, "Like Jesus Christ." Jesus is a character ultimate.

The last fundamental tendency of the universe is the Eighth: The tendency to transfer the basis of authority from the without to the within—from compulsion to impulsion. That tendency comes to its full fruition in Jesus when He said, "It is for your advantage that I go away, for if I do not go away, the Counselor will not come to you; but if I go, I will send him unto you . . . when the Spirit of truth comes, he will guide you into all the truth" (John 16:7, 13). His guidance would now be from within. The basis of authority would be within them. "Can ye not of yourselves judge that which is right?" He was creating not puppets but persons, not persons who cringe before the Creator but who create with the Creator. This is the end of creation. To create sons, made in His image, free as He is free, so that they too can create along with Him and share His ruling authority because it is a gift of grace and because it is won from within. What a Redeemer and what a Redemption! Worthy of God!

O God, our Father, when we think of it all it leaves us speechless and breathless, but thankful to our depths. May our lives be one continuous manifestation of our thankfulness. We can never repay to Thee, but we can relay to others. Amen.

AFFIRMATION FOR THE DAY: *"O the depths of the riches and wisdom and knowledge of God!" And, oh, the wonder of His redemption!*

"THE CONCRETE CHRIST"

In preparing some of my books to be put out on the bookstalls of India in a cheap, paperback edition, I read again *The Christ of the Indian Road,* my first book, and which to my surprise went to over a million copies and was translated into over thirty languages. This book was written thirty-eight years ago. A second World War has been fought, and world-shaking movements have arisen. But when I reread the chapter with the above title, I felt that this chapter deserved a place with additions, but no corrections, in this my last book—so far!—so that first and last the emphasis is the same. He is "the Concrete Christ."

Jesus, the mystic, was amazingly concrete and practical. Into an atmosphere filled with speculation and wordy disputation, where men were "drunk with the wine of their own wordiness," He brings the refreshing sense of practical reality. He taught, but He did not speculate. He never used such words as "perhaps," "maybe," "I think so." Even His words have a concrete feeling about them. They fell upon the soul with the authority of certainty—self-verifying.

He did not discourse on the sacredness of motherhood—He suckled as a babe at His mother's breast, and that scene has forever consecrated motherhood.

He did not argue that life was a growth and character was an attainment. He "increased in wisdom and in stature, and in favor with God and men" (Luke 2:52).

He did not speculate on why temptation should be in the world—He met it, and after forty days' struggle in the wilderness He conquered, and "returned in the power of the Spirit into Galilee."

He did not discourse on the dignity of labor—He worked at a carpenter's bench and this makes the toil of the hands honorable.

O Jesus, Thou dost not merely tell us of the way, Thou art the Way, not by claim alone, but by demonstration that Thou art the Way by the way Thou didst act. We see the Way at work, and what a sight! Amen.

AFFIRMATION FOR THE DAY: *Blessed are your eyes which see, and more blessed are you if you do what you see.*

HE DID NOT DISCUSS IMMORTALITY—
HE RAISED THE DEAD

We continue looking at the concrete Christ. He did not discourse on the necessity of letting one's light shine at home among kinsfolk and friends—He announced His program of uplift and healing at Nazareth, His own home, and those who heard "wondered at the words of grace which proceeded out of his mouth."

As He came among men he did not try to prove the existence of God—He brought Him. He lived in God, and men looking upon His face could not find it within themselves to doubt God.

He did not argue, as Socrates, the immortality of the soul—He raised the dead.

He did not speculate on how God was a Trinity—He said, "If it is by the Spirit of God that I cast out devils, then the kingdom of God has come upon you" (Matt. 12:28). Here the Trinity—"I," "Spirit of God," "God"—was not something to be speculated about, but was a working force for redemption—the casting out of devils and the bringing in of the Kingdom.

He did not teach in a didactic way about the worth of children—He put his hands upon them and setting one in their midst tersely said, "Of such is the kingdom of God," and He raised them from the dead.

He did not argue that God answers prayer—He prayed, sometimes all night and in the morning "the power of the Lord was present to heal."

He did not paint in glowing colors the beauties of friendship and the need for human sympathy—He wept at the grave of his friend Lazarus.

He did not discuss the question of the worth of personality as we do today—He loved and saved persons.

O Jesus, Lord and Friend, we watch Thee in action and we see how to live. Teach us Thy secret, for if we do not know how to live we miss the one thing in life. So we watch Thee with breathless interest and our deepest devotion. Amen.

AFFIRMATION FOR THE DAY: *I would be saved from being interested only in personality and not in persons.*

THE DIVINE ILLUSTRATION

Jesus did not discourse on the equal worth of personality—he went to the poor and outcast and ate with them.

He did not argue the worth of womanhood and the necessity of giving them equal rights—He treated them with infinite respect, gave to them His most sublime teaching, as to the woman at the well, and when He rose from the dead He appeared first to a woman.

He did not teach in the schoolroom manner the necessity of humility—he girded himself with a towel and washed his disciples' feet.

He did not prove how pain and sorrow in the universe could be compatible with the love of God—He took on Himself at the cross everything that spoke against the love of God, and through that pain and tragedy and sin showed the very love of God.

He did not discourse on how the weakest human material can be transformed and made to contribute to the welfare of the world—He called to Him a set of weak men, as the Galilean fishermen, transformed them, and sent them out to begin the mightiest movement for uplift and redemption the world has ever seen.

He wrote no books—only once are we told that he wrote and that was in the sand—but He wrote upon the hearts and consciences of people about Him and it has become the world's most precious writing.

He did not point to a utopia, far off and unrealizable—He announced that the kingdom of heaven is within us, and is "at hand" and can be realized here and now.

We do not find him arguing that the spiritual life should conquer matter—he walked on the water.

O Blessed Conqueror, Thou hast conquered matter and Thou hast conquered me—both of them miracles. Make me a miracle of Thy grace this day, conquering where I cannot conquer and making me love where I cannot love. Amen.

AFFIRMATION FOR THE DAY: *When He conquered my wayward will by His love, that was a greater miracle than conquering matter.*

HE LOVED

We continue "The Concrete Christ." John sent to him from the prison and asked whether He was the one who was to come or do they look for another. Jesus did not argue the question with the disciples of John—He simply and quietly said, "Go tell John what you see, the blind receive sight, the deaf hear, the lame walk, and the poor have the gospel preached to them." His arguments were the facts produced.

He did not discourse on the beauty of love—He loved.

He greatly felt the pressing necessity of the physical needs of the people around him, but he did not merely speak on their behalf, he fed the five thousand people with five loaves and two fishes.

He did not speak only in behalf of the Gentiles—He goes across the lake and fed the four thousand, made up largely of Gentiles and ate with them as a kind of corporate communion.

They bring to him a man with a double malady—sick in body and stricken more deeply in his conscience because of sin. Jesus attended first of all to the deeper malady and said, "Thy sins are forgiven thee." In answer to the objections of the religious leaders, He said, "Whether is it easier to say . . . Thy sins be forgiven thee; or to say, Arise, and take up thy bed, and walk? But that ye may know that the Son of man hath power on earth to forgive sins, (he saith to the sick of the palsy,) ' . . . take up thy bed, and go thy way into thine house' " (Mark 2:9-11 KJV). The outward concrete miracle was the pledge of the inward.

He did not argue the possibility of sinlessness—He presented himself and said, "Which of you convinceth me of sin?"

O Jesus, Lord of all, we thank Thee that Thy method was different—Thou didst not declare so much as demonstrate. And the demonstration is more convincing than any delaration could ever be. We thank Thee. Amen.

AFFIRMATION FOR THE DAY: *I shall have no maladies rooted in wrong attitudes of mind or emotions.*

"SONS OF FACT"

Jesus has been called the Son of Fact. We find striking illustration of his concreteness at the judgment seat. To those on the right He does not say, "You believed in me and my doctrines, therefore, come, be welcome in my Kingdom." Instead He said, "For I was an hungered, and ye gave me meat: I was thirsty, and ye gave me drink: I was a stranger, and ye took me in: Naked, and ye clothed me: I was sick, and ye visited me: I was in prison, and ye came unto me." These "sons of fact," true followers of His, were unwilling to obtain heaven through a possible mistake and so they objected and said, "When saw we thee an hungered, and fed *thee?* or thirsty, and gave *thee* drink? When saw we thee a stranger, and took *thee* in? or naked, and clothed *thee?* Or when saw we thee sick, or in prison, and came unto thee?" And the Master answered, "Inasmuch as ye have done *it* unto one of the least of these my brethren, ye have done *it* unto me" (Matt. 25:35-40 KJV). He was not only concrete Himself, He demanded a concrete life from these who were His followers.

He told us that a human soul was worth more than the whole material universe, and when He had crossed a storm-tossed lake to find a storm-tossed soul, ridden with devils, He did not hesitate to sacrifice the two thousand swine to save this one lost man.

He did not merely ask men to turn the other cheek when smitten on the one, to go the second mile when compelled to go the one, to give the cloak also when sued at law and the coat was taken away, to love our enemies and to bless them—He Himself did that very thing. The servants struck him on one cheek, He turned the other cheek, and the soldiers struck Him on that; they compelled Him to go one mile from Gethsemane to the judgment hall—He went two, even to Calvary. They took away His coat at the judgment hall and He gave His seamless robe at the cross and in the agony on the cross he prayed, "Father, forgive them."

O Blessed Illustration of all Thy saying, going even beyond all Thou hast said, teach me Thy secret, and more, give me Thyself to live within me so that I can do what Thou didst so graciously do—do it by Thy grace. Amen.

AFFIRMATION FOR THE DAY: *One deed is worth a hundred words.*

ILLUSTRATIONS THAT ILLUSTRATE

He did not merely tell us that death need have no terrors for us—He rose from the dead, and lo, now the tomb glows with light.

Many teachers of the world have tried to explain everything—they changed little or nothing. Jesus explained little and changed everything.

Many teachers have tried to diagnose the disease of humanity—Jesus cures it.

Many teachers have told us why the patient is suffering and that he should bear it with fortitude—Jesus tells him to take up his bed and walk.

Many philosophers speculate on how evil entered the world—Jesus presents Himself as the way by which it shall leave.

He did not go into long discussions about the way to God and the possibility of finding Him—He quietly said to men, "I am the Way."

Many speculate with Pilate and ask, "What is truth?" Jesus shows himself and says, "I am the Truth."

Spencer defines physical life for us as response to environment—Jesus defines life itself by presenting Himself and saying, "I am the Life." Anyone who looks upon Him knows in the inmost depths of his soul that he is looking on Life itself.

Jesus said, "But ye shall be baptized with the Holy Ghost not many days hence (Acts 2:5 KJV), and not many days hence Peter could rapturously say, "This Jesus God raised up, and of that we all are witnesses. Being therefore exalted at the right hand of God, and having from the Father the promise of the Holy Spirit, he has poured out this which you see and hear" (Acts 2:32-33 RSV).

Everything He said He did—and more. For His life was greater than His words. Words never have had such weight of meaning.

Blessed One, Thou dost pour blessings upon us beyond our fondest dreams and our highest imaginations. We never dreamed or thought that God was like this. But now that we see who Thou art, we give this all to Thee. Amen.

AFFIRMATION FOR THE DAY: *Grace is written across all I think, say, do, and am—nothing but Grace.*

JESUS THE CONCRETE WORD

Jesus did not try to prove heaven to his disciples—He went up into heaven before their very eyes.

He said to His disciples that the rulers of the Gentiles lord it over their subjects but among them it shall not be so. He that would be great among them should be the servant of all. And when He came into Jerusalem announcing His messiahship He came riding on an ass's colt. He rode into His kingdom on the lowliest of beasts.

He did not say anything about being Lord of nature—He spoke to the winds and the seas, and they obeyed Him.

He said to His disciples that in the New Order revenge should be abolished—the Old Testament limited revenge—one eye for one eye—He abolished it. When the Samaritans would not receive Him because His face was set to go to Jerusalem and the disciples wanted to call down fire upon them—He rebuked them "and went to another village."

When His disciples asked, "Who did sin, this man or his parents that he should be born blind?" Jesus dismissed both hypotheses—He showed them how "The works of God could be made manifest" even through suffering and disability. Then He proceeded to illustrate in His own life the principle of using suffering, turning the worst into the best—He took the worst thing that could happen to Him, namely His death, and turned it into the best thing that could happen to the world, namely its redemption.

Jesus was the Concrete, for He was the Word become flesh. Had He been the Word become word He would have spun theories about life, but since He was the Word become flesh He put shoes on all His theories and made them walk.

O Lord and Savior, I hear Thee speak and when I do I hear more than I hear—I see—see the meaning of Thy words in what Thou art. Theory and practice were one in Thee. And Thy practice makes luminous Thy theory. I thank Thee. Amen.

AFFIRMATION FOR THE DAY: *I see it can be done—it was done in Him, and it can be done in me, by His grace.*

WHAT JESUS CHRIST MEANS TO ME

We come to our closing week together. The whole of what we are saying in the book is that teaching must become testimony, or it ceases to be teaching. So I close this book with a testimony.

When the attack upon Pearl Harbor took place I was in Urbana, Illinois, and was to speak that afternoon in a University convocation on "Peace." I had just come from weeks and months of efforts at Washington to head off the war. As I walked down the steps of the hotel on my way to the Convocation I heard the excited voice of a radio announcer telling of the attack upon Pearl Harbor. Here I was on the way to speak on peace and peace was gone. I announced to the great crowd what I had heard over the radio, news to most of them, a shock to all. I told that shocked audience that obviously I could not speak on peace, for peace was gone, but I would speak on, "What Christ means to me." When that world of peace which we had tried to build up had crashed, did anything remain? Yes, all the values, the real values, of my life were intact, for "Jesus Christ was the same yesterday, today and forever." When things crashed He remained.

A thousand students stayed that afternoon to know the steps to find Christ and to take them, for they knew that they could not walk out into a shaken world of war without an Unshakable Center.

The war was won, but the peace has not been, so we are still in a very shaken world. So I give my witness again in this shaken situation as to what Christ means to me. It seems the only befitting way to end this book. For unless the message of this book has become real to the messenger—real in experience—it all ends in the Word become word. I will tell you how it became flesh in me—imperfectly of course, but real as far as it has gone.

O Lord and Savior, may the message we bring be not merely a message, but a message embodied in the messenger. May what we say be deep speaking to deep, heart speaking to heart, and may at the end we see Christ and not the messenger. Amen.

AFFIRMATION FOR THE DAY: *I am grateful that I, a very imperfect follower of a very perfect Lord, have Someone to talk about, for He is my message.*

JESUS CHRIST MEANS TO ME
FIRST OF ALL REDEMPTION

The first thing Christ means to me is redemption. I met Him first at an altar of prayer. I came there with nothing to offer except my moral and spiritual bankruptcy. To my astonishment He took me, forgave me, reconciled me to God, to myself, to my brother man, to nature, to life, and sent my happy soul singing its way down the years. A Hindu said to a friend of mine, "I believe in prayer, but it is a very deep belief on the part of us Hindus that prayer cannot do anything about the past—the past must be paid for now or in a coming reincarnation." But the prayer of repentance and surrender to Jesus Christ did something about the past—it was gone, wiped out as though it belonged to another person, now dead, a new one alive in his place.

I have described in *Christian Maturity* that when the church in which this happened moved to another place, they cut the altar at the place where I was converted and made it into a prayer desk and put it in the new Church with an inscription on it: "At this place Stanley Jones knelt and was converted," and urging others to do the same at the same spot. Tradition says that Zacchaeus used to come to water the tree where he found Christ. Well, I go periodically and kneel, at least once a year, at this spot and water the place with my tears of gratitude where I first saw the Light and the burden of my heart rolled away.

I was in a plane and the stewardess passed around a card on which was the question, "What do you think of our meals?" and I wrote, "Too good for a ransomed sinner." She threw her head back and laughed, but I meant it. It is the undertone of my life—everything is seen in the light of being a ransomed sinner. After sixty years I've never gotten over the wonder of it. "By the grace of God I am what I am."

Dear Savior, I wonder if I will ever get over the wonder of being a ransomed sinner. Nor do I want to get over it. It sends me to my knees and to the highest heaven. It fills me with humility and hallelujahs. I thank Thee. Amen.

AFFIRMATION FOR THE DAY: *Grace is written across all I have and all I am—Grace and Gratitude.*

RESOURCES AND GUIDANCE

The second thing Jesus Christ means to me is resources. I ran for about a year after my conversion under cloudless skies, and then I ran into stormy weather. But the storms were within—deep within, from the fact of an unredeemed subconscious. My conscious mind was converted in conversion, but apparently my subconscious was not. So a crisis ensued. In that crisis I surrendered all I knew—the conscious, and all I didn't know—the subconscious. And then something happened. When I arose from my knees a quiet but profound joy possessed me. I knew the Holy Spirit had moved into the subconscious and had cleansed it, coordinated it with the conscious. So now conscious and subconscious were under one control—the control of the Holy Spirit. The Holy Spirit was redemption extended to the subconscious, the applied edge of redemption—applied to the deepest urges—to self, sex, the herd. Don't misunderstand me—these urges are still there, and can be and are the source of temptation. But they were under a new control, and, if I cooperated by surrender and obedience, the resources were adequate for life. So the second thing that Jesus Christ means to me is resources.

The third thing He means to me is guidance. My life had become, not a self or circumstance-guided life, but a God-guided life. In all the great crises, and in the smaller crises—and more, in the daily round, I have felt a Hand not my own on the helm. Not automatically, I can still insist on my way, can take the helm myself—and pay the penalty. But He never leaves me, and takes over again, with my penitent consent, when I'm about to go on the rocks. And I've found it profoundly true, in the words of a group, "Where God guides, God provides."

O Son of God, we're grateful that we need not fumble and stumble through life. Thy superior wisdom is at our disposal, and thy trustable love will never let us go. We are not at loose ends and a pattern is being woven. I thank Thee. Amen.

AFFIRMATION FOR THE DAY: *He who redeemed my life will guide my life—I shall not falter nor fail—He remembers and He has resources.*

ADEQUACY—THE POWER
TO MAKE EVERYTHING CONTRIBUTE

Before I leave this matter of guidance let me add this one incident out of thousands: When, after finishing college, I was faced with what to do with my life, I knelt before a chair, spread out a letter on the chair, and said, "Now, Lord, I've got to answer this letter from the Mission Board. It may settle my life work. I'm ready to go anywhere, at any time, to do anything, if you will let me know what it is. What is it?" The Inner Voice replied, "It is India." I arose from my knees and said, "It is India." It was settled. Fifty years later I knelt before a chair in that same room and thanked Him for the guidance and for the years spent working out that guidance. It has turned out perfectly. His will if accepted as "good," will turn out "acceptable," and finally "perfect."

The fourth thing that Jesus Christ means to me is adequacy, the power to use everything that comes. I do not ask for special treatment, to be God's spoiled child (though sometimes I wonder if I'm not) but to be able to take what comes, good, bad, and indifferent, and make something out of it. A blind man in our Ashram in India said, "The quinessence of Stanley Jones is his belief that you can not merely bear everything that happens, but use it, to rescue out of everything some good." But I was a long time learning that secret. After a period of fumbling it came as a revelation through the Scriptures: when you are delivered up before courts and magistrates "it shall turn unto you for a testimony." The injustice that brought you before courts can be used for a testimony. The injustice becomes opportunity. In Jesus everything is opportunity. So I do not ask for special treatment, or for exemptions, I ask for adequacy to use what happens and make something out of it. Everything, literally everything, furthers those who follow Christ.

O Lord and Master, I thank Thee for Thy mastery of me, and through that mastery of me my power to master everything that happens. Mastered, I master. It is so simple and yet so effective. Am I grateful? Amen.

AFFIRMATION FOR THE DAY: *I can bear everything for I can use everything.*

JESUS CHRIST MEANS EDUCATION

The fifth thing Jesus means to me is education. I've always felt uneducated. I have nothing but a college degree, and from a small college at that. I have some honorary degrees but I've felt uneducated when in company with the really educated. When M.A.'s and Ph.D.'s get their degrees by dissertations on "The Theology of E. Stanley Jones," my reaction is, "'Have I a theology?" What theology I have is a by-product of evangelism among the intellectuals of India and other parts of the world. An author of twenty-three books? It all seems a mistake, for I never intended to be an author. I simply write when I see a need and the urge is upon me. Then somehow I must be educated. The secret is in Jesus. He is the Awakener—Awakener of the total person, including the mind. Since I've never felt educated I've made life and people educate me—a lifelong process. My mind has become a magnet, so I pull from every person, every situation, some information, some truth to further me. And as I am compelled, or impelled to give, so I am compelled to get in order to give. An Alpine guide was buried in an avalanche. On his tombstone were put the words, "He died climbing." If any inscription should be put on mine, it might be, "He died learning." For Jesus has given me the Counselor, and He keeps me alive to life. Another secret is perhaps this—that I've found it is easier to act yourself into right thinking than to think yourself into right acting. In other words, "He that is willing to do shall know of the teaching."

This all leads us back to the Word become flesh. If the Word does not become flesh it ceases to be word—it becomes words, which means it becomes nothing. So Jesus Christ being the Truth awakens me to search for truths which invariably lead me to the Truth.

O Truth, I thank Thee that Thou art keeping me on the stretch to know more of truth. Convert my mind every day from error to truth, from lower truths to higher truths, from truths to the Truth. In Thy name. Amen.

AFFIRMATION FOR THE DAY: *Truth will take me by the hand today and will bring me to His feet.*

MY CODE IS A CHARACTER

The sixth thing Jesus Christ means to me is health. I don't make that first, but as a by-product of all I've said before, health emerges. In a health crisis a few years ago He said to me: "In Me you are well and whole." It was important for it meant that if I stepped out of Him into resentments, fear, self-preoccupation, and guilt I was not well, and I was not whole. I can only be "well" as long as I am "whole," and I am "whole" only as long as I remain in Him.

The seventh thing Jesus Christ means to me is that my code is a character, that Character is Jesus Christ Himself. You can outgrow a code but you never outgrow a character if that character is a Divine Character. The more you see the more there is to be seen. He is an unfolding Revelation—forever with you and forever beyond you. There is a surprise around every corner, life is popping with novelty, never a dull moment.

And He lets me see nothing less than my Heavenly Father. When an H-bomb was exploded with its blinding flash, a physicist said that it reminded him of a passage from the Bhagavad-Gita: "If the radiance of a thousand suns were burst into the sky, that would be like the splendor of the Mighty One." But that is not the revelation of God I get in Jesus. Jesus is God's Transformer, transforming Him from blinding light that would sear us, into the glory of God as seen in the face of Jesus Christ—that doesn't sear us, it saves us.

They tell us that lazer light can carry information: "Each five-thousandth of a second burst of light can theoretically be made to transmit coded information that would be equivalent of 200,000 words." Jesus is that lazer light who in one split second of an act can reveal to us the Father and be of more use to us than all the piled-up words of philosophy of the ages.

O Lord Jesus, Thou dost not blind me with Thy radiance—Thou dost beckon me with Thy love. Thou dost not deafen me with Thy thunder—Thou dost speak in the still small voice, and God the Eternal is in that still small voice. Amen.

AFFIRMATION FOR THE DAY: *The Lowly God enters in at lowly doors, but when He does He reveals the most High God. Only God can afford to be humble.*

IN HIM I HAVE EVERYTHING

The eighth thing Jesus Christ means to me is the kingdom of God—God's total answer to man's total need. Without this fact of the Kingdom our faith would be a personal allegiance to a Person—it would lack total meaning, individual and corporate. But with Jesus and the Kingdom one—He is the Kingdom—then "all authority" is in Him both "in heaven and on earth." I belong to the sum total of Reality and the sum total of Reality belongs to me.

Ninth, Jesus Christ means to me eternal life. I don't get it hereafter, I have it now in Him. I am sure of heaven, for I'm sure of Him. To be in Him is to be in heaven wherever you are. So whether I live or die, so-called, is a matter of comparative indifference.

Tenth, Jesus Christ means to me a divine-human fellowship in the church. I put this last, not first. The church has been the mother of my spirit—at her altars I found Christ. When I found Christ I found the church. But I do not belong to the church, though I'm a member of it—I belong to Christ—the church belongs to me—a gift of Grace. The most precious fellowship the world holds.

Eleventh, Jesus Christ means to me self-surrender. Not a self-surrender once and for all—it is that—but a continuous moment-by-moment surrender of my self and my problems as they arise. I say to Him, "I am Yours and this problem is Yours, tell me what to do about it." One morning early at what I call my Listening Post, He said, "You are Mine, life is yours." I saw its amazing sweep, so I asked Him to repeat it. He did. I belong to Him; life with all its problems and possibilities belongs to me; I can master it. One morning as I got out of bed, I said to myself, "Stanley, how are you?" And I found myself replying, "Well, I am His." That settled everything. So when I have Jesus Christ—The Word become flesh, I have Everything. For it has me—has me with the consent of all my being. "See the Christ Stand!" "I commend my Savior to You."

O Redeemer, we cannot give to Thee this, that, and the other, for nothing less than our very all is befitting. So we offer to Thee our all, and lo, we have Thy all. And what an All! It fills heaven and earth and me—with Glory. Amen.

AFFIRMATION FOR THE DAY: *"And we all, with unveiled face, beholding the glory of the Lord, are being changed into his likeness from one degree of glory to another; for this comes from the Lord who is the Spirit"* (II Cor. 3:18).